GOVERNING THE FROZEN COMMONS

GOVERNING THE FROZEN COMMONS

The Antarctic Regime and
Environmental Protection

Christopher C. Joyner

UNIVERSITY OF SOUTH CAROLINA PRESS

© 1998 University of South Carolina

Published in Columbia, South Carolina, by the
University of South Carolina Press

Manufactured in the United States of America

02 01 00 99 98   5 4 3 2 1

Library of Congress Cataloging-in-Publication Data

    Joyner, Christopher C.
      Governing the frozen commons : the Antarctic regime and
    environmental protection / Christopher C. Joyner.
        p. cm.
    Includes bibliographical references and index.
    ISBN 1-57003-239-4. —ISBN 1-57003-274-2 (pbk.)
      1. Antarctic Treaty system. 2. Antarctica—International status.
    I. Title.
    KWX70.J694 1998
    341.2'9—dc21   97-45360

For Nancy, Kristin, and Clayton
for reasons only they know
and for
All who would preserve the Antarctic commons
for future generations

CONTENTS

ILLUSTRATIONS

PREFACE

The global commons are large areas of the planet situated beyond the reach of national sovereignty. The ocean, deep seabed, atmosphere, outer space, and polar regions are usually said to qualify as such commons areas. While technological innovations have enabled interventions into these commons regions, national jurisdiction there is ambiguous, polemical, or ineffective. These circumstances allow the global commons to remain open to use by any state or persons having the requisite technological capability.

Antarctica is often thought of as a global commons area. The issues pertaining to the Antarctic transcend traditional boundaries of the states involved in the region. The Antarctic area does indeed involve a set of global issues. No single state or corporate group of actors is capable of resolving the persistent environmental problems associated with global commons spaces. As global issues affect the Antarctic environment, there is also the imperative to deal with environmental problems in the near term—i.e., to control pollution, conserve natural resources, and limit the impact of increasing numbers of people visiting the region. There is, in addition, the fact that resolution of these commons issues requires policy action by responsible governments acting alone and in concert. It is here where the notion of an international regime becomes salient for Antarctic law and politics.

In terms of international relations theory, the concept of regimes for governing commons spaces aims at a middle ground between anarchy and world government. Regimes involve the acceptance by a group of states of a community of laws and legal notions. Regimes involve not only the mutual respect and recognition of various rules for regulating the behavior of involved governments, they also generate a common loyalty among those governments to abstain from prohibited conduct within the sphere of the regime. In this regard, a commons area that is mutually and equitably administered within the context of scientific knowledge, and leads to the development of a legal conscience through a regime, can produce rules of law. That is, through the creation of legal obligations in specific issues areas, international regimes serve to close gaps in the international legal order. The Antarctic presents a region with such relevant issue areas. This study, therefore, appraises and determines the regime-like qualities of the special arrangements negotiated for governing the frozen South.

In general, this study explores four analytical perspectives. First, it seeks to determine which relevant actors are involved in managing the Antarctic commons and the linkages that exist between them. Second, a serious attempt is made to ascertain what prevailing values are operating in the Antarctic for managing the area, and to explain how the relevant actors have responded in this century to those values. Third, and critical to explaining the policy process for governing the Antarctic, the analysis investigates the policies adopted by these actors for the Antarctic commons and the means used to determine whether and how policies should be applied in the region. Fourth, the study strives to point out the futures represented in the values and policies of actors interested in the Antarctic and the means through which they can be planned and carried out.

The volume is intended for the general reader and the scholarly investigator. The first chapter describes the Antarctic setting in order to place the region into geographical, legal, and geopolitical perspectives. Chapter 2 appraises the nature of a global commons in order to determine whether the Antarctic region qualifies as such an international area. The third chapter evaluates the Antarctic Treaty as the legal mechanism for governing the polar South, specifically, the treaty-based institutions it has created to make the system function. Chapter 4 arranges the legal mechanisms and institutions in the Antarctic Treaty system into a conceptual model to explain the evolution and unique character of the Antarctic regime that now regulates activities in the frozen South. Chapters 5 through 7 address fundamental man-made challenges confronting the Antarctic region. The fifth chapter examines policies and institutions devised by the states to ensure resource conservation and management in the Antarctic, especially for the circumpolar ocean. Chapter 6 highlights various contemporary threats to environmental protection and preservation and also assesses the adequacy of efforts taken thus far by states to redress and prevent those threats. The prominent need to maintain the principle of free scientific research and cooperation in the Antarctic is treated in chapter 7, as are concerns over environmental damage done by scientific stations and the implications posed by large numbers of tourists visiting Antarctica. Chapter 8 critically examines the legal, economic, and political implications of Antarctica being declared part of the common heritage of mankind, having a status legally analogous to that now for the deep seabed or, more arguably, for the moon and other celestial bodies. Last, some conclusions are posited about the future of the Antarctic as a global commons and the prospects for the Treaty system successfully being able to manage the area's critical issues of resource conservation, environmental protection, and jurisdiction over national activities.

Finally, this is not a neutral book. While the facts and data are objectively presented, the views expressed argue for conservation and protection of the Antarctic commons. Little of commercial value will be gained by the area's exploitation, and much stands to be lost from the resultant pollution, resource depletion, and degradation of the regional environment. I happen to believe that the existing measure of international order in the world does offer the ability to cope with protection and conservation of the environment in the frozen South, if the major governments acting in the region are politically willing to make it happen. The present study is a modest contribution to the discussion of why and how the international cooperative enterprise that presently governs the frozen commons should be sustained for the benefit and enjoyment of this and future generations.

ACKNOWLEDGMENTS

This study is the product of a long-standing collaboration between the author and several important influences that merit acknowledgment. At the outset, special mention must be made of the Antarctic Cooperative Research Centre (Antarctic CRC), which generously afforded me the opportunity to visit the University of Tasmania during April–June 1994 as a research fellow to begin the research for and writing of this study. I owe much to many people in "Tasi." An enormous debt is owed to Bruce Davis, for his personal concern and professional hospitality in making my stay in Hobart such a socially pleasant and intellectually meaningful experience. Richard Herr in the Department of Political Science gave unselfishly of his time to prompt my thinking through the merits of regime theory and its particular application to the Antarctic context. David Agnew of CCAMLR Headquarters was very helpful in pointing out to me the complex difficulties of biological interdependencies in the Antarctic marine ecosystem. The willingness of Andrew Jackson of the Australian Antarctic Division to contribute his personal insights on Antarctic diplomacy was much appreciated indeed. My thanks go to Garth Paltridge, director of the Antarctic CRC, and the staff of the Institute for Antarctic and Southern Ocean Studies (IASOS) for making me feel so welcome in their intellectual home. Special thanks are also owed to Robert Hall for sharing his insights on regime theory and to Marcus Howard, Lorne Kriwoken, Julia Green, and Jennettee Johensen for our many conversations on Antarctic law and regime behavior.

Coincident with my research experience in Tasmania was the visit to Hobart in April 1994 by Willy Østreng, Olav Schramm Stokke, and Davor Vidas of the Fridtjof Nansen Institute. Their visit was part of the collaborative enterprise known as the International Antarctic Regime Project (IARP), which critically assessed the effectiveness and legitimacy of the regime governing Antarctica. This workshop experience contributed much to clarifying and crystallizing my thoughts on the theoretical distinctions between the Antarctic Treaty System and the Antarctic regime, and was vital to elucidating that conceptual process. I am genuinely grateful for their collective and individual contributions to that end. But most of all, I am grateful for their personal friendship.

Valuable financial assistance came from Georgetown University through an Academic Grant for Research Development during the summer of 1997. I am very grateful for that support. In addition, the Department of Government at Dartmouth College provided a quiet, yet stimulating environment during the summers of 1995 and 1997 when much of the work on this manuscript was completed. The hospitality of friends and colleagues in the Dartmouth community is likewise appreciated, especially that of Gene Lyons and Oran Young.

I have learned and profited much from friends, students, and officials in Washington, D.C. Several colleagues provided support and encouragement, in particular Anthony Arend and Charles Pirtle, whose friendship has been a principal influence on my intellectual efforts at Georgetown. Joseph Lepgold also made helpful comments about the chapter on regime formation. Many thanks are due George E. Little, my teaching assistant during 1995–96 at Georgetown University, for his assistance in preparing the bibliography. A considerable debt of gratitude is owed to Tamara Cofman Wittes, my research assistant for 1996–98, who patiently waded through my prolix verbiage to make it more cogent and comprehensible, and who offered valuable suggestions concerning reorganization of the manuscript. Thanks, too, for her talents at drawing graphics.

I have also enjoyed and benefited immensely from conversations over the years with other Antarctic scholars and practitioners who were willing to discuss our mutual interests. Lee Kimball, Tucker Scully, Anthony Bergin, Bill Bush, John Heap, Don Rothwell, M.J. Peterson, Peter Beck, and Ethel Theis were notably helpful in clarifying and making better sense out of Antarctic law and policy.

I am particularly grateful to Marvin Soroos, my friend and editor at North Carolina State University. It was he who initially asked me to contribute a study for the series on global commons regimes at the University of South Carolina Press. I would not have written this book had it not been for his suggestion, and I would not have finished it without his encouragement. While I appreciate Marvin's confidence in asking me to write the volume on Antarctica, I am even more grateful for his admirable patience and understanding in waiting for the completion and revision of a long-overdue manuscript.

Most important, my family is owed special appreciation for putting up with my capers at the computer at all hours of the early morning, and for tolerating my wanderings around the world in search of the Antarctic grail. My wife, Nancy, endured this project as it dragged on year after year, as did my daughter, Kristin, and my son, Clayton. All of them have been patient above and beyond the call of familial duty, and for that I am genuinely grateful. The volume is dedicated to them for their unflagging love, forbearance, and emotional support over the years.

This volume is also dedicated to all those who work to keep the Antarctic a pristine natural wonderland, in particular, the Antarctica Project and the Antarctica and Southern Ocean Coalition (ASOC). These organizations have acted as an intellectual magnet for maintaining my interest in Antarctic law and politics long after I might have moved on to other subjects of inquiry. I have learned much from their newsletters, reports, and analyses concerning developments in Antarctic law and environmental politics. Their public and private efforts to conserve and protect the frozen commons have served as a genuine inspiration for this intellectual inquiry. Jim Barnes and Beth Clark deserve special mention for being so helpful in this regard.

Notwithstanding the intellectual debts and truly cooperative enterprise that this study represents, responsibility for any deficiencies resides with the author. This work remains my own product, and any errors of commission or omission are mine alone.

Chapter 1

INTRODUCTION

The Antarctic is the last great wilderness on Earth. The only continent that remains free from significant human intervention, Antarctica constitutes about 10 percent of the Earth's land surface and is covered by a massive ice sheet three miles thick in some places. The southern circumpolar seas account for nearly 10 percent of the world's ocean space and are home to an abundance of marine life.

The Antarctic is also a region of extremes. It is the highest, driest, windiest, coldest, remotest, most desolate place on the planet. Yet the brutality of the Antarctic environment is paradoxically coupled with fragility. Both the terrestrial and marine ecosystems in the Antarctic are particularly sensitive to outside perturbations. Serious damage to these areas by human activities may have far-reaching effects, for example, on the global climate, ozone depletion, or world fishery resources. Concerned governments have made serious efforts over the past four decades to prevent potentially disruptive activities from affecting the Antarctic. The story of those efforts and their implications for Antarctic law and politics are the focus of this study.

This chapter has three purposes. First, it describes the geophysical nature of the Antarctic to give the reader greater appreciation of the continent, its circumpolar seas, and the natural resources in the region. This treatment clarifies the global commons character of the Antarctic and underlines the high stakes at risk for governments in the area. Second, the chapter assesses the historical evolution of national claims to the Antarctic. The intention is to demonstrate the reality of the claims in the minds of claimant states and to evaluate whether those claims to the

Antarctic meet the traditional tests under contemporary international law for obtaining valid sovereign title to territory. Finally, the chapter introduces the system of international agreements that has emerged since 1959 for managing the Antarctic. The relevant treaty agreements that currently shape rules and norms for regulating state conduct in the region are set out, with a view to determining whether the integrated nexus of those agreements constitutes an international regime for managing the Antarctic commons area.

GENERAL FEATURES

The Antarctic area encompasses both a continent and an ocean. The south polar region includes the continent of Antarctica proper, several oceanic islands and their continental shelves, as well as the circumpolar Southern Ocean. Perhaps most appropriate as a boundary for demarcating the northern reaches of the Antarctic area is the Antarctic Convergence, sometimes called the Polar Front. The Convergence is a belt of ocean space, fifty kilometers wide at points, where Antarctic waters meet subantarctic waters, creating an identifiable biological zone of nutrient upwelling. The principal reason for using the Convergence as the Antarctic periphery is that it represents a natural breakpoint for most Antarctic influence on the global marine ecosystem and for the impacts of human activities on Antarctic natural resources. Within the Convergence area, natural and geophysical processes occur that are unique to the Antarctic. Still, there are certain problems in using the Convergence for a demarcation line. For one, its boundary varies considerably, meandering between latitudes 50° and 62° south. It is also irregularly shaped and randomly cuts across important fishing grounds, whaling regions, and krill fields.[1]

The Southern Ocean has been notorious throughout maritime history for its high winds and rough waters, and for the dangers associated with floating ice. Indeed, the wide expanses of the Southern Ocean, especially the thick girdle of ice surrounding the continent, have remained the major obstruction for ships sailing to Antarctica. Often labeled the "Roaring Forties," "Furious Fifties," and "Shrieking Sixties" after their latitudes, these seas are a storm belt of gale-force winds, dense fog, and ice-infested waters.[2] Such harsh conditions historically made the circumpolar southern seas into an impenetrable moat surrounding an ice-clad continental fortress. The Antarctic consequently remained mostly ignored and little explored into the nineteenth century. Only recently have the international implications of Antarctic activities been appreciated, primarily in response to demands on its natural resources, the creation of new technologies, and concerns over global environmental degradation.

ANTARCTIC GEOGRAPHY

The Continent

Antarctica is permanently ice-bound and isolated and thus remains the least inhabited and hence the most pristine continent on our planet. The continent of Antarctica covers the South Pole. It is the southernmost of the seven continents and the fifth largest in size. Covering some 14.2 million square kilometers (5.5 million square miles), Antarctica occupies one-tenth of the Earth's land surface, or an area approximately the size of the United States and Europe combined.[3] The continent is compact and nearly circular in shape, except for an outflaring of the Antarctic Peninsula (which juts northward toward Tierra del Fuego in South America some 600 miles distant) and the indentations of two major embayments, the Ross and Weddell Seas. These indentations are so large that they give the continent a pear-shaped profile. The Antarctic coastline, extending some 30,010 kilometers (18,648 miles), is covered by a mixture of glacial ice and pack ice floes.

The massive Antarctic ice sheet conceals the geology of the continental bedrock below. The continent is actually divided by the Transantarctic Mountains into two geological portions of unequal size, Eastern and Western Antarctica. Eastern Antarctica, sometimes referred to as Greater Antarctica or the Gondwana Province, is predominantly situated in the eastern longitudes and is mainly comprised of an ancient Precambrian continental shield that is perhaps three billion years old. The ice mantle overlying the eastern segment comprises one mass and is dominated by a high ice-domed plateau, under which the South Pole and the Transantarctic Mountains are located. The fact that Eastern Antarctica consists of a solid land mass covered by a single dense ice sheet suggests that this portion of the continent has been and will remain geologically stable.[4]

Western Antarctica, known as Lesser Antarctica or the Andean Province, lies entirely in the western longitudes. This smaller segment includes the Antarctic Peninsula and the Ellsworth Mountains, which boast the continent's highest elevations. Geological evidence suggests that the Ellsworth Range is similar in structure to the Andes Mountains in South

America. This finding has prompted speculation by geologists that a submarine mountain chain links the continental mainland of South America with Antarctica. Even more significant is that Western Antarctica, under the ice, consists of an archipelago of mountainous islands containing both old and young geological fragments. With the Weddell Sea on the Atlantic side and the Ross Sea on the Pacific, the western ice sheet that overlies both land and ocean water acts as glacial cement between these rock fragments. This situation, however, suggests inherent conditions of instability and has provoked concern over the possibility that, should a global warming trend occur, the ice sheet over Western Antarctica might melt.[5]

Uplifted by its massive snow and ice mantle, Antarctica is the Earth's highest continent, with an average elevation of 1,850 meters (5,550 feet). This nearly doubles the median elevation of Asia, the second-highest. Without its ice sheet, however, Antarctica's elevation would average only around 500 meters. The polar ice sheet's tremendous weight depresses the fringes of the Antarctic continent to depths of 400 to 600 meters, thus making the continental shelf exceedingly deep and narrow. There are also extensive depressions and troughs, some which plummet 1,000 meters beneath the Antarctic ice.[6]

Nearly all of Antarctica's coastal seas lie within the deep continental shelf areas. The broadest of these continental shelves, which are located in the western Weddell Sea and in the southern Ross, Amundsen, and Bellingshausen Seas, extend out as far as 480 kilometers. In other places—for example, off Queen Maud Land—there is practically no evidence of a shelf region, as the continent drops off abruptly to the abyssal plain under the sea below.

Climate and Meteorology

Antarctica's extreme weather and climatic conditions have prompted the continent's well-deserved description as a great "crystal desert." These conditions are made even more severe by frequently prevailing high winds. The wind chill factor (i.e., the cooling force of the atmosphere) adds to the oppressive environmental conditions. Antarctica has the distinction of being the coldest continent, where the lowest temperature on record, −128.6° F, was measured at the Soviet's Vostok station on July 21, 1983.[7] Temperatures on the continent vary greatly according to location, time of day, and type of season. Summer temperatures may climb as high as 52° F (11° C) in the northern tip of the Antarctic Peninsula, the warmest part of the continent. However, mean temperatures during the coldest months (July and August) vary from -30°C on the coast to -70°C in the interior polar plateau.[8] In the coastal regions, the Southern Ocean casts a moderating effect upon continental temperatures.

Coastal regions nonetheless can be hit by violent bursts of strong wind. Cold, dense air blows down the steep slopes from the interior highlands, especially in East Antarctica. These surface airflows, known as katabatic winds, can become fiercely turbulent and sweep up loose snow to create localized blizzardlike conditions, although these are not considered true blizzards simply because no precipitation is falling and the upper atmosphere remains clear.[9] Wind speeds of up to 90 miles per hour are common along the coast.

The frigid air, constant subfreezing temperatures, high winds, snowstorm conditions, and dense fog in Antarctica combine to produce the harshest climate on the planet. Still, there is only scant precipitation on the continent. Annual rates of precipitation vary from 300 to 500 millimeters (1.2 to 2 inches of water equivalent) near the eastern Antarctic coast to a 1000 millimeters (4 inches) and more in coastal areas of the near eastern Antarctic and subantarctic islands. Precipitation in the interior averages only about 30 to 50 millimeters.[10] This situation reveals an intriguing paradox of nature: Antarctica has locked up in its polar ice cap nearly three-fourths of all the world's fresh water resources; yet the continent receives less precipitation than the Sahara Desert. Despite being the world's most abundant storehouse of fresh water, Antarctica is the driest place on the planet.

Flora and Fauna

The frigid desert climate and the dominant ice mantle have relegated to Antarctica an impoverished, primitive community of cold-tolerant terrestrial plant life. About 800 species of land vegetation have been discovered, of which some 350 are lichens. These indigenous flora are well adapted to Antarctic survival, with some found growing inland 500 meters from the South Pole. About 100 species of mosses and liverworts are found in coastal areas, along with molds, yeasts, fungi, and algae. Only two flowering plant species have been discovered on the continent, on the far northern tip of the Antarctic Peninsula. No higher vegetation, such as shrubs, grasses, or herbs, exists there, and Antarctica is the only continent without trees.[11]

Animal life on Antarctica is less climatically tolerant and less readily dispersed than the continent's plant life. There are no indigenous land vertebrates in the Antarctic. Terrestrial microfauna are mainly protozoans (approximately thirty species) or arthropods—mostly mites, springtails, and lice. The largest native animal on the continent is a wingless midge called the belgica, which grows to a length of about three millimeters.[12]

The Ice Sheet

Antarctica's ice sheet, the largest and oldest ice mass on the planet, covers about 98 percent of the southern continent. This enormous glacial sheet rises to form a massive ice dome over the center of the continent. The average thickness of this tremendous ice cap is around 2000 meters (6500 feet), with some places in the interior reaching depths of 4500 meters.[13] It is this massive ice dome that accounts for Antarctica having the highest average elevation on Earth.

The Antarctic ice sheet, with a volume calculated at 30 million cubic kilometers (7 million cubic miles), contains 75 percent of the Earth's fresh water and about 90 percent of the world's ice.[14] If the whole ice sheet were to melt, global sea levels would rise some sixty meters and relief from this massive weight would elevate the Antarctic rock surface by 200–300 meters.[15] Ice lost by the constant flow of the glacial sheet coastward is replenished by new precipitation, though it is scanty. Only one seasonal river, the Onyx, forms on the continent as melt water from the Lower Wright Glacier in the Ross Dependency empties into the basin of Lake Vanda near McMurdo Sound. The Onyx flows only during the summer months, over a course running less than thirty kilometers.[16]

Ice Shelves

Antarctica's relatively circular shape is produced by the dominant influence of the ice cap, which not only covers the land mass but also extends out over the coastal waters. These protrusions of the ice cap, called ice shelves (or "ice barriers" by early explorers), are not merely extensions of continental ice. Rather, they are floating ice sheets that became melded together as they were squeezed into bays or trapped behind island-bound jetties. Such floating shelf ice is unique to Antarctica, and more than one-tenth of the sheet protrudes beyond the continent's mainland as ice shelves.

Antarctica's ice shelves, which average 185 meters in thickness, are formed mainly from the extrusion of continental ice and snow accumulation. Their thinnest ends lie open to the sea. The thicker interior portions are fixed to the continent by glacial ice, which also serves to replenish and reinforce the extended shelf ice. Antarctica's ice shelves move continually seaward at a rate of about one meter per day. This process of glacial creep is caused by the downward gravitational pressure of snow accumulated at the ice-domed center of the continent.[17]

Ice shelves are thickest near the shoreline, with depths approaching 1,300 meters. The largest of these formations, the Ross Ice Shelf, makes up about 30 percent of all the shelf ice in Antarctica. The Ross Shelf covers some 414,400 square kilometers (160,000 square miles) of ocean space—an area approximately the size of France—and ranges in thickness from 150 to 3,000 meters. The Filchner Shelf and the extensive shelf areas off Marie Byrd Land and Queen Maud Land cover another 932,400 square kilometers (360,000 square miles) of ocean space.

Ice shelves can become unstable as sea water warms their margins. Wave action and the ocean swell may create cracks in a shelf, and large portions may then break off into the ocean. This calving process produces massive tabular icebergs, really gigantic ice islands that vary from 200 to 300 meters in thickness and from a few hundred meters to more than 100 kilometers in length (about the size of Connecticut). They drift northward with prevailing currents until they melt in latitudes between 50° and 60° south. While the average giant tabular iceberg survives about four years, some have been tracked for considerably longer periods.[18]

THE SOUTHERN OCEAN

Sea Ice

The physical feature that most clearly distinguishes the Southern Ocean from other ocean areas is the pervasive presence of ice. Glacial ice, primarily ice shelves and giant tabular icebergs, is far more prevalent in Antarctic waters than in the Arctic. Antarctic sea ice thus exerts an extraordinary influence in circumpolar southern waters.[19]

Pack ice most prominently affects the Southern Ocean. Each year the circumpolar waters undergo a cyclical process of freezing and melting. In winter the pack ice area surrounding the continent expands out to 56° south latitude in the Atlantic and 64° south latitude in the Pacific to encompass an area of some 20 million square kilometers. By austral summer's end, the ice pack contracts back to an area of approximately 4 million square kilometers. This annual growth and retrenchment of pack ice constitutes the largest seasonal process in the world's oceans. The Southern Ocean's ecosystem is synchronized with this perennial pack ice phenomenon, which nearly doubles the size of the Antarctic continent during the winter months from 18 to 34 million square kilometers.[20] Antarctica in essence becomes a continent pulsating with the seasonal advance and retreat of sea ice.

Winds and currents constantly push against the Antarctic pack ice. Because of its massive extent, the pack ice has significant impacts upon the heat exchange between the ocean and the atmosphere. In this way, the process of pack ice formation affects global weather patterns and climate.

The general distribution of sea ice in the Southern Ocean and its undulating seasonal changes are well known. Satellite imagery provides continuous measurement of the variations in Antarctic ocean ice formations. Even so, only meager data are available about Antarctic ice pack dynamics, leaving the precise geophysical properties of pack ice and the growth and decay process of the sea ice field less than fully explained.

Certain characteristics of the Antarctic ocean ice field have been discovered, however. Contrary to expectations, sea ice does not grow and decay in a simple north-south pattern of progression and regression. Rather, ice growth proceeds erratically and irregularly, especially offshore the Ross and Weddell Seas' ice shelves. More significantly, the extensive ice cover over the Southern Ocean reflects solar radiation, thus obstructing radiant heat from penetrating the sea water. These conditions affect the quantity and quality of biological production, since shading from the ice cover impedes primary production in the water column below. Finally, the process of sea ice formation can affect the stability of the water column below. Ice that crystallizes from sea water is near pure, meaning that, in ocean areas where sea ice forms, salts are not accumulated in the ice. The water adjacent to the ice consequently increases in salinity, which in turn increases the density of the water, leading this high-salt water to sink relative to the rest of the water column. This process contributes to the formation of heavy bottom water. Conversely, as sea ice melts, the salinity of adjacent water decreases and the water column becomes restabilized.[21]

Patterns of sea ice growth and decay are strongly affected by both atmospheric and oceanic circulation. In addition, the fluctuating size of this tremendous girdle of shifting pack ice tends to complicate the relationship between ice and land. There are substantial geophysical differences between continental ice shelves, which are permanent and quasi-stationary, and pack ice, which is only semipermanent and drifts with the currents and winds of the Southern Ocean. The implications of these differences for the Antarctic continent, however, remain uncertain.

Living Marine Resources

The Southern Ocean's food web is unique among the world's oceans. The southern seas have long been touted as rich in nutrients; one prominent marine biologist three decades ago posited that the productivity of Antarctic offshore waters was 400 percent greater than the average primary productivity for the ocean generally.[22] More recent scientific findings have questioned how extensive primary production actually is in the Southern Ocean and have suggested that the availability and production of biomass (i.e., the amount of living matter) vary considerably throughout the region.

Antarctic waters are notable for having major ocean current systems, huge frontal zones that separate waters with different properties, and seasonally varying degrees of ice cover. Each of these characteristics influences the distribution and production of marine life at all levels of the Southern Ocean's ecosystem. At its lowest level, organic primary production in the Southern Ocean varies considerably with the availability of phosphates, nitrates, and silicates. In this connection, among the most significant factors affecting primary production and its seasonal variation in the marine polar South are light and ice. Near-total darkness prevails for one half of the year, near-continuous daylight for the other half. The reach of ice-covered areas of the Southern Ocean ranges over the year from some 2.6 million square kilometers in March to around 18.8 million square kilometers in September. Since little sunlight is able to penetrate the ice cover, the photosynthetic process is inhibited, and the amount of primary production is impaired. Even so, the constant churning of the Southern Ocean's waters creates persistent upwelling of nutrient-enriched bottom water, which stimulates photosynthesis, especially along Antarctica's continental shelf and in the Antarctic Convergence zone. It is here that phytoplankton are produced in profusion, zooplankton abundantly swarm, and larger predators in the marine food chain come to feed.

Krill

The foundation species for the Antarctic marine ecosystem is krill, a two-inch-long shrimplike crustacean that swarms in vast shoals of the Southern Ocean. Krill is the major Antarctic "prey" species, a central dietary component for many higher forms of life. Krill is found all around the Southern Ocean, although it is not uniformly distributed. Major concentrations are found just north of the Antarctic Peninsula. Other areas attracting large krill swarms include the Ross Sea, the Amundsen Sea, the Bellingshausen Sea, the waters around South Georgia Island, the Scotia Sea just north of the Orkney Islands, the waters around the South Shetland Islands, and the waters west of the South Sandwich Islands.[23] Krill are absent north of the Antarctic Convergence, making them as unique to the Antarctic marine ecosystem as they are central to it.[24]

The krill-based ecosystem is efficient and remains the key link to bioproduction in the Southern Ocean. Large krill swarms attract large populations of whales to the Antarctic, as well as fish, seals, and sea birds. The large biomass available in these swarms suggests that krill might also be worth exploiting for large-scale human consumption. But living resources in the Antarctic—be they krill, seals, whales, or fish—cannot sustain intense, prolonged exploitation after virgin stocks are depleted. The exploitation problem is complicated further by the fact that seals, sea birds, penguins, fish, and whales all compete for the same primary food supply, krill. Prudence suggests that more scientific study is needed before krill stocks are harvested in substantial quantities from the Southern Ocean, given the potentially profound impacts on the Antarctic marine ecosystem.

Fish

The Southern Ocean does not contain dense stocks of fish, especially when compared to krill and other living marine resources. But those around Antarctica are distinctive. Of 20,000 species of modern fishes worldwide, only 120, representing twenty-nine families, are found south of the Antarctic Convergence. Of those, three families are the primary fish species in the Southern Ocean region: (1) the *Nototheniidae*, a codlike species; (2) the *Chaenichthyidae,* the so-called "ice fish"; and (3) the *Myctopidae,* or lantern fish, which swim just south of the Antarctic Convergence.[25]

Antarctic cod is the dominant group, comprising nearly 75 percent of all species and possibly accounting for 90 percent of the total fish population in Antarctic waters. These cod tend to concentrate in waters above the Antarctic continental shelf and continental shelf areas surrounding various island groups.[26] Of potential Antarctic fish, the cod are perhaps most attractive. Hence, it was not surprising that the Soviet Union conducted extensive fishing operations in the region during the 1960s and 1970s.

Data on fish in the Southern Ocean are sketchy, speculative, and often include marine areas beyond the Antarctic. It is known that many indigenous species of demersal (i.e., bottom-swimming) fish in subantarctic waters migrate to the Antarctic Convergence to feed on zooplankton. For example, southern blue whiting and Patagonian hake have frequently been located around the South Shetland and South Orkney Islands during the summer season. Antarctic fish are relatively small and swim mostly above the continental shelves of islands. While they do not have a large influence on the Antarctic marine ecosystem, fish do play an important role in the food chain for Antarctic mammals. At the same time, their slow growth and longevity rates make Antarctic fish stocks highly susceptible to overexploitation.

Squid

Antarctic cephalopods may be important to the marine ecosystem, but how much so remains uncertain. Some seventy-two species of squid are found in Antarctic waters, mostly pelagic (i.e., ocean-swimming) varieties that feed on krill.[27] Since squid are fast-swimming, active predators and are difficult to catch, sampling difficulties have hindered scientists from gathering reliable data on the total squid population, its biomass, or its distribution. Estimates of squid populations and their distribution have been extrapolated from the stomach contents of sea birds, seals, and whales. Despite the inadequacy of such sources, these estimates show that squid are important in the diets of sperm whales, seals, penguins, pelagic birds, and certain fish.

Birds

Land areas in the Southern Ocean support considerable bird life, which is integral to the ecology of the Antarctic. Given the vast extent of ocean space and the lack of ice-free areas, it is not surprising that nearly all Antarctic bird life comes from marine groups that are well adapted to ice, especially penguins, albatrosses, and petrels.

While some fifty bird species are known to appear in the Southern Ocean area, only thirty-five of them breed south of the Antarctic Convergence. Even so, what the Antarctic area lacks in quantity of bird species it more than compensates for in numbers. The number of birds is estimated to exceed 200 million individuals.[28] Most species are breeders in large colonies, with some having millions of pairs. Of these, penguins are the most numerous, accounting for as much as 65 percent of the bird stock. Three species of penguins—chinstrap, Adelie, and macronic—have in recent years experienced rapid population growth. Their numbers may exceed 10 million pairs—or a total population double that—and may account for 90 percent of the Antarctic region's total bird life biomass. Penguins' dominant numbers among Antarctic birds suggests that they are a key component in the Antarctic marine ecosystem.[29]

The significance of seabirds in the Antarctic marine ecosystem mainly comes in their role as predators: Antarctic seabirds can eat as much as 115 million metric tons of krill annually—with 85 percent of that consumption attributed to penguins—in addition to great amounts of squid and fish. Birds eat as much as baleen whales and almost half as much as seals. The massive consumption of fish and krill by Antarctic seabirds ensures their salient place in the Southern Ocean's marine community.[30] Much remains to be learned about the abundance, distribution, and habits of bird life in the Antarctic. The distribution of Antarctic seabirds appears to be affected by oceanographic and environmental factors, especially island location, oceanic fronts, pack-ice zones, ice shelves, and what ice-free areas are available for breeding.

Seals

Six species of seals live south of the Antarctic Convergence. Of these, only the crabeater, leopard, Ross, and Weddell seals are considered true Antarctic species in that their life cycles are intimately associated with ice zones. Antarctic fur seals and southern elephant seals are land breeders and rarely venture into areas of pack ice. They inhabit pelagic regions in lower latitudes and breed principally on subantarctic islands.[31]

In the Antarctic, crabeater seals hold the most ecological significance due to their abundant population and pervasive role as krill predators. At least 12–15 million crabeaters inhabit the Antarctic, accounting for one-half of the total world seal population and 80 percent of the total world seal biomass.[32] Moreover, crabeater seals are preeminent among predators of krill, possibly consuming as much as 106 million metric tons per year—equivalent to three times the amount of krill consumed by all whale species combined.[33]

Other Antarctic seal populations are smaller but still prevalent in circumpolar waters. Estimates of Weddell seals vary from 200,000 to 800,000, leopard seals number around 440,000, and there are some 220,000 Ross seals. Elephant seals may have a population of 750,000, and the number of fur seals in 1997 probably exceeded 2 million.[34] The total stock of Antarctic seals could exceed 25 million. In the aggregate, seals might consume as much as 130 million tons of krill, 10 million tons of squid, and 8 million tons of fish. These predator relationships suggest that seals exert fundamental influences on the Antarctic ecosystem.[35]

Whales

Antarctic waters seasonally support the largest stock of whales in the world ocean. Most baleen (filter-feeding) whales and adult sperm whales migrate between tropical breeding grounds and polar feeding regions. They spend summers in the Antarctic, feeding off krill and other rich plankton in the circumpolar waters. With the approach of winter and the formation of dense pack ice, whales migrate north to warmer seas around the equator. Here they breed in tropical waters until late spring, when the migratory cycle begins anew.

Six species of baleen whales are found seasonally south of the Antarctic Convergence: blue, fin, sei, minke, humpback, and southern right. In addition, one species of large-toothed whale—the sperm whale—and eleven species of smaller cetaceans—including beaked and toothed whales, the pygmy right whale, and the killer whale—also inhabit southern polar waters.[36]

Estimates of the whale population come from annual surveys conducted by the International Whaling Commission, but these are based only on actual sightings and are therefore suspect. Only about 500 blue whales and about 2,000 fin whales are believed to remain. Sei whales also may number around two thousand, with estimated populations of humpback and right whales put "in the low thousands." The minke whale probably has a population as high as 500,000. Since "no reliable method for surveying sperm whale numbers has yet been implemented in the Antarctic, their abundance cannot be estimated."[37] What is known, though, is that whale numbers remain severely depressed when compared to their populations at the turn of the century.

SOVEREIGNTY IN ANTARCTICA

The legal and political status of Antarctica throughout this century has been ambiguous and subject to dispute. Before its discovery in the early nineteenth century, the continent was uninhabited and belonged to no one. No universally accepted treaties or legal principles governed activities in the region or defined jurisdiction over territory and resources. Antarctica was viewed mainly as an ice-bound wasteland, a curiosity, the most frigid, inaccessible, forbidding region on Earth. The continent was considered *terra nullius*, literally a no-man's-land, a frozen ice-clad land mass at the bottom of the world.

Progression of Antarctic Claims

Beginning in 1907, however, seven governments progressively asserted pie-shaped claims to tracts of Antarctica as portions of their own national territories. While these claims persist today, they have not been recognized by any other states in the international community.

Great Britain was the first government to declare national sovereignty in the Antarctic and articulated its claims in a King's Letters Patent of 1908.[38] This royal proclamation declared the formal organization of the Falkland Islands Dependencies and was augmented in 1917 by a second Letters Patent that clarified the precise geographical extent of Britain's claim.[39]

Today, officially designated the British Antarctic Territory, the British claim in the Antarctic includes "Graham Land" on the Antarctic Peninsula and certain island groups in the Southern Ocean, namely, the South Orkneys, South Shetlands, South Georgia, and South Sandwich group. Although vigorously disputed by Argentina, British claims to these Antarctic lands are legally premised on discoveries made by British explorers over three centuries. The first reported discovery of land in the Antarctic is believed to have been South

Georgia in 1675 by a British merchant, Anthony de la Roche. A century later that island was "rediscovered" by the English captain James Cook, who in January 1775 claimed it in the name of King George III. In the same month Captain Cook also discovered the South Sandwich Island group. In 1819 William Smith discovered the South Shetlands and claimed them for the British Crown. The first sighting of the Antarctic coast, probably along Trinity Peninsula, is credited to Edward Bransfield, a Royal Navy officer, in 1820. The South Orkney Islands were discovered and claimed for Great Britain by George Powell in late 1821. In early 1832 Capt. John Biscoe circumnavigated the Antarctic continent and visited the Palmer archipelago. During 1841–43 Sir James Clark Ross also circumnavigated the continent, charted some 800 kilometers of coastline along Victoria Land, discovered Ross Island, and located the northern edge of the Ross Ice Shelf. In January 1843 Sir Ross landed on the eastern shore of Palmer Peninsula and claimed Ross Island and all "contiguous lands" for the British Crown.[40]

By an Order-in-Council in 1923, Great Britain formally claimed a sector encompassing the Ross Dependency and placed it under the administration of New Zealand.[41] In 1933 a similar order was issued that asserted sovereignty over one-fifth of the continent on behalf of Australia.[42]

Now an independent state, New Zealand claims the Ross Dependency for itself. The legal grounds for its claim are couched in discoveries by British explorers, particularly those by Adm. James Ross in 1841 and the expeditions between 1901 and 1909 by Robert Scott and Earnest Shackleton. Further support for New Zealand's claim presumably derives from the title asserted by Great Britain prior to 1923.

The Australian Antarctic Territory is the largest national claim to the continent. Two principal legal bases support Australia's claims to Antarctica. First, there are certain acts of discovery made by both British and Australian explorers, beginning with Capt. James Cook's voyage in 1770–75 and highlighted by the expedition of Sir Douglas Mawson in 1910–11. Second, the assertion is made that the Australian presence on the continent is one of continuous occupation, purposeful administration, and proper control. An Australian decree in 1936 ratified its Antarctic claim.[43] Hence, by the mid-1930s Great Britain and its two former colonies had officially lodged sovereignty claims to nearly two-thirds of the frozen continent.

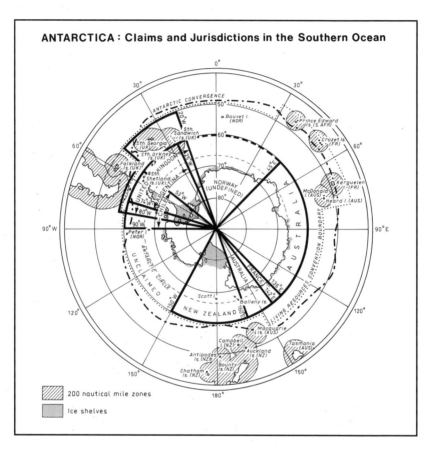

Figure 1.1

Other states quickly joined in the competition for Antarctic territory. In 1924 the French annexed Terra Adelie (Adelie Land) in East Antarctica as well as several islands in the Southern Ocean, among them Kerguélen and Crozet.[44] French claims to these lands were legally predicated on their discovery by Dumont d'Urville in 1840 and on the expeditions of J. B. Charcot in 1903–05 and 1908–10. Yet French motivations were more geopolitical; France was increasingly concerned about British intentions on the continent and wanted to protect fishing rights around French-claimed subantarctic islands. French administration of Adelie Land was initially placed under the governor general of Madagascar. Even so, the extent of that claim remained imprecise until 1938, when a government decree formally set out its geographical coordinates.[45] The French claim is notable on two counts: first, it bisects Australia's huge sector; and second, it is the smallest slice of claimed territory on the continent.

In 1939 Norway claimed Queen Maud Land, situated between the British and Australian sectors.[46] The legal basis for the Norwegian claim was "geographical work done," presumably that by Roald Amundsen in his race to the South Pole during 1911–12. Unlike other Antarctic claims, however, Norway's claim hinged less on discovery than actual occupation and historical use of the circumpolar seas by its national fleets. Norway had earlier annexed the subantarctic islands of Bouvetoya (1928) and Peter I (1931) off West Antarctica to support whaling activities in the Southern Ocean.[47] Norway's Antarctic claim is unique in that it has neither northern nor southern end points. This is especially intriguing since Amundsen, the first man to reach the South Pole, had laid claim to the polar plateau in December 1911 for King Haakon VII of Norway.[48] That claim was never legally substantiated by the Norwegian government, however. The decision by Norway not to claim a full sector, or pie slice, of Antarctic territory is premised on a practical geopolitical reason: To acknowledge the validity of the sector as a device for demarcating polar territory in Antarctica would imply that the sector theory might legitimately apply to the Arctic too. But this would compromise Norway's vital territorial interests in the Arctic. The Soviet Union (now Russia) has long asserted a sector claim to Arctic territories such that the Norwegian claim to the Svalbard Archipelago is placed at a geographical disadvantage.[49] Norway's sovereignty proclamation in the Antarctic thus carefully sidestepped assertion of a sector-shaped claim there in order to protect its greater geostrategic and legal interests in the North.[50]

The earliest claims to Antarctica were made by European powers. The onset of World War II, however, broadened interest in the Antarctic, and two non-European states soon joined the ranks of territorial claimants to the frozen continent. The first of these was Chile. In 1940 the Chilean government formally proclaimed its sovereignty over "Territorio Chileno Antartico."[51] The legal bases for Chile's claim are several, though weak. Modern title is said to have accrued from the 1493 Papal Bull *Inter Caetera*, augmented by the 1494 Treaty of Tordesillas, under which Pope

Alexander VI divided the Western Hemisphere between Spain and Portugal. Chile contends under the theory of patrimony that it inherited legitimate claim to title over Antarctic lands when it gained independence from Spain in 1810.[52] Chile maintains, moreover, that as the country closest to the polar South, it should enjoy a preferential right of claim to territory there. The argument is also made for effective occupation, albeit only since 1947, when the Chilean government began to perform certain administrative acts intended to buttress legitimacy of its claim to sovereignty on the continent.[53] Significantly, Chile's claim overlaps areas claimed by both the United Kingdom and Argentina on the Antarctic Peninsula.

Argentina was the second non-European state to assert sovereignty in the Antarctic. Argentina's claim evolved during the 1940s under the government of Juan Perón and was first formally articulated in certain Argentine maps published in December 1946.[54] The Argentine claim, known as "Antartida Argentina," covers much of the Antarctic Peninsula and extends northward to encompass the South Orkney Islands, the South Shetlands, South Georgia, and the South Sandwich island group.[55] Importantly, all Antarctic territories claimed by Argentina are disputed by Great Britain.

Argentina has advanced its legal case for Antarctic claims on four grounds. First, the uninterrupted maintenance since 1904 of Argentina's Laurie Island weather station in the South Orkneys is said to constitute sufficient effective occupation to qualify for territorial sovereignty throughout the entire region.[56] As "evidence" of the efficacy of this occupation, Argentina has performed numerous symbolic and ceremonial acts in the region (e.g., depositing property plaques; designating postmasters, coroners, and local magistrates; issuing Antarctic territory postage stamps; and even birthing children) that purportedly demonstrate "actual administration" of its territories.[57]

Second, Argentina also relies upon the doctrine of *uti possidetis juris* (patrimony, or the law of inheritance) to justify its inheriting valid legal title over Antarctic lands from Spain.[58] Again, the supposed substantiation for this rests upon the Papal Bull *Inter Caetera* of 1493 and the Treaty of Tordesillas of 1494.[59] Modern international law, however, does not recognize as binding the authority of these religious edicts proclaimed five hundred years ago.

A third basis for Argentina's claims to the Antarctic is propinquity, that is, its geographical proximity to the continent. That Argentina and

Chile lie closest to Antarctica purportedly furnishes to those governments a special right to claim territory in the polar South.[60] No universally accepted principle in international law, however, corroborates this basis for claim.

Finally, Argentina maintains that it possesses a special geological affinity with the Antarctic region. That is, since the Andes Mountains form a continuous chain under the Southern Ocean that links South America to the Antarctic continent, Argentina contends that it is entitled to claim geologically appertained areas.[61] Modern international law, however, fails to find support for these legal contentions. These are theoretical arguments tailored conveniently to Argentina's geographical situation. They are not principles or norms of international law premised on recognized international agreements or accepted state practice.

The seven national claims to Antarctica have generated considerable controversy, not only over their own precise legal status, but also because of the political and economic implications sovereignty claims have for the continent. By their very essence, moreover, these claims to national sovereignty on the continent challenge any consideration of Antarctica as a commons area. Some assessment, therefore, of the legal merits of these national claims made to Antarctica seems warranted.

Legitimacy of Antarctic Claims

Until the eighteenth century, discovery remained the preeminent means for acquiring title to territory. Discovery in international law traditionally meant more than visual sighting of new lands. For discovery to convey title, international law also required that physical possession be taken of the territory and that symbolic acts be continuously performed in order to demonstrate the lawful authority of the claimant state over that territory.[62] As a consequence, discovery alone furnished only inchoate title, which became regarded as insufficient for sustaining the legitimacy of a territorial claim under international law. Actual control over a territory (and its native inhabitants, if any) remained necessary for sovereign ownership. Thus, merely sighting some hitherto unknown Antarctic land, going ashore, planting a flag, and proclaiming title in the name of a foreign regent was not enough. International law required that, following an act of discovery, a process of effective occupation be evident over that Antarctic land.[63]

Effective occupation remains the legal touchstone upon which modern title to territory is sustained. Effective occupation cannot be instantly achieved. Although not precisely defined, international law maintains that some period of time must pass during which occupation is demonstrated. For occupation to be effective it must also be continuous; a government must be in place, functioning, and controlling; and the peaceful exertion of territorial sovereignty must be adapted to the particular conditions of the claimed land.[64]

The physical challenges of Antarctica make effective occupation almost impossible to achieve. Permanent settlement by nationals of a state must be evident for possession of Antarctic lands to be considered legitimate under contemporary law. This means that the discovering state must at least attain and exercise authoritative control over the territory. To be accorded the status of "occupied" for purposes of eventual claim, an Antarctic territory must be used such that the "occupier" clearly and convincingly demonstrates the process of occupation.[65] That this condition has occurred in the Antarctic seems at best arguable.

Claimant states also have been unable to sustain any colonization that might qualify as a condition of permanent settlement. The human population in Antarctica is comprised almost entirely of visiting scientists from nonclaimant states, not colonists from claimant states. What few "colonists" there are hardly have sufficient political and economic relationship with Antarctica to justify exclusive claims to the region.[66] Settlement of an Antarctic territory is thus essential, though not necessarily sufficient, for sustaining the effectiveness of that occupation. This observation prompts an obvious question concerning the status of lands with environmental conditions so harsh and forbidding that the usual requirements for obtaining effectiveness cannot be fulfilled. Should international law make exceptions to the effectiveness-of-occupation norm for regions deemed to be uninhabitable? No clear consensus exists on this issue.[67]

Finally, the legal situation in the Antarctic remains clouded by the ambiguity and suspicion of the national claims. Resorting mainly to discovery and special circumstances for justifying Antarctic claims fails to conform to customary standards under modern international law for acquiring sovereign rights to territory. At present, these caveats render the legal status of the claims contentious and vague to all governments save for the claimant states.

ISSUES AND CHALLENGES

Antarctica is the last pristine continent. It is the planet's largest unbroken wilderness, the only ecosystem virtually untouched by humans. Yet parts of Antarctica are now feeling the impacts of human activities. Above the continent is an open wound of manmade chemical pollution, the ozone hole. Over the past half-century, scientific bases on the continent have accumulated trash nearby, abandoned hazardous wastes in unmarked barrels, and incinerated garbage in open fires. Millions of gallons of raw, untreated sewage are pumped each summer from the United States McMurdo Station into the sea. Environmentalists fear that such threats could contaminate Antarctica's unspoiled wilderness and destroy its value as a natural global laboratory—a place that scientists can study as a baseline to ascertain how humans and pollution are affecting the planet.

Concern over national activities in the Antarctic is not new. During the early 1950s the United States, the United Kingdom, and Australia became wary regarding the Soviet Union's intentions in the region and the prospect that the Cold War might spread to the cold continent. The Soviet Union expressed intense interest in Antarctica and asserted its intention to participate in any international legal arrangement for the area.[68] But the successful International Geophysical Year in 1957/58, with its cooperative scientific effort on the continent, catalyzed diplomacy to craft a specific agreement aimed primarily at ensuring scientific cooperation and free exchange of information about Antarctica. This treaty was the seedbed for what has evolved into the Antarctic Treaty System, the constellation of international agreements now governing the frozen South.

THE ANTARCTIC TREATY SYSTEM

The area south of 60° south latitude is governed under the legal framework established by the 1959 Antarctic Treaty.[69] As a multilateral accord, the Antarctic Treaty is given high marks for its success in mandating demilitarization and denuclearization of the area, as well as in promoting free scientific research and cooperation and peaceful settlement of disputes. The Antarctic Treaty has worked well to promote science and provide for exclusively peaceful uses of Antarctica. It accommodates sovereignty claims by sidestepping them and allows for on-site, surprise inspections as its means of monitoring and enforcement.

At present, twenty-six governments participate as decision-makers, or Consultative Parties (ATCPs), under the Antarctic Treaty.[70] Representatives of ATCP governments convene annually to set recommended policies for their nationals to observe in the Antarctic. By 1998 the ATCPs had adopted some 228 "recommendations" on issues ranging from environmental issues, meteorology, and agenda-setting to logistics, telecommunications, scientific research, and protected areas.

The 1959 agreement provides for no direct measures to preserve or protect the Antarctic environment, either on the continent or in the circumpolar seas. The initial attempt by the ATCPs to remedy this deficiency came in 1964, with the adoption of specific policies for making the area of the Antarctic Treaty a "Special Conservation Area." Known as the Agreed Measures for the Conservation of the Antarctic Fauna and Flora,[71] this was the first instrument supplementing the Antarctic Treaty that was especially designed to protect and conserve the Antarctic marine environment.

A second major step was taken in 1972 to protect marine life in the Southern Ocean with the promulgation of the Convention for the Conservation of Antarctic Seals.[72] Though intended to limit the vulnerability of Antarctic seals to commercial exploitation from overharvesting, the agreement also strived to "promote and achieve the objectives of protection, scientific study and rational use of Antarctic seals, and to maintain a satisfactory balance within the ecological system."

Among the Antarctic Treaty System (ATS) appendages, by far the most comprehensive in scope is the Convention for the Conservation of Antarctic Marine Living Resources (CCAMLR).[73] Negotiated in 1980, CCAMLR entered into force in 1982 and was crafted to apply "to the Antarctic marine living resources of the area south of 60° South Latitude and to the Antarctic marine living marine resources of the area between that latitude and the Antarctic Convergence which form part of the Antarctic marine ecosystem."[74] The purpose of CCAMLR is to preserve all Antarctic marine living resources, including fish, crustaceans (i.e., krill), creatures on the continental shelf, and bird life.

From 1982 through 1988 the ATCPs negotiated a special treaty to regulate prospecting, exploration, and development of mineral resources in the Antarctic. Consensus came in June 1988 on the text for a new minerals agreement, and in November 1988 the Convention on the Regulation of Antarctic Mineral Resource Activities (CRAMRA) was opened for signature in Wellington, New Zealand.[75] Even so, objections from environmental activists worldwide and the withdrawal of key governments from the agreement process shelved CRAMRA before it could enter into force.

The most recent addition to the ATS, the Protocol to the Antarctic Treaty on Environmental Protection,[76] was adopted and opened for signature on October 4, 1991, by the Consultative Parties in Madrid, Spain. The Environmental Protection Protocol supplies a legal blueprint for preservation and protection of the Antarctic.

The Antarctic Treaty, since its entry into force in 1961, has led to the creation of a regime for governing human activities in the Antarctic. This study assesses the political, environmental, and legal considerations that indicate just how well Antarctica has been managed as a global commons region. The analysis explains the nature of the Antarctic Treaty regime, evaluates how it functions to govern the polar South, and ascertains the major challenges that confront it in the future.

Chapter 2

THE FROZEN COMMONS

Antarctica is fashionably described as a global commons. While perhaps self-evident, that conclusion is complicated both by political realities and conceptual difficulties. For example, what is meant by the term *global commons*? What criteria in international law are necessary for an area to be considered a global commons? What peculiar legal and political implications, if any, flow from the notion of global commons? Are geographic, economic, political, and environmental features in the polar South such that they can legally qualify the Antarctic region for such a "commons" status? To set the stage for this analysis, one should understand what factors distinguish a global commons and how those factors relate to the south polar region. That is the purpose of this chapter, which will be accomplished by examining the concept of global commons; clarifying its meaning under international law; and determining whether economic, political, and environmental earmarks of commons areas properly relate to the Antarctic region.

At the close of the twentieth century, environmental concerns have become serious issues for international reflection and debate. As early as 1972 the Stockholm Declaration produced from the United Nations Conference on the Human Environment[1] had formally recognized the global, interdependent character and severity of environmental threats. Two decades later the Rio Declaration from the United Nations Conference on Environment and Development (UNCED or the Earth Summit) went further by directly linking global environmental problems with international economic development. By 1992 the world environment was being threatened in several ways, with increasingly severe strains placed on commons areas. Among the areas being seriously affected was the Antarctic.

The reach of environmental problems pervasively beyond the limits of national jurisdiction highlights this notion of the global commons. Yet the global commons concept remains ambiguous. It can vary with a particular region or resource, and it can generate disparate economic and political ramifications depending on how, when, and where it is applied. Careful thought, therefore, is required on the nature and disposition of the global commons notion, particularly since policies for addressing problems in such commons areas will also vary accordingly. This holds especially true for unique regional ecosystems, of which the Antarctic clearly is one.

This chapter examines the concept of the global commons, its meaning in international law, and its relevant economic and political ramifications for world order. From this analysis, the significance of designating the Antarctic, the most pristine region on Earth, as a global commons can be better appreciated. In addition, the political, legal, and environmental implications of assigning a status to an area can be assessed, along with the special place Antarctica holds for future generations.

THE CONCEPT OF GLOBAL COMMONS

Impressions of a global commons range from simplistic, elegant statements to broad, far-reaching generalizations. Certain factors suggest whether an area might aptly qualify as a global commons. Among these are the following: the ways, means, and circumstances used to delimit an area; the degree of national legitimacy attached to property title, ownership rights, sovereignty claims, and jurisdictional reach within the area; the extent to which control, regulation, and management of the area are needed; the degree of access granted persons to the area and its resources; the distribution of costs and benefits accrued from activities in the area; and the decision concerning whether an area should be conserved or exploited.

PROPERTY AND JURISDICTION

The global commons have been described as those portions of the planet that lie beyond the limits of national jurisdiction.[2] Such a definition underscores the "globalness" of the area and evokes the "law of international spaces,"[3] in contrast to specific rules for governing local or state territory. Largely omitted from this consideration, however, are critical concerns pertaining to ownership and use, as well as legal scope and practical impacts.[4]

Other definitions build on the traditional notion of a commons as pastureland owned and managed jointly by people who directly benefit from it.[5] This view portrays the global commons as a space containing natural resources that belong to everyone, and which are intended for the benefit of all peoples.[6] The global commons thus includes those areas on or above the planet that lie beyond the territorial and jurisdictional reach of states.[7] These areas cannot be appropriated as parts of national territory, and states may not impose on them extraterritorial laws or policies to secure resources from the area. In this view, no recognized sovereignty claims may intrude into the global commons, principally since such an international area is not legally susceptible to national appropriation.

A global commons may also be construed in economic terms of resource use, or as "common property" or "common pool" resources.[8] Such a commons area might exist where the cost of maintaining and exercising property rights exceeds the benefits of doing so, given the physical difficulties of appropriation and the mobility or dispersal of local resources.[9] Such a situation might apply, for example, to fish or whales in the high seas or creatures on the sea floor, but not to minerals on the deep seabed or ice in the Antarctic ice cap.

A commons area may also be viewed as a space over which there is no exclusive title and which remains free from national or international regulation.[10] Thus, the "indivisibility"[11] of a global commons suggests that the area is not owned or being managed, which raises questions about the area's legal status and how it should be governed. Such considerations also point up the need for some kind of international decision-making body, perhaps without exclusive title but holding the authority to manage that commons area. This situation would require setting out goals and objectives of an international agency, for instance, the adoption of special rules for protecting and conserving the commons as opposed to permitting open, unrestricted exploitation and development. The area would remain a global commons, internationally managed so that all peoples might benefit from its use. The global character of a commons area, however, does not necessarily mean global management. Regional administration may be more appropriate and more efficient in some instances.[12]

The notion of global commons appears more properly construed as a legal precept. It is broader than the notion of "common property resource" (CPR), which carries economic implications in terms of physical characteristics. While a global commons might contain common property resources (e.g., the world's oceans have fish, krill, and manganese nodules), a CPR would not necessarily be a global commons in the legal sense.[13] A more satisfactory explanation of a modern global commons suggests the need for a special legal regime to regulate and manage activities affecting a region or its resources, unlike the commons area of a simple cow pasture in nineteenth-century England.

Global commons areas have certain geographical, economic, legal, and administrative attributes. Their use by one person or state will present costs for all. International institutions can be established to redress those costs, and they can also seek to optimize use of that commons area.[14] But each global commons remains unique. Each commons area has its own particular set of geophysical characteristics and political problems, and each will be affected by its own economic conditions and perceived solutions.

LOCATIONS AND USES

Among the areas traditionally considered global commons have been oceans, atmosphere, polar regions, and outer space.[15] Each area can be broken down into various aspects of commons use as well. For instance, the world ocean contains numerous commons features in its high-seas fisheries, outer continental shelf energy resources, deep seabed manganese nodules, ocean floor geothermal energy, and in being a global sink for waste disposal.[16] Admittedly, the "commons" character of such resource considerations is arguable and can produce conflicting economic and political interpretations for both user and conservationist.

Important geophysical distinctions exist as well. In the polar regions, the Arctic has physical and legal characteristics unlike those of Antarctica. The Arctic is a mediterranean ocean enclosed by sovereign states; the Antarctic consists mainly of a continent surrounded by the open Southern Ocean.[17] The atmosphere and outer space have different physical properties. The atmosphere includes the troposphere above the Earth (where weather patterns begin), as well as the stratosphere (where the ozone layer is located), the mesophere, and beyond.[18] While no universally agreed upon legal ceiling has been placed on how high up airspace extends, the upward limit suggested by legal treatises ranges between 50 and 100 miles.[19] Though extending far beyond the Earth, outer space may be regarded as a global commons because of its "global" effects on the earthbound and because humans use outer space. In this regard, distinct commons regimes have been suggested for the moon and other celestial bodies,[20] outer space itself,[21] the geostationary orbit,[22] and even the broadcast frequency spectrum.[23]

The global commons notion has been extended to nonphysical dimensions as well. Computer networks such as the Internet have been depicted as an "information commons," analogous to how information on a mainframe computer operates in a way common to all devices on the network.[24] Similarly, the electromagnetic spectrum might also be considered an international commons phenomenon, absent attributes of sovereign control or national ownership.

Certain national natural resources, the use (or abuse) of which could produce profound impacts worldwide, have also been depicted as global commons resources. For example, pervasive destruction of tropical forests has raised international concern on account of the critical role these forests play in the oxygen cycle. The implication here is that tropical forests, especially those in Brazil's Amazon region, should be considered "common heritage resources" and made subject to international norms like those for global commons areas. The reasoning here is plain enough. Tropical forests absorb massive amounts of carbon dioxide and produce massive amounts of oxygen to sustain life on Earth. The diminishing area of forest land permits carbon dioxide in the atmosphere to build up, which may aggravate global warming while also reducing the amount of oxygen produced by photosynthesis. As a result, global impacts of excessive deforestation prompted developed governments during the early 1990s to propose initiatives aimed at curbing deforestation. Notwithstanding objections from developing countries that the trees, wildlife, and lands in these tropical forests were integral parts of their sovereign territories,[25] this common concern was voiced to protect a "global" commons resource.[26]

Deforestation activities also threaten biological diversity, which can be viewed as a resource having worldwide implications.[27] Plants and insects in tropical rain forests may hold the key to producing important drugs of the future, and many species are endangered because of practices such as poaching and clear-cutting. At the 1992 UNCED Conference, 160 governments signed the Biodiversity Treaty, which requires developed states to compensate developing countries for conservation and permits the latter group to share in the fruits of genetic research and development.[28] In this view, Earth's entire biomass can be interpreted as a "common concern" for the international community as well.[29]

THE COMMONS PROBLEM

The problem fundamental to the global commons concept, often expressed as the "tragedy of the commons," can vary among these areas. Indeed, the particular dynamics of how a commons area is misused or abused may actually contribute to how that commons is defined.[30] Garrett Hardin's famous essay, "The Tragedy of the Commons,"[31] explains the principal dynamic of commons abuse in the setting of a typical English village commons green. This pasture, open to all, is able to sustain cattle herds for many years with a stable population. Ultimately, though, populations increase. Each individual herdsman rationally seeks to maximize his own gain. He reasons that he will benefit for every additional cow that he grazes in the commons space, with the cost of that use dissipated among all the herdsmen. But each additional cow actually contributes to the progressive deterioration of the commons. Other herdsmen will follow the same logic and will add cows, seeking to optimize their personal gain. In this way, rational individual action leads to irrational collective action by bringing about the inefficient use and eventual destruction of the commons.[32]

Another aspect of the commons dilemma is the problem of "public goods."[33] Public goods are those goods to which access cannot be limited. Thus, those who do not contribute to creation of such goods can still share in the benefits. In the commons green situation above, the commons area and its grass resources represent the public goods. A rational person can make greater personal gains by excessively using these public goods (i.e., the commons), but others will lose if they restrain their activities. If many restrain their use of the area, those few who seize the advantage and put more cattle on the green (the "free riders") will have more cattle to sell at more profit. Assuming that cattle sales remain profitable, the herdsman who (responsibly) refrains from putting more cattle on the commons green will eventually reap less profit at the marketplace. Similarly, the fisherman who exercises restraint by conserving resources must depend on others to do likewise, lest the resource disappear altogether. Competition in the free market can ultimately *undermine* market outcome. Thus, in the public goods model, a central authority may seem desirable for compelling all users to refrain from overexploiting limited, albeit public resources.[34]

Whether overloading, depleting, or polluting a commons, the fundamental logic runs the same: In the absence of genuine cooperation and actual enforcement, prevailing strategies by users are inclined toward misuse, and eventually abuse, of the commons area. If global commons are to remain economically productive, they must remain environmentally solvent. To that end, regimes must be devised and effectively implemented for the sustainable management of those areas.[35]

A global commons can be determined by the area's location, the area's physical susceptibility to exclusive ownership, and the particular set of implicit or explicit rights and responsibilities related to the area. Certain attributes thus define a global commons area, among which are included most, but not necessarily all, of the following: (1) The area is physically and legally situated beyond the limits of national jurisdiction. (2) There are no recognized or valid national sovereignty claims that appertain to the area. (3) The area is presumed to be indivisible, and not politically enclosable, thus inviting the need for it to be regulated by a group of concerned states, rather than by one government. (4) The absence of individual state ownership or national sovereignty may imply universal access to the area. (5) The effects of abuse or mismanagement of the area are experienced universally; this includes both the costs caused by degradation of the area or depreciation of its resources, as well as the beneficial effects arising from protection, conservation, or sustainable management practices. (6) The risk to the commons area increases when states or their nationals conduct activities there. The scope of global commons areas, the potential for pervasive environmental harm from abuse, and the predisposition of states to adopt policies of national self-interest highlight the need for more international cooperation and perhaps even more multilateral management institutions.

INTERNATIONAL LAW CONSIDERATIONS

The legal status of activities in a commons area can be distinguished in terms of management practices, depending on whether that area is owned by no one or owned by everyone. States have designed particular rules and general principles for conduct in international spaces. The application and enforcement of those rules and principles, however, vary according to the type of commons approach in place. Four principal approaches in modern international law pertain to status and "ownership" of international spaces: (1) *res nullius;* (2) *res communis;* (3) the common heritage of mankind concept; and (4) *res publica*. Each approach carries relevance for the contemporary notion of the global commons.

Res Nullius

The concept of *res nullius* means "the property of nobody."[36] The legal construct of *terra nullius*, then, refers to land that has no owner (since *res* refers to a thing and *terra* is that thing). In the absence of an owner, title of ownership or sovereignty over that land will accrue to the first lawful taker, namely, the one who is able to demonstrate sufficient legal authority and control—i.e., a valid legal claim to title—over that territory. This can be a tricky proposition. Legal control becomes vested in the actual demonstration of sovereignty—in establishing permanent settlement—which requires more than mere discovery of the land. Control requires evidence of a claimant's ability to administer and regulate activities throughout the land.[37] Thus, while the situation for *terra nullius* might appear straightforward, it actually remains murky.

Consider the comparison between the Arctic and Antarctica. The Arctic is not land but rather a huge ice cap floating on an ocean. Antarctica, on the other hand, is mostly land but with much of the continent depressed below sea level by the tremendous weight of an ice mantle three miles thick in places. Yet, because the continent is considered *terra firma*, seven states have asserted pie-slice sector claims of national sovereignty to portions of Antarctica. Ultimately, the consequence of applying *res nullius* to Antarctica is to admit that these claims might merit legal credibility. That admission thus far has not been forthcoming.

Such contentions rest on even shakier ground when applied to other global commons, such as the atmosphere, high seas, or outer space. *Res nullius* applies only when the *res* is capable of being enclosed, with the potential of being placed within the territorial jurisdiction of some state. To be sure, no one can claim to have discovered the atmosphere, or the oceans, or outer space. Nor can anyone occupy more than only a tiny portion of those regions. Similarly, the exercise of controlling authority over such spaces remains impracticable. Sovereignty must be plainly demonstrated by the ability to regulate. Given this pragmatic prerequisite, *res nullius* is not a useful device for establishing the legal condition of a global commons area.

Res Communis

The concept of *res communis* provides a legal contrast to *res nullius*. While both notions refer to property owned by no one, *res communis* implies that the property may be available for use by everyone.[38] Practically speaking, the designation of *res communis* has applied more readily to commons such as the oceans or atmosphere that elude sovereign possession or national enclosure. While sovereignty claims or private appropriation do not legally occur under *res communis*, the clear implication is that of an open access regime. Anyone who can use the area may do so. Under *res communis*, states with the available technology and resources may exploit that commons area, provided that any specified obligations of resource conservation and environmental protection are aptly observed.

As legal concepts, neither *res nullius* nor *res communis* preclude appropriation or use. Both notions implicitly furnish legal means by which a commons area may be exploited. In the case of *res nullius*, benefits lawfully go to the first taker. In the case of *res communis*, benefits may accrue to any and all who are able to use the commons area or its resources. In this regard, a distinction should be noted between the commons space and the particular resources in that space. A fishery region in the high seas would be *res communis*, and thus open to fishing by any and all persons. The individual fish caught in that region, however, would be considered *res nullius*, susceptible to being lawfully taken by the first fisherman to make the catch. In any event, neither approach redresses the situation where states or individuals might acquire lawful rights to use the commons but lack the requisite capabilities to exercise those rights. Absent these capabilities, commons areas are unlikely to serve tangible economic benefits.

Common Heritage

The common heritage of mankind (CHM), though sometimes confused with *res communis*, is actually more far-reaching in its intended scope. The CHM concept, which has attained little international credibility through state practice as an accepted legal regime, functions mainly as a principle of international treaty law.[39] Still, common heritage has enjoyed an astonishing rise into the mainstream of international law, having been philosophically conceived and politically introduced only three decades ago.[40]

Common heritage resembles *res nullius* and *res communis* in certain ways. For one, the commons are not owned by any person, group, or sovereign. For another, access to the commons is not restricted. Important distinctions, however, are found in the distribution of benefits and management of the regime. There is also is a shift in focus from the state to humankind as a whole, as all peoples become the legal entity that manages and benefits from activities in the commons area.

Several fundamental tenets define the CHM concept.[41] First, the commons area beyond the limits of national jurisdiction is not subject to national appropriation, since presumably it is owned by all.[42] Second, common spaces under a CHM regime must be used exclusively for peaceful purposes.[43] Third, scientific research must be free, open, and not damaging to the environment. Benefits of such scientific research should go to all humankind, not just to particular governments. Fourth, economic benefits from a CHM regime must be shared with all peoples, as opposed to only certain persons, corporations, or governments. In this context, economic demands of developing countries suggest a certain redistributive justice implicit in CHM to ensure that greater benefits might be allocated to poorer countries.[44] Fifth, exploration, exploitation, and use of the commons must benefit not only present peoples but also future generations. The commons are considered areas to be held in trust for future use, not just regions to be exploited for present needs.[45]

The common heritage concept strives to embrace all humankind, not simply states. The inference follows, then, that a common heritage management regime cannot rely on the prospects for continued cooperation among governments. Instead, CHM would require some kind of international administration over a commons area, theoretically done by all peoples but practically performed through a supranational management and monitoring agency.[46] Typical of such an institution is the International Seabed Authority created under the 1982 UN Law of the Sea Convention.[47] Regardless of structure, the management regime would be relegated to regulating that particular commons area beyond the limits of national jurisdiction.

Recent efforts have been made to apply the CHM notion to outer space and the moon,[48] as well as to Antarctica.[49] In this regard, the common heritage concept, like the regimes for *res nullius* and *res communis*, essentially furnishes a legal device for exploiting resources of the commons. Such exploitation becomes fundamentally necessary if that regime is to redistribute global wealth successfully, as the New International

Economic Order ideology of the 1970s might have had it. Not surprisingly, then, arguments made for common heritage stressed more the immediate political and economic returns, rather than legal propriety or ethical considerations for future generations.[50]

None of these concepts—*res nullius, res communis*, or even common heritage—aims to set as priority considerations the necessity to conserve resources and protect the environment of a global commons area. Each legal regime remains limited in its application. Common heritage remains especially constrained by little acceptability in state practice, so much so that its asserted status as a principle of customary international law can aptly be called into question.

Res Publica

The prospect of a "public heritage of humankind,"[51] or the *res publica*[52] notion, seems more appealing given the limitations of legal alternatives for jurisdiction over a global commons. Such a public heritage or *res publica* regime appears appropriate for those global commons that are not enclosable. Protection of the commons area would be placed above other considerations. A public heritage regime would permit free access to the commons, similar to the regimes for *res nullius, res communis*, and common heritage (though in the CHM case, only with permission of the management authority). Still, that access would be regulated by some international institution to prevent abuses and degradation of the commons area. In this sense the *res publica* regime takes on a status legally analogous to that of internal rivers and waterways. These areas may be used by anyone but are policed and maintained by the state. Under *res publica*, a commons area essentially becomes a public trust.[53] This notion of *res publica* being a public trust might find considerable appeal if applied to the Antarctic region.

To preserve the environmental integrity of a global commons area, public access must be reasonably controlled. Historically, granting private property rights over resources may have fostered efficient use, since each owner tended to use his share more efficiently. The steady process of enclosure in Britain was premised on this idea.[54] While this approach could apply to land or stationary regions such as Antarctica, it would seem less suitable for areas having fluid, more dynamic characteristics, such as the ocean or atmosphere.

A commons area generally lacks exclusive ownership. But this situation can vary. Shared lakes, wells, inner-city markets, grazing areas, and farms are treated as commons areas in some communities. These localized commons zones, mostly prevalent in developing countries, are owned communally and are self-governed for mutual benefits of the user community.[55] But such local commons actually involve forms of restrictive enclosure. Joint ownership rights are conferred to that community but are withheld from all others. This is contrary to the notion of global commons. A global commons may not be transformed into the private province of a select group which excludes the rest of the world. Global commons areas should not be monopolized by a few. They are to be shared by all.[56]

ECONOMIC CONSIDERATIONS

Global commons do exist. The responsibility for managing them through international legal agreement is shared by many, if not all states. Such a situation generates significant economic implications, which arise from treaty-based and customary legal obligations as well as from the national self-interests of governments. Each global commons area has unique physical and legal attributes, and each also has special economic attributes.[57]

Certain economic factors arise from and impinge upon issues affecting global commons areas. Over the past two decades these considerations have centered on the conflict between industrialized developed states of the Northern Hemisphere and poorer developing countries of the Southern Hemisphere. This complex political-economic relationship has been strained even further by the connection between environmental protection and economic development, which has been severely tested by broad changes in the global economy.

The end of the Cold War permitted world politics in the 1990s to turn away from East-West ideological rivalry, allowing for economic concerns between the North and South to receive closer attention. The South's concerns are reflected in the so-called New International Economic Order (NIEO), which stemmed largely from UN General Assembly proclamations during the 1970s.[58] Specifically regarding resources, the NIEO philosophy maintains that each state has full and permanent sovereignty over natural resources in its territory. As for the global commons, NIEO advocates would adopt the doctrine of common heritage of mankind. This thesis asserts that if greater economic equity among states is to be promoted, any resources, revenues, and other benefits derived from commons areas should be shared with developing southern countries, since they lack the North's economic and technological wherewithal to exploit global commons resources on their own.[59]

While NIEO aspirations and the common heritage concept remain linked, the prospects for realizing either have dimmed markedly over the past decade. True, CHM has emerged as a treaty-based principle of international law. The entry into force on 16 November 1994 of the UN Law of the Sea Convention attests to that.[60] Even so, the CHM concept still lacks acceptance as a customary legal norm, as internationally substantiated by state practice. Moreover, tensions between the need to develop and the need to protect the environment have become prominent concerns for most governments. Setting aside the ideological blinders of the NIEO, the 1992 UNCED Conference demonstrated that economic development and environmental protection are inseparable goals, which can be reconciled philosophically and politically through international law. Such environmentally sensitive economic development became translated at UNCED in 1992 as "sustainable development," meaning "development that meets the needs of the present without compromising the ability of future generations to meet their own needs."[61] This definition sets as chief priorities for national governments the need to develop economically while at the same time limiting harm to Earth's environment by human activities.

Sustainable development as a policy recommendation emerged from multilateral efforts to manage global commons areas. Yet, neither the notion nor the strategy has escaped criticism. The concept of sustainability may be too conservative, since it does not proactively seek ways to use the environment more efficiently, such as harnessing solar power or tapping thermal energy.[62] The harsh economic critique suggests that the principle of sustainable development mainly serves the rich, since that policy would insist that governments of poorer states manage the environment better but permit affluent states to go about their polluting, wasteful ways. Critics put it more bluntly when they ask, "Whose common future is to be sustained?"[63] Regarding vast areas of natural wilderness such as Antarctica, one is tempted to add, "And at what price?"

Management of a global commons area carries economic implications. Indeed, no cost-benefit policy analysis applies universally to every global commons area, since each government's policies can vary widely for each commons area.[64] In economic terms, then, problems of the global commons differ in the distribution of net costs and benefits. Assessing each global commons problem is necessary to determine whether unilateral action would be effective, or what incentives might spur economic cooperation. In short, each state confronts its own public policy choices for each commons area.[65] The main economic consideration is this: For each global commons and every management policy, a different set of costs and benefits exists. Concerns for equity in one commons area may suggest answers that are not compatible with solutions deemed economically more efficient for another commons. What might be economically prudent for the oceans and the atmosphere might not aptly apply to Antarctica or the moon. The need for governments to identify and assess costs and benefits therefore becomes necessary, not only for efficient or equitable solutions, but also to get solutions that distribute costs more equally and allow for greater cooperation to minimize cheating.[66]

Managing a global commons area requires financial resources. Treating the environment as a never-wasting asset with infinite value makes it difficult to meet costs and attract political support to protect and conserve a commons area. The costs versus benefits ratio of a commons area's exploitation must be weighed and choices deliberated.[67] Interestingly enough, this has been the pattern generally followed by governments involved in managing activities in the Antarctic.

One legal device for managing activities in the commons is the "polluter pays" principle, which requires that a polluter pay for environmental damage caused by his actions. Intuitively, this approach seems fair. There are, however, problems of application. For one, the polluter is simply permitted to buy his way out of trouble, which means that the dirty means of production can still be profitable after compensation is paid for damage caused by pollution. For another, the "polluter pays" notion removes incentives by potential victims to seek measures aimed at protective or preventive action, which could be more efficient in dissuading further acts by the polluter.[68]

Suggestions have also been made that governments should reduce their production of pollutants based on the percentage output of how much pollution they produce domestically. While perhaps more equitable when compared to indices linked to a state's level of economic development, this option seems intrinsically unfair, since it sustains the advantage of industrialized countries to pollute more. It is also inefficient, since reductions may be cheaper in one country than in another. It might be less costly for a developed state to cut back five tons of pollutants than for a less efficient country to cut back only one ton.[69]

Regardless of which commons, how costs and benefits are distributed, or who pays for pollution, such global environmental issues are still inextricably linked. Processes of ozone depletion, global warming, and deforestation are all intertwined with conditions that affect the Antarctic area. These global processes interact with one another and Earth's climate generally, producing changes that can adversely impact on Antarctica. It is not far-fetched to imagine that accelerated widespread deforestation could contribute to the aggravation of global warming, which then leads to climate changes, which would produce melting of the Antarctic ice cap, which would then cause global sea level rise. Thus, in gauging costs and benefits, the ultimate level of analysis is not the individual state; rather, it must be the planet. This permits the scope of these problems to be more accurately accessed and implementation of global solutions to be more adequately addressed.

POLITICAL CONSIDERATIONS

If international solutions to perceived threats to global commons areas are to be found and implemented, governments will have to make significant reforms in international law and economic priorities. Such changes suggest the need for establishing global regimes to manage environmental conditions in global commons areas. Governments must begin to "redefine security"[70] and should realize that managing global commons areas inevitably means accepting limitations on national sovereignty. Accepting that may not be easy, especially in the wake of violent ethnic nationalisms that have arisen in developing countries since the end of the Cold War. Still, for international regimes to manage problems in global commons areas effectively, governments must genuinely commit themselves to that international effort. The Antarctic experience attests that such commitment and political will can produce successful results.

Certain philosophical themes in the southern tier's perspective have surfaced along with the global commons concept. One apparent theme suggests a pervasive sense of communitarianism, which probably derives from many small commons areas on which the entire community depends.[71] In a community, common values such as the need to maintain viability of a local common pool resource are shared. International communitarianism also seems consistent with the notion of sustainable development. Theoretically, then, a communitarian spirit might be marshaled to overcome feelings of private rights in deference to a sense of international entitlement. Rooted in the New International Economic Order philosophy, this view advocates that developed states should share with developing countries any resources or benefits derived from a global commons area, as well as be more generous by giving to poorer countries greater amounts of technology and foreign aid.

Theory does not always dovetail with political reality, however. Such NIEO considerations brought values sharply into conflict. Use of increased technology transfer, foreign aid, and international resource sharing to benefit developing countries conflict with free market principles that now guide the world economy and on which industrialized countries depend. NIEO developmental aspirations thus invited debate over the morality of distributive justice, or the immorality of environmental harm resulting from unrestricted industrial growth. In the United Nations during the 1980s, this debate touched on the question of Antarctica and often generated more political heat than legal light.

The effectiveness of international law does not rest on morality. It is propelled by considerations of national interest and political pragmatism. Thus the political process for producing an international consensus of values remains crucial for devising appropriate policy means to address global commons issues. In short, commons areas will be better protected by prudent policies of environmental reason and legal obligation than by an economic ideology driven by aspirations of redistributive justice.

POLITICAL GOALS AND VALUES

The goals of governing global commons areas may vary, depending on the relative balance of power in political institutions or the processes at hand. All governments presumably support environmental protection and sustainable development in the abstract. But the economics of managing each global commons area differs. Moreover, resultant international law or agreed upon policies are determined from political processes. The point here is that global treaty making is a protracted, arduous task. During the negotiation process international environmental conditions can seriously deteriorate. Thus while agreements for managing a global commons evolve, they are more likely to produce effective policies if problems can be addressed seriatim, as a reasonable progression of critical issues. This progressive approach is being increasingly adopted. The "convention-with-additional-protocols" method of treaty making has become a vehicle for managing global areas, with the Antarctic and law of the sea being notable recent examples.[72] International agreements, as opposed to national legislation, appear better suited for meeting problems of global commons areas. While such instruments often prescribe conduct in commons regions, they usually do not require causal links to be found between action and injury. Serious, specific provisions for fixing liability are not always included in international environmental agreements for commons areas. Moreover, the costs of deviance from such accords are set comparatively low.[73]

In the "convention-cum-protocol" approach, an initial consideration involves how to define the nature of the problem with an international agreement that may be nonbinding but which represents a clear legal commitment to resolve that problem. National scientific programs are then expected to generate concern about the problem and determine how much public response is needed to correct it. For example, scientific research done during negotiation of the 1979 Long-Range Transboundary Air Pollution Treaty[74] also laid the diplomatic groundwork for the 1985 Vienna Convention on the Protection of the Ozone Layer[75] for reducing chlorofluorocarbon emissions, which later gave rise to its more effective 1987 Montreal Protocol.[76] The Climate Change Convention[77] that emerged from the 1992 Rio Summit likewise followed this model, as it omitted specific targets and timetables in favor of more general commitments to reduce greenhouse gas emissions,[78] with its Kyoto Protocol of December 1997.

This process of adding protocols invites the risk of politicizing issues, however. Developed states might be tempted to monopolize relevant scientific information for their own negotiating advantage. Science is power. Science generates public and state action, and can form the basis of agreement on an issue. Most international negotiations on global commons areas are reluctant to proceed without scientific consensus on the nature of the core problem and the most appropriate means to resolve it. Whereas technology may assist in solving a problem, science increases understanding about it.[79]

Like technology, though, most scientific knowledge and capability is controlled by advanced states, especially those in the West. This advantage gives these governments a weighted, sometimes preponderant capacity to shape the environmental debate. Developed governments can argue (consonant with their interests) that insufficient scientific information is available to proceed with restrictions on, for example, acid rain or greenhouse gas emissions.[80] It also gives those same governments the political capability to assume international leadership in fashioning agreements for specific environmental concerns. This latter course has plainly been the pattern for scientific and technological developments affecting the Antarctic area.

After the initial agreement for managing a global commons area has entered into force, follow-on agreements and protocols can be formulated for dealing with more specific issues. The 1959 Antarctic Treaty clearly fits this pattern with its constellation of subsequent agreements, as does the 1982 UN Convention on the Law of the Sea (with the adoption of its 1994 Implementation Agreement) and the 1985 Vienna Convention on the Protection of the Ozone Layer (with its 1987 Montreal Protocol).

The resort to "soft law" is often criticized for its nonbinding quality. Yet, such "soft law" remains useful for promulgating principles and reinforcing customary international law. It is precisely because such international resolutions and declarations containing broad normative statements lack binding enforcement authority that governments can be attracted to sign on to an agreement.[81] Such "soft" legal accords are often negotiated for global commons issues that affect many states, particularly when scientific consensus on critical issues is lacking. The logic of pragmatism dictates "soft law" as a suitable remedy. The more states in the negotiation, the more difficult it usually is to obtain a universally satisfactory agreement.[82] Resorting to soft law provides interim hortatory measures that indicate where the law may eventually be headed. The critical factor here is the conduct of states and the willingness of governments eventually to adopt in practice legal principles that they were unwilling to adopt earlier as binding policy.

Two fundamental problems often encumber agreements on global commons areas: monitoring of activities and enforcement of provisions. Monitoring is vital if cheating is to be prevented and treaty violations are to be detected. One model of effective monitoring can be found in the 1959 Antarctic Treaty, in which unannounced, on-site inspection of any scientific station is permitted. Requiring that specified data be collected and submitted to a central authority can also influence government behavior. Similarly, satellite surveillance of commons areas enhances global monitoring of harmful activities, for example, ocean dumping, pollution output, ozone depletion, and drift-netting activities.[83]

Governing a global commons implies some degree of control over the area, particularly as resources in the commons are exploited. Enforcement, however, remains a real difficulty for international agreements, as with all law. So-called "war-room environmentalism" would have an international police agency defend the environmental integrity of the commons, by military force if necessary.[84] While that scenario seems far-fetched, some form of sanction remains essential to induce compliance and foster cooperative action. Attempts to impose economic sanctions for environmentally harmful actions usually flounder, though, and actually have been formally condemned as unlawful interference in restraint of international free trade.[85]

As connections are tightened between economic development and environmental integrity, compliance with international environmental agreements should increasingly be linked to incentives rather than coercion. Efforts by more affluent governments to use aid, grants, technology, and other assistance as inducements to developing countries should enhance their compliance with international environmental agreements.[86] Strengthening the United Nations Environmental Programme (UNEP) is necessary for more effective governance in global commons areas. The UNEP was established to inject environmental considerations into United Nations activities, but it remains a weak agency within the UN system, having a meager budget, small staff, and little political influence in the organization.

The prospects for increasing interstate cooperation in the global commons should improve precisely because these are commons areas and the costs of compliance are disseminated among many governments. More successful agreements are reached when concerns involve potential threats and the real prospects for developing natural resources are unknown. In the long run, preventive agreements are more successful than reactive policies, which are fashioned after environmental damage has begun. The 1959 Antarctic Treaty and the 1967 Outer Space Treaty furnish examples of successful preclusive agreements.[87]

THE BALANCE SHEET

The cardinal principle of sovereignty underpins rights that states seek to assert in global commons areas. That is, states claim a sovereign right to perform activities within their sovereign territories, regardless of what impacts might be produced on the commons. In this regard, permanent sovereignty by a state over its natural resources remains a basic tenet of international law. The state's sovereign right to conduct its foreign policy without external interference is also a fundamental guarantee of international law.

Sovereignty, as a hallmark of modern international law and the contemporary state system, has not disappeared. As a legal attribute, sovereignty still means supreme authority, independence, and rule of the state. Sovereignty also provides for the state's exclusive jurisdiction over activities within its territory and the related duty for other states to refrain from interfering in another state's internal or external affairs. The tendency by governments to pursue national sovereign prerogatives without duly considering their international ramifications causes global gridlock. It reflects the reluctance of governments to cooperate in halting environmental abuse and deterioration in commons areas for the sake of exploiting the region for their own short-term economic gains. Such a strategy is internationally shortsighted and environmentally regrettable.

But also stemming from the concept of global commons is the inference that absolute national sovereignty may be declining. As more states engage in more international agreements and become legally bound to greater numbers of international obligations, the degree of absolute freedom enjoyed by states is diminished. The increasing nexus of international obligations means the concomitant lessening of states' abilities to pursue unilateral sovereign policies. Such a trend seems encouraging for greater cooperative management of global commons areas. Perhaps nowhere else in international experience has this perception been better demonstrated than in the Antarctic. Since 1959 intense considerations of national sovereignty in Antarctica have been set aside by seven states to allow for greater international cooperation with several other nonclaimant states in governing the region.

Managing global commons areas ultimately becomes a behavioral problem,[88] and individuals and governments must act responsibly and assertively. From such pressures impetus is given to governments to take international action. Nongovernmental organizations frequently convey public opinion. For democratic governments, the rise of environmental issues in local politics, through green movements or simply consciousness raising, is a dynamic political development in the management of global commons areas. It is this concern over the need for governments to exercise responsible behavior in global commons areas that underpins the integrity of the Antarctic Treaty System. Indeed, the rise of such ecological consciousness since the 1960s has driven the development of a special body of regional law and policy for the polar South.

The Earth's commons areas are integrated. The oceans, atmosphere, outer space, and the Antarctic are ecologically interdependent. This natural fact again highlights a salient reality in international environmental law: While states remain the primary actors, Nature does not recognize international boundaries, and man-made pollution transcends them. Moreover, the individual state is not capable of being the lone legal agent for addressing problems global in scope. A resolute, concerted international response is required for implementing solutions to problems affecting global commons areas.

Global commons areas legally belong either to no one or to everyone. Commons regions belong to no state or group of states. In the actual practice of states, the Antarctic situation today reflects these fundamental conditions particular to global commons areas. But claims of national sovereignty by seven states, though at present not overtly exercised, persist for portions of the continent. Accordingly, it becomes important to determine to what extent the Antarctic aptly qualifies as part of the global commons, and how that situation affects development of an international regime to manage the area.

ANTARCTICA AS A GLOBAL COMMONS

Antarctica has been described as a "special kind of commons" or a "disputed commons."[89] Even so, its status as a global commons area sometimes is questioned, largely on account of the competing claims by seven governments for sovereignty on the continent. Determining the status of Antarctica as a global commons area therefore involves assessing the nature of a global commons vis-à-vis the nature of the regime governing the continent. The fact remains, however, that no two global commons areas are exactly alike. Moreover, the natural and legal situations of the Antarctic plainly intimate that the region qualifies as a global commons area. The constellation of international agreements comprising the Antarctic Treaty System (ATS) also implies attributes of a global commons regime.

Recall that for an area to qualify as part of the global commons, certain features should apply:

1. The area is physically and legally situated beyond the limits of national jurisdiction.

2. No valid sovereignty claims can apply to the area.

3. The area is geophysically indivisible and not practically enclosable. It thus may be more appropriately governed by a multilateral regime, rather than just one state.

4. Universal access to the area is implied by the absence of individual ownership or demonstrated national sovereignty, or by the concept of *res communis*.

5. Effects of use/management or abuse/mismanagement (i.e., the benefits or costs) of the area are experienced universally. This includes both negative effects of exploitation and depreciation as well as beneficial effects of protection, conservation, or preservation.

6. The area probably requires international management schemes for resource conservation. Left unregulated, global commons areas are often invaded by extractive technologies and chemical pollution, leading to serious environmental degradation of their resources from abuse and overuse. Management of the commons through international legal institutions then becomes necessary to ensure ecological protection and resource conservation.

Other characteristics are present in global commons areas as well. For one, contemporary international politics over their use have been shaped mainly by economic controversies between the North and the South and the quest for sustainable development worldwide. For another, acts of national sovereignty in a commons area can undermine prospects for conflict resolution, as they discourage international cooperation. Another feature is the use of international agreements to promote development of legal principles and rules for regulating states' activities in that area. Additionally, there is the essential need to attain near-universal compliance and enforceability by states of those principles and rules in the commons area. Further, nongovernmental organizations often assume prominent roles as environmental watchdogs over global commons areas. And finally, the formation of appropriate policies for managing a commons area remains dependent upon new scientific information and the sympathetic politics of science. While all of these features are not always present for every global commons area, many are for nearly all cases. Managing the global commons must accordingly take them into close account.

Sovereignty Considerations

The status of sovereignty claims to Antarctica remains the key sticking point for determining whether the continent should be legally considered *terra nullius* (land belonging to no one) or *terra communis* (land belonging to everyone). This question invites pondering whether Antarctica can, as a practical matter of international law, be lawfully claimed by any state.[90]

Not all of Antarctica rests on firm ground. As mentioned earlier, much of subglacial Eastern Antarctica resembles a depressed, ice-covered archipelago. Further, about 10 percent of the continent's ice sheet actually extends beyond the continent as massive ice shelves. Antarctica as a consequence is not geologically *terra firma* as a whole and cannot therefore qualify literally as *terra nullius* in its entirety. Most of the continent's surface and its seaward margins are ice, which might be called *glacia firma*. This invites the intriguing query as to whether frozen water can qualify as having the same legal status as land for purposes of acquiring valid claim to sovereign title over territory.[91]

Competing claims to national sovereignty on Antarctica are premised on the continent's having the legal status of *terra nullius*, bolstered by the absence of an indigenous human population there. Other conditions required for establishing valid claim to title—and hence the right of sovereignty—override the fact that a lawful agent discovered some territory in the name of a sovereign state. A sovereign must demonstrate that administrative state functions actually exist in that new territory and that delimitation of the territory is not disputed.[92] When applied to Antarctica, these standards do not appear to have been adequately met. Harsh environmental conditions on the continent have rendered governmental regulation, administrative control, and continuous occupation thus far impossible.[93] True and effective occupation, demonstrated through permanent settlement, remains to be convincingly demonstrated in Antarctica by any claimant government. Sovereignty claims legally premised on Antarctica being a *res nullius* are therefore questionable.

In addition, claims to sovereignty in Antarctica clearly remain controversial. In fact, the contentious nature of conflicting claims to the continent necessitated creation of an ingenious legal linchpin in the 1959 Antarctic Treaty—namely, the Article IV provision that sets sovereignty claims aside.[94] Article IV finesses the sovereignty conundrum as it requires governments to put aside the legal effects of sovereignty claims as a precondition for participating in the agreement.[95] While Article IV also prevents sovereignty claims to Antarctica from being "prejudiced," which implies that they had some credibility to begin with, such claims have not been accepted by any governments other than the claimants in state practice.[96] Moreover, Antarctic claims are not perfectible while the treaty is in force; they may not be enlarged, reinforced, "perfected," or bolstered by those states' activities. National assertions to sovereign title remain shelved, through an agreement that works as a political device but one that has worked successfully for nearly four decades. Under the present legal arrangement, claims to sovereignty in Antarctica today appear more as political artifacts than viable constructs in international law.

Significantly, the Antarctic Treaty assumes sovereignty as a principle fundamental to Antarctic affairs. Parties to the treaty are sovereign polities engaging in the sovereign right to join international agreements. But for legal and political purposes on the continent, sovereignty's presence is neither paramount nor pervasive. So long as the Antarctic Treaty remains functioning as a legal instrument, and so long as the parties comply with its provisions, the Antarctic can be viewed legally as lying beyond the limits of recognized national jurisdiction, absent any lawfully recognized national sovereignty claims. In the view of contemporary international law, then, the continent under the Antarctic Treaty has become indivisible. Permission is not required from claimant governments to move from one claimed sector to another; passports are not required to visit various national bases around the continent; non–Antarctic Treaty governments may lawfully send their own scientists to the Antarctic without permission from any Antarctic Treaty party, claimant or otherwise, to conduct scientific investigations anywhere in the region. Antarctica under the 1959 Treaty is to be an area open to all, for the scientific benefit of all.

The absence of effective administrative control by individual states over Antarctica clearly implies the absence of valid territorial sovereignty over the continent, which produces the lack of recognized legitimate territorial jurisdiction in the area. Hence, Antarctica not only lies beyond the limits of national jurisdiction, it also lies beyond the limits of any state's ability yet to demonstrate, define, develop, or enforce sufficient national jurisdiction to merit a valid claim to title over territory.

Free Access

Perhaps regarding Antarctica as *res communis* would be more appropriate.[97] Central to this legal notion is that access to the commons area is free and open to all peoples. Yet, since the 1960s certain restrictions have evolved through the Antarctic Treaty System that clearly curtail that access for ATS parties. Specially protected areas; specially managed areas; various historic sites; bans on mining or drilling activities on or around the continent; closing fishing areas and setting limits on where, when, and how much harvesting of certain species can be done—all these measures are specifically intended to limit access for express purposes of resource protection and conservation. Hence the argument that Antarctica cannot be a commons, either in the literal or legal sense. The region is being controlled by a select group of governments, making international law and Antarctic policy explicitly for themselves and implicitly for the international community.

But free access to a commons area is not necessarily beneficial. In fact, open, unregulated access, especially if resource exploitation were freely undertaken, might quickly desecrate a commons area or deplete its living resources. Consider ocean dumping or air pollution, as well as the plight of whales during this century. Limiting access, either by strict human regulation or by the natural force of harsh environmental conditions, can protect a commons. Antarctica mirrors this situation. Although legal limits on access are imposed by the ATS, formidable natural obstacles exist as well. In the first event, the treaty provides admission to the ATCP group only to governments who can demonstrate "substantial scientific research activity"[98] in the Antarctic. Even so, to conduct activities in the Antarctic requires considerable scientific knowledge and technological capabilities, performed under extremely harsh conditions. As with ocean mining and outer space exploration, few governments can afford the financial luxury to engage in such efforts.

Environmental conditions aside, the Antarctic Treaty does permit free and open access to all to further the chief benefit and primary export of Antarctica, namely, scientific research. The Antarctic Treaty remains open to all members of the United Nations.[99] The Antarctic marine living resources agreement does permit parties access to resources of the Southern Ocean, albeit subject to conservation regulations regarding seals, marine living resources, and international whaling instruments. States party to these agreements are not required to share profits from any harvested resources with any others, thus falling short of common heritage of mankind principles. In all these endeavors, however, the open access to scientific research and cooperative exchange remains special and preeminent, indicative of a kind of international commons regime.

Twenty-six of the forty-three states now party to the Antarctic Treaty are Consultative Parties having full rights of decision-making. Seventeen parties are observer states. The treaty requires that access to the Antarctic not be restricted and that access should be guided toward uses that are compatible with a uniquely fragile ecosystem. Regarding minerals exploitation, the present Antarctic Treaty regime aspires not to be one of inequitable free access but rather one of equal nonaccess. ATCP parties have agreed to forfeit the legal right to explore for and exploit minerals found in or around the continent. The Antarctic Environmental Protection Protocol contains this provision, which when in force, will apply to all parties of the Antarctic Treaty.

An important caveat is needed here. The agreements comprising the Antarctic Treaty System legally apply only to those governments which have willingly consented to accept them. As explained in chapter 3, states not party to these instruments are not legally obligated to comply with their specific limitations and restrictions, although they still enjoy free, unrestricted access to the continent, its circumpolar seas, and their natural resources. The ATS agreements legally bind only their parties; they do not generate international legal obligations for all states whose nationals might visit the Antarctic.

Obstacles to free, open access to the Antarctic area even greater than legal obligations in agreements are found in the region's extreme climate and frigid environment. These are natural conditions about which humans can do little or nothing. Antarctic ice, wind, and cold, augmented by the legal fiats requiring responsible use, have combined to produce a more effective regime for protecting and conserving the Antarctic commons area.

Distribution of Costs and Benefits

Antarctica resembles a global commons area in another profound way: Both the costs of its destruction and the benefits of its use and protection for scientific research are global in scope. This is particularly true for global climate change, world weather patterns, and the circulation of wind and ocean currents worldwide.

Antarctica remains a valuable research center. As discussed in chapter 7, the ice sheet contains the climate record of the planet. The region's temperature extremes are useful for studying the effects of cold on creatures and their biological abilities to adapt. The physical hardships of living in Antarctica provide a social and psychological laboratory for studying human behavior under extreme conditions of solitary isolation.

The area furnishes globally shared natural benefits as well. The massive Antarctic ice sheet interacts with ocean and air currents and influences climate around the world. The great capacity of Antarctic ice to reflect solar radiation prevents Earth from overheating. However, to the degree that the ice sheet is melting, global warming might be enhanced by the loss of that Antarctic reflecting power. Antarctica, given its sensitivity to environmental change, serves as a global early warning system for climatic change. Detection of the ozone hole above Antarctica, therefore, might be a harbinger of more serious problems for the rest of the planet.

Multilateral or Supranational Management

As for all global commons areas, considerations of national sovereignty affect the management of Antarctica. Still, various proposals advocating a more internationalized strategy for protecting the Antarctic add to its credibility as a global commons area. One approach is to establish a condominium for Antarctica—that is, to create an international arrangement of shared rights and duties, with several states capable of exercising rights of sovereignty. Such an arrangement would mean pooling governing responsibilities among involved states but would not require any state to relinquish prior claimed rights. Still, a new institution would be needed to manage and enforce agreed upon policies under a condominium.[100] Suggestions for such a new international institution have taken different approaches, including proposals for an Antarctic Public Heritage Agency,[101] an Antarctic Environmental Protection Agency,[102] or a new organization analogous to the International Seabed Authority.[103]

Another suggestion would have the United Nations declare Antarctica an international trusteeship territory.[104] The UN Trusteeship Council might be resurrected to form a Trusteeship Commission on the Global Commons, on which would sit governments having vested interests in the Antarctic.[105] This mechanism would be an international clearinghouse for developing norms, standards, and rules to deal with specific problems affecting commons areas.

Other proposals would designate Antarctica as an internationally protected environmental sanctuary, or "world park."[106] Implementation of such a plan would not be difficult for the Consultative Parties and would cut short future controversies between developed and developing countries over sharing Antarctic resources. No exploitation activities could go forward, and no resources would be commercially available to share. The recent addition of the Environmental Protection Protocol to the Antarctic Treaty System might be viewed as contributing to this world park approach.[107]

Similarities to Global Commons Regimes

The regime now administering activities in the Antarctic resembles in political and economic dynamics other global commons regimes. This fact also reinforces the conclusion that Antarctica should be considered part of the global commons.

Like the deep seabed and the moon, Antarctica was touted by developing countries as part of the common heritage of mankind. This was done so that economic benefits and revenues derived from exploiting its mineral resources might be used for development opportunities in those poorer countries. As analyzed in chapter 8, developing countries not only vigorously advocated during the 1980s that the common heritage concept be applied to Antarctica, but also posed demands for greater access to the "Antarctic Club" and asserted that more extensive technology transfer was necessary so that they could acquire the scientific expertise needed to operate in Antarctica. While these ambitions were largely not met, and no special international Antarctic authority was created, important changes were made in the ways and means by which the Antarctic Treaty functioned.[108]

Nongovernmental organizations have influenced Antarctic affairs, especially by publicly advocating more impartial investigation, environmental monitoring, and scientific research. Certain of these NGOs have even attained observer status in ATS proceedings and participate as self-appointed conservators of the Antarctic global commons.[109] In this connection, however, scientific research has taken on a role for Antarctic politics that is more pivotal than for other global commons: It remains the Antarctic's most valuable resource. Without constant accumulation of new scientific data, protection of the Antarctic environment and conservation of its living resources are not possible. Scientific research and the exchange of that information are the foundation stones for the "commonness" of Antarctica, and they provide the cardinal motive for governments to cooperate in the region.[110]

CONCLUSION

The status of Antarctica as part of the global commons has, until recently, been largely ignored and undervalued. While not significant in terms of human habitation or cultural development, the Antarctic still warrants serious policy consideration and focused geopolitical attention. The sheer size and physical dimensions of the area; the far-reaching impacts exerted by Antarctica on the Earth's climate, atmosphere, and oceans; the potential for exploiting living and mineral resources; and, the fact that the continent contains 90 percent of the world's surface freshwater in its ice cap—these considerations make the future of Antarctica and its circumpolar seas a salient consideration for contemporary world politics, as well as for sustaining the environmental integrity of the planet.

The status of sovereignty on the continent remains a legal conundrum for both Antarctic Treaty parties and the international community. Permanent settlement to effect occupation is a necessary precondition for sovereignty; effective occupation is essential for establishing sovereign title to Antarctic polar areas—these conditions have not changed in international law. If anything, the process of territorial acquisition has been sharpened and clarified by modern state practice. No compelling argument can justify jettisoning the fundamental requirements for territorial occupation on account of extraordinarily harsh environmental conditions. This remains the case for the Sahara Desert, the Arctic, and the island of Greenland. It should remain the case for the continent of Antarctica as well.

While Antarctica is extremely inhospitable for humans, this should neither cloud not skew overarching principles of modern international law. For sovereignty to exist in fact, it must be demonstrated in fact. People must live there, work there, and exist there in a civil society with recognized territorial borders and a functioning local government. Lands whose status cannot fulfill these conditions of occupation fail the test of practicality required for legitimate sovereignty. Scientists from at least twenty-six states, most of whom are nationals of nonclaimant states, visit the Antarctic temporarily for purposes of scientific research and investigation, not to colonize or establish permanent residency. Thus, the "inhabitants" in the Antarctic are scientists, not colonists, leaving the lawfulness of title to territory for Antarctic lands left open to question.

In the absence of recognized validity of any claims to title on the frozen continent, the principle of effective occupation presents the most appropriate means for securing title to territory in Antarctica. As the basis for acquiring sovereignty in Antarctica, effective occupation though permanent settlement remains the essential legal prerequisite condition. Thus far, in the legal view of the international community, that condition in Antarctica remains unfulfilled. To the extent that national sovereignty is practiced in the Antarctic, it can be found in the scientific stations where laws and regulations follow the flag of the state sponsoring that facility. But for the ice-clad continent as a territory, the existence or exercise of national sovereignty appears to remain more legal fiction than actual fact.

The Antarctic region is part of the global commons. Accordingly, in recent years the need has arisen for new international law to manage increased human activities there. The rest of this study examines that need. In the process, special attention focuses on efforts to protect the environment and to establish a management regime that is guided by legal norms for regulating human conduct and the use of natural resources on, in, and around the Antarctic continent.

Chapter 3

GOVERNANCE STRUCTURES

The Antarctic commons is governed by a special legal arrangement that has evolved, bit by bit, over the past four decades. Known as the Antarctic Treaty System (ATS), this constellation of legal agreements has been incrementally constructed by a particular group of governments so as to integrate each new treaty for the Antarctic with previous ones.

This chapter examines the legal agreements that make up the Antarctic Treaty System. It analyses the regulatory nature of each agreement, as well as the regulations' connections to similar provisions in other ATS agreements. From this assessment one can see the political and legal intricacies of the ATS, the specific links between the agreements, and their purposeful integration into a composite whole. The Antarctic Treaty System thus emerges as a complex legal regime, comprised of a cluster of subregimes, that aims at regulating governments and the activities of their nationals in the Antarctic commons.

EVOLUTION OF THE 1959 TREATY

The 1959 Antarctic Treaty is the core legal instrument in the Antarctic Treaty System. It serves as the legal hub for an international regime to manage national activities in the Antarctic commons. The origins of the Antarctic Treaty can be traced to the dispute during the 1940s among the United Kingdom, Argentina, and Chile over their overlapping sovereignty claims to the Antarctic Peninsula. The United States, in seeking to resolve this conflict, suggested in 1948 that a moratorium be placed on all sovereignty claims in the region and that consideration be given to putting the continent under the administration of a United Nations

Trusteeship.[1] Argentina and the United Kingdom opposed any solution that might compromise their territorial sovereignty in Antarctica. Chile, on the other hand, reacted in a more conciliatory fashion and proposed the Escudaro Declaration, which would have held sovereign claims in abeyance for five years, during which time international scientific cooperation would be encouraged.[2] This suggestion by Chile became the progenitor for what became a multilateral legal regime to regulate activities on and around Antarctica.

Several developments helped set the international political stage for the 1959 Washington Conference that eventually adopted the Antarctic Treaty. For one, an attitude change took place among the seven claimant states. During the International Geophysical Year (IGY) of 1957/58, participating governments agreed tacitly on the need to cooperate in a spirit of scientific amity and agreement. The friendship and cooperation that emerged from the IGY fostered a belief among claimant governments that disputes over sovereignty could be set aside in the interest of peace and mutual scientific benefits.[3]

A second development was the expansion of international interest in Antarctica. By the mid-1950s Antarctica became an area of concern among states that historically had demonstrated little interest in the region. For example, in 1956 India suggested that the "Question of Antarctica" be inserted on the agenda of the United Nations General Assembly.[4] The suggestion went nowhere, however.

The third, and perhaps most critical, development was the ascendancy of the United States and the Soviet Union as dominant players on the Antarctic continent. The United States exerted a major influence over Antarctica, not only because of its numerous scientific activities there but also because of its preponderant presence there. Presumably, the United States might make its own national claim in the Antarctic, if it deemed this to be necessary. The Cold War rivalry of the superpowers played out in the South Pole as the Soviet Union insisted that it participate equally in Antarctic affairs, especially in activities related to the IGY. The launch of Sputnik in 1957 furnished compelling evidence to Western analysts that Antarctica merited strategic importance, and the continent, it was feared, might be used by the Soviets as a strategic base for launching ballistic missiles aimed at Western states. The Soviets established more scientific stations than any other IGY participant during 1957/58, in every claimed sector of the continent. The Soviets' assertion of a historical right to make a claim in Antarctica,[5] and the possibility that they one day might exercise it, raised further concerns among the United States and other claimant states regarding future governance of the continent.[6]

These international concerns led to negotiations during the spring and summer of 1959 among the twelve governments that had participated in the 1957/58 IGY. These negotiations culminated in the Washington Conference and the promulgation of the Antarctic Treaty on December 1, 1959. The agreement entered into force for those twelve states on June 23, 1961. With that, the seed for the Antarctic Treaty System had sprouted.

THE ANTARCTIC TREATY SYSTEM NEXUS

The Antarctic Treaty

The Antarctic Treaty is the core of the ATS. Its provisions supply the normative themes, rules, and procedures that have progressively evolved into an internationally functional regime. The Antarctic Treaty asserts relatively modest objectives. It was designed chiefly to facilitate scientific cooperation and to ensure that activities in the Antarctic are dedicated to peaceful purposes. A secondary purpose of the treaty is to ensure the "preservation and conservation of living resources in Antarctica."[7] This phrase is the lone reference to conservation in the entire Antarctic Treaty.

The preamble to the Antarctic Treaty sets the tenor for the whole treaty system, reaffirming the fundamental premises on which the agreement was negotiated. The preamble stresses the aspirations of the treaty: that the continent be used exclusively for peaceful purposes; that it not become the scene or object of international discord; that the driving spirit of scientific research and cooperation continue; and that the treaty's promotion of international harmony contribute to furthering the purposes and principles of the UN Charter.[8] Article I tersely reasserts the obligation to use Antarctica only for peaceful purposes. It prohibits any measures of a military nature, including bases and fortifications, maneuvers, and testing of weapons. The only permissible exception from demilitarization of the region is the use of military personnel or equipment for scientific research, logistical, or other peaceful purposes.[9]

Antarctica is established as a continent for science. Harking back to the IGY, Article II guarantees freedom of scientific investigation and cooperation, subject only to provisions in the treaty. Article III seeks to implement the scientific cooperation called for in Article II. Parties are committed to exchange plans for their scientific programs in Antarctica, exchange scientific personnel between expeditions and stations, and make freely available the results and observations of scientific activities in the region.[10] To promote scientific cooperation, the treaty also encourages working relations with specialized agencies of the United Nations and other organizations with a scientific or technical interest in Antarctica.[11]

The conundrum of disputed sovereignty in Antarctica is addressed in Article IV. This provision is divided into two parts. The first and most intricate paragraph is intended to assure parties that nothing in the treaty is to be interpreted: (a) as a renunciation of a previously asserted claim; (b) as a renunciation or lessening of any basis for assertion of a territorial claim; or (c) as prejudicing the position of any party as regards its recognition or nonrecognition of any other state's claim or basis for claim.[12] This provision circumvents the sensitive sovereignty issue by freezing the status of claims on the continent—not only for the seven original claimants but also for the United States and Soviet Union as potential claimant states. The rationale for dodging the sovereignty issue is to integrate claimant, nonclaimant, and potential claimant states within the same multilateral agreement. This is necessary since the treaty impacts so directly on Antarctic sovereignty. Through such legal legerdemain, all the principal parties are able to cooperate without compromising their actual or potential sovereignty claims. The claimant states are accommodated by subparagraph 1(a), described above, and the United States and Soviet Union are consigned by subparagraph 1(b). The most troublesome of the claims—the assertions made by Argentina, Chile, and the United Kingdom overlapping the Antarctic Peninsula—are specifically redressed through subparagraph 1(c).

The second part of Article IV negates the impact of sovereignty claims during the treaty's duration. It asserts that no new claim or enlargement of an existent claim may be asserted while the treaty remains in force. Moreover, no acts or activities that occur while the treaty is in force may constitute a basis for any state "asserting, supporting, or denying a claim to territorial sovereignty in Antarctica or create any rights of sovereignty in Antarctica."[13] This facet of Article IV ensures that the status of sovereignty claims on the continent remains unaltered throughout the Antarctic Treaty's duration. In effect, then, sovereignty considerations are shelved to prevent them from complicating or undermining successful operation of the treaty.

Article IV is the legal "flexi-glue" that allows the Antarctic Treaty to work for governments who hold diametrically opposed positions on the contentious question of sovereignty over the continent. By agreeing to disagree on the status of the continent—and by pledging in 1959 not to change the legal status quo—parties to the Antarctic Treaty increased both their political maneuverability and their diplomatic confidence.

Article IV is the lubricant that permits the Antarctic Treaty to function, but it also prevents resolution of the sovereignty conundrum on the continent. For that reason, the provision has been criticized as creating a "purgatory of ambiguity" that does little, if anything, to contribute toward a solution.[14] Such criticism, however, presupposes that the sovereignty issue *can* be resolved. A solution cannot emerge as long as the claimant states persist in asserting their sovereign possession of territory in Antarctica. Article IV at least dampens the energy with which states pursue claims and fosters meanwhile an atmosphere of cooperation between claimant states that may ease future negotiations over sovereignty.

Another obvious legal difficulty with Article IV is that it does not apply to all states. Governments not party to the Antarctic Treaty are not bound to the moratorium on claims or exercise of sovereign rights in the region. As a consequence, a nonparty state could lawfully proceed with activities aimed at establishing an eventual basis for asserting a sovereignty claim. That has not happened thus far, nor does it appear likely in the future because of the harsh Antarctic conditions and the high costs for conducting activities there.

But such criticisms ignore the chief purpose of Article IV, namely, to provide a politically workable arrangement for states with competing claims and mutually supportive claims, and for states that deny legal respect for those claims. Since 1961 this proviso has functioned successfully as a modus vivendi for the states party to the Antarctic Treaty. It permits those governments to participate in the whole Antarctic Treaty System and allows states to give national allegiance to an international Antarctic regime. In sum, Article IV accomplishes a fundamental aim of the treaty relationship: to accommodate the sovereignty issue and permit the treaty to function by effectively setting out a moratorium on claims. That cardinal achievement should not be lost in all the criticism.

Article V of the Antarctic Treaty prohibits nuclear explosions and the disposal of nuclear wastes in Antarctica. It is important to realize, though, that Article V does not expressly prohibit the use of nuclear energy on the continent.[15] Particularly notable about this provision is that it established the Antarctic area as the first, and indeed the most extensive, nuclear weapons–free zone in the world. Even more impressive, when Article V is set in tandem with Article I of the treaty, Antarctica is rendered a completely demilitarized area—in effect, a zone of peace covering nearly one-tenth of the Earth's surface. This stands as a truly remarkable accomplishment given that the treaty was negotiated in 1959 and entered into force in 1961, during the tensest times of the Cold War between the United States and the Soviet Union.

Article VI fixes the jurisdictional reach of the treaty to the area south of 60° south latitude, inclusive of all ice shelves. The provision guarantees, moreover, that nothing in the treaty will prejudice or affect the rights or exercise of rights of any state on the high seas in the treaty area. High-seas freedoms, therefore, are explicitly preserved for all states.[16] The provision on high-seas rights has certain problematic legal implications for the Antarctic Treaty parties. Literal interpretation of Article VI suggests that the treaty applies to all waters south of 60° south, but with no effect on high-seas freedoms. But what are the legal implications for those waters directly offshore the claimed portions of the continent? Are they subject to national jurisdiction, territorial claim, or the proclamation of exclusive economic zones? This conundrum involving contemporary law of the sea zones remains unanswered.[17]

Article VI implicitly distinguishes between ice shelves and high seas. It suggests that under the treaty, ice shelves are to be considered neither as land nor ocean space. Rather they should be treated as sui generis, a unique geophysical form unto themselves. While this distinction may appear to lessen confusion over the legal status of ice fringes along the continent, Article VI does little to clarify the legal status of waters under the ice shelves, especially the massive Ross and Ronne formations. This ambiguity cannot help but invite problems of competing jurisdictional interpretation when considered in view of subsequent developments in the modern law of the sea, especially the creation of 12–nautical mile territorial seas and 200–nautical mile exclusive economic zones under the now-activated 1982 UN Convention on the Law of the Sea.[18]

Contracting parties to the Antarctic Treaty are permitted under Article VII to inspect each other's stations and activities in the Antarctic. This provision, of course, aims to foster cooperation and ensure that obligations in the treaty are being fully observed by state parties. What makes this stipulation so notable is that the inspection procedures enable unannounced, open access to all sites in Antarctica, including stations, installations, and equipment, as well as ships, aircraft, and personnel at points of cargo discharge or embarkation.[19] Again, considering the timing of the treaty's enactment during the Cold War, the significance of this provision should not be minimized. Between 1963 and 1997 fifteen governments conducted thirty-one inspection missions, visiting at least 170 bases or ships representing the nationality of every state active in the Antarctic.[20]

Article VII also requires the exchange of information between parties on matters concerning expeditions to and within Antarctica, as well as on stations occupied by nationals and any military personnel or equipment needed to support scientific research.[21] This desire to facilitate information exchange was a legacy of the productive cooperative experience during the IGY period. Parties exchange information on a broad range of topics, including logistical problems, measures needed to protect living resources, conditions affecting living resources, tourism, telecommunications facilities, and meteorology.[22]

Jurisdiction over nationals in Antarctica is dealt with in Article VIII. To sidestep the problematic sovereignty issue, contracting parties maintain jurisdiction over their own nationals who are designated observers, scientific personnel, or staff members.[23] Should jurisdiction over nationals become the object of dispute, the respective parties are required to consult together so that a mutually acceptable solution can be reached.[24]

The administration of the Antarctic Treaty and the procedure for convening Antarctic Treaty Consultative Party Meetings (ATCMs) are found in Article IX. Governments that participate in these meetings are known as the Antarctic Treaty Consultative Parties (ATCPs). From 1961 through 1994 the ATCPs convened nearly every two years at sites that rotated among the ATCPs' capitals.[25] Since 1994 ATCMs have been held annually.[26] The Antarctic Treaty conspicuously provides for no independent institutional structure or secretariat.[27] The only permanent decision-making institution in the treaty structure is the Consultative Party Meeting. Article IX also distinguishes among parties to the Antarctic Treaty by categorizing their status on three levels: (1) original ATCPs—the original members of the treaty who are enumerated in the preamble; (2) ATCPs that have become parties by accession and have qualified for ATCP status by conducting substantial scientific activity in Antarctica; and (3) other parties that have acceded to the treaty.[28]

The first category, the original ATCPs, includes the states that took part in the Antarctic phase of the IGY. Seven of these are claimants—Argentina, Australia, Chile, France, New Zealand, Norway, and the United Kingdom. The remaining five are nonclaimants—Belgium, Japan, Russia (the former Soviet Union), South Africa, and the United States. These twelve governments retain a right to attend and participate in discussions and policy formulation during ATCMs by virtue of being founding members of the treaty.

The second category of parties includes those states that have acceded to the treaty and become ATCPs by fulfilling the Article IX, paragraph 2 requirement of demonstrating their "interest in Antarctica by conducting substantial scientific research activity there, such as the establishment of a scientific station or the dispatch of a scientific expedition." Since 1961 fifteen states have acquired this special ATCP status, which comes only with the unanimous approval of all the current ATCPs. In chronological order, the governments admitted to ATCP status include: Poland (in 1977), the Federal Republic of Germany (in 1981), Brazil (in 1983), India (in 1983), China (in 1985), Uruguay (in 1985), the German Democratic Republic (in 1987), Italy (in 1987), Spain (in 1988), Sweden (in 1988), Finland (in 1989), the Republic of Korea (in 1989), Peru (in 1989), Ecuador (in 1990), and the Netherlands (in 1990). The reunification of the Federal Republic of Germany and the German Democratic Republic in 1990 reduced the number of add-on ATCPs to fourteen.

The third category of states includes those that have acceded to the treaty but have yet to meet the qualification of "substantial scientific activity" set by Article IX. Known as Non-Consultative Parties, these seventeen states are entitled to attend ATCMs as observers only. As of 1998 the following states are Non-Consultative Parties: Denmark (since 1965), Romania (since 1971), Bulgaria (since 1978), Papua New Guinea (since 1981), Hungary (since 1984), Cuba (since 1984), Greece (since 1987), the Democratic People's Republic of Korea (since 1987), Austria (since 1987), Canada (since 1988), Colombia (since 1989), Switzerland (since 1990), Guatemala (since 1991), the Ukraine (since 1992), the Czech Peoples' Republic (since 1993), Slovakia (since 1993), and Turkey (since 1996).[29]

The treaty envisioned that ATCMs would provide a forum for the Consultative Parties to exchange information and consult on matters of common interest concerning Antarctica. The chief reason for convening ATCMs, though, was to allow parties to engage in "formulating and considering, and recommending to their governments, measures in furtherance of the principles and objectives of the Treaty."[30] As set out in the treaty, these "measures," which only become effective when approved by all ATCP governments,[31] may pertain to:

(a) use of Antarctica for peaceful purposes only;

(b) facilitation of scientific research in Antarctica;

(c) facilitation of international scientific cooperation in Antarctica;

(d) facilitation of the exercise of the rights of inspection provided for in Article VII of the treaty;

(e) questions relating to the exercise of jurisdiction in Antarctica;

(f) preservation and conservation of living resources in Antarctica.[32]

This list of issue areas for consideration by ATCMs is not exhaustive. Any matter of common interest may be placed on an ATCM agenda.

The resolutions adopted by the Consultative Parties at ATCMs from 1961 through 1995 were known simply as "Recommendations" and represented policy decisions taken by the ATCP states as a group. Recommendations were adopted by consensus[33] and were supposed to create a legally binding obligation for ATCP states. Legal uncertainties, however, surround the status of various recommendations that have not been specifically approved by all ATCP governments. Also unclear are the legal effects of previous recommendations on states who become parties to the Antarctic Treaty after the adoption of those recommendations and who have not formally adopted them.

To help remedy these uncertainties, the XIXth ATCM meeting in Seoul, Korea, in 1995 agreed to distinguish recommendations according to three categories. (1) "Measures" are texts approved by all ATCPs and intended to be legally binding as recommended for approval in accordance with Article IX of the Antarctic Treaty. The Measures category reflects the original intent of the term recommendations. Since 1995 nine "measures" have been adopted, pertaining mostly to management plans and protected areas. (2) "Decisions" concern internal organizational matters and become operative upon their adoption at an ATCM. Since 1995 two "decisions" have been adopted, including one that formalized this revision in the status of traditional recommendations. (3) Finally, there are "resolutions," which are nonbinding, hortatory texts adopted at ATCMs. Since 1995 nine "resolutions" have been adopted, largely dealing with logistical issues. Consensus agreement by the ATCPs is still required for the adoption of each new category of recommended text.

Decisions at ATCP meetings are only somewhat authoritative. While measures decided upon at ATCMs require consensus approval of all present, they are considered to be only recommendations to governments.[34] Those measures adopted do not become effective as official Antarctic Treaty policy, however, until all ATCP governments have approved them through their municipal procedures, either through ratification processes or domestic legislation.

The Antarctic Treaty did not establish an international organization with a specific institutional structure endowed with legal personality to deal with Antarctic Treaty matters. The absence of a secretariat and the requirement that recommendations must be adopted unanimously by ATCPs clearly highlight the central concern by claimant states that their sovereignty in Antarctica be protected. No state can be outvoted. Every ATCP government retains the right of veto. Retention of such veto power supplies ATCPs a valued safeguard for their national political interests but has not been a bar to ATCP decision-making. Since 1959 at least 228 "recommended measures" have been adopted by the ATCPs, including twenty-three texts in the three new categories described above.

The Antarctic Treaty also aspires to connect Antarctic affairs with broader international institutions. Parties pledge to undertake efforts in the Antarctic that are consistent with the United Nations Charter and not contrary to the principles and purposes of the treaty.[35] Further, specific provision is made for dispute settlement in the region. Should a dispute arise between parties regarding interpretation or application of the treaty, those parties are obliged to consult together to seek resolution of the problem. The treaty suggests means for peaceful solution of a dispute, including but not limited to negotiation, inquiry, mediation, conciliation, arbitration, and judicial settlement. If a satisfactory solution still is not forthcoming, then states are called upon to submit the issue to the International Court of Justice, provided that consent is given by all parties to the dispute.[36]

The Antarctic Treaty may be modified or amended at any time, provided that all Consultative Parties unanimously agree to do so and go on to ratify the changes.[37] The treaty also provides for a thirty-year review conference.[38] Beginning thirty years after the treaty came into force (i.e., after June 23, 1991), any Consultative Party may call at any time for such a conference. Modifications or amendments to the treaty could be passed at such a conference by a majority of contracting parties if a majority of the Consultative Parties is included as well. Withdrawal from the treaty is permitted under Article XII, though it is a complex process. Any party can initiate withdrawal proceedings by failing to ratify modifications or amendments approved at a review conference. If after two years such modifications or amendments have not entered into force, then a party may give notice of withdrawal from the treaty. Withdrawal would take effect two years after notice is received by the depository government (i.e., the United States).[39]

Article XIII provides terms for ratification of and accession to the treaty by any state that is a member of the United Nations and registers the treaty with the UN Secretariat pursuant to Article 102 of the UN Charter. Finally, official languages of the treaty are stipulated in Article XIV as English, French, Russian, and Spanish, with each version being held equally authentic.

The Antarctic Treaty was originally drafted as a framework agreement for cooperation in international scientific research. Since the Treaty entered into force in 1961, however, state parties have increasingly been required to deal with more difficult concerns, especially issues pertaining to resource exploitation.

In the thirty-six years since its entry into force, the Antarctic Treaty has evolved from a rather modest international legal document with fourteen articles and twelve signatories into the framework for a robust Antarctic Treaty System, a multifaceted regime for managing one-tenth of the Earth's surface. Through legal instruments that support and are supported by the 1959 Treaty, the ATS successfully addresses a number of fundamental issues that affect management of the Antarctic commons but which were not foreseen in 1959. The normative themes that unite the 1959 Treaty and subsequent legal agreements are described below.

Normative Linkages

The Antarctic Treaty establishes the normative framework for the regime system. Among the norms most prominent in Antarctic Treaty affairs are the peaceful use of the continent, scientific cooperation, and continuance of international harmony in Antarctica. These are fundamental to the 1959 agreement and are echoed in the later ATS agreements.

The norm of peaceful use contains two cardinal rules. The first is nonmilitarization of the Antarctic continent and its circumpolar waters. No military forces, bases, maneuvers, or weapons are permitted in the Antarctic, except for naval vessels or military aircraft used for logistical support operations.[40] The second rule is that of nonnuclearization. No nuclear weapons or tests are allowed within the Antarctic Treaty area.[41] To enforce these rules, specified inspection procedures have been adopted, implemented, and repeatedly used by state parties to verify compliance with the treaty provisions.[42]

Also central to the Antarctic Treaty is the norm for scientific cooperation among member states.[43] Science is the main business in the region. Securing scientific cooperation among all governments active in the Antarctic is thus critical to all activities on the continent and to making each and every agreement in the ATS work. Treaty provisions, as well as informal state practice, promote free exchange of scientific information and freedom of scientific investigation in the Antarctic.[44]

The Antarctic Treaty makes little mention of environmental concerns in the region. Within the last two decades, however, protection and conservation of the environment has emerged as a salient normative consideration in Antarctic affairs. The pristine nature of Antarctica makes it a natural laboratory for studying global climatic trends and world pollution patterns. The value of such an environment demands its protection. States are also concerned to prevent the Antarctic commons, one-tenth of the Earth's surface, from becoming degraded and polluted and its living resources from being overharvested.

The rules to ensure protection of the Antarctic environment are still emerging. One key issue is assigning liability for damage. If a natural or juridical person commits an act that results in environmental degradation, the ATCPs are beginning to agree that that person should be responsible for making restitution in a fair, just, and prompt manner. Thus, a consensus is emerging among the Antarctic states around the polluter pays principle—if you pollute, you pay for the environmental cleanup or for ecosystem restoration. Another important environmental issue is conservation of the Antarctic ecosystem. Principles of conservation are being promoted by closing zones to fishing and by regulating harvesting seasons. These liability and conservation measures are intended to bolster appreciation for the aesthetic value of a pristine wilderness. Such protective principles are critical considerations in the ATS agreements linked to the Antarctic Treaty.[45]

ATS INSTRUMENTS

The following section describes five major legal instruments that promote the norms embodied in the 1959 Antarctic Treaty, particularly the norm of environmental conservation. The section lays out the provisions of each instrument as well as its normative and institutional linkages to the 1959 Treaty. In this way the ATS can be appreciated as a web of overlapping and mutually reinforcing agreements that together govern state behavior in the Antarctic commons.

The Agreed Measures

The Antarctic Treaty never attempted to deal comprehensively with all problems that might confront the treaty regime. Those future concerns could be addressed by ATCMs within the Article IX authority of making recommendations. Among the earliest attempts to do this concerned the issue of "preservation and conservation of living resources,"[46] only briefly mentioned in the 1959 Treaty.

At the third ATCM in 1964 in Brussels, the Consultative Parties adopted Recommendation III-VIII, the Agreed Measures for the Conservation of Antarctic Fauna and Flora.[47] The Agreed Measures, as suggested by its title, has as its broad objective to conserve fauna and flora in Antarctica. As set out in its preamble, the Agreed Measures also has three subsidiary objectives: (1) to protect Antarctica's indigenous fauna and flora from man's increasing activities on the Antarctic continent; (2) to foster collaborative scientific research; and (3) to encourage "rational use" (which is left undefined) of Antarctic fauna and flora. Toward these ends, the Agreed Measures declares the Antarctic Treaty area to be a "Special Conservation Area" and aims not just to bind states party to the Antarctic Treaty, but also to influence the actions of third parties, including members of expeditions and scientific stations from states not party to the Antarctic Treaty.[48]

The Agreed Measures entailed a recommendation adopted by the ATCPs according to Article IX of the Antarctic Treaty and was produced at a formal Consultative Meeting, adopted by the ATCPs, and approved as policy by their governments. The Agreed Measures, in short, was a direct product of the Antarctic Treaty process, and its implementation and enforcement were left to the authority of national governments.[49] Governments are expected to administer the system of permits allowing the taking of native mammals and birds,[50] oversee entry into specially protected areas,[51] and control introduction of nonindigenous plants and animals into the Antarctic.[52]

Enforcement of the Agreed Measures is likewise left to national authorities. International monitoring is enabled through the exchange of information among states.[53] The Agreed Measures requires exchange of statistics on the numbers of native birds and mammals captured or killed, information on the status of those fauna, and judgments as to the degree to which a species' protection might be needed. Consonant with the 1959 Treaty's lack of centralized institutions, reporting takes place directly between national governments.

The Scientific Committee on Antarctic Research (SCAR) is the sole international institutional body used by the Agreed Measures to analyze data exchanged between the parties. Beginning in 1970, the ATCPs invited SCAR to publish and gather information exchanged and prepare reports on the status on species.[54]

The continued reliance on national means for implementation and enforcement limits the effectiveness of the Agreed Measures. However, it also highlights the persistent reluctance among ATCPs to entrust a designated institutional regime to oversee effective implementation of the instrument. As discussed earlier, this reluctance stems from the desire among ATCPs to sidestep jurisdictional questions. Another limitation of the Agreed Measures is the unwillingness of ATCPs to affect the high-seas rights guaranteed in the Antarctic Treaty. The regime for the 1964 recommendation is restricted to land, ice shelves, and the airspace above them[55] and likewise echoes Article VI of the Antarctic Treaty in asserting that "nothing in these Agreed Measures shall prejudice or in any way affect the rights, or the exercise of the rights, of any state under international law with regard to the high seas within the Antarctic Treaty area."[56] For the Agreed Measures, then, conservation stops at the edge of the ice. This self-imposed restriction was intended to avoid infringing on the ATCPs' own exercise of high-seas rights, which include the freedom to fish.

The ATCPs are accorded the special right to amend the Agreed Measures (which they did in 1991 through Annex II to the Madrid Protocol), including emendation with annexes.[57] While modification could occur through diplomatic channels,[58] actual practice has been for amendments to be adopted at regular ATCMs in the form of recommendations.

The Seals Convention

During the mid-1960s a pilot Soviet sealing expedition in the Antarctic area aroused concern among the ATCPs over the threatening possibility that commercial sealing might return to the circumpolar high seas. This threat fell outside the legal purview of the Agreed Measures, which only protected seals on the continent, on its ice shelves, and on islands within the Antarctic Treaty area. The ATCPs convened a special conference in London on the seals issue, though outside the framework of the Antarctic Treaty. The decision to hold a special, non-ATCP session was made for two main reasons. First, conservation of seals did not fall within the scope of the 1964 Agreed Measures. Second, ATCPs felt that the conservation of seals might be of interest to states other than themselves.[59] Even so, only ATCP states participated in the conference, most having no intention of harvesting Antarctic seals.

The product of the London conference, the Convention for the Conservation of Antarctic Seals, was opened for signature on June 1, 1972, was signed by all twelve participant ATCPs, and entered into force in 1978.[60] The Seals Convention applies to the seas south of 60° south latitude, though it may also be applied to sea ice floating northward of that parameter.[61] The principal objective of the 1972 Seals Convention is to establish effective conservation measures that prevent decimation of Antarctic seals should harvesting activities be revived by some state.

To pursue conservation, the Seals Convention coordinates the exchange of information and provides for scientific assessments of species' health.[62] Like the Antarctic Treaty and the Agreed Measures, the Seals Convention identifies SCAR as the agency to perform those roles.[63] Provisions in the Annex require each contracting party to provide information either to other contracting parties and to SCAR or to SCAR alone. SCAR is to assess the data, make recommendations regarding the effects of sealing on species sustainability,[64] and notify the depository state (i.e., the United Kingdom), which is to report to contracting governments if permissible catch limits for any species might be exceeded. The harvesting state is then supposed to estimate for SCAR the date on which permissible catch limits might be reached and then take "appropriate measures to prevent its nationals and vessels under its flag from killing or capturing seals of that species after the estimated date until the Contracting Parties decide otherwise."[65]

Concern over restricting high-seas activities is reaffirmed in Article 1, which sets application of the Seals Convention "to the seas south of 60° South Latitude." Seals are protected within the Antarctic Treaty's ocean space under this agreement. The Seals Convention excludes from its application the continent and its ice shelves, which are areas covered by the 1964 Agreed Measures.

The 1972 Convention on the Conservation of Antarctic Seals contains clear links to the Antarctic Treaty. In addition to its clear necessity as a means for fulfilling the conservation objective left incomplete in the 1959 Treaty, the Seals Convention makes direct references to the Antarctic Treaty in its preamble. Paragraph 1 of the preamble specifically recalls the Agreed Measures adopted under the Antarctic Treaty, to which the Seals Convention is an adjunct. In the convention provisions, Article 1(1) sets the same jurisdictional scope for the new instrument as the Antarctic Treaty (i.e., 60° south latitude). It also affirms that the contracting parties accept as obligatory Article IV of the Antarctic Treaty.[66] In Article 4(2) the Contracting Parties are required to inform SCAR about the purpose and content of special permits they issue for killing or capturing seals. Article 5 stipulates that contracting parties must provide to SCAR information on how they are acting to implement the Seals Convention. These provisions expressly link the Seals Convention with SCAR, the same international scientific committee that has responsibility for facilitating scientific cooperation among the ATCP governments.[67] Also significant is that paragraph 4 in the Annex attached to the Seals Convention sets out special sealing zones. Closure of those zones in that Annex is tied to "paragraph 2 of Annex B to Annex 1 on closings in the Report of the Fifth Antarctic Treaty Consultative Party Meeting," thereby asserting the formal link to the Antarctic Treaty.[68]

The Antarctic Marine Living Resources Convention

A milestone agreement for preserving and protecting the integrity of the Antarctic seas ecosystem is the Convention on the Conservation of Antarctic Marine Living Resources (CCAMLR).[69] Negotiated in 1980, CCAMLR entered into force in April 1982.[70] Despite earlier ATCP concerns over extending the scope of international regulations to the high seas, the purpose of CCAMLR is to regulate a high-seas activity, namely the harvesting of living marine resources. The conservation agreement applies to all marine living resources within the Antarctic ecosystem and "related and associated ecosystems," covering an area roughly bounded by the Antarctic Convergence, which differs from the northern 60° south latitude boundary in other ATS instruments.[71]

CCAMLR, unlike the legal instruments discussed previously, creates an administering institution. The Commission for the Conservation of Antarctic Marine Living Resources makes and regulates policy and is accorded legal personality with privileges and immunities.[72] The Commission can promulgate binding conservation measures[73] through the decision-making procedures set out in CCAMLR.[74] As of 1998 the Commission had twenty-three members: Argentina, Australia, Belgium, Brazil, Chile, the European Community, France, Germany, India, Italy, Japan, the Republic of Korea, New Zealand, Norway, Poland, the Russian Federation, South Africa, Spain, Sweden, the Ukraine, the United Kingdom, the United States, and Uruguay. These include all states fishing in southern waters save two—Panama and Bulgaria. Bulgaria is an acceding state to the Convention and joined the Commission in 1995.[75] Policies of the Commission are decided by consensus among the parties.[76] The consensus rule, adopted to accommodate the position of the Antarctic claimants, also coincides with the interests of fishing states, who wish to retain some discretion over the exercise of their activities in the region.

The Antarctic Marine Living Resources Convention establishes a special advisory body, the Scientific Committee, that functions as "a forum for consultation and co-operation concerning the collection, study and exchange of information with respect to marine living resources. . . ."[77] A full-time secretariat for CCAMLR is headquartered in Hobart, Tasmania, to administer the organization's bureaucratic responsibilities.[78]

The Convention links CCAMLR institutions to external agencies through explicit directives for cooperation. The Commission and the Scientific Committee are charged with cooperating, "as appropriate," with the Food and Agriculture Organization and other UN specialized agencies. These two CCAMLR bodies are also supposed to work with intergovernmental and nongovernmental organizations, including SCAR, the Scientific Committee on Oceanic Research, and the International Whaling Commission.[79]

The jurisdictional reach of CCAMLR is impressive. Through its ecosystemic approach (described more fully in chapter 5), the Convention encompasses all "the marine living resources" of an area and covers all species of living organisms, including seals.[80] CCAMLR is not meant to apply so much to the *area* south of the Antarctic Convergence as it does to the living marine resources found *within* that area, in this respect differing from the Antarctic Treaty and the Seals Convention, which focus more on a given area of land and sea than on the resources that area might contain.[81] CCAMLR overlaps in jurisdiction with the Antarctic Treaty, the Agreed Measures, and the Seals Convention, and its provisions make its relationships to those instruments explicit. CCAMLR likewise acknowledges the International Whaling Convention, but by expressly excluding it from the family of ATS agreements.[82]

CCAMLR, like the 1959 Treaty, had to be carefully designed to accommodate the disparate positions of states as regards sovereignty claims. The extended scope of CCAMLR northward beyond 60° south latitude, to encompass areas where certain island groups were situated, aroused fresh concerns. Some of these islands had disputed sovereignty claims; others did not.

The Commission distinguishes between different maritime zones in the area that it circumscribes. Thus, understandings in the Convention formally acknowledge rights by France to apply national conservation measures to waters around Kerguélen and Crozet Islands. These understandings recognize France's right to use its own national measures to regulate these zones[83] but preserve the effective scope of CCAMLR's jurisdiction.

CCAMLR makes explicit linkages to previous Antarctic instruments. In the language of CCAMLR's preamble, the stipulation is made that conservation of Antarctic marine living resources requires international cooperation with "due regard" for the provisions of the Antarctic Treaty.[84] Specific recognition, moreover, is given to "the prime responsibilities of the Antarctic Treaty Consultative Parties for the protection and preservation of the Antarctic environment and, in particular, their responsibilities under Article IX, paragraph 1(f) of the Antarctic Treaty in respect of the preservation and conservation of the living resources of living resources in Antarctica."[85] Reference also is made to the Agreed Measures and the Seals Convention.[86] Thus, at the outset CCAMLR clearly acknowledges its debt to other Antarctic Treaty instruments and preserves the treaty norm that ATCPs have primary authority over activities within the area.

Article III of CCAMLR unites that agreement with the Antarctic Treaty. Contracting parties to CCAMLR agree in this provision that "they will not engage in any activities in the Antarctic Treaty area contrary to the principles and purposes of that Treaty and that in their relations with each other, they are bound by the obligations contained in Articles I and V of the Antarctic Treaty."[87] Article IV of CCAMLR, which concerns territorial sovereignty and coastal state jurisdiction, asserts that within the Antarctic Treaty area, all contracting parties, irrespective of their status as parties to the Antarctic Treaty, are bound by Articles IV and VI of that instrument. The obligations underlined here are important, as these two provisions respectively set aside national claims to the continent and guarantee to all states without prejudice the exercise of high-seas rights within the area. These articles likewise bind even non-ATCPs to obey provisions of the 1959 Treaty.

Another connection to the Antarctic Treaty is made in CCAMLR's Article V. This provision confirms that contracting parties not party to the Antarctic Treaty "acknowledge the special obligations and responsibilities" of the ATCPs for the protection and preservation of the environment within the Antarctic Treaty area.[88] Article V also obliges contracting states not party to the Antarctic Treaty to observe "as and when appropriate" the Agreed Measures and other recommendations adopted by the ATCPs "in fulfilment of their responsibility for the protection of the Antarctic environment from all forms of harmful human interference."[89] The Convention sets special relations with the International Convention for the Regulation of Whaling[90] and the Seals Convention, as CCAMLR stipulates that nothing in it can derogate from the rights and obligations of contracting parties under those latter agreements.[91]

Institutions created under CCAMLR also establish links to other ATS instruments. Paragraph 5 of Article IX, which concerns functions of the Commission, asserts that this body is charged with taking "full account of any relevant measures or regulations established or recommended" by Antarctic Treaty Consultative Party meetings. In setting out functions of the Scientific Committee, Article XV stipulates, inter alia, that this body "shall have regard" for "scientific activities conducted within the framework of the Antarctic Treaty."[92] In defining CCAMLR's relations with other international organizations, Article XXIII asserts that the Commission and the Scientific Committee "shall co-operate with the Antarctic Treaty Consultative Parties on matters falling within the competence of the latter."[93] Finally, CCAMLR's dispute settlement provisions in Article XXV were extracted nearly verbatim from Article XI of the Antarctic Treaty. CCAMLR actually improves on that dispute settlement by providing in the Annex to the Convention for an arbitral tribunal.

The Antarctic Minerals Convention

From 1981 through 1988 the Antarctic Treaty Consultative Parties (ATCPs) met to produce a special regime that would regulate the prospecting, exploration, and exploitation of mineral resources in the Antarctic should these activities occur there.[94] Agreement came in June 1988 on the text for a new minerals treaty, and in November 1988 the Convention on the Regulation of Antarctic Mineral Resource Activities (CRAMRA) was opened for signature in Wellington, New Zealand.[95] By 1990, however, the ATCPs had abandoned this minerals agreement in favor of negotiating an instrument for more comprehensively protecting the Antarctic environment.

The Wellington Minerals Conventionis an impressive document containing sixty-seven articles and an annex for an arbitral tribunal. While not a detailed mining code, the treaty created a complex regulatory framework for mineral activities. Four institutions comprised the CRAMRA regime: (1) an Antarctic Minerals Commission was to be the forum for making executive policy decisions and was to set rules and designate through consensus any areas to be opened for exploration and development;[96] (2) a Special Meeting of States Parties open to all parties to the Antarctic Treaty was to give advice to the Commission on any decision to open an area;[97] (3) an Advisory Committee was to advise the Commission and Regulatory Committees on matters requiring scientific, technical, and environmental expertise about Antarctic mineral activities—although not a decision-making body with binding powers, the Advisory Committee was created to provide special opportunities for consultation and cooperation;[98] and (4) Regulatory Committees were to be established for each geographic area the Commission designated for possible minerals exploration and development activities.[99] These mechanisms were designed to play central roles in a minerals management arrangement. CRAMRA allocated broad powers to the Regulatory Committees, including approval of applications for exploration and development permits, approval of management schemes (that is, the contracts between operators and the Convention's regulatory authority), as well as inspection and the power to suspend minerals activities in an area.[100] Establishment of a secretariat for CRAMRA was also viewed as likely for coordinating bureaucratic affairs to manage the regulation of minerals activities on the continent.[101]

CRAMRA provided a specific framework to regulate Antarctic minerals activities. To this end, the Minerals Convention created new institutions, set out impressive environmental restrictions, and established legally binding procedures to ensure that minerals activities could only go forward with the consensus approval of all contracting parties. The minerals agreement provided for inspection, monitoring, reporting, compulsory settlement of disputes, access to courts, and suspension of activities causing unacceptable damage to the environment.[102]

Though now politically moribund and legally inert, the Antarctic Minerals Convention is hardly politically or organizationally irrelevant for the ATS. The Minerals Convention represents by far the most extensive, most protracted, most complex agreement negotiated by the Consultative Parties to regulate state activities in the Antarctic commons. It was, moreover, negotiated over seven years through a Special Consultative Meeting process under the Antarctic Treaty arrangement. The institutional links to the Antarctic Treaty are consequently unmistakable and could be highly significant for the future of the Antarctic Treaty System, especially should minerals development in the Antarctic ever become seriously contemplated.[103]

Paragraph 14 of the Final Act identifies members of the CRAMRA Commission[104] by reference to those states defined in Article IV, paragraph 1(a) of the Antarctic Treaty (i.e., the claimant states). The members of the Commission mentioned in Article 29(2)(b) are those referred to in Article IV (1)(b) of the Antarctic Treaty (i.e., the two states having a basis for claim, namely the United States and the Soviet Union [Russia]). In short, the governments responsible for negotiating and implementing the Minerals Convention were defined in that agreement as the same parties identified as principal players in the Antarctic Treaty.

In the first paragraph of CRAMRA's preamble "the provisions of the Antarctic Treaty" are recalled. The second paragraph then asserts that the parties are convinced that the Antarctic Treaty System "has proved effective in promoting harmony," and the third paragraph reaffirms that it is in the interest of mankind that the Antarctic Treaty area continue to be used exclusively for peaceful purposes. While the fourth paragraph notes that "exploitable mineral resources may exist in Antarctica," the fifth paragraph then underscores the "special responsibility" of the ATCPs to ensure that all activities in Antarctica "are consistent with the purposes and principles of the Antarctic Treaty." Finally, the sixth paragraph asserts that any regime for Antarctic mineral resources must not only be consistent with Article IV of the Antarctic Treaty, it must also be without prejudice and acceptable to those states that assert rights or claims of territorial sovereignty in Antarctica.[105]

CRAMRA's Article 2 sets out the objectives and general principles of the agreement. This provision asserts that "This Convention is an integral part of the Antarctic Treaty system, comprising the Antarctic Treaty, the measures in effect under that Treaty, and its associated separate legal instruments, the prime purpose of which is to ensure that Antarctica shall continue forever to be used exclusively for peaceful purposes and shall not become the scene or object of international discord."[106]

In implementing CRAMRA, parties must ensure that mineral activities take place in ways that are "consistent with all the components of the Antarctic Treaty system and the obligations flowing therefrom."[107] Regarding mineral resource activities, Article 2 of CRAMRA acknowledges the "special responsibility" of the ATCPs to protect the environment, as well as the need to: protect the Antarctic environment and its dependent and associated ecosystems; respect the significance for and influence of Antarctica on the global environment; "respect other legitimate uses" of the continent; respect Antarctica's value for science and aesthetic and wilderness qualities; ensure safety of operations in Antarctica; promote "fair and effective participation" by all parties; and "take into account the interests of the international community as a whole."[108] Thus, for example, Article 2 commits the State Parties to protect not only the continent but also "its associated and dependent ecosystems."[109] To fulfill such a commitment necessarily implies respect for and observance of the mandates established by the Agreed Measures, Seals Convention, and CCAMLR.

Several of CRAMRA's provisions are purposefully crafted to ensure coincidence with the Antarctic Treaty's jurisdictional scope. For example, in defining CRAMRA's area of application, Article 5 fixes it as "the Antarctic Treaty area," that is, the area south of 60° south latitude.[110] This provision neatly aligns CRAMRA with the same jurisdictional scope as the Antarctic Treaty. Likewise, CRAMRA binds the Antarctic Treaty's Consultative Parties to international cooperation and participation in implementing the Minerals Convention.[111] Also important, CRAMRA stipulates that it will not affect the operation of Article VIII of the Antarctic Treaty, which provides that observers used for inspections shall be subject only to the jurisdiction of the contracting party of which they are nationals.[112] Finally, as with all formal ATS instruments, CRAMRA sets aside contrary state positions on claims as provided for in Article IV of the Antarctic Treaty.[113]

Unlike other ATS instruments, CRAMRA contains a special provision, Article 10, intended to promote consistency among the components of the Antarctic Treaty System. In its first paragraph Article 10 specifically commits parties to ensure that mineral resource activities are consistent with the Antarctic Treaty, the Seals Convention, CCAMLR, and the measures effected pursuant to those agreements. Similarly, paragraph 2 mandates that CRAMRA's Commission "shall consult and cooperate" with the ATCPs and contracting parties to both the Seals Convention and CCAMLR. The Commission, moreover, is admonished to avoid "any interference with the achievement of the objectives and principles" and "inconsistency" with those same agreements. Article 10 thus emerges as the legal and policy link that expressly binds all the ATS legal instruments into a package arrangement. In the event that mineral resource activities ever did go forward, the ATCPs and other parties to CRAMRA would be legally obliged to cooperate with the contracting parties of these other instruments and to adhere to the principles of those agreements.

The fact that nearly all the same states are parties to all these various instruments only increases the effectiveness of Antarctic governance attained by formally linking these agreements together. First, linkage commits all parties to a set of overlapping, mutually reinforcing legal relationships within the ATS. Second, that relationship works to ensure consistency among ATS instruments so that no activities in the region impinge upon environmental management, protection, or conservation in the Antarctic area.[114]

Concern over protected areas is also manifest. Antarctic mineral activities are prohibited in any Specially Protected Area or Site of Special Scientific Interest designated under Article IX (1) of the Antarctic Treaty.[115] CRAMRA's Commission is charged with bringing any decision on mineral resource activities that affects protected areas to the attention of the ATCPs, the contracting parties of the Seals Convention and CCAMLR, and to SCAR.[116]

Growing directly out of the Special Consultative Meeting process, CRAMRA's operation turned on the participation of the ATCPs. This is made clear in the composition and functions of the CRAMRA Commission. The Commission's principal membership would be comprised of "each Party which was an Antarctic Treaty Consultative party on the date when this Convention was opened for signature."[117] Two other categories of membership are also provided for, namely: (1) parties "engaged in substantial scientific, technical or environmental research" in the Convention's area; and (2) parties sponsoring mineral resource exploration or development during the phase an operation's Management Scheme is in force.[118] A non-ATCP party that wished to participate in scientific, technical, or environmental research had to declare its intent to abide by any recommendations pursuant to Article IX (1) of the Antarctic Treaty.[119] This stipulation further linked CRAMRA to the Antarctic Treaty and would have bound such parties to the environmental principles set out in the 1964 Agreed Measures. Similarly, a special "observer status" in the Commission was afforded to any contracting party to the Antarctic Treaty that was not a party to CRAMRA.[120]

A special Scientific Advisory Committee was also proposed under CRAMRA. Any nonparty state that was a contracting party to the Antarctic Treaty or to CCAMLR would be permitted to enjoy observer status to that body.[121] CRAMRA also created a special Meeting of States Party, which granted observer status to any contracting party to the Antarctic Treaty that was not party to CRAMRA.[122]

Finally, under the complicated system for establishing the ten-member Regulatory Committees, the ATCPs were again purposefully integrated into CRAMRA's functions. All ATCPs were made eligible for membership on these committees.[123] In fact, the minerals convention expressly stipulated that four committee members must come from among claimant states and six members must come from among nonclaimant states, two of which would be the United States and the Soviet Union (now Russia).[124] Article 29, paragraph 7 closes the provision regarding Regulatory Committees by asserting that "Nothing in this Article shall be interpreted as affecting Article IV of the Antarctic Treaty." Appreciating the intricacy of the Commission and Regulatory Committees in CRAMRA's operation, the ATCPs safeguarded CRAMRA against any interpretation that might have jeopardized the legal balance between claimants and nonclaimants in the Antarctic Treaty System.

The Wellington Convention made notable contributions to the Antarctic Treaty System: it completed the resource protection regime under the ATS—along with those instruments for fauna and flora, seals, and living marine resources; it provided regulations and environmental standards to govern minerals activities; and it furnished a consensus approach for regulating mineral activities that might impinge upon sensitive questions of national sovereignty and environmental protection in Antarctica. CRAMRA supplied innovative environmental provisions, chief among them the principle that one might not proceed with mineral activities unless sufficient information were available about exploration.[125] Even so, the existence of sufficient information had to be verified by the agreement of all parties.

Despite the intricacy of its provisions and the diligence with which they were negotiated, the Wellington Convention was never legally consummated as part of the Antarctic Treaty System. Critical doubts about the negotiated minerals regime were translated by environmentalists into potent political weapons. Most disturbing to conservationists was that the Wellington Convention was viewed as permissive. They argued that having a minerals treaty in force would not be a deterrent to minerals development but rather would, in fact, serve as a prominent catalyst for eventual development activities. There was a fear that CRAMRA, by default or by design, would become the slippery slope leading to exploitation and development of mineral resources in the Antarctic. Two governments essential for the implementation of CRAMRA, Australia and France, announced in May 1989 that they would not ratify this agreement, therefore preempting any possibility of the mineral convention's entry into legal force.[126]

The Madrid Environmental Protocol

The demise of CRAMRA opened the diplomatic door for the ATCPs to consider and negotiate a far more significant instrument for comprehensive environmental protection of the Antarctic. Emerging out of three special ATCP meetings in Viña del Mar, Chile (November–December 1990), and Madrid, Spain (April and June 1991), came an environmental protocol to the Antarctic Treaty, a new instrument for preclusive restoration in the polar South.

On October 4, 1991, the Protocol on Environmental Protection to the Antarctic Treaty[127] was adopted and opened for signature by the ATCPs in Madrid, Spain. This agreement stands among the most comprehensive, far-reaching multilateral environmental instruments ever promulgated. It is futuristic and commonsensible, and it provides a legal blueprint for conservation throughout the Antarctic. The Madrid Environmental Protocol also signals a profound reversal in the ATCPs' intentions for the Antarctic. Whereas during the late 1980s the policy of the Consultative Party group had leaned toward possible exploration and development of Antarctic minerals and hydrocarbons, by late 1991 the ATCPs had bound themselves to a general legal obligation to protect and conserve the continent and its circumpolar seas.

The Madrid Protocol provides for comprehensive regulation over activities affecting the Antarctic environment. It sets up standards for conducting human activities on and around the continent that integrate the confusing nexus of recommendations, codes of conduct, and different international conventions having varied legal effects. It establishes a framework through which ATCPs can fill gaps in protection as needs arise. It aims to promote consistent regulation that will result in more rational application of environmental standards.[128] The Protocol ensures that no minerals development by ATCPs can lawfully take place on Antarctica or in its circumpolar waters within the foreseeable future. This prohibition means that Antarctica is not likely to be degraded by minerals or hydrocarbon development or transportation activities on or around the continent. Nor are natural habitats of Antarctic living marine resources likely to be disrupted or destroyed by such activities for at least fifty years.[129]

The Protocol creates a new institutional body, the Committee for Environmental Protection (CEP),[130] on which each party to the Protocol is entitled to a seat. The CEP is intended to oversee compliance with the Protocol but lacks independent capabilities, power to compel enforcement through sanctions, and decision-making authority. The Committee's chief function is, therefore, to provide advice and formulate recommendations to ATCP meetings concerning implementation of the protocol and its annexes.[131] As in the Agreed Measures, governments party to the Protocol are responsible for ensuring compliance.[132]

Five annexes are attached to the Protocol. Annex I sets procedures for environmental impact assessment (EIA), a major achievement of the Protocol.[133] Annex II restates the need for conservation of Antarctic fauna and flora and updates the Agreed Measures.[134] The third annex pertains to waste disposal and waste management.[135] It grew out of the 1975 Code of Conduct for Antarctic Expeditions and Stations Activities[136] and from Recommendation XV-3, which upgrades the 1975 Code.[137] The fourth annex concerns "Prevention of Marine Pollution"[138] and is directly linked to the International Convention for the Prevention of Pollution from Ships, as amended by its 1978 Protocol (MARPOL 73/78).[139] In October 1991 at the XVIth ATCM in Bonn, Germany, a fifth annex to the Protocol was adopted that simplifies and significantly expands the scope of the Antarctic protected area system.[140] It also supplies an integrated approach to the creation and management of protected areas in the Antarctic. The annexes "form an integral part" of the Protocol and were all adopted in line with Article IX of the Antarctic Treaty.[141]

The Madrid Protocol consolidates the previous piecemeal ATS environmental protection measures into a single instrument under the Antarctic Treaty. In the process, the Protocol provides channels for revising and improving detailed measures as circumstances evolve. The Madrid Protocol is legally a protocol appended to the Antarctic Treaty, negotiated and promulgated by the governments party to the Antarctic Treaty. Article 4 of the Protocol expressly integrates that instrument with the Antarctic Treaty, as it stipulates:

1. This Protocol shall supplement the Antarctic Treaty and shall neither modify nor amend that Treaty.

2. Nothing in this Protocol shall derogate from the rights and obligations of the Parties to this Protocol under the other international instruments in force within the Antarctic Treaty system.

These two statements unmistakably reveal the Protocol to be a full, direct, and integral legal addition to the Antarctic Treaty, and it is expected to operate consistently with all other components of the Antarctic Treaty system. Article 5 obligates parties to consult and cooperate with "the Contracting Parties to the other international instruments in force within the Antarctic Treaty system and their respective institutions." The plain purpose here is to ensure that goals and values of the Protocol are met, and to avoid "any interference with the achievement of the objectives and principles of those instruments or any inconsistency between the implementation of those instruments and of this Protocol."[142]

The Protocol's preamble states as its aims to "strengthen the Antarctic Treaty system so as to ensure that Antarctica shall continue forever to be used exclusively for peaceful purposes and shall not be the scene of international discord." The preamble also points up the "special legal responsibility of the Antarctic Treaty Consultative Parties to ensure that all activities in Antarctica are consistent with the purposes and principles of the Antarctic Treaty," and recalls "the designation of Antarctica as a Special Conservation Area and other measures adopted under the Antarctic Treaty system to protect the Antarctic environment and dependent and associated ecosystems." To highlight the legal links, the preamble then reaffirms the "conservation principles of the Convention on the Conservation of Antarctic Marine Living Resources" and asserts that the contracting parties desire to "supplement the Antarctic Treaty" in order to develop a comprehensive regime for the protection of the Antarctic environment and dependent and associated ecosystems that serves the interest of mankind as whole.

The Protocol's environmental principles apply to the planning and conduct of all activities in *the Antarctic Treaty area*.[143] This same jurisdictional ambit is used for the requirements of cooperation among parties (article 6), environmental impact assessment (article 8), inspection procedures (article 14), emergency response action (article 15), and liability for damage to the environment (article 16). In sum, the Protocol has within its provisions specific institutional links that make it by intent, design, and definition a constituent part of the Antarctic Treaty and its family of associated international agreements.

CONCLUSION

The operation of the Antarctic Treaty System rests on the normative and institutional relationships and dependencies among its parts. The Antarctic Treaty System integrates ingredients, procedures, and products. Ingredients consist of governmental resources, technology, and perceived social and political gains that might be made. Procedures include the decision-making apparatus, administrative means, and communication channels that make the system function. Products are the policies made and benefits gained. The result of this multinational, interdependent arrangement of international agreements is the Antarctic Treaty System. The ATS instruments furnish the normative and procedural frameworks for a general Antarctic regime, which is intended to promote certain expectations of government behavior. When the ATS regime works successfully, it provides predictability in state behavior and more order and stability in Antarctic affairs.

The Antarctic Treaty System has evolved over the past three decades, pushed by the need to respond to new challenges, most significantly from various national and private efforts to exploit resources in the Antarctic commons. The ATCPs' response has come through new international agreements initially designed to conserve living marine resources but more recently aimed at protecting the Antarctic environment. The chapters that follow examine the achievements and deficiencies of these regulatory agreements for the Antarctic region, with a view to drawing lessons for other commons areas.

Chapter 4

REGIME DYNAMICS

Specialized international regimes, such as that for managing the Antarctic commons, are created by states in order to resolve specific problems of interstate interaction. Regimes are desirable when governments confront situations that a single state or a small group of states cannot adequately cope with alone. Areas of global concern, such as environmental protection or issues requiring complex coordination—for example, air travel or international commerce—demand greater interstate cooperation and a more regularized and intricate set of expectations for behavior than are present in everyday international relations. Consequently, states form more interdependent associations in order to enable their interactions to produce conditions or outcomes that all the concerned governments desire. International regimes are typically understood to mean "rules, norms, principles and procedures around which actor expectations converge in a given issue area."[1] In the Antarctic context, the regime governing states' expectations has been formalized and internationalized in the 1959 Antarctic Treaty and the procedures it creates, along with subsequent associated agreements negotiated for the conservation and protection of Antarctic resources.

This chapter examines the theoretical dimensions of the international legal framework adopted for governing the Antarctic commons, i.e., the creation and operation of the Antarctic Treaty regime. Toward this end, the conceptual nature of an international regime is first considered. The chapter then applies traditional international relations theories of regimes to the Antarctic context. The aim here is to demonstrate the complicated, multidimensional nature of the regime formulated by governments over the past four decades to manage activities in the Antarctic commons. Finally, the chapter examines how the regime operates in practice and what contributions the Antarctic experience can make to the theory of regime formation.

THEORETICAL CONSIDERATIONS

States cooperate to reduce uncertainty and minimize risks. If states could not form expectations about their own and others' future behavior, international relations would truly approximate the chaotic anarchy that neorealist scholars view as normal. In fact, interests that states share in avoiding the consequences of pure anarchy in particular issue-areas lead them to form regimes as a basis for shared expectations.[2] International regimes, now formalized in multilateral treaties, govern such mundane issues as international mail delivery and air passage, as well as such critical areas as treatment of diplomats, protection of human rights, and the conduct of war. Increasingly, states also form regimes to achieve some commonly held objectives that are unattainable without international cooperation. For example, the complex interdependence of international economics and industrial activities in tandem with the truly global nature of threats to the environment have made collective action by states essential to deal with contemporary ecological problems.[3]

But cooperation does not necessarily mean that states have achieved a harmony of interests. States may come to cooperate because their interests on a given issue converge, because working together gains them more (or costs them less) than working apart, because they value what they can gain from cooperation more than what sustaining a regime may cost them, or for some combination of these or other reasons.[4]

In general, regimes are easier to sustain once they are formed than they are to form at the outset.[5] In order to fulfill their coordinating function, regimes need not be formal. As Stephen Krasner has observed, in some situations, "So long as everyone agrees to drive on the right side of the road, little more is needed."[6] But in issue-areas that are complex and require coordination across a broad range of state activities to provide the desired outcome, the rules and procedures that make up an international regime are most efficiently expressed and enforced through a formal institution. Institutions aid interstate cooperation by lowering the costs of certain necessary transactions between states. This is done by making clear to all participants the costs and benefits each incurs from cooperation or defection and by easing enforcement of the regime's rules by making defections known and by linking cooperation in one issue-area to cooperation in others. States often create their coordinating institutions through the medium of international law, which adds the force of its own rules and norms.[7]

DEFINING A COMMONS REGIME

Two essential rationales explain the need for creating regimes to manage global commons areas. First, some goals may be better or more easily attained if sought through cooperation among states. Second, better coordination of activities among states can be accomplished through norm-creating institutions established by regimes.[8] International regimes thus become social creatures that generate normative guidelines and rules for their members.

An international regime consists of norms, rules, principles, and procedures designed to help states coordinate their action toward the achievement of particular values.[9] But the ingredients necessary for creating and maintaining an international regime to govern a global commons are not easily defined. Because of the particular characteristics of commons problems, and because global commons regimes are usually couched in international legal terms, their norms, rules, principles, procedures, and values differ in scope, content, and application from those of other, less formal regimes. Nor do they convey equivalent obligations. The institutional means through which these obligatory ingredients are devised and imposed remain key to the lawful character and functions of the regime.

A *value* is something states esteem for its own sake, something they desire.[10] When states' values agree, one can speak of an international value, which reflects some generally accepted judgment of what is desirable or undesirable in the life of states. In short, international values reflect international principles, standards, or qualities that are considered desirable in the international relations among states. In the case of the polar South, such values would include the region's wilderness, scenic and aesthetic qualities, peaceful condition, the conduct of scientific research there, and appreciation for the historic and pristine qualities of the Antarctic commons. These are the commonly held objectives of the states that developed and maintain the Antarctic Treaty System (ATS).

The development of norms in a given issue-area is essential for establishing an international regime. A *norm* here means an authoritative standard of acceptable or unacceptable behavior for the international community.[11] Norms are prescriptions for behavior that relate to rights and responsibilities of individual governments and can help states identify roles and conduct they can expect from others in the international system. Norms may be contained in formal rules (i.e., explicit norms) or in informal understandings (i.e., implicit norms). In either event norms prescribe social goals that are desirable for the international community and outline what policy means are acceptable for achieving them.

Norms carry behavioral expectations that often translate, in international legal terms, into moral and ethical imperatives. Norms supply for governments the rules for international intercourse, that is, a code of conduct. When used as the basis for state behavior, norms can evolve into comprehensive and fundamental law. Norms widely adhered to may become fundamental truths and hence accepted legal doctrine.[12] For governments involved in the Antarctic, for example, norms would include such concepts as only peaceful uses for the continent, nonnuclearization of the region, free access to and exchange of scientific information, peaceful settlement of disputes, and conservation and protection of the circumpolar environment.

Rules are prescribed orders or specific maxims agreed upon by states as a group to govern their individual conduct.[13] Rules constrain the practices of governments in their international relations. In an international legal arrangement like the Antarctic Treaty System, rules are framed and adopted explicitly for governing that body's conduct and that of its members. Rules in the Antarctic Treaty regime are explicit, either laid out in the Antarctic agreements or by the Consultative Parties in their meetings. They include prohibitions against military behavior (e.g., no building of military bases or fortifications, no conducting maneuvers or weapons tests), banning nuclear explosions, and forbidding disposal of radioactive waste materials in the region. Other, more recent rules include prohibitions against mining or drilling for minerals and regulations governing fishing for certain species in certain areas at stipulated times. Future rules that have been agreed to but are not yet in force include the need to conduct environmental impact assessments and supply sufficient information on activities so that decisions on their permissibility might be made by the appropriate authority. In addition, rules for governing operations in the Antarctic commons regime are manifold and are well illustrated by the two hundred–plus recommendations that have been adopted by Consultative Party Meetings since 1961.

Principles refer to fundamental "beliefs of fact, causation, or rectitude"[14] that serve as a guide for states in determining what a given regime can accomplish. Antarctic-related regime principles might include such beliefs as "overfishing endangers the marine environment" (leading logically to rules for governing fishing), "pollution degrades the health of the ecosystem" (leading logically to rules to prohibit pollution-causing activities), or "ozone depletion causes skin cancer" (leading logically to a ban on chlorofluorocarbons).

Finally, decision-making *procedures* are vital if an international regime is to function and adapt to changing international conditions and circumstances.[15] Such procedures indicate what norms or principles underlie the regime and lay out how the rules of the regime will be determined. The procedures for policy-making in the Antarctic generally revolve around the Consultative Party mechanism, its evolved process for decision-making, and the various institutional arrangements created by new treaty instruments that have entered into force. Among the latter would be included the Seals Commission and the CCAMLR Commission and its Scientific Committee. Procedures that will likely become functional soon are those associated with the Madrid Protocol's Committee for Environmental Protection. Less likely to enter into operation are the procedures established in the CRAMRA treaty for its Commission and Regulatory Committees.

Establishment of a global commons regime may occur in yet another context. International regimes strive to make more predictable and controllable what states (or their nationals) regularly do in a commons area. Commons regimes aim to control national activities in an international space, which can enhance stability and promote more order among state actors.[16]

Regime Cohesion

When governments work closely together in a special relationship over long periods, they develop certain habits of compliance. They also develop implicit expectations concerning mutual rights and obligations. These habitual patterns of compliance and expectations furnish the foundation for trust and credibility among governments in their relationships. Such habits of compliance give rise to a sense of stability in intergovernmental relationships, and hence contribute to regime cohesion. In this way, the habits and "cognitive expectations" that the regime generates in states help to bolster the regime itself, as well as contribute to stabilizing international relations generally.[17]

An association of states is able to maintain a degree of order, predictability, and activity through regime cohesion.[18] As a multistate association gains cohesiveness, members and institutions become tightly linked together such that the group operates as a single unit to make decisions and carry out policies. Regime cohesion is the process through which the states in an international association become linked together by common norms, values, rules, and principles.[19]

Regime cohesion appears to evolve in two fundamental ways. First, substantial interaction between states on an issue builds up a shared store of experience within the association of states, which in turn can lead to normative cohesion. That is, as several governments coexist together, a set of basic values becomes fostered among members of that association. This mirrors the situation among the original Antarctic Treaty parties during the decade of the 1960s. States' shared principles and values regarding the Antarctic were applied to specific situations, leading to the development of norms to direct the association's actions. As jointly held goals were pursued by states in the association, these governments came to agreement about what goals were desirable and about how to achieve them.[20] This process of an interstate association functioning to build values and norms into cohesive bonds can be called regime institutionalization.[21] In the case of the Antarctic Treaty states, such a process crystallized during the 1970s and has continued to evolve since then. The Antarctic Treaty System has become a formalized explicit regime, having special international institutions to perform the functions necessary for maintaining regime cohesion.

When governments decide to seek shared interests and values through a regime, they integrate the regime's norms and principles into their own decision-making structures in a process of socialization. As states act out their roles as responsible members of the regime and are rewarded by other states' approbation and by the benefits of cooperation, this socialization process is reinforced. A state can, through the process of socialization and role enactment, come to view its interests in issue-areas of the regime and its interests as a responsible regime participant as being tightly interwoven and even identical.[22] The process of regime socialization has occurred throughout the evolution of the ATS but can be seen especially during the 1980s as the number of regime members doubled and new governments had to be educated about the norms, rules, and processes of the system. That this education process was effectively carried out is evidenced by the regime's continued operation.

The degree of cohesion in an institutionalized regime has two dimensions. The first, normative cohesion, depends in part upon the degree of consensus regarding basic values the regime is meant to pursue (and the absence of strong competing values). In addition normative cohesion depends on the development of an internally consistent set of regime norms that can guide state behavior. Still a third factor is the degree of congruence between values and norms; whether adherence to the regime's norms permits values to be realized. Normative cohesion can also be influenced by how effectively norms are integrated into a institution's rules and procedures to make the activities of its member states reflect its underlying basic values. Finally, cohesion can be affected by the degree to which individuals have become socialized to the regime, meaning that governments have internalized fully the regime's shared values and common norms.

A second dimension of regime cohesion is functional cohesion. Functional cohesion refers to the relationships among governments in the regime. Members of the regime become specialized in activities and functions necessary to the regime's achievement of shared goals. Task specialization, in turn, makes actors increasingly interdependent, spurs intensive exchange transactions, and thus binds the members closely in networks of functional relationships. To preserve and enhance these relationships, regime members create rules and procedures to coordinate and regulate exchange activities. In these ways, the regime spreads and deepens.[23]

The extent of functional cohesion achieved by a regime association depends on a number of factors. One factor is the degree of task specialization among members of the regime. Another is the extent of reciprocal exchange relationships among the interdependent components. Functional cohesion may also depend on the creation of adequate and consistent procedural rules for the exchange of functions, as well as on the effectiveness of administrative units in coordinating and regulating exchange networks. Finally, the regime association must establish reciprocal flows of information that permit rules to be understood clearly by all members and problems affecting the interrelationship to be expeditiously addressed. Examples of such problems include enforcement of rules against a deviant state member and a change in the environment that alters the behavior necessary to achieve the regime's goals.[24]

Conformity to a commons regime means compliance with its rules. Sometimes rules may not be appreciated, especially by a government that had little or no influence in making them. Still, as a regime member, that government inherited normative obligations. By joining the Antarctic Treaty, governments voluntarily agree to obey the norms and principles set up by the regime. For most ATS governments most of the time, it is preferable to live by the rules of the Antarctic Treaty regime than to engage in deviant behavior and antagonize other participating governments. Once its legitimacy as primary norm provider was established, the ATS was able to guide and influence member states of the regime more authoritatively, since those states were expected to comply with those norms. Within the Antarctic Treaty System's legal culture, provisions that are agreed upon (i.e., laws) act as formal, explicit, and politically enacted rules for maintaining those norms.[25]

Institutions and Processes

The Antarctic Treaty System supplies the institutional foundation for the multistate Antarctic regime. This loose-fitting series of arrangements operates as a composite whole. The ATS contains two features that structure the international regime for managing activities in the Antarctic: (1) substantive legal agreements that bind states to certain values, norms and procedures; and (2) established practices that enable member governments to fulfill the obligations in the agreements. These elements combine to provide the normative and procedural nexus for the Antarctic commons regime.

Substantive Components

Substantive legal agreements between states comprise the regime's institutional body. These substantive components include both those agreements already in force and those in the process of entering into force. The ATS agreements already in force spell out norms and principles that guide the regime, as well as create legally binding obligations. Central among these instruments is the 1959 Antarctic Treaty,[26] which serves as the constitutive instrument of the regime, furnishes the legal foundation for the international institution called the ATS, and stands as the source of legal authority for all subsequent measures adopted by the participating states. Other important legal sources for the ATS are recommendations from Antarctic Treaty Consultative Meetings (ATCMs).[27] These meetings and recommendations flow from the decision-making process specified in the Antarctic Treaty and include policy, planning, and consultation measures. The recommendations are adopted through consensus by the Antarctic Treaty Consultative Parties (ATCPs), the group of states (currently numbering twenty-six) that convenes annually to set policy directives for activities in the Antarctic.[28] Particularly notable among these recommendations is the 1964 Agreed Measures for the Conservation of Antarctic Fauna and Flora, which first set out in detail conservation goals to guide state conduct in the Treaty area.[29]

Two special agreements have been adopted and are in force based on the authority of the Antarctic Treaty. First, some ATCPs promulgated the 1972 Convention for the Conservation of Antarctic Seals[30] to limit the vulnerability of Antarctic seals to commercial exploitation. While admittedly bolstered by the nonprofitability of sealing as a commercial activity, the Convention has contributed to dissuading states party to it from harvesting seals in the region.[31] The second agreement is the 1980 Convention on the Conservation of Antarctic Marine Living Resources (CCAMLR).[32] As discussed previously, CCAMLR is designed to promote conservation and prudent management of living resources (mainly krill and fish) in the Southern Ocean. Though enjoying only mixed success early on, CCAMLR is now making important contributions to both the theory and practice of ocean resource management.[33]

Substantive agreements only recently in force are legally binding upon the ATCPs or other parties to the Antarctic Treaty. They institute legal obligations that many Antarctic Treaty states must follow. Chief among these new law-making instruments is the 1991 Protocol on Environmental Protection to the Antarctic Treaty,[34] along with its five annexes, which entered into force on Januray 14, 1998. Respectively, these annexes specify policies governing state activities relating to environmental impact assessment, conservation of Antarctic fauna and flora, waste disposal and waste management, prevention of marine pollution, and protection and management of the Antarctic area.[35]

One Antarctic agreement that might be placed in the category of "instruments in progress" is the Convention on the Regulation of Antarctic Mineral Resource Activities (CRAMRA).[36] The legal status of the minerals agreement is literally that of a treaty still in progress, undergoing the procedural processes of signature and ratification among ATCPs. Nevertheless, the prospects for this agreement being approved in the foreseeable future as a formal, binding addition to the Antarctic Treaty System seem remote.

Procedural Components

In addition to substantive rules, norms, and principles discussed, the ATS governing the Antarctic commons includes procedures by which states party to the regime can make decisions. The procedural elements of the ATS specify the ways and means that permit this collection of states to operate as an integral decision-making unit and achieve jointly held goals.

The ATS is rooted in individual and common interests of states, and defined by the terms of those issue-oriented agreements which make it up. The original Antarctic Treaty parties eschewed creation of a formal organization to manage affairs affecting either treaty relations or impacts upon the legal regime. Nor is there yet a permanent secretariat to manage operational affairs of the ATS or to coordinate implementation of policies adopted by member governments.

Explicit provision for group decision-making, however, is made in Article IX of the Antarctic Treaty. This article provides for periodic meetings of representatives of the Consultative Parties to the Treaty (i.e., the ATCPs) in order to exchange information, consult together on matters of common interest pertaining to the Antarctic, and consider, formulate, and recommend to their governments measures to further the principles and objectives of the treaty. These "recommendations" generally regulate state activities related to those areas of cooperation listed in the treaty.[37] The Antarctic Treaty Consultative Meetings (ATCMs) are the main arena through which states coordinate their policies and thereby further develop the Antarctic regime. The treaty therefore gives to a self-designated group of states the legal competence to initiate and formulate law and policy governing state activities in the Antarctic. Although the law and policy formulated affect only the activities of the ATCP governments, those laws and policies have political and legal ramifications for the entire international community, especially by promoting international scientific cooperation, legal norms for environmental protection and conservation, and safety and logistical procedures.

Special Consultative Party Meetings have also been used to design and negotiate new agreements. These meetings permit the ATCPs to reach decisions and act upon them without having to wait for the approval of an ATCM recommendation. At least eleven such Special Consultative Meetings have been convened. The First (in London, 1977), Third (in Buenos Aires, 1981), Fifth (in Canberra, 1983), Sixth (in Brussels, 1985), Seventh (in Rio de Janeiro, 1987), Eighth and Ninth (in Paris, 1988 and 1989), and Tenth (in Viña del Mar, 1990) were all convened to consider applications from states who desired Consultative Party status as provided for under Article IX, paragraph 2 of the Antarctic Treaty. The Second Special Meeting, which had three formal and four informal sessions, convened between 1978 and 1980 for the purpose of negotiating the text of the Convention on the Conservation of Antarctic Marine Living Resources. The Fourth Special Consultative Meeting met in twelve sessions between 1982 and 1988 to negotiate the text of the Convention on the Regulation of Antarctic Mineral Resource Activities. The Eleventh Special Meeting, which convened in four sessions during 1990–91, met to consider a comprehensive environmental agreement and produced the text for the Protocol on Environmental Protection to the Antarctic Treaty and its annexes.[38] Special Consultative Meetings are arranged in ad hoc fashion and may be scheduled in train with regular ATCMs or held separately, depending on the circumstances. Meetings of Experts are also frequently convened on various matters. Such gatherings are not authorized to make recommendations to ATCP governments, but their reports may serve as the basis for proposing recommendations at ATCMs.

The Scientific Committee on Antarctic Research (SCAR), a body established by the International Council of Scientific Unions, is designed to formulate and coordinate Antarctic research programs. Despite being a nongovernmental institution, SCAR operates in practice as the scientific agency of the Antarctic Treaty System, and its reports and advice are seriously considered by all appendages of the ATS. Another important procedural component of the ATS is the Commission for the Conservation of Antarctic Marine Living Resources, which meets annually. The Commission is responsible for making CCAMLR effective as a conservation tool. Toward that end, the Commission coordinates national scientific research programs to design more prudent conservation polices for the Southern Ocean, especially by setting catch limits on various marine living resources south of the Antarctic Convergence.

A certain paradox thus envelopes the Antarctic Treaty System. The central goal of this family of agreements is to attain stability in the relationships among its component elements, the member states. Yet the ATS relies on complex interactions between its multiple parts to achieve this end. Such a process creates constant change within the system. The ATS is thus a dynamic creature, and the participating states negotiate when necessary to regularize their activities and the relations between the regime's various components.

LEGAL CULTURE OF THE ATS

The Antarctic regime is a product of the legal culture of its collective membership. This special legal culture stems from the patterns of involvement by member governments in Antarctic affairs. Due to the socialization process outlined above, signing on to one or more of the Antarctic agreements and becoming legally associated with the regime makes a state more closely connected to the regime's legal culture. Membership in the ATS implies specific roles for a state within the international community and creates expectations of that government. Membership thus conveys legal rights and obligations and creates political relationships between states through the Antarctic Treaty agreements in which they all participate.

Analysis of the ATS legal culture enables one to assess the relationships the regime creates among states, evaluate mechanisms that generate support for the regime's norms and values, and gauge the potential of the regime for fulfilling the needs of member states. As a multistate association the ATS can function as an international actor. To the extent that this process occurs, it does so through the collective ATCP membership, though often at meeting levels below the full ATCM. Even so, the international legal culture of the ATS reflects the social behavior of the regime under which the law operates.[39]

Rules for common behavior bind the Antarctic Treaty System together. Essential for making those rules work is the ingredient of trust. Indeed, the high degree of trust and confidence among ATS member governments on Antarctic issues is one reason the ATS is able to function so effectively. Continued trust among those governments closely collaborating on Antarctic affairs contributes significantly to producing their expectations that an Antarctic regime will help them meet their national goals.[40]

The Antarctic Treaty System and its legal regime are not static; they experience change, growth, and decay. The ATS can mature, adapt, and evolve; or failing that, it can stagnate, resist, and decay. What might prompt a multitreaty system like that governing the Antarctic commons to decay? Sometimes a persistent pathological conflict can destroy the very reason for the system's existence. For instance, certain members might pursue an ambition that was rejected by other member governments and might therefore come to obstruct the system's cooperative enterprise toward shared objectives. Steady degeneration of the system's operation might lead to frustration in policy, disorganization in planning, and increased, more widespread tendencies toward noncooperation. Issues that might give rise to such a scenario include the persistent sovereignty issue, the conflicting claims situation in Antarctica, and the prospective discovery of some valuable mineral resource in or around the continent. Any of these, singly or in combination, could touch off intense rivalries among ATCP members and threaten the regime's future.[41]

Clearly, multitreaty systems like the ATS do not function in conditions of complete harmony and cooperation. Some conflict among the collective membership is inevitable. Conflict at times may prove healthy for a system, since in a zero-conflict situation, change and adaptation are less likely and a system may experience decay through a sense of institutional atrophy. Conflict can force productive reassessments and can result in redirection of regime policies and priorities.[42]

Since 1961 when the Antarctic Treaty entered into force, the ATS has undergone certain periods of creative tension. Member ATCP governments have been able to transform the energy generated by conflict into productive changes to the regime. This was true when resolving disagreements over fishing and conservation policies in CCAMLR during the 1980s. It was true during debates during the mid-1980s (in the UN General Assembly) about opening up the secretive ATCP meetings to Antarctic Treaty Non-Consultative Parties and generating more information for nonparty developing countries. It was true during the lag between the collapse of the Antarctic minerals treaty (CRAMRA) in 1989 and completed negotiation of the Madrid Protocol in 1991. When the collective ATCP membership is able to take advantage of conflict and transform it through legal instruments into more elaborate cooperation, then the Antarctic Treaty

System matures into a broader and potentially more successful enterprise. In the process, the legal regime for managing the Antarctic is also strengthened and the cooperative interactions between parties are reinforced.

The Antarctic Treaty System has a teleological character: It was designed to accomplish specific goals. To do this successfully, the ATS integrates into its policy-making procedures regular means of incorporating feedback from the membership. Readings must be constantly taken by ATCP governments of how successfully various issues are being dealt with by treaties in the ATS. Information is gathered and means devised to evaluate the performance of the ATS and its component treaties as regards the success in attaining their intent and purposes. For an Antarctic regime to function effectively, each agreement within the Antarctic Treaty System must mesh in its design to attain common regime objectives.

Still, it seems unlikely that an organization made by fallible humans, much less one founded on the basis of sovereign national state interests, can ever be wholly self-directed or self-correcting. In the Antarctic Treaty System, perhaps the best one can hope for is that member governments will be able to recognize and correct errors by continually reconsidering policy and adapting behavior accordingly.

THE ANTARCTIC REGIME MODEL

The normative rights and duties, rules and procedures laid out in the Antarctic Treaty and associated agreements combine to constitute an Antarctic regime. As explained in detail earlier, the Antarctic Treaty System consists of six basic parts: (1) the Antarctic Treaty; (2) various recommendations adopted by the ATCPs (including the 1964 Agreed Measures); (3) the 1972 Seals Convention; (4) the 1980 Antarctic Marine Living Resources Convention; (5) the 1991 Antarctic Environmental Protocol, with annexes, which has just been ratified by ATCP governments; and (6) the Antarctic Minerals Convention, which for the indefinite future has been intentionally set aside in legal limbo. Each appendage of the ATS was created separately for its own particular reasons. Each component agreement generates its own subregime with its own particular norms, rules, regulations, and procedures. Each of these subregimes, however, has been successively linked through its own treaty provisions to other treaties in the ATS.

The core of this network of clustered Antarctic subregimes is, of course, the Antarctic Treaty. This agreement furnishes the central norms for governing activities in the Antarctic and makes it possible for the other treaties to operate within the ATS. In addition, the Antarctic Treaty generates and sustains norms for the cluster of outlying subregimes. The model in Figure 4.1 depicts the cluster of Antarctic agreements as a cohesive regime. Each treaty of the regime cluster generates its own subregime, and all the subregimes are linked—with common goals, norms, and procedures—to the parent regime produced by the Antarctic Treaty. The subregimes are also linked to each other, and the legal agreements share elements that link them tightly together, creating a family of clustered legal regimes.

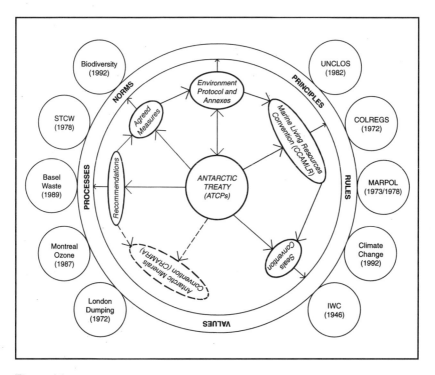

Figure 4.1
The Antarctic Treaty System Regime

This cluster of Antarctic regimes may be conceived in a three-dimensional sense as spherelike, with the Antarctic Treaty at the core. The agents operating the Antarctic Treaty (and governing the entire Antarctic Treaty System as well) are the Antarctic Treaty Consultative Parties, whose governments, in effect, decide law and policy for the region. The six principal legal instruments comprising the ATS are joined together by spokes of communication. Feedback that sustains norms and adapts functions flows reciprocally between the Antarctic Treaty and its offspring agreements. As a consequence, the subregimes of various ATS treaties are constantly being nourished by normative and regulative reinforcement flowing from the parent Antarctic Treaty regime. Similarly, since each subregime's norms and procedures support the others, the entire normative structure of the regime is sustained, and in this manner the ATS regime's cohesion is maintained and strengthened.

The grand regime for the Antarctic commons is produced by the cumulative sense of interests, rights, obligations, and legal suasion generated by the aggregate of norms, procedures, principles, and rules that flow from the Antarctic Treaty to the subregimes created by the ATS instruments. The Antarctic Treaty System regime is the integrated composite of all the separate regimes created by the legal instruments of the Antarctic Treaty System.[43] The grand regime for managing the Antarctic commons contains a number of concentric regime layers. The foundation layer (or core) is the Antarctic Treaty's regime, i.e., the special regime produced by the 1959 instrument alone. A second layer consists of the integrated composite of subregimes created by those international agreements especially negotiated and adopted by the ATCPs as parts of the Antarctic Treaty System. This outer layer is the Antarctic Treaty System regime. A third layer of regimes includes the composite ATS regime plus those external subregimes generated by various non-Antarctic legal agreements on issues of special relevance for governments operating in the Antarctic. The combined layers of the Antarctic Treaty, its family of agreements, and the other external instruments affecting international activities in the Antarctic commons may simply be called the Antarctic Regime.

As indicated in Figure 4.1, however, the Antarctic Treaty System regime is neither self-contained nor all-inclusive. Certain other international agreements external to the ATS touch on its issue-areas and legally affect the ATS regime. The supplementary roles played by these ancillary agreements add to the normative strength and legal viability of the entire regime that governs activities throughout the Antarctic commons. Among the international agreements that intersect with and augment the ATS regime are:

1. The Convention for the Regulation of Whaling, originally negotiated in 1931 and reconsolidated in 1946.[44] This convention set up the International Whaling Commission, a body which sets catch quotas for whaling and has the authority to call an end to a particular whaling season as soon as the quotas are filled. As a consequence, Antarctic waters are famous as a whale habitat.[45]

2. The United Nations Convention on the Law of the Sea, which was opened for signature on December 10, 1982, and entered into force on November 16, 1994.[46] This convention regulates activities in the world's oceans, including the circumpolar Southern Ocean. Especially important to the Antarctic are new laws regulating offshore territorial limits, environmental protection, fishing and conservation, and freedoms on the high seas.[47]

3. The 1973 International Convention for the Prevention of Pollution from Ships, with its 1978 Protocol, which entered into force October 2, 1983 (MARPOL 73/78).[48] Under this convention the Antarctic Treaty area was declared a special area. Annex IV to the Madrid Protocol provides detailed reference to the intimate relationship between the MARPOL system and the regime established by the Madrid Protocol.[49]

4. The 1972 Convention on the Prevention of Marine Pollution by Dumping of Wastes and Other Matter (the London Dumping Convention), which entered into force on August 30, 1975.[50] This convention obligates parties to prohibit the dumping of noxious wastes at sea (prohibited wastes are enumerated on a blacklist) and to submit specific authorization for dumping other types of wastes (on a "gray list"). The provisions of the London Dumping Convention clearly apply to the Antarctic Treaty area.[51]

5. The 1972 Convention on the International Regulations for Preventing Collisions at Sea (COLREGS), which entered into force on July 15, 1977.[52] This convention is concerned mainly

with the conduct and movement of ships relative to other ships in conditions of poor visibility in order to avoid collisions. The common standards for light and sound signals enumerated in the COLREGS are important in the stormy seas of circumpolar Antarctic waters.

6. The UN Framework Convention on Climate Change, concluded in Rio de Janeiro in June 1992.[53] This convention assumes a gradual approach toward an ambitious goal, namely stabilizing greenhouse gases in the atmosphere at levels that will not disturb the global climate system. Under the Madrid Protocol, regular and effective monitoring is supposed to facilitate early detection of possible unforeseen effects of human activities on the Antarctic environment and its dependent and associated ecosystems, whether those activities occur within or beyond the Antarctic Treaty area.

7. The Convention on Biological Diversity, concluded in Rio de Janeiro in June 1992 at the United Nations Conference on Environment and Development.[54] This agreement aims at the conservation and sustainable use of biological diversity, including those species in the Antarctic region. Such diversity is critical, according to the principles of the convention, for the evolution and maintenance of life-sustaining systems of the biosphere. The obligation to preserve Antarctic biological diversity is a major ambition of the Madrid Protocol.[55]

8. The Convention for the Protection of the Ozone Layer, concluded in 1985,[56] and the Protocol on Substances that Deplete the Ozone Layer, which was concluded in Montreal in 1987,[57] underscore the strong concern shared by Antarctic Treaty parties about depletion of the ozone layer and especially about the ozone hole above Antarctica.

9. The Convention on the Control of Transboundary Movements of Hazardous Wastes and Their Disposal, concluded at Basel in 1989, is directly linked to the Antarctic.[58] Article 6 of this convention states that its parties agree not to permit the export of hazardous wastes or other wastes for disposal within the area south of 60° south latitude, regardless of whether or not such wastes are subject to transnational movement.

Though outside the family of Antarctic Treaty agreements, these nine instruments still exert salient political influence and legal suasion upon the ATCPs. Since these agreements affect the legal obligations of most governments active in the Antarctic, they perforce have some influence upon regimes governing state activities in that commons region. In the regime model in Figure 4.1 the impact of these external instruments is depicted as their intersection with the periphery of the umbrella regime created by the Antarctic Treaty System.

Antarctic Regime Sociology

The Antarctic Regime is a product of interactions between states and is visible in state actions that are within or guided by the regime's governing rules and norms. States participate in the Antarctic Regime mainly through participation in the Antarctic Treaty Consultative Party (ATCP) group. Member governments are socialized to the regime as they acquire knowledge, motivation, and capabilities from the ATCP group experience. While it is true that member governments pursue their own national interests in Antarctic matters and work to maximize their individual gains through the ATS, governments learn to participate in Antarctic Treaty System processes. Because they receive recognition for contributions made to enhance those processes, members thus become motivated to strengthen compliance with regime norms and rules. They also contribute in this way to enhancing regime cohesion.[59]

The Antarctic Treaty System is comprised of a combination of international legal agreements acting in concert. The linkage of issues across these treaties creates a chain of mutual interdependencies for the participating states. The collection of special international agreements on the Antarctic provides the essential foundation for governments to associate, meet, and decide on norm-based policies for governing the Antarctic commons. The Antarctic Treaty is the parent agreement that has spawned offspring agreements, each of which generates its own subregime of norms, rules, principles, values, and procedures. These may be considered *cradled sub-regimes* that, due to their overlapping memberships and areas of concern as well as formal and informal connections, combine to form a densely woven regime network. The ATCP group is the main organizational association through which governments jointly administer these interlinked cradled Antarctic subregimes as, in effect, a composite regime.

The Antarctic Treaty System regime is more than just the sum of the rights and duties of states as enumerated in a series of legal instruments. Viewed through the lens of legal agreements, the ATS appears mechanistic and purely functional, but the ATS regime connects states in deeper ways. The varied legal provisions of the Antarctic Treaty give rise to a dense network of reciprocal interactions among states in a variety of related institutions and across a variety of issues. Through this sustained shared experience, a certain sense of mutual obligation and shared interest arises among the participant governments. This mutual, collective obligation furnishes the normative cement that binds the Antarctic Treaty System regime together. It creates in effect an Antarctic normscape for ATCP governments.

Three aspects of this grand Antarctic Regime help define it for the states involved and for the observer: area, component parts, and issue orientation. First, there is the Antarctic region. The Antarctic Treaty System's umbrella regime encompasses activities within the area south of 60° south latitude, except for the CCAMLR subregime, which extends up to the Antarctic Convergence at around 50° south latitude. The focus of the ATS regime is thus the Antarctic and the special needs of that area. Second, there are the values, rules, norms, principles, and procedures articulated in the several Antarctic treaties. Third, the nature of the Antarctic Regime is affected by the various priority issues regarding the region with which states have been concerned and for which they have created the various subregimes. Within the ATS arrangement, discrete regimes have been successfully created for the conservation of Antarctic fauna and flora, seals, and living marine resources (i.e., krill and fish), as well as for the protection of the Antarctic environment. A subregime for Antarctic mineral resource development was also successfully negotiated, but sufficient support among ATCPs could not be marshalled for its entry into legal force. Yet each treaty, and the subregime to which it gave rise, was purposefully designed to operate interdependently with the other subregimes and to reinforce the other agreements, while at the same time avoiding conflict with the principal objectives of other agreements.

Norms in the ATS regime are both proscriptive and prescriptive. Proscriptive norms are negative; they forbid an action. Examples might be the norm against military uses of the Antarctic continent or prohibition on the testing of nuclear weapons within the treaty area. Prescriptive norms, on the other hand, assert what should be done and are designed to create a consensus among participating states behind certain objectives. Examples of prescriptive norms might include the right of open, on-site, unannounced inspections of research stations on the continent or the free exchange of scientific research and information.

ATS regime norms set out accepted, legitimate, and expected patterns of conduct for participating governments. While these norms for guiding states' conduct in the Antarctic are institutionalized in legal agreements and in decisions of the ATCP governing mechanism, this institutionalization occurs within a social context of states constantly observing and interacting with each other around the same set of issues and agreements. While the extent to which states view compliance as obligatory may vary from situation to situation and from rule to rule, nonetheless, governments participate in an ongoing process of remaking the ATS regime, and the socialization and voice for their own interests engendered in this role lead them to comply with regime norms. Compliance within the Antarctic Regime context involves informal practices as well as formal rules. Because of changing circumstances governments adhering to the Antarctic Regime must be willing and able to adapt their own policies and national behavior. In other words, governments must retain sufficient flexibility in their policies to meet unforeseen demands in the Antarctic. This ability has permitted the progressive adoption of new ATS agreements, with new norms, rules, institutions, and procedures to deal with new problems affecting Antarctic situations. In addition, compliance can involve informal international practices. These can implicitly strengthen bonds of cohesion in the entire system—and those of the regime as well.

As well as through informal practices, compliance is often produced in an indirect manner. For example, it can result from publicizing and documenting a decision's objective, which is made scientifically unfettered by political considerations. Enforcement operates in various kinds of settings, though it is often carried out through diplomatic pressure at ATCMs. Control within the ATS is exerted more by communication through diplomatic channels and following through than by coercive management or sanctions. Considerable pressure is also applied at ATCMs, more informally than formally, internationally between sessions. Such intercessional pressure comes through diplomatic channels, communications, correspondence, and nongovernmental organizations.

Although informal and indirect practices can have their effects, compliance in the Antarctic Treaty System regime occurs largely through formality, custom, and coordination. Governments have developed regularized ways of doing things in the ATS, and such accepted patterns of conduct have produced expectations of behavior and thereby contributed to defining how things should be done.

The relative influence of Consultative Party governments is exercised most prominently in ATCMs, and the ability to control Consultative Meetings (i.e., the relative power of actors) is keyed to a number of factors. First, there is the influence of personalities. The force of a diplomat's personality and his ability to pull strings and make things happen during a meeting carry considerable clout among ATCP delegates. A person who is regarded as a positive institutional memory also commands respect and attention. Arthur Watts and John Heap of the United Kingdom, Tucker Scully of the United States, Rüdiger Wolfrum of Germany, and Chris Beeby of New Zealand clearly have played leading personal roles in Antarctic law and politics during the past two decades. In addition, the ability to communicate in English is fundamental to speaking and being heard at ATCMs, since English is the common language, the "default" language as one diplomat put it. Other factors may also contribute to perceptions of a government's special prominence among the ATCPs. Among these are a state's status as a claimant, or its high degree of scientific investment in Antarctic activities, or its impressive level of technological expertise.[60]

The outcome of an ATCM really depends on how many levers are pulled, by whom, and in which direction. In other words, the outcomes of Consultative Meetings are not necessarily based on quality or quantity of debate. Rather, the products derive more from the power of personalities, the personal deals struck, and the language used to consolidate an agreement. In this sense, informal controls within the ATS regime operate quite effectively.

The ATS regime is earmarked by developed division of labor and differentiated institutions. The regime produced by the Antarctic Treaty System is a human product, subject to human limitations. The tendency, however, may be to regard such normatively grounded arrangements as having a fixed character. Actually, the ATS regime, like other regimes for managing common spaces, must be dynamic and adaptable if it is to succeed in a rapidly changing world.

ANTARCTIC REGIME BEHAVIOR: RULES OF THE GAME

What makes the regime produced by the Antarctic Treaty System authoritative for its member governments? To a great extent the answer lies in that regime's ability to stimulate efficacy and demonstrate legitimacy to that group of states. *Efficacy* and *legitimacy* emerge as key concepts underpinning the functional operation of the regime produced by the Antarctic Treaty System.

Efficacy refers to the compelling impact that the regime exerts on ATS members. If the actions of member governments are influenced by the norms, principles, and rules of the ATS regime, then the regime matters.[61] The efficacy of the ATS regime may be conveniently considered from the perspective of goal attainment. Efficacy implies causation. To be effective means to get results, to cause wanted reactions, or to produce intended responses toward the attainment of some desired end. The efficacy of the ATS regime can thus be measured by the degree to which the regime contributes to the resolution of those problems it was created to address.

To be effective in the real world, regimes must, first of all, make explicit the goals and objectives of their mission. The legal arrangement of agreements setting out the Antarctic Treaty System should clearly designate the regime's mission and define long-range goals toward accomplishing that mission. To a considerable degree, the ATS has succeeded. In so doing, it has enhanced the efficacy of each individual agreement and the regime package as a whole.[62] Whether the ATS regime is effective in achieving its stated goals depends on the degree to which member states follow the course of action the regime prescribes for them and how well they make use of the group's decision-making procedures that the regime sets up. As discussed below, the Antarctic regime enjoys a high degree of compliance, which greatly enhances its efficacy.[63]

Legitimacy concerns the manner in which the ATS regime is regarded by the international community. It also refers to the degree to which states view the ATS regime as applicable (i.e., its perceived relevance and lawful credibility) to the problems it is meant to address and the degree to which states view it as acceptable (i.e., appropriate for the tasks states face). A regime state's view as acceptable should not be challenged by other competing regimes.[64] The degree of legitimacy is reflected by appraising policy reactions in the attitudes and behavior of states party to agreements in the ATS. More than that, however, legitimacy may be more aptly demonstrated by the attitudes and conduct of governments outside the Antarctic Treaty System, through the intensity of their criticism or approval, challenge or acceptance, opposition or support, and recognition or defiance of the regime's intentions, policies, and prescriptions.

The legitimacy of the ATS regime may be a matter of degree. The impact of domestic considerations upon regime formulation ought not to be overlooked, nor should the causal relationships between effectiveness and legitimacy. Antarctic regime norms often take the form of legitimately shared guidelines for accepted and expected patterns of conduct by ATCP governments. Norms underpinning the cluster of Antarctic regimes are marked by gradual development; that is, norms are rules of behavior that have evolved and gradually gained popular support over time. That certain desired practices have been repeatedly followed by ATCP governments in the Antarctic has given rise to norms of conduct and served to set the course for legitimate behavior.[65]

Within the context of the ATS regime, legitimacy does not strictly mean legality. The legitimacy of the ATS regime does not turn merely on its lawful nature, on whether that regime was created and performs in a permissible manner. Nor should it be inferred that the legitimacy of the ATS regime necessarily means justice. The notion of legitimacy for the Antarctic regime turns more aptly on its obligatory attraction, on the magnetic sway that the regime exudes among governments party to the Antarctic Treaty in pulling together their conformity to the regime's norms, rules, and principles. Legitimacy explains why member governments choose to respect the composite Antarctic regime and adapt the conduct of their foreign policies accordingly. Like efficacy, then, legitimacy can be evaluated by the degree to which ATCP governments comply with the regime's norms and rules absent any means of coercion or forcible inducement.[66]

REGIME COMPLIANCE

The record of compliance by ATCP governments with the Antarctic regime may be better than that for any other international agreement this century. For nearly four decades the Antarctic Treaty has functioned without a single serious violation of its norms, rules, principles, or procedures reported by its member governments. Several general reasons for this may be suggested.

First, there are rewards for compliance. The Antarctic regime itself offers opportunities for participants to receive positive outcomes and benefits. The treaty arrangement offers a neutral ground for cooperation. Some governments may feel that they want to be good international citizens, so they comply with regime obligations. Some may want to work with other governments in order to gain influence among them or to receive "favors" in return for compliant behavior beneficial to others. Membership in and compliance with the Antarctic Treaty brings international prestige and respect. Participating in the Consultative Party Meetings provides an exclusive forum for communicating on important international issues, as well as the possibility of exclusive opportunities for ATCP governments. During the 1980s twelve states sought and received ATCP status.[67] Most were enticed to seek Consultative Party membership mainly by the prospect of sharing in the development of an Antarctic minerals regime. The ATS regime, apparently, affords states with opportunities to accomplish goals and establish reciprocal relationships that they deem to be in their national interests. That governments see benefits to be gained by international cooperation and that they associate themselves with a formal cooperative mechanism enhance prospects for greater stability in international relations affecting the regime's areas of concern.

States' support of the ATS regime's approach to sovereignty on the continent is an example of this willingness to cooperate. Both claimant and nonclaimant states benefit from the status quo sovereignty provision in Article IV of the Antarctic Treaty. The claimants' policy inclination is to protect their long-term interests in the region, viz., to maintain the option of claiming national sovereignty there. The Antarctic Treaty enables that. As a consequence, claimant states are disposed to support the treaty regime since it meets that key interest. What alternatives are there to the Antarctic Treaty by which states can preserve their claims of sovereignty? On the one hand, acting directly to support these claims would be distracting and enormously costly for those governments, never mind that international challenges would surely be made against them. In addition, asserting and defending jurisdiction would require heavy investments in physical resources and political capital. Compliance with the treaty regime, on the other hand, makes protecting sovereign interests in the Antarctic affordable.

A similar situation holds for nonclaimant states. A regime whose rules preclude conflict over sovereignty considerations makes it possible for nonclaimants to enjoy the benefits of multinational scientific research and international cooperation, without having to worry about whose territory is being encroached upon. For an example of another reward, compliance can lead governments to better relations with their constituent nongovernmental organizations that are concerned with the Antarctic. Governments generally prefer to broaden the domestic consensus behind their actions. The bottom line for ATCP governments thus seems clear.

A second reward of participation in the ATS regime is that compliance permits acquisition of special knowledge, training, and skills. Regime compliance brings with it access to new scientific data and technology pertaining to the Antarctic and with possible applications in other areas. Scientific research and exchange—hallmarks of international cooperation in Antarctica—supply tangible glue that helps keep the ATS regime in place. Governments that comply can participate in international meetings and scientific programs. The acquisition of knowledge and technology related to a global commons area contributes to a state's national power.

Benefits are not equal for all states, however. Less technologically sophisticated ATCPs are likely to benefit more than the ATCPs who are more advanced and who furnish most of the technologies used in the region. Scientifically advanced states can use expertise as a carrot to entice other governments to participate in Antarctic Treaty scientific activities, with the hope that those governments might be brought as parties into formal compliance with the treaty arrangement. The willingness of ATCPs to distribute gains unequally in order to attract new adherents to the regime was evident when Australia assisted India and China with their scientific programs during the 1980s before those governments joined the Antarctic Treaty. A similar intention also prompted Australia to offer its assistance to Pakistan in the latter state's Antarctic scientific research in 1991. That invitation, however, bore little fruit, as Pakistan opted to remain outside the Antarctic Treaty Regime.[68]

Third, compliance enables information exchange that is beneficial to all participants. Scientists and government officials share information and technology with nationals from other ATCP states. Information sharing through the ATS regime includes the exchange of U.S. scientific personnel, the exchange of Australian data on polar medicine, shared use of Australia's heavy overland machinery, and learning more about Italy's alternative energy systems and waste management systems. Increased cooperation in Antarctic matters can spill over into other areas of international contact, producing greater reciprocal relationship, confidence, and trust. This is not only true for exchange of scientific information, but also for new information concerning fishery and resource management (particularly among CCAMLR states), cold weather survival, and logistical operations. In addition, information exchange among ATCPs is increasing the global knowledge base about global climate change, sea level rise, and ozone depletion—all issues that seriously affect the entire international community.

A fourth inducement for states to comply with the ATS regime is that penalties or losses might be incurred for noncompliance. Concern over the possibility of punitive sanctions for noncompliance could theoretically induce members to comply. Even so, ATCP governments have not seriously contemplated adding such sanctions to the Antarctic Treaty System regime.[69] Thus far, then, governments need not calculate the political losses for deviating from ATS regime norms in order to ensure that they outweigh potential benefits gained from noncompliance.

The relative lack of concern among ATCP governments over noncompliance may be explained by the manner in which the ATS regime operates. Three examples make the point. First, in 1985 the French decided to build an airport at Point Geologie, in Adelie Land, just offshore the continent. In the process of doing so, they destroyed penguin rookeries on islands that were blasted away for the runway. The evidence at the time strongly suggested that provisions in the Agreed Measures had been breached in the process, yet no sanctions (or even formal admonitions to halt the runway) were imposed by other ATCPs against France for those violations. Rather, the attitude among other ATCP governments was that this was a French concern, being carried out in the claimed French sector. If the French said that they were in compliance with the Agreed Measures, then that explanation was sufficient for other ATCP governments. No punitive measures, formal or informal, were taken against the French. Environmentalists branded this incident a failure on the part of the ATCPs to protect treaty norms and Antarctic values. The ATCPs, however, regarded their nonaction as a small environmental price for long-term regime cohesion.[70]

A second example is the opening of the Chinese Great Wall station in 1981. To celebrate the occasion the Chinese brought in several doves, a species not indigenous to the Antarctic, which were released on the continent to inaugurate the station. Some Chinese also brought their pet dogs to Antarctica, and others were seen kicking penguins around as footballs for sport. All three activities plainly breached the Agreed Measures, and each presumably could have been cause for ATCP governments to protest vigorously or impose penalties against the Chinese. Neither of those options happened. Rather, national station administrators from neighboring bases undertook low-level, informal consultations with the station director of the Chinese facility and informed him of the wrongdoings. Each problem was subsequently corrected. The point here is plain: Compliance with conservation norms is treated as an educative process. Norms and rules in the ATS regime are not viewed by member states as black-or-white situations that give cause for punitive sanctions.[71]

A third example concerns management and conservation of fishery resources in the Southern Ocean under CCAMLR. It was widely known during the 1980s that Soviet fishermen failed to provide accurate data on fish and krill catch counts. Similarly, Soviet representatives were often hesitant to agree to conservation measures that might restrict opportunities for their ships to fish in circumpolar seas. This Soviet attitude nixed the consensus needed in the CCAMLR Commission for adoption of those measures. But with the collapse of the Soviet Union in 1990 and the radical deterioration of the Russian economy since then, the diplomatic situation in the Commission was dramatically altered. Russia could now measure the cost of obstructing CCAMLR economically, as aid desperately needed from the West could be held as a bargaining chip against Russia's actions in Commission meetings. Prior to 1991 fewer than 20 conservation measures had been adopted by the CCAMLR Commission. Since then more than 117 measures have been adopted, many of which curtail fishing in areas heavily visited by Russian trawlers.[72] Again, the ATS practice here is clear: Heavy-handed diplomatic punishments or sanctions are not the preferred means of inducing compliance with rules and norms in the Antarctic Treaty System regime. More subtle measures of persuasive influence are favored by member states and have tended to produce more impressive results. The ATS thus operates through methods of persuasion rather than compulsion, through education among its governments about ATS regime norms rather than by punitive sanctions when a breach occurs.[73]

Intraregime Cooperation

Several factors contribute to cooperation in the Antarctic Treaty System and enhance the efficacy and legitimacy of its composite regime. First are incentives. In situations where the reward structure is explicit and where improvements in policy position are considered important, the perceived gains made by policy coordination around a new agreed-upon standard can enhance cooperation. When ATCP governments see cooperation as the means to desired policy ends, they strive to maximize the joint rewards obtained through cooperation.

Second, clear and ongoing communication among member governments improves the regime's efficacy and legitimacy. Active communication works to ensure accurate perceptions of other governments' policies. Communication may also help member states to understand other states' motivations. Clear communication thus reduces the likelihood of conflict or competition between member states who wrongly believe their actions or intentions are at odds with one another or with the regime. In addition, if the tone of communication between parties is positive, the states involved may be encouraged to pursue further cooperation.

Interstate communications regarding Antarctic issues take place largely through the institutions set up by the ATS agreements. Prior to 1994 formal meetings of the Antarctic Treaty Consultative Parties were held once every two years, but these meetings are now convened annually. The CCAMLR Commission also convenes annually, as does SCAR. Numerous intersession meetings and scientific workshops are held frequently. International conferences are convened by academic bodies to discuss Antarctic science, law, and policy. During these occasions government representatives from ATCP states frequently engage in informal consultations with one another to exchange information and ideas about Antarctic matters. All these meetings—formal and informal, governmental, scientific, and academic—promote the intensive and direct communication among scientists and diplomats that facilitates cooperation among ATCP governments. In the process, such contacts also tend to reinforce norms adopted by the regime.[74]

The possibilities for cooperation in ATS arrangements can be strongly affected by government perceptions. Governments pay close attention to motives and intentions. If one government perceives another's behavior to stem from a genuine desire to cooperate, the former may choose to cooperate with the latter in order to obtain mutual benefits. If, however, actions by one government are interpreted by another as coming from an ambition to manipulate or exploit a situation, then the latter government may spurn cooperative overtures and instead react competitively. In the absence of good communication, and sometimes in spite of it, the critical factor is not the actual intent or motivation of a government. It is rather the perception of that behavior by the reacting state and the attribution of motive and intent. Importantly, a government's proclivities either to cooperate or to compete with other governments can influence attributions about it. Tendencies to cooperate can influence perceptions of that state and expectations about the government's behavior.[75]

Third, the size and complexity of an association also can influence the ability to bring about cooperation.[76] As the number of governments participating in ATS agreements increases, the ability to secure cooperation among all those governments on any one issue may be more difficult. In 1961, when the Antarctic Treaty entered into force, there were twelve original parties. Now there are forty-three parties, of which twenty-six are members of the policy-making ATCP group. Universal cooperation is generally harder to obtain as the number of members and the complexity of the association increase. Moreover, as a regime arrangement grows more complex in size and membership, so too does the opportunity increase for at least one member to adopt a selfish view. States within a larger, more complex association may also encounter less pressure for cooperation because of the greater diffusion of responsibility among its membership. These general rules can apply specifically to the Antarctic Treaty System regime.

Still, one must be mindful that governments and individual representatives who are longtime practitioners of the Antarctic Treaty Consultative Party process have greater reservoirs of political power and engender more respect for their ideas than newer, less experienced members. Original members have institutional memories, know how the rules of the regime operate, and are able to pull the right political levers to get their desired policy results. This capability tends to produce greater cooperation in ways that most benefit longtime members.[77]

During the 1980s, when a raft of new states rushed to join the Antarctic Treaty Consultative Party group, concern arose among some original Antarctic Treaty governments over the regime's efficacy. In a consensus decision-making process, they feared, the more states that participated, the more likely it was that one government might play the role of spoiler. This concern seemed particularly acute since leading Third World countries—India, China, and Brazil—had recently joined the treaty and might attempt to politicize the common heritage issue within the ATCP group.[78] This scenario did not occur. Why not? The answer is simply because those three governments valued their own expected gains in the Antarctic Treaty process more than the common heritage notion then being pushed by Malaysia. Each new ATCP government now had a vested interest, with considerable power, within the select group of ATCP states. Concern over ATCP membership size waned with the recognition that new members had more to gain by preserving the ATS than by trying to destroy it.

Fourth, reciprocity tends to work within an association as a general norm. A government tends to behave toward others as other governments behave toward it.[79] Reciprocity in ATS dealings generates much goodwill, although relatively few opportunities are available for it. Emergency assistance, rescue operations, and transfer of medical supplies from one station to another are salient examples of reciprocity opportunities. The tendency nonetheless has been to turn to the government having the best capabilities, and that has often been the United States. Still, governments, like individuals, usually feel obligated to return favors (and, for that matter, insults). In the course of Antarctic affairs, initial cooperation usually begets further cooperation, which produces a reenforcing and self-perpetuating positive cycle of goodwill and collaboration.[80]

CONCLUSION

The Antarctic Treaty System has given rise to a regime that governs that commons area. Governments have developed norms and rules for regulating activities in the Antarctic by progressively assimilating them into international legal arrangements. This formation of a commons regime from the 1959 Antarctic Treaty has come about in an ad hoc manner, through an association of Antarctic Treaty agreements. The Antarctic Treaty System's nexus of agreements has produced a cluster of regimes for maintaining order and managing national activities in the Antarctic. Indeed, the evolution of a commons regime for the polar South has come to reflect patterned interactions and relationships among the various Antarctic agreements. Each individual instrument, with its norms, rules, principles, and procedures, can be considered a discrete subregime of the ATS regime.

There is an overarching, or parent, regime generated by the Antarctic Treaty itself. The gradual recognition that certain issues were not adequately addressed in the Antarctic Treaty led the ATCPs subsequently to negotiate new agreements, producing cradled subregimes to deal with special concerns: in 1964 the conservation of Antarctic fauna and flora; in 1972 the conservation of Antarctic seals; in 1980 the conservation of Antarctic marine living resources; and in 1991 comprehensive environmental protection in the Antarctic. Recall, too, that an unsuccessful attempt was made in 1988 to regulate development of Antarctic mineral resource activities.

From the Antarctic experience, a number of theoretical observations can be gleaned for global commons regimes. The first suggests that, at a minimum, two critical considerations appear necessary for a commons regime to function properly. First, the ways and means for intergovernmental cooperation must be available and open among the parts of a multilateral organization. Second, officials in states participating in the regime must have the political will to make that cooperation happen, accomplish the values desired, and abide by the norms endorsed by the regime. If these decision-makers are not willing to make cooperation and compliance happen, both the efficiency and legitimacy of the regime will come into question.

In the case of the Antarctic, treaty law has given rise to establishing a cluster of regimes that have evolved to define the rights and duties of governments and circumscribe their activities in the polar South. For a global commons regime to be realized, then, there must be the express international intent to create operative norms for regulating national activities on specific issues in a commons area.

The regime in the Antarctic suggests a point about the defining characteristic on which common space regimes pivot. The rationale for creating international commons regimes is not concern over a commons space, but rather over the effects of certain state activities *in* that space. Regimes are devised and operate according to a perceived international need to regulate state activities that affect an issue-area of general international concern. Whether they are activities affecting the Antarctic, oceans, airspace, outer space, human rights, or the conduct of war, the body of norms, rules, principles, and procedures designed to deal with those activities will constitute the regime for that issue-area.

The Antarctic experience makes clear that not only will the degree of international cooperation determine the effectiveness of compliance with a regime's mandate, but also the level of compliance will affect the willingness of governments to cooperate within that regime. For Antarctica, it is important to examine what makes cooperation among interested parties not only possible but also desirable. Why do national governments involved in Antarctic affairs want to abide by multifaceted international obligations generated by the Antarctic Treaty's regime? As shown above, doing so benefits their national interests.

A state's motivations to remain within the ATCP group are also influenced by the real-world goals of that group. States participate in the ATCP group as a means to an end. Attraction to the Consultative Party group depends on how well a government's national interests can mesh with the goals the ATCPs lay out. A government's willingness to remain in that association will also depend on how successful the ATCP group is in accomplishing its objectives while accommodating that government's interests.

Certain forces may discourage an ATCP state from defecting from the regime, even if that government is not pleased with certain policies or is dissatisfied with the direction in which the ATS appears headed. Simply put, the costs of leaving are viewed as too great. Governments have invested high political, economic, and diplomatic stakes in the ATS, and there are no realistically available regime alternatives. Hence, to leave is in effect to abandon the political capital invested in the system and also to risk becoming alienated from the only group of states that has successfully made policy for the Antarctic commons since 1961. That price of omission is considered far too exorbitant, even among the most dissatisfied ATCP governments.

The regime generated by the Antarctic Treaty System is marked by interdependent interaction. The efficacy and legitimacy of the regime persuade Antarctic governments to remain in the group. Key as a positive force for increasing compliance with the ATS regime are the mutual benefits and opportunities that accrue from ATCP group participation. Simply put, personalities matter; people make decisions and regime policy. When decision-makers in different governments respect each other and become closely connected by bonds of friendship, community, and dedication to mutual purposes, the prospects for regime cohesion tend to increase. To a considerable degree, this has been the diplomatic situation among Antarctic Treaty governments over the past four decades.

Chapter 5

RESOURCE CONSERVATION AND MANAGEMENT

The Antarctic commons covers one-tenth of the Earth's surface, including the continent of Antarctica, several islands, and the Southern Ocean. As mentioned earlier, the southern commons can be delimited by the Antarctic Convergence, which meanders around 50° south latitude and encompasses some 20 million square miles of land and sea. The Convergence effectively forms a biological barrier: very few species migrate beyond it. It is thus a natural boundary within which to manage the tremendous resources of the Antarctic commons.

Natural processes within the Antarctic have already been disturbed by man's activities. Ozone depletion over Antarctica has dramatically highlighted the continent's importance for the entire planet. Antarctica and the Southern Ocean interact in critical ways that influence the Earth's weather, air, and ocean currents. Should global warming proceed and the Antarctic ice sheet melt, the world's sea level could rise some sixty meters (two hundred feet), inundating most islands and inhabited coastal regions on every continent.[1] The impacts of human activities upon the Antarctic environment must therefore be considered within a global context.

As the ability to exploit living and nonliving resources throughout the Antarctic commons increased, so also did the need for regulatory regimes to conserve those resources and protect the Antarctic environment. Conservation is the planned management of resources or the environment of an ecosystem to prevent their exploitation, pollution, destruction, or neglect. Through such measures conservation aims to ensure that those resources and that ecosystem are preserved for future use.

Acknowledging these concerns, this chapter examines the environmental stakes in the south polar region. It evaluates the legal arrangements of the ATS to assess the strengths and weaknesses of the regimes that were created to conserve, manage, and preserve the environmental integrity of the Antarctic commons. This analysis indicates how far ATCP conservation and protection policies for the Antarctic commons have progressed and how far they still must go to attain success as a conservation regime.

BACKGROUND

The Antarctic commons is a unique ecosystem that depends on a fragile balance of natural processes which, if disrupted, could cause serious consequences for the entire planet. Intensified scientific, economic, and tourist activities have created threats for the Antarctic environment that have necessitated special measures to conserve and manage natural resources in the region. Conservation of resources was not a significant concern of the Antarctic Treaty drafters in 1959; only casual reference is made in Article IX, paragraph 1(f) to the "preservation and conservation of living resources" but without distinction from protection of the Antarctic environment. Likewise, protection of the environment is aided indirectly by provisions in the Antarctic Treaty concerning the prohibition of military activities (Article I, paragraph 1), bans on nuclear explosions, and regulations on the disposal of radioactive wastes (Article V, paragraph 1). However, conservation is not embraced as a coherent strategy distinct from environmental protection.

The Antarctic Treaty's broad reference to "preservation and conservation of living resources" as a "matter of common interest" placed the issue within the scope of the policy recommendations by the Consultative Parties. As a consequence, the fundamental principles for preservation and conservation of Antarctic resources initially came as Consultative Party recommendations of a preventative nature. Coming in the 1970s and 1980s, these measures were designed to preclude damage to the Antarctic environment and were adopted by the Consultative Parties in line with suggestions by the Scientific Committee on Antarctic Research (SCAR).[2]

Since entry into force of the Antarctic Treaty in 1961, the policies of the ATCPs toward the south polar commons have evolved along two tracks. The first aimed at conservation and management, while the second (which will be treated in chapter 6) focused on protection of the environment. The purpose of this first policy track was to prevent living resources from being overexploited by conserving and managing those resources in the Antarctic, both on land and at sea. These efforts crystallized in the Agreed Measures on the Conservation of Antarctic Fauna and Flora in 1964, the Convention on the Conservation of Antarctic Seals in 1972, and the Convention on the Conservation of Antarctic Marine Living Resources (CCAMLR) in 1980. Each of these resource conservation instruments evolved with its own strengths and deficiencies. Moreover, the lessons learned in implementing each agreement helped better the protective qualities of its successors.

CONSERVATION ON LAND

The first significant effort to establish a conservation regime for the Antarctic came in 1964 as the Agreed Measures for the Conservation of Antarctic Fauna and Flora.[3] The Agreed Measures, promulgated as a Consultative Party recommendation, focuses on plants and animals indigenous to the continent and obligates Antarctic Treaty governments (and their nationals) to abstain within the treaty area from "killing, wounding, capturing or molesting of any native animal or native bird, or any attempt at any such act, except in accordance with a permit."[4] Governments are also supposed to take "appropriate measures" to minimize "harmful interference" with native mammals or birds and to prohibit bringing into the Antarctic any species of plant or animal not indigenous to the region.[5]

The Agreed Measures also created a system for protecting certain areas and sites that has become central to Antarctic environmental management. The Agreed Measures established Specially Protected Areas (SPAs), which are areas of "outstanding scientific interest" that are accorded special protection "in order to preserve their unique ecological system."[6] Consistent with preserving the Antarctic environment, the ATCPs in 1972 designated two new categories for preservation. First, Sites of Special Scientific Interest (SSSIs) were established through Recommendation VII-3 to protect areas where scientific investigations might be disturbed by accidental or intentional human interference.[7] Second, provision was made for Sites of Historic Interest (SHIs) in Recommendation VII-9 to preserve historical locations and monuments.[8] To strengthen the Agreed Measures, at the Fifteenth ATCM in Paris in 1989 the category of "Specially Reserved Areas" was adopted to set aside areas of outstanding geological, glaciological, geomorphological, aesthetic, scenic, or wilderness value.[9] Finally, "Multiple-Use Planning Areas" were set up to redirect human activities where and when they threatened to interfere with or harm the environment.[10]

Enforcement of the Agreed Measures is left to national authorities, and the exchange among ATCPs of information on monitoring is required.[11] The Agreed Measures also requires ATCPs to exchange statistics on native birds and mammals captured or killed, the status of those species of fauna, and the degree to which their preservation requires their protection. Again, responsibility for reporting is left to national governments.

The effectiveness of the Agreed Measures was, at least initially, limited by the ever-present issue of conflicting claims to the continent. In 1964 sensitivity remained over sovereignty claims, making the ATCPs reluctant to deal with questions of jurisdiction or to implement policies except through national authorities. Continued reliance on national means to implement the Agreed Measures highlighted the inhibition of claimant Consultative Parties against entrusting a designated institutional authority with the responsibility of overseeing conservation policies on the continent.

Another limitation of the Agreed Measures was the unwillingness of the ATCPs to encroach upon high-seas rights, which are guaranteed in the Antarctic Treaty. The scope of the Agreed Measures is restricted to the land, ice shelves, and airspace below 60° south latitude.[12] That scope was circumscribed even further as the Agreed Measures echoed the Antarctic Treaty in asserting that "nothing in these Agreed Measures shall prejudice or in any way affect the rights, or the exercise of the rights, of any state under international law with regard to the high seas within the Antarctic Treaty area."[13] In the Agreed Measures, then, conservation stops at the edge of the ice. This self-imposed limitation by the Consultative Parties was intended to avoid hampering the exercise of their own high-seas rights, including the freedom to fish.

Two other instruments are relevant for setting preservation and protection standards for activities affecting the south polar environment. The Code of Conduct for Antarctic Expeditions and Station Activities[14] was adopted in 1975 as a recommendation that governments should follow "to the greatest extent feasible." The code addressed waste disposal, environmental impact assessment, the introduction of alien species and the disturbance of native fauna. In 1979 the ATCPs also adopted the Statement of Accepted Practices and the Relevant Provisions of the Antarctic Treaty.[15] While not binding, this environmental measure reaffirms the ATCPs' recognition of their "special responsibility" in the Antarctic. These governments are expected to ensure that their nationals visiting the Antarctic protect the environment, conserve wildlife, respect the ban on pelagic sealing and waste disposal, and protect historic monuments and sites of specific scientific interest. Expeditions from ATCPs are also required to give notice to scientific stations that might be visited.

CONSERVATION AT SEA

The continent of Antarctica is nearly barren of indigenous life. The Antarctic seas, in contrast, are among the world's most biologically productive. Yet the Antarctic Treaty curiously omits mention of managing the use of Antarctic ocean resources. To compensate for this omission in the face of increased fishing activities since 1970, Antarctic Treaty parties focused their conservation efforts on the living resources in the Southern Ocean.

The Seals Convention

The first major international conservation agreement in the Antarctic commons was the 1972 Convention for the Conservation of Antarctic Seals.[16] This instrument, which entered into force in 1978, protects six seal species—southern elephant, leopard, Weddell, crabeater, Ross, and southern fur.[17] Catch limits are also set for crabeater, leopard, and Weddell seals.[18] Under the convention, any seal harvests must be limited so that the "optimum sustainable yield" from a species is not exceeded and so that a satisfactory balance is maintained within the Antarctic ecosystem. The Seals Convention recognized that scientific research is needed to ensure that harvests are kept at a sustainable level. As the Convention's preamble asserts, "Every effort should be made both to encourage biological and other research on Antarctic seal populations and to gain information from the research and from the statistics of future sealing operations."[19]

The Seals Convention included minimal procedures by which to carry out its mandate, and the roles for contracting parties to the Seals Convention parallel the roles of the Consultative Parties under the Antarctic Treaty; contracting parties to the Seals Convention may adopt additional measures for conservation, scientific study, and "rational and human use of seal resources,"[20] mirroring the treaty's Article IX, paragraph 1. Certain disparities in membership qualifications are also apparent between the Antarctic Treaty and the Seals Convention. For one, all contracting parties to the Seals Convention are equal; no distinction is made between Consultative and Non-Consultative Parties. In addition, accession to the Seals Convention is by invitation only, with that invitation issued by consent of all the contracting parties.[21] The Antarctic Treaty, on the other hand, remains open to accession by any state that is a member of the United Nations.

The perceived need for a separate Seals Convention revealed that the Consultative Parties felt incompetent (and were unwilling) to control certain activities on the high seas, such as pelagic sealing. The ATCPs' perceived incapacity led them to negotiate a separate treaty agreement to conserve seals rather than to enforce a solution under the Antarctic Treaty that claimed in principle to protect seals through the Agreed Measures. The unwillingness of the ATCPs to limit their high-seas freedoms reveals two important points. First, the ATCPs are not legally competent to restrict the exercise of rights to the high seas, including the taking of living resources, by nationals of states not party to the agreement. Even the 1972 Convention's restrictions on sealing in high seas pertain only to states contracting to the convention, not to all governments whose nationals might be engaged in sealing operations. The second point is that this reluctance to limit rights to the high seas under the Seals Convention was self-imposed by the ATCPs. These governments decided that the Seals Convention should be legally consonant with the respect for high-seas rights flowing out of Article VI in the Antarctic Treaty. This arrangement, though, produced an unusual situation. One creature living in the Antarctic was made subject to two separate conservation regimes, depending on whether it was on land and ice shelves, or lying on pack ice or swimming in the high seas. The Agreed Measures protected seals in the former case, the Seals Convention in the latter. For seals in the high seas, moreover, limited commercial sealing is permitted. The Agreed Measures offers no similar opportunity to sealing states, providing seals on the continent with total protection from hunting.

The Seals Convention marked a new threshold in the ATCPs' strategy to conserve Antarctic commons resources, particularly in the circumpolar seas. The legal nature of Antarctic Treaty recommendations was deemed inadequate by itself to produce binding conservation obligations. By designing, negotiating, and formally ratifying special multilateral agreements on the conservation of Antarctic living resources, the ATCPs sought to enhance the legal weight of those commitments. As noted in chapter 4, the overlapping issue-areas and memberships of these different treaties means that each reinforces the other and contributes to a holistic Antarctic regime.

The Convention on the Conservation of Antarctic Marine Living Resources (CCAMLR)

During the 1970s the Consultative Parties became aware that there were risks associated with exploiting living resources in Antarctic waters. The Seals Convention directly grew out of that concern. Similarly, concern over the exploitation of marine living resources was raised beginning with the Seventh ATCM in 1972. At the Eighth ATCM in 1975 the ATCPs agreed, in Recommendation VIII-10, on "the need to promote and achieve within the framework of the Antarctic Treaty, the objectives of protection, scientific study and rational use" of Antarctic marine living resources.[22] ATCP governments also requested that the Scientific Committee on Antarctic Research (SCAR) develop a research plan for the Antarctic Ocean.

Responding to this request, SCAR set up a special working group on living resources of the Southern Ocean and launched an international research program called BIOMASS (Biological Investigations of Marine Antarctic Systems and Stocks). The principal objective of BIOMASS was to acquire better understanding of the composition of the Southern Ocean ecosystem and the relationships among its species. At the Ninth ATCM in 1977 the Consultative Parties agreed to negotiate a new convention and to include within its scope resources that were not commercially exploitable. To that end, Recommendation IX-2 called for increased cooperation in scientific research, particularly for BIOMASS investigations by the ATCPs. Interim guidelines were also proposed for conserving Antarctic marine living resources, including measures to increase the exchange of catch statistics so as to facilitate "the greatest possible concern and care in the harvesting of Antarctic Marine Living Resources."[23] Finally, Recommendation IX-2 called for convening of a Special Consultative Meeting to negotiate a "definitive regime" to conserve marine living resources throughout the entire Antarctic ecosystem.[24]

In 1980 the Convention on the Conservation of Antarctic Marine Living Resources (CCAMLR) was promulgated. CCAMLR aims to control exploitation of living resources in the Southern Ocean by creating a regime to manage conservation of those resources;[25] under CCAMLR *conservation* is defined as "rational use."[26] CCAMLR is concerned with more than fishing activities. The convention uses an "ecosystem approach" for managing the Antarctic commons. That is, if any species is harvested, then due regard must be paid not only to the impact of harvesting on the target species but also its impact on the marine ecosystem as a whole.[27]

Jurisdiction

CCAMLR establishes the largest targeted conservation zone on Earth. Through its ecosystem approach, the convention encompasses all "the marine living resources" of the Antarctic area; broadly defined, CCAMLR covers all living organisms in the Antarctic marine commons.[28] But CCAMLR is not meant to apply so much to the *area* south of the Antarctic Convergence as to the *living marine resources* in that area. In this respect, CCAMLR differs from the Antarctic Treaty and the Seals Convention, which focus more on activities in the area of 60° south than on resources per se.[29]

CCAMLR's jurisdiction overlaps with the Antarctic Treaty, the Agreed Measures, and the Seals Convention. Yet CCAMLR takes into account the International Whaling Convention and expressly excludes it from the family of Antarctic Treaty System agreements,[30] thus acting as a bridge between the Antarctic regime and other international regimes governing the high seas.

CCAMLR was negotiated to accommodate disparate ATCP positions on sovereignty in the Antarctic. CCAMLR's scope north of 60° south latitude raised concerns regarding certain sub-Antarctic island groups. Some of these had disputed sovereignty claims (viz., South Orkney, South Georgia, South Sandwich, and the South Shetland Islands), while others did not (viz., Prince Edward, Crozet, Kerguélen, McDonald, and Heard Islands). To address the issue of competing sovereign claims, CCAMLR reiterates Article IV in the Antarctic Treaty as its own Article IV, with two significant modifications. First, the moratorium on claims is adjusted to account for CCAMLR's extended jurisdiction north of 60° south latitude to the Antarctic Convergence. Second, CCAMLR's Article IV specifically states that nothing in the agreement shall prejudice "any right or claim or basis of claim to exercise coastal jurisdiction under international law within the area to which this Convention applies."[31] This new language was added to accommodate those parties (in particular, France and Australia) whose claims to islands within the Convergence were not in dispute but whose exclusive economic zones overlapped with the ambit of CCAMLR's jurisdiction. Understandings were negotiated into the Convention that acknowledged rights by France to agree to application of the conservation measures to waters around Kerguélen and Crozet Islands. These understandings recognized France's right to use its own national measures to regulate fisheries,[32] notwithstanding CCAMLR's jurisdiction cutting across those zones.

Institutions

The institutional structure created by CCAMLR makes it the most complex of the ATS's conservation instruments. The Commission for the Conservation of Antarctic Marine Living Resources, CCAMLR's policy-making and regulatory body, was established with legal personality, privileges, and immunities.[33] The Commission drafts and adopts binding conservation measures through consensus.[34] Resort to consensus for decision-making in the Commission was done by the ATCPs to accommodate and protect the position of the claimants. Consensus also permitted fishing states—in particular, Japan and the then Soviet Union—to control their own fishing activities in the region. An advisory body, the Scientific Committee, was also created to collect, study, and facilitate exchange of state-held information on marine living resources.[35]

Participation in CCAMLR is open to states and other competent international entities not party to the Antarctic Treaty. While farsighted in conservation appeal, CCAMLR also reinforces for the ATCPs the legal fact that they cannot regulate lawful fishing activities of nonparty states on the high seas. CCAMLR's membership is therefore intended to be broader, and CCAMLR encourages accession by "any State interested in research or harvesting activities in relation to the marine resources to which this Convention applies."[36]

A special process has evolved for Commission meetings, which traditionally last for two weeks. The Commission initially convenes in plenary session to open the meeting, then goes into recess. During the recess the Standing Committee on Administration and Finance (SCAF), the Standing Committee on Observation and Inspection (SCOI), and the Scientific Committee convene separately to discuss, debate, and finalize reports to be presented to the Commission. At the beginning of the second week, the Commission reconvenes in plenary session to consider reports from the committees. The reports are discussed, proposed measures are considered, and the plenary takes action.

Conservation Procedures

Conservation measures are usually adopted in the following manner. First, the need for a measure is identified, often from a national background paper or the work of the Scientific Committee. Inspiration for new conservation measures usually originates in one or several delegations, which draft measures they think merit approval. During its annual meeting the Commission responds to national papers that identify problem areas. One or two persons from the sponsoring delegations draft the formal proposal and circulate it informally to other delegations to solicit unofficial reactions. During this process sponsoring delegations can get a sense of whether their measure might be approved or should be abandoned.

If the other delegations respond well, the measure then goes to the Commission plenary for discussion. The Commission may comment on the proposal and even ask that some language be redrafted. It is also possible that a delegation might voice objections in the plenary. Usually, however, once a measure reaches the Commission plenary, it has secured informal approval from all delegations and has achieved the consensus necessary for adoption. According to CCAMLR, conservation measures should be based on the best scientific information available.[37] However, decisions on matters of substance (e.g., conservation measures) still require consensus in the Commission.

Enforcement of conservation measures is key to the effectiveness of CCAMLR's resource management system. A conservation measure is agreed upon in principle by members, and if no objection is registered within 90 days, it becomes binding upon members 180 days thereafter.[38] Since 1988, however, measures taken for the fishery around South Georgia have become binding immediately after adoption due to the severe depletion of fish stocks there.[39]

The Ecosystem Approach

The ecosystem approach is the principal conservation innovation of CCAMLR. Core conservation principles in CCAMLR require that: (1) exploited populations must not be allowed to fall below a level that ensures they can sustain their greatest net annual increase; (2) depleted populations must be restored to such levels; (3) ecological relationships between harvested, dependent, and related species must be maintained; and (4) risks of changes to the marine ecosystem that are not reversible over two or three decades must be minimized.[40] These principles are the four pillars that support the ecosystem approach to living resource conservation and distinguish CCAMLR from other marine resource management regimes.

Under CCAMLR, management of fishing must not only conserve targeted species, it must also consider the impact of harvesting on creatures that prey on and compete with the target species. Hence, scientific research becomes essential for fulfilling the goals of the ecosystem approach and for implementing conservation policies throughout the Antarctic marine commons. The consensus model of decision-making, however, can impede adoption of policies that scientific data indicate are necessary. For example, since 1984 the Scientific Committee has advocated strict regulation of finfishing, a policy that received approval each year from the Commission. Even so, opinions became polarized between fishing and nonfishing states, so much so that consensus on more rigorous conservation measures was not possible though 1990. General progress on conservation measures has thus come about slowly.

Fishing countries (mainly Japan and the Soviet Union) contended that any scientific advice would be uncertain, since scientific information was wanting. Fishing states contended that conservation measures should not be adopted with such scanty scientific data. The necessary data, not coincidentally, could be provided only by the fishing states themselves. Nonfishing CCAMLR members, meanwhile, argued that it was preferable to err on the side of caution, even absent detailed data. It was better to adopt reasonable conservation measures, they said, than to risk letting fishery stocks decline below sustainable levels. Precautionary action was more desirable than no action at all.

The Commission thus remained frustrated on fishing conservation policies until the late 1980s. While most Commission members advocated implementing new conservation measures, a few fishing nations motivated by short-term economic interests created a policy-making impasse. It is important to understand, nonetheless, that CCAMLR did not preside over the drastic depletion of fishery stocks in the Southern Ocean; depletion had already occurred. But the Commission remained stymied from halting the decline—and thus facilitating the recovery—of stocks that were depleted before CCAMLR ever entered into force.

Given this history of obstruction, it is worth asking whether out of respect for the wishes of only one or a few, the principle of consensus decision-making can carry too exorbitant a price for all. Decision-making by consensus demonstrated that cost by paralyzing the Commission for more than half a decade. One must be mindful, though, of the real world of international politics. The fact remains that no formal decision-making procedure can compel governments to accept policies or enforce conservation measures that they perceive as contrary to their national interests. Had decision-making in CCAMLR been by majority vote, the fishing conservation measures simply would have been ignored by the major finfishing states.

The CCAMLR Ecological Monitoring System (CEMP)

The twin purposes of CCAMLR are conservation of living resources in Antarctic waters and maintenance of their ecological relationships. CCAMLR thus aims to ensure that exploitation of living resources is not detrimental to natural predators.[41] At the urging of its Scientific Committee, the Commission established in 1985 an Ecosystem Monitoring Program (CEMP). The objectives of CEMP are:

> to detect and record significant changes in critical components of the ecosystem, [and] to serve as the basis for the conservation of Antarctic Marine Living Resources. The monitoring system should be designed to distinguish between changes due to the harvesting of commercial species and changes due to environmental variability, both physical and biological.[42]

The program was set up to get advice and data on managing certain species, with two key considerations: first, how to determine whether a predator is affecting the availability of a prey fish species; and second, how to determine whether some change in a predator's population is related to the availability of a fishery. Scientists can now determine what both fishery and predator species are doing. They have yet to discover, however, the precise ecological links between the two.

CEMP aims to detect changes in key components of the Southern Ocean's ecosystem and to distinguish between changes caused by commercial harvesting and those caused by natural circumstances. Since 1985 this approach has been used to monitor selected species of seals and seabirds that are harvested and to assess the impacts of environmental factors on them,[43] and in 1991 the Commission adopted a special conservation measure protecting seal island sites used in CEMP.[44]

CEMP's activities further the conservation objectives in Article II of CCAMLR. Since it is not possible to monitor all organisms and their ecological interactions, CEMP selectively identifies key species and special environmental variables in Antarctic waters that are highly sensitive to changes in the availability of food (e.g., reproduction cycles, growth conditions, feeding behavior, abundance of species, and distribution of populations). Information from monitoring these variables, along with fishing data and biological data taken from catch samples, are studied to determine how well CCAMLR's conservation principles are working to manage fishing activities in circumpolar seas.[45]

CEMP was designed to monitor the availability of food to predators. Its greatest focus is on krill, in particular *Euphausia superba*, since krill are critical in the Antarctic ecosystem as the principal food of fish, seabirds, seals, and whales. Yet krill have also become a principal target for commercial fishing in the Antarctic marine commons. The primary consumers of krill that CEMP monitors are seals, seabirds, and whales. These species were selected as predator indicators in the belief that changes in their numbers would take place if substantial decreases occurred in the amount of available krill. The availability of considerable knowledge about their biological behavior, underlined by their importance in the Antarctic marine ecosystem, also influenced the choice of these species for CEMP monitoring.

Monitoring sites were chosen on the basis of proximity to known fishing grounds, the presence of predators, and the availability of substantive research on those areas. CEMP in the late 1990s is focusing on three study regions: the areas around South Georgia, Prydz Bay, and the Antarctic Peninsula.[46] If CEMP is to be scientifically successful, data from different sites and different seasons must be comparable. Standardized methods for monitoring predators, devised in cooperation with SCAR, are applied at each site. Once CEMP puts in place standard monitoring methods for all environmental variables, then information on prey and predator species can be collected and submitted to the CEMP Working Group for its advice to the Scientific Committee of CCAMLR. More experience with baseline standards and monitoring procedures is required, however.

CEMP uses "feedback management" to assess and adjust levels of harvesting so that desired conditions in the ecosystem can be sustained. This process requires monitoring critical facets of an ecosystem (e.g., the population dynamics of krill stocks and prey species), as well as the conduct of the fishery. Such data are used by the Scientific Committee to advise the Commission on how the ecosystem might be affected by harvesting krill. The Commission can determine from these appraisals which strategies are best suited for conservation measures in a particular situation.[47] Feedback management thus contributes much toward CCAMLR's aims. It permits monitoring to operate more effectively and furnishes data sufficiently early for the Commission to take action toward sustaining the conservation objectives contained in Article II of CCAMLR.[48]

Two main factors explain why CCAMLR applies CEMP data in its fishery management strategies. The first is that the ecosystem approach explicitly attempts to ensure that exploitation of living resources does not adversely affect natural consumers. This feature distinguishes CCAMLR starkly from traditional fishery management agreements, which focus on survival of one species only and have often failed to prevent gross overexploitation because they waited too long before acting. Once overexploitation was recognized (or acknowledged), critical damage had been done, and it was too late to restore either the target species or the depleted population of its natural predators. A second reason given for using CEMP data is more pragmatic. If CCAMLR governments actually commit substantial time and money to the CEMP, then CEMP must operate as a viable program.[49] The application of CEMP findings to making CCAMLR conservation policies will supply tangible evidence of the program and its financial and scientific value.

CEMP remains an ambitious program. The quality of its results depend on the quality of its science and the degree of support it receives from participant governments. CEMP could add much to the knowledge base about Antarctic marine living resources and enhance opportunities for their conservation. The critical indicator of CEMP's influence, however, will be in how much the program's findings influence decisions within the Commission—a consideration that ultimately depends on how much individual governments appreciate the validity of those findings. In this connection, the success of CEMP ultimately depends on the number and eagerness of the CCAMLR states that become involved in and contribute to CEMP's programs.

Fishery Exploitation in the Antarctic Ocean

Finfish

Until the 1980s fishing in Antarctic waters was conducted almost exclusively by fleets from former Eastern Bloc states. Large-scale harvesting of finfish was begun in 1969/70 by the Soviets around South Georgia and around Kerguélen Island in the next year. Poland, the former German Democratic Republic, and Bulgaria also fished these waters beginning in 1977. After the 1977/78 season fishing activities moved south. These areas yielded good catches until the early 1980s, when harvests fell off rapidly. Japan began fishing in the Indian Ocean sector and gradually shifted toward the Pacific. Today nearly all Japanese fishing activities are concentrated in the South Atlantic. Fishing along the Antarctic coasts, meanwhile, has only reached exploratory levels.[50]

Finfishing has mirrored patterns for whaling in the Southern Ocean, but on a more collapsed timescale. Like whaling, then, finfishing in the southern waters went through stages of discovery, exploitation, and depletion of stocks. Depletion of demersal fish stocks, especially Patagonian toothfish and lantern fish, began in the late 1980s. Lanternfish harvesting was halted in the 1991/92 season and has not resumed since then for financial, rather than biological, considerations.[51] Longlines were introduced in 1985 to catch Patagonian toothfish and came into full commercial operation around South Georgia in 1988/89 and around the Kerguélen Islands in 1991. Longline fisheries are responsible for killing many sub-Antarctic albatrosses and petrels in the course of their operation[52] and have contributed to a steady decline in the populations of these birds over the past two decades.[53] In 1995 Commission members adopted Conservation Measure 29/XIV specifically to reduce the incidental mortality of seabirds due to the longline fishery.[54]

By 1997 more than 3 million tons of finfish had been taken from the Southern Ocean. More than 2.8 million tons had been taken from the Atlantic sector, and of that, 1.8 million tons (or 84 percent) were caught around South Georgia.[55] Of the 924,000 tons harvested in the Indian sector, 872,000 tons (or 94.4 percent) were fished around the Kerguélen Islands.[56] The depletion of fisheries worldwide is creating greater interest in the resources of the Southern Ocean. In response to domestic pressure from fishermen in New Zealand, Australia, and South Africa, state parties to CCAMLR agreed to open four new fisheries for 1996/97 in the Southern Ocean—three for Patagonian toothfish and one for squid.[57] Conservation groups had hoped the precautionary principle would prevail, i.e., that fisheries would be limited in scope so that scientific data could be collected to determine whether the stock could support commercial harvests. The Commission opted otherwise, moving in November 1996 to set commercial harvest limits between 1,980 and 2,200 tons.[58]

Other recent developments affecting fisheries in the Southern Ocean give cause for concern. Numerous reports from the 1994/95 and 1995/96 seasons suggest that Argentinean and Chilean fishing boats exceeded quotas for Antarctic toothfish in the South Atlantic. To discourage such illegal activities, the United Kingdom in 1993 had declared a two-hundred-mile management zone around South Georgia and the South Sandwich Islands. A Fisheries (Conservation and Management) Ordinance enacted by the United Kingdom provides for comprehensive fisheries regulation with the zone, consistent with the conservation measures adopted by the CCAMLR Commission. While some Chilean vessels have been impounded by the United Kingdom, illegal fishing activities persist. At the XVth Meeting of the CCAMLR Commission in November 1996, Chile reported taking legal action against two vessels, and Argentina reported imposing fines and suspending fishing permits against five of its vessels.[59] But the initial declaration of the management zone was challenged by Argentina, which claims sovereignty over the same groups of islands. Indeed, both the Argentinean and Chilean governments have discouraged their nationals from applying to the United Kingdom for fishing permits, since this would recognize British sovereignty in the region. Such a strategy, however, also permits illegal fishing activities to continue.

The complications in South Atlantic conservation raise two concerns. First, the Patagonian toothfish still has not recovered from being overfished in the 1980s, and excessive overfishing makes sustainable management of its stocks even more difficult. Second, the dispute between Britain and Argentina has halted negotiations between those governments over conserving South Atlantic fisheries. The resultant tensions could spill over into CCAMLR and undercut its ability to reach consensus on conservation measures for sustainably managing Antarctica's circumpolar marine living resources.[60]

Krill

Exploratory fishing for krill as a commercial resource began in the early 1960s, but it was not until the 1973/74 season that krill harvests reached commercial levels.[61] Early krill harvesting operations were centered in Atlantic waters east of South Georgia, around the South Orkney Islands, and off the northern coast of the South Shetlands.[62] Krill catches reached a maximum annual take of 500,000 tons in 1981/82.[63] Since then catches have fallen off considerably, mainly due to difficulties in processing krill and to a shift toward finfishing. In 1990/91 around 350,000–400,000 tons of krill were caught,[64] but catch levels since have been markedly lower—from 83,800 tons in 1992/93 to 88,776 tons in 1993/94, 118,714 tons in 1994/95, and 95,040 tons in 1995/96. Much of this decline is because neither Russia nor Chile is fishing for krill, due to depressed market conditions.[65]

The Soviets, traditionally the leading fishing nation in the Antarctic seas for both finfish and krill, usually favored the South Atlantic fishing grounds and were responsible for 85 percent of the krill caught in the region. However, domestic market and economic conditions forced Russia to halt krill fishing operations in 1992, and they have not resumed since.[66] In 1991, the final year for the Soviet Union, its fishing fleets harvested 275,495 tons out of a total reported catch of 357,538 tons of Antarctic krill.[67] In 1996 Japan took more than 60,546 tons, Ukraine's take fell off to 13,338 tons (from a high in 1995 of 51,325 tons), and Poland reported a catch of 20,610 tons. Japan and the lesser fishing states will likely maintain these levels.[68] In 1995 and 1996 Panama, a nonmember of CCAMLR, reported to the Commission that it had caught 141 and 496 tons of krill, respectively. The Commission responded to this activity by encouraging Panama to join CCAMLR and to abide by the relevant conservation measures.[69]

The total quantity of krill reported harvested from 1981 to 1997 slightly exceeds 5.1 million tons, of which more than 90 percent came from Atlantic-sector waters.[70] This quantity of krill appears considerably less than the species' estimated global sustainable yield. Even so, because krill swarms are so locally concentrated (usually in areas where breeding predators feed), precautionary limits on permissible catches have been adopted by Commission members. In the South Atlantic the annual limit in 1997 is 1.5 million tons, with a provision that should the catch reach 620,000 tons (the highest recorded annual catch), stricter limits will be imposed. A precautionary limit of 390,000 tons now also applies to the Prydz Bay/Enderby Land coast.[71]

A particularly noteworthy CCAMLR conservation regulation was adopted in 1991. Conservation Measure 32/X set precautionary catch limits of 1.5 million tons per year for krill in the Atlantic sectors.[72] The Commission has given high priority to setting additional precautionary catch limits for krill elsewhere in the Convention area and to adopting special conservation measures that ensure that sufficient krill are kept available to meet the needs of predators. While the impact of this measure is not fully quantifiable—and thus not subject to direct attribution—the biomass estimate of krill has recently been revised upward some 3–5 million tons,[73] a significant increase over estimates in previous years.

Greater concern may be warranted in the long term over the future fishing strategies of certain large developing countries. In particular, were India and China to begin serious krill fishing, their efforts could have significant impact upon krill stocks in the Southern Ocean. With India's population currently exceeding 950 million and China's at 1.4 billion, it is conceivable that either or both of these Asian giants could turn to Antarctic fish or krill stocks to supplement their national protein needs. Even so, neither India nor China today has a credible fishing fleet that can harvest and process vast quantities of fish or krill in Antarctic waters; nor has either government indicated its intentions to embark on such a project. For the foreseeable future, then, large-scale fish or krill harvests by Indian or Chinese fishermen probably remain more fancy (or fear?) than fact.

The biological connection between krill fishing and conservation of other marine species is important.[74] The Antarctic Peninsula and South Orkney Islands krill fisheries are located within one hundred kilometers of major predator colonies. The peak fishing season occurs between December and March, when bird colonies are undergoing the critical breeding and postfledgling periods. Overharvesting krill in nearby predators' feeding grounds could seriously disrupt prey bird species. A similar situation exists for both seals and birds around South Georgia, Heard, and McDonald Islands.[75]

Large-scale krill fishing has an additional dangerous consequence for marine conservation. Krill are caught midwater, using fine mesh trawl nets, and during harvesting krill nets catch thousands of juvenile fish. The extent of these by-catches is unknown, as is the quantity of by-caught species that are actually harvested. The biological concern, though, is that such by-catches could threaten other predator species, for example, the mackerel icefish found along the South Georgia shelf.[76]

Crabs

Harvesting stone crabs is a relatively recent activity in Southern Ocean fisheries. Exploratory harvesting has so far proceeded in waters around South Georgia and the Shag Rocks. In July 1992 a U.S. ship harvested crabs using pots around South Georgia, specifically on the Scotia Ridge. Catch rates were good, and the three-hundred-ton catch limit set by CCAMLR was easily attained. Crab fishing continued through the 1995/96 season, but when the vessel failed to complete the experimental harvest regime by 1996, its fishing permit was revoked by the United States.[77] The crabbing venture's profitable outcome is likely, however, to attract more Aleutian-based U.S. fishermen and others from Argentina and Chile using long-line fishery techniques.[78]

Ecosystem Implications

The growth of commercial fisheries in the Southern Ocean threatens the entire Antarctic marine ecosystem. How well these renewable resources can be conserved depends on how well several complex and often interrelated factors can be accommodated. Perhaps most important is krill's role as the foundation species for the Antarctic marine food web. Mammals, birds, fish, and squid in the Antarctic marine commons depend on krill, either directly or indirectly. Therefore, overharvesting krill could have multiple impacts, including: (1) the number of competing species might increase, leading to replacement of krill as the dominant herbivore in the Antarctic marine food web; (2) the recovery of depleted whale populations, which eat krill, might be halted; (3) independent populations of seals, birds, fish, and squid might shrink; and (4) krill populations might decrease below sustainable levels.

Many species that prey upon krill have long life spans, low potentials for reproduction, and unknown populations in the circumpolar seas. These uncertainties complicate any analysis of impacts krill depletion would have on these predator populations. Delayed reactions by prey species to krill depletion could take decades to correct, assuming that any destructive changes could in fact be reversed.

A further consideration is how little information is available on the Antarctic ecosystem. Data on krill biology and ecology, as well as on krill competitors and predators, are inadequate to predict confidently what quantities of a marine species might be taken without depleting it or skewing the biological relationships among associated species in the marine ecosystem. So long as such information is lacking, conservation measures will not be reliable.

The Antarctic ocean commons cannot remain in a pristine condition. Human activities, especially fishing, influence this natural system. A disturbed ecosystem adds certain risks and exacerbates the difficulty of managing Southern Ocean fisheries—though the extent of these influences is not known. To address the conservation challenge in light of these complexities, the ATCPs have assumed international responsibility for managing the Southern Ocean.

Recent Conservation Measures

Improvement in the implementation of stronger conservation measures for fish stocks during the 1990s became possible due to a more constructive dialogue between the Commission and the Scientific Committee. This improved relationship resulted from several conditions: increasing accumulation of biological data from fisheries; acquisition of additional data from fishery-independent analyses; and increasing accommodation of the Soviet Union (and later Russia) to reporting and voting responsibilities. This last change was due to the domestic economic constraints on Russia's distant water fishing fleets, coupled with its desire to obtain more foreign aid from the very states who were nonfishing members of the Commission.

CCAMLR's Conservation Grid

A gridlike management map was designed in 1983 to help implement CCAMLR's conservation system. The northern boundary line designating CCAMLR's area of concern coincides with the biological Antarctic Convergence. For further precision and convenience this area is subdivided into subareas and divisions. Within the Southern Ocean conservation area, seventeen subareas are delimited on scientific grounds so as to account for various biologically discrete stocks.[79] The origins of this breakdown can be traced to the publication by the Food and Agriculture Organization (FAO) in 1972 of a classification system for living marine resources.[80] The FAO also issued during the 1970s a series of identification sheets arranged by oceanic region to facilitate identification of aquatic species, to assist in standardizing names, and to provide information on maritime characteristics and potential for resource exploitation.[81] See figure 5.1.

In this worldwide sector system catch statistics were reported by fishing states to FAO in terms of species and tons caught in specifically designated areas. Boundaries for these areas were decided either on biological grounds or to coincide with the areas of competence of regional fishery commissions. At the time these areas were delineated, practically no fishing activity was occurring in the Southern Ocean. Scant fishing activity produced few worries, and the northern limits of the Antarctic fishing area were thus decided rather arbitrarily. But with increased Antarctic fishery activities during the mid-1970s, certain difficulties surfaced in interpreting catch data in overlapping areas, especially around South Georgia and Kerguélen Island. Hence there arose the need for designating new areas for collecting fishing statistics.

To overcome this problem, FAO suggested in 1976 that the Antarctic fishery statistical areas should have their northern boundary at the line of latitude (to the nearest five degrees) closest to the Antarctic Convergence. In the Indian and Atlantic Ocean areas major sections are subdivided into subareas and divisions in order to give a finer breakdown of principal fishing areas.[82] In the conservation grid since adopted by CCAMLR, longitude lines are indicated every ten degrees from south to north to designate the length of the grid sectors. For the breadth of the sectors, latitude lines are drawn every five degrees east to west. For simplicity, consistency, and professional continuity CCAMLR scientists studying the Southern Ocean have adopted the numerical designations originally used by the FAO for the CCAMLR map.[83]

Today six statistical subareas on the CCAMLR map have been deemed most critical for finfish conservation attention. These are statistical areas numbered 48.1 (around South Georgia), 48.2 (around the South Orkneys), 48.3 (around the South Shetlands and offshore the Antarctic Peninsula), 58.5.1 (around the Kerguélen Islands), 58.4.2 (off Prydz Bay) and 58.41 (in the Eastern Indian Ocean sector). Those subareas that appear to be less critical for conservation attention are numbers 48.5

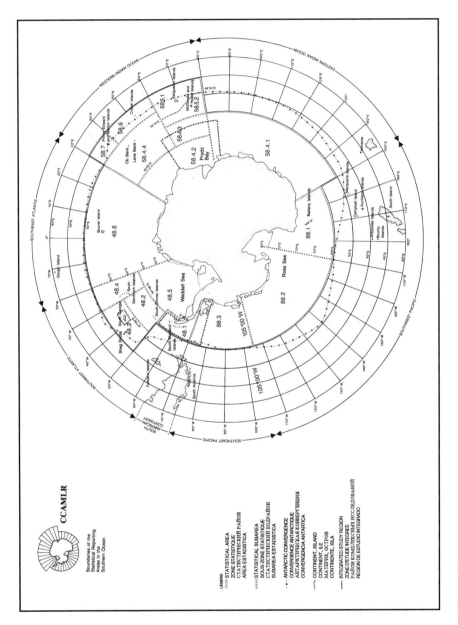

Figure 5.1

(encompassing the Weddell Sea), 48.6 (in the South East Atlantic), 58.4.4 (in the Ob Bank and Lena Bank), 58.4.3 (in the mid-Western Indian Ocean sector), 58.7 (around Prince Edward Island) and all of 88 (which includes all the Pacific Ocean sector).[84]

At present, the fishery most depleted is that for *N. Rossii* (a codlike species) around South Georgia and the South Shetlands. The specific reason(s) for the drastic decline of this species of cod remains unclear. Populations of seals have expanded tremendously in these same regions, so seals, or penguins, may be eating enough larvae of the cod species to depopulate it. These predator conditions, coupled with overharvesting during the 1970s, appear to have produced such a drastic decline in the *N. Rossii* population that the species has not yet been able to recover.[85]

While krill are known to be distributed throughout the Convention area, commercial krill fishermen have tended to concentrate their harvesting operations in three major statistical areas in the Antarctic commons. These areas are in the Atlantic sector (Statistical Area 48), the Indian Ocean (Statistical Area 58) and the Pacific Antarctic (Statistical Area 88). In response to this heavily concentrated fishing, CCAMLR in 1991 adopted precautionary catch limits for krill in the Atlantic sector.

The krill experience furnished an important step toward achieving precautionary management in an uncertain biological environment. It underscores the logic that preclusive action of some kind may be at times necessary before sufficient scientific data on an environmental situation can be obtained or assessed. Put tersely, the reactive management policies of the 1980s are now viewed by Commission members as unduly capricious. Such reactive policies might be sufficient to remedy a declining situation, but they are unable to deal adequately with severe threats to the Antarctic marine ecosystem. The Commission has apparently concluded that it is more prudent to act on some conservation policies immediately than to wait for more data and possibly pay an exorbitant environmental price later.

On a separate conservation track, the CCAMLR Commission in 1990 endorsed the objectives of General Assembly Resolution 44/225 (1990) concerning large-scale pelagic drift nets, agreeing that such drift-net fishing should not be allowed into the Convention area. If enforced, that prohibition would practically exclude the entire Southern Ocean from large-scale pelagic drift-net fishing by CCAMLR members.[86]

The Commission also agreed that members which have not accepted or ratified Annex V of the MARPOL 73/78 Convention should take steps to do so and to ensure that their vessels operating within the Convention area are in compliance with provisions of Annex V (especially dispersal of synthetic materials, e.g., ropes and fishing nets). Annex V of MARPOL 73/78 asserts that it is unlawful to discard garbage from ships, in particular plastics such as synthetic ropes, synthetic fishing nets, and plastic bags.[87]

Beginning in 1991 members contemplating opening a new fishery within the CCAMLR area must notify the Commission in advance. Information must be provided on the type of fishery, target species, fishing methods, region, and biological information on dependent and associated species.[88] This information is to be evaluated by the Scientific Committee to assess potential yields and risks of opening up such a fishery.[89] Recent examples of such fisheries include the U.S. crab fishery close to South Georgia and Chile's new fishery for Patagonian toothfish around the South Sandwich Islands.[90]

A CCAMLR system for vessel inspection was put in place in 1989/90. Beginning in 1991 inspectors are authorized to board vessels to observe and inspect catch, nets, fishing gear, and harvesting activities.[91] Problems with CCAMLR inspections are evident, however. The remoteness of the fishing grounds, logistical difficulties, and high costs for maintaining inspection vessels require strong national commitment to make the system work (such as efforts by France in its claimed Kerguélen fishing zone). However, such national commitment is often wanting. Another problem is that inspectors are not appointed by the Commission; they are designated by each government to inspect that state's own vessels. This means that monitoring may be prejudicial in favor of fishermen. During the 1991/92 season sixteen of eighteen inspections performed were by inspectors aboard vessels of their own nationality.[92] During the 1990/91 season Soviet inspectors carried out 150 CCAMLR-related inspections, but reports to the Commission were not submitted on the proper CCAMLR reporting forms, making interpreting the findings difficult.[93]

Inspections by Great Britain in 1996 discovered illegal fishing activities around South Georgia and in waters around South Africa's Prince Edward Island. While this lack of compliance is disturbing, the fact that inspections caught these violators speaks well of the system. Governments have also moved closer to adopting the use of vessel monitoring systems (VMS) on board fishing boats. While infringements on sovereign rights remain a concern, CCAMLR members in 1998 appear increasingly inclined to adopt VMS to improve control over fishing vessel activity and contribute to enforcement of conservation measures.[94]

Current Conservation Issues

Between 1982 and 1996 at least 117 conservation measures were approved through consensus by the Commission. Many have been overtaken by other measures, have lapsed, or have intentionally not been renewed. In 1997 the number of CCAMLR conservation measures in force totals 40.[95] In addition, the Commission has adopted two special "resolutions." The first, Resolution 7/IX (1990), advocates the need to cease large-scale pelagic drift-net fishing in the CCAMLR Convention area. The second, Resolution 10/XII (1993), responds to concerns over the harvesting of straddling stocks occurring "within and outside the Convention Area" and urges members to fish "responsibly, in accordance with conservation measures."

The Commission's adopted and implemented measures continue to fulfill the conservation function of CCAMLR. Directed finfishing in the Atlantic sector has been prohibited for all species save mackerel icefish, Patagonian toothfish, and lantern fish within the subarea of South Georgia.[96] Other measures adopted and implemented include mesh-size restrictions for fishing nets, the designation of areas closed to fishing, closed seasons for catching particular species, by-catch provisions, limitations on the use of longline fisheries, and requirements for notification regarding bottom trawl fishing activities.[97]

A serious concern for CCAMLR in 1998 is the discovery of illegal fishing activities in the Convention area. During the 1995/96 season illegal fishing for Patagonian toothfish moved from the waters around South Georgia and the Shag Rocks to the exclusive economic zone surrounding Prince Edward Island. At least twenty vessels were reported to be fishing straddling stocks in these waters, including ships from Vanuatu, Panama, Portugal, and South Africa.[98] Since 1994 several activities that contravene conservation measures, especially fishing out of season, have also been reported by Chile and Argentina. To their credit, these governments have taken legal action against a number of their nationals' apprehended vessels, including fines, confiscation of catches, and suspension of fishing permits.[99]

The primary responsibility for implementing conservation measures falls to member governments. Thus, enforcement of CCAMLR relies on the good faith of governments in complying with and enforcing its rules. The Convention does not provide for sanctions or penalties against a party that is unwilling or unable to implement or enforce conservation measures on its nationals. This deficiency in CCAMLR's structure weakens the efficacy of the Commission's conservation measures.

In the face of these challenges to Southern Ocean fisheries, four principal strategies can be suggested to ensure stronger compliance with CCAMLR conservation measures: (1) Marine protected areas in the Southern Ocean must be agreed upon. Such protected areas would include waters where fishing was prohibited, areas contiguous to seabirds' breeding and nesting sites, and offshore fish nursery areas. Governments that claim subantarctic islands (viz., France, South Africa, Australia, New Zealand, and the United Kingdom/Argentina) must be encouraged to support protected areas on these islands for seabirds. (2) The CCAMLR Commission must be encouraged to change the toothfish fishing season in order to decrease the incidental morality of seabirds. This would involve beginning the season earlier, when there is less bird activity. (3) Governments must be convinced that their interests are best served by enforcing their nationals' compliance with conservation measures, especially against illegal fishers. (4) Governments should be encouraged to require a Vessel Monitoring System (VMS) on board their fishing vessels; mandatory use of VMS would help control the location of vessels to ensure that their harvesting operations were conducted in areas not closed to fishing.[100]

Assessment

CCAMLR, on balance, is a successful conservation instrument. No fishery in the Southern Ocean is left uncovered by the Commission's conservation measures. The Commission has adopted particularly strong conservation efforts to decrease incidental mortality rates.

The Commission inherited a situation in which the total catch of demersal fish was thirty thousand to forty thousand tons a year. By 1980 most stocks had already been depleted to levels less than 30 percent of their estimated original biomass level. Stocks of only two significant species—the mackerel icefish and Patagonian toothfish—had evaded serious depletion. But icefish around South Georgia (in Statistical Area 48.3) had suffered a major biological collapse, the cause for which remains unknown.[101] CCAMLR, in other words, inherited a situation in which standing stocks in the Antarctic area were in very poor condition. However, most stocks since 1980 have recovered. Only two—C. *Gunnari* and *N. rossii*—continue to struggle in their recovery rates. No Commission member has suggested reinstating fishing for these species, probably because there is neither great potential for profit nor are the fish stocks sufficiently attractive.[102]

Effective conservation requires improved fishery data. Data on fish stocks come from national governments—usually the states doing the fishing—and such data can be fudged. For example, various species that are caught can be lumped together for convenience. Such practices skew scientific objectivity for the sake of harvesting expediency and present misleading accounts of stock conditions. Also, since fishing data come from fishing states, those governments must provide adequate financial support to analyze and monitor data scientifically. Securing money to support those activities, however, becomes increasingly difficult as nations tighten their budgets for all Antarctic scientific activities. Without adequate funding, analysis of fishery data is likely to be left undone.

Given the delays in adopting fishing conservation measures, some argue that consensus decision-making weakens CCAMLR. Even so, once a measure is approved by consensus in the Commission, no member government can go back on the decision. In a majority-rule decision-making system, a government may object and declare its unwillingness to be bound by a decision. The consensus process precludes that opportunity. The objector system is not used in CCAMLR, except on rare occasions when technical inabilities might prevent a government from meeting its obligations. States do not even formally object to proposed measures because the measure's sponsors would not permit that point to be reached in the Commission's deliberations. In the consensus process a sponsor will abandon a measure rather than be pushed into a situation where a formal objection would kill it. In sum, the Commission plenary serves as an opportunity to negotiate compromise positions, not to force some issue to a divisive vote.

Another encumbrance on CCAMLR's effectiveness concerns the mechanics of the inspection system. The present CCAMLR inspection system relies on opportunity as the means for its action. That is, if a U.S. Coast Guard vessel is sailing to Antarctica and en route it should happen across a trawler of another Commission state that is fishing, then U.S. personnel can board that trawler and inspect it for possible conservation violations. Thus, inspections are done haphazardly, without any scheme of regular visits or scheduled observation. This inspection by happenstance, determined by the chances of passage and geography, however, does not ensure compliance with conservation measures. In addition, while Commission governments can inspect a vessel of any member state, their jurisdiction does not extend to fishing vessels of nonparty countries, such as those from Ukraine during 1991–94 or Panama since 1996. Accordingly, the Commission invited those governments to attend meetings as official observers and urged them to join CCAMLR as soon as possible.[103]

CCAMLR still must confront the issue of straddling stocks on the high seas. Certain species, especially the toothfish and lantern fish around South Georgia Island—as well as krill around the Kerguélens and Patagonian toothfish around Prince Edward Island—straddle Convention and non-Convention areas, swimming northward from within the Convergence into the high seas, beyond CCAMLR's protective jurisdiction. In high-seas waters whole stocks might be caught legally, which could devastate these species. Although the Commission in 1993 adopted a special "resolution" calling for members to fish responsibly within and outside the Convention area[104] and a new global fishery agreement for straddling stocks on the high seas was promulgated in 1995,[105] the issue of straddling stocks in subantarctic waters remains a salient concern.

Thus, commercial fishing in the Southern Ocean remains a difficult and costly venture. There are only slight profit margins; there are considerable natural obstacles; and there is great scientific uncertainty. CCAMLR restrictions on fishing season, location, or permissible catch levels can interfere so much with safe, efficient, or preferred fishing practices that fisheries become uneconomic and therefore less than sustainable. For the foreseeable future, exploiting Antarctic fisheries is apt to be viewed more as a commercial risk than a lucrative economic opportunity.

The Antarctic Marine Ecosystem

A popular scientific notion in the 1970s suggested that an annual excess of krill had resulted from the decline of baleen whales in southern waters. This supposition led to a related hypothesis that the krill surplus was responsible for steady increases in the populations of other Antarctic krill predators. The scientific consensus at the time was that this surplus Antarctic krill fishery would be able to sustain harvests of

60 million tons annually, nearly equal to the total annual fish catch of all species at that time.[106]

Scientific understanding of krill biology and ecology has improved considerably over the past two decades. While the quantity and distribution of krill cannot yet be estimated with precision, the notion of a krill surplus has evaporated. It is now known that uncontrolled depletion of krill, especially if concentrated in localized areas, could actually be ruinous for krill predator populations. Of greater concern, since prey species are found at every level of the Antarctic marine food chain, overharvesting krill could detrimentally affect the entire Antarctic ecosystem.

For food-chain dynamics in the Antarctic ocean commons to be understood—and for living resources to be prudently managed—both the low efficiency of the pelagic system's food chain and the variations in its key elements must be addressed.[107] This relationship points to a paradox that affects the ecology of living resources in the circumpolar waters: Strategies for effectively managing Antarctic resources must be grounded in realistic expectations of being able to accomplish that goal, but living resource potential in the Antarctic cannot accurately be gauged until clear scientific analysis has determined the extent of those resources. For Antarctic marine living resources, then, the fundamental problem is how can statistical data for biomass in the Antarctic/Southern Ocean region be interpreted accurately without knowing precisely how many living resources are located where, at any one time. No easy answers are available. Given the harsh Antarctic conditions, errors and gross inaccuracies will occur. Statistics are usually averages and can often vary with whatever sampling technique is used to obtain the data. Inconsistencies also occur from the means of calculation used.[108]

Such conditions complicate the scientists' ability to assess the data and draw conclusions on the habits of living resources in the Southern Ocean, and they also cloud knowledge about the region's ecology. This makes CCAMLR's ability to manage resource conservation prudently in the Antarctic commons all the more difficult. It is likewise important that many Antarctic living marine resources, especially seals and birds, use the continent for breeding habitats. While Antarctica supports only a scanty, primitive community of indigenous terrestrial life, the integrity of the continent's environment, in particular coastal regions, must be protected if the seal and bird populations that visit there are to survive.

CCAMLR's Balance Sheet

Management and conservation of living resources in the Antarctic commons can only work as well as the weakest data assumptions that support such policies. Present theories of Antarctic marine dynamics often rest on incomplete information. If CCAMLR's conservation objectives are to be realized, then its Scientific Committee must be capable of predicting accurately the effects of harvest levels and strategies on target, dependent, and associated species. Success of conservation efforts is keyed to management policies that: (1) restore and maintain the ecological balance between target, dependent, and related species; (2) foster rapid recovery of depleted whale and fish populations; (3) prevent wasteful use and depletion of dependent and associated populations, as well as target species; and (4) protect breeding areas and other habitats of biological importance to target, dependent, and related populations.[109]

Acquiring reliable data on which to base decisions is essential for these management strategies to succeed. In particular, CCAMLR's Scientific Committee must furnish to the Commission more information on various factors affecting the ecosystem. But policy considerations in the Antarctic are severely complicated by significant gaps in information. More knowledge is needed about the influence of currents, eddies, and gyres on the distribution of nutrients, phytoplankton, krill, and organisms higher in the tropic scale. Better data on pack-ice dynamics could reveal much about nutrient cycling and biological productivity. Little is known about the physical, biological, and demographic factors that affect the abundance, productivity, and distribution of krill. More research is necessary on the location and feeding habits of whales within the Antarctic commons. Likewise, better data on the distribution, abundance, reproductive cycles, and feeding habits of seals, fish, birds, and squid in the Southern Ocean must be accumulated. CEMP is intended to close these information gaps and thus contribute to more prudent conservation policies for the Antarctic marine ecosystem.

CONCLUSION

The Antarctic marine commons is the largest and most conspicuous coherent ecosystem on Earth. It is also distinctive for the critical role that krill plays in the region's tropic webs. Krill remains the principal prey for many species of whales, seals, penguins, seabirds, squid, and fish, and is the foundation species for many organisms in the Antarctic marine commons.

The tragic history of efforts to exploit living marine resources in the Southern Ocean clearly reveals problems with single-species management in an ocean commons. CCAMLR states have realized over time that interactions of one species with other components of the ecosystem must be taken into account. The concern in the Antarctic marine commons involves more than managing further exploitation in an ecosystem that has already been disturbed, mainly through the depletion of its whale populations during this century. The focus of future exploitation, requiring redoubled conservation efforts, is krill, the primary food source of most higher organisms within the ecosystem.

CCAMLR is the first international fishery agreement that monitors the effects of commercial activities on an entire ecosystem. As such, it is an important step toward improved conservation of marine resources. Still, the Antarctic experience over the past three decades suggests that conservation of living resources can only come from purposeful management of the commons in the polar South. The conservation process grows and improves through learning. It involves complicated efforts to maintain ecological processes and life support systems in order to preserve biological diversity and ensure sustainable use of species and ecosystems. Accordingly, time and research are necessary to acquire increased awareness about interrelationships between species within the Antarctic commons ecosystem.

Conflicting economic priorities of CCAMLR member governments during the 1980s hampered that organization's ability to work effectively toward conservation in the Antarctic. Since 1990, however, those tensions have largely abated, and states parties have demonstrated greater commitment to the adoption and implementation of conservation measures. Even so, the bottom line for CCAMLR as a conservation instrument remains clear: The convention will only be as effective as member states want it to be. Time will tell just how full and sincere the extent of their commitment has been.

Chapter 6

ENVIRONMENTAL PROTECTION AND PRESERVATION

The south polar commons reaches to the Antarctic Convergence, far beyond the legal scope of the 1959 Antarctic Treaty.[1] Yet the treaty provides no direct measures to preserve or protect even the commons environment within its jurisdiction, much less the more extensive area beyond. The ATCPs pursued two strategies to correct this deficiency. First, they undertook during the 1970s to enact special measures for conserving living resources in the circumpolar marine ecosystem. Key to this conservation strategy was setting limits on which, where, and how much of those resources could be exploited, and then managing activities to ensure that those limits were observed. This conservation and management strategy was analyzed in chapter 5.

As human activities intensified, a second strategy for environmental preservation became necessary. The ATCPs adopted instruments during the late 1980s and early 1990s to protect the Antarctic commons environment by prohibiting certain activities. Protection aims to shield the environment from harm or injury, i.e., to preserve the integrity of the environment against human activities in the region. The ATCPs thus initially sought to create a minerals treaty during the 1980s, with a view to setting a regulatory regime in place if ever Antarctic minerals development should go forward. When agreement on that regime floundered during 1989 and 1990, those governments then redirected their course and negotiated a new instrument for comprehensive protection of the Antarctic environment.[2]

The Protocol on Environmental Protection to the Antarctic Treaty (also called the Madrid Protocol) was adopted by the ATCPs and opened for signature on October 4, 1991, in Madrid, Spain.[3] Produced in less than two years of negotiations, the Protocol and its five annexes represent one of the most comprehensive, far-reaching multilateral environmental agreements ever concluded: a legal blueprint for protecting the Antarctic commons environment. No less important, the Madrid Protocol also signals a profound shift—indeed a reversal in course—in the ATCPs' intentions for the Antarctic. In late 1988 the Consultative Party group appeared headed toward adopting policies that might permit exploration and possible exploitation of Antarctic minerals and hydrocarbons. By late 1991 the ATCPs had committed themselves legally to protect and preserve the continent and its circumpolar seas.[4]

Negotiation of the Madrid Protocol followed considerable debate, tension, and frustration among the environmental, conservationist, and scientific communities and within the ATCP group itself. A fundamental source of disagreement centered on the intended status of the area: Should the Antarctic be susceptible to exploitation by a special regime to regulate future mineral resource activities or should that region be legally declared an international wilderness conservation zone—in effect, a world park administered by the ATCPs under strict rules and regulations to promote environmental protection? This argument forecasts the main themes of this chapter, namely to assess what standards have been adopted for protection and preservation of the Antarctic, to appraise the Madrid Protocol's attributes and deficiencies, and to ascertain whether recent developments in environmental law contribute toward transforming the Antarctic commons into a de facto world park.

The chapter is divided into three sections. In the first section the evolution and content of the Protocol and its annexes are examined as the framework for environmental protection in the Antarctic commons, followed by assessment of how well these provisions legally complement and reinforce the Antarctic Treaty regime. The second section appraises the potential contributions of the Madrid Protocol to Antarctic environmental protection and preservation. In so doing, however, deficiencies in the Protocol for protecting the environment are pointed out, as are the shortcomings of viewing it as a charter that transforms Antarctica into a world park. Finally, the chapter suggests some conclusions about the Madrid Protocol's future role in establishing the Antarctic commons as a world conservation zone.

EVOLUTION

The Protocol on Environmental Protection and its annexes were not negotiated in isolation. Coming more than thirty years after the original Antarctic treaty, the Protocol was designed mindfully to supplement and strengthen the entire family of Antarctic Treaty instruments. Indeed, the Protocol implicitly relies upon these other instruments for both political and legal support. Likewise, the environmental purposes of the other Antarctic treaties are further realized in the Madrid Protocol.

The Protocol emerged out of the diplomatic wreckage left by disagreement over the need for an Antarctic minerals convention. From 1982 through 1988 the ATCPs negotiated a special regime to regulate prospecting, exploration, and development of mineral resources in the Antarctic, should such activities ever occur there. Agreement by all Consultative Parties on the text for a new minerals accord came in June 1988, and in November 1988 the Convention on the Regulation of Antarctic Mineral Resource Activities (CRAMRA) was opened for signature in Wellington, New Zealand.[5] The Wellington Convention, however, despite its attributes as a preclusive management regime, was stillborn. Critical concerns had been left unresolved by the proposed minerals regime, and these were translated by environmentalists into potent political weapons. Environmentalists viewed the Wellington Convention as an incentive for states to exploit minerals resources in the Antarctic. Its entry into force would have lifted the policy of voluntary restraint and effectively made commercial mining lawful. Clearing the way to mine legally would, critics argued, promote prospecting. Prospecting could then lead to mineral discoveries, which would give rise to additional exploration and growing exploitation. That pattern, the environmentalist movement claimed, would inevitably produce environmental degradation.[6]

The Wellington Convention was derailed in June 1989, as two states with pending sovereign claims on the continent, Australia and France, opted not to sign the agreement. This decision broke the unanimous position of the ATCPs in favor of the agreement and threatened the new regime with irrelevance should Australia and France ignore its provisions. Thus, these two defections effectively scuttled the mineral convention's likelihood of entering into legal force.[7]

Environmental considerations may well have figured into Australia's decision against signing a minerals treaty for the Antarctic. Four publicized environmental disasters in polar waters early in 1989 no doubt seized the Hawke government's attention: On January 28 the Argentine supply ship *Bahia Paraiso* hit rocks offshore the U.S. Palmer Research Station on the Antarctic Peninsula, spilling some 250,000 gallons of diesel fuel into the sea. The accident killed thousands of krill and scores of penguins and other seabirds, and ruined several scientific projects along the coast. On February 7 the British resupply ship HMS *Endurance* hit an iceberg near Deception Island, reportedly causing an oil spill in Esperanza Bay. On February 28 the Peruvian research vessel *BIC Humboldt* ran aground and leaked oil in Fildes Bay, off King George Island. These three Antarctic episodes paled in comparison to the Arctic disaster on March 24, when the tanker *Exxon Valdez* struck a reef off Prince William Sound, Alaska, spilling some 11 million barrels of crude oil into the frigid waters and killing thousands of otter, birds, and fish as it washed ashore along a forty-five-mile pollution zone.[8]

The environmental disaster of the *Exxon Valdez* in the Arctic paradoxically became a media bonanza for Antarctic environmentalists: It dramatically demonstrated the risks of transporting crude oil in frigid waters. Domestic political considerations and the desire to retain Australian sovereign influence in its Antarctic sector claim were preeminent motivations behind Australian prime minister Robert Hawke's decision. However, the pervasive international publicity generated by the Alaskan ecocatastrophe clearly bolstered the decision by the Australian government to oppose the minerals treaty.

The French and Australian defection led the evolution of the ATS down a new path. By shelving the minerals treaty, the ATCPs could turn their attention to comprehensive protection of the Antarctic environment. Resentment among some Consultative Parties over the breakaway Australian and French policy reversal gave way to new aspirations to protect the environment in the polar South. Prior to the October 1989 XVth Antarctic Treaty Consultative Party Meeting (ATCM) in Paris, Australia and France circulated a joint proposal calling for comprehensive measures to protect the Antarctic environment and its dependent and associated ecosystems.[9] Stimulated by this development and sensing the futility of CRAMRA's prospects, four other states—Chile, New Zealand, the United States, and Sweden—submitted draft proposals for comprehensive protection measures at the Paris meeting.[10] From this impetus came the decision to convene a special ATCM in Viña del Mar, Chile, and the group met from November 19 to December 6, 1990.

The stated purpose of the Viña del Mar meeting was to discuss development of a comprehensive regime for protecting the Antarctic environment, but the discussions were dominated by impasse over the minerals issue. In the session's closing hours, however, a Draft Protocol on the Antarctic Environment was submitted on a personal basis by Norway's Rolf Trolle Andersen. The so-called Andersen Draft supplied the necessary compromise provisions for a broad Antarctic environmental regime and was adopted as an unofficial working draft text for subsequent sessions of the Eleventh Special Consultative Meeting.[11]

THE MADRID PROTOCOL

The Madrid Protocol on the environment obligates parties to consider the Antarctic (defined as the area south of 60° south latitude, inclusive of ocean space) as a "natural reserve devoted to science" and commits them to comprehensive protection of the region's environment.[12] ATCP governments are obliged to pursue policies that preserve and protect Antarctica's fragile ecosystem, both on land and at sea. The preamble to the Protocol reaffirms the special responsibility of the ATCPs "to ensure that Antarctica does not become the scene or object of international discord." It also recalls "the designation of Antarctica as a Special Conservation Area . . . to protect the Antarctic environment and its dependent and associated ecosystems."

The premise undergirding the Protocol is stated in Article 3:

The protection of the Antarctic environment and dependent and associated ecosystems and intrinsic value of Antarctica, including its wilderness and aesthetic values and its value as an area for the conduct of scientific research, in particular research essential to understanding the global environment, shall be fundamental considerations in the planning and conduct of all activities in the Antarctic Treaty area.[13]

This statement marks a notable advance over previous Antarctic law, which was made to apply only to Antarctic Treaty states in the conduct and support of their scientific activities. The Protocol applies to *all* governmental and nongovernmental activities of state parties, including tourism by their nationals.

Building on this premise, Article 3 then articulates three guiding principles for protecting and preserving the Antarctic ecosystem:

(a) activities in the Antarctic Treaty area shall be planned and conducted so as to limit adverse impacts on the Antarctic environment and dependent and associated ecosystems;

(b) activities in the Antarctic Treaty area shall be planned and conducted so as to avoid:

(i) adverse effects on climate or weather patterns;

(ii) significant adverse effects on air or water quality;

(iii) significant changes in the atmospheric, terrestrial (including aquatic), glacial or marine environments;

(iv) detrimental changes in the distribution, abundance or productivity of species or populations of species of fauna and flora;

(v) further jeopardy to endangered or threatened species or populations of such species; or

(vi) degradation of, or substantial risk to, areas of biological, scientific, historic, aesthetic or wilderness significance;

(c) activities in the Antarctic Treaty area shall be planned and conducted on the basis of information sufficient to allow prior assessments of, and informed judgments about, their possible impacts on the Antarctic environment and dependent and associated ecosystems and on the value of Antarctica for the conduct of scientific research.[14]

To achieve these objectives, the Protocol requires "regular and effective monitoring" to assess the impacts of ongoing activities, as well as to substantiate predicted impacts.

Article 3 also furnishes legally binding principles for protecting and conserving the Antarctic ecosystem. These principles, which relate to the entire Antarctic Treaty System, include the following: (1) parties are obligated to meet specific environmental standards and to limit insofar as possible adverse impacts on the environment; (2) parties are obligated to give priority to scientific research in Antarctica and to preserve Antarctica for global research; (3) parties are obligated to ensure that human activities are planned and carried out on the basis of information sufficient to permit prior assessments of their possible impacts; and (4) parties are obligated to conduct environmental monitoring.[15]

Article 7 of the Madrid Protocol places a flat prohibition on all mining activity in Antarctica: "Any activity relating to mineral resources, other than scientific research, shall be prohibited."[16] This ban, however, is not made permanent, and the Protocol permits modification or amendment at any time, provided all ATCPs agree by consensus.[17]

The Protocol establishes a new institution, the Committee for Environmental Protection (CEP). The chief function of the CEP is to provide advice for ATCP meetings to consider in implementing the Protocol and its annexes.[18] Specifically, the Committee furnishes advice on:

(a) the effectiveness of measures taken pursuant to this Protocol;

(b) the need to update, strengthen or otherwise improve such measures;

(c) the need for additional measures, including the need for additional Annexes, where appropriate;

(d) the application and implementation of the environmental impact assessment procedures set out in Article 8 and Annex I;

(e) means of minimizing or mitigating environmental impacts of activities in the Antarctic Treaty area;

(f) procedures for situations requiring urgent action, including response action in environmental emergencies;

(g) the operation and further elaboration of the Antarctic Protected Area system;

(h) inspection procedures, including formats for inspection reports and checklists for the conduct of inspections;

(i) the collection, archiving, exchange and evaluation of information related to environmental protection;

(j) the state of the Antarctic environment; and

(k) the need for scientific research, including environmental monitoring, related to the implementation of this Protocol.[19]

The Committee was created to supply advice to ensure that rules governing environmental restraint are interpreted uniformly and consistently. The CEP, moreover, serves as a forum for investigating controversial environmental matters, for assisting in the preparation of environmental impact statements, and for reaching common interpretations of key terms and threshold levels in the Protocol.[20] The Committee, however, lacks authority to enforce compliance with the Protocol, or to define mandatory environmental conservation zones, or to send out inspection or monitoring agents to conduct oversight of human activities in Antarctica. Put tersely, the CEP is only an advisory organ; it has no decision-making authority over environmental policy.

Compliance is left to governments party to the Protocol, who are obliged to take "appropriate measures" to that end.[21] To foster compliance, inspections may be carried out by any government "to promote the protection of the Antarctic environment and associated ecosystems, and to ensure compliance with this Protocol." Governments may inspect stations, installations, equipment, ships, and aircraft within the Antarctic Treaty area.[22] The Protocol also creates an Antarctic Arbitral Tribunal for mandatory dispute settlement, continuing the pattern of appending sophisticated mechanisms for dispute resolution to ATS instruments.[23] Advance environmental impact assessment is also mandatory for proposed activities in the Antarctic.[24] In addition, the Protocol provides for emergency response plans in case of accidents[25], and each party is responsible for reporting annually on its progress to implement the Protocol,[26] including notifications[27] and contingency plans.[28]

THE ANNEXES

Appended to the Protocol are five annexes that deal respectively with environmental impact assessment, conservation of fauna and flora, waste disposal and waste management, marine pollution, and protected areas. As stipulated in the text, these annexes "form an integral part" of the Protocol and were adopted in accordance with Article IX of the Antarctic Treaty.[29] They also furnish the principal themes for protection and preservation of the Antarctic commons.

Annex I: Environmental Impact Assessment

Environmental impact assessment (EIA) in the frozen South involves evaluating a planned activity's likely impact on the Antarctic environment. Gauging potential impacts of human programs and policies in the Antarctic remains essential to protecting that environment. Assessment procedures should be included in a state's planning process to ensure informed decisions on activities in the Antarctic Treaty area. If environmental assessment is to succeed as a prophylactic, all activities proposed for the Antarctic must be reviewed, be they research programs by scientists, logistical support activities by governments, or sight-seeing visits by tourists.

The 1959 Antarctic Treaty does not provide binding rules that require cooperation on impact assessment or analyses in advance of major construction projects, but such procedures were recommended in 1973 by the Scientific Committee on Antarctic Research (SCAR).[30] This proposal would have required the circulation of assessments to SCAR and concerned governments for comments on their adequacy. The idea, however, was rejected by the Consultative Parties and replaced with a more limited recommendation that contained a Code of Conduct for Antarctic Expeditions and Station Activities.[31] In 1985 SCAR reiterated its recommendation for a mandatory environmental assessment procedure to the XIIIth ATCP Meeting,[32] but this proposal also failed to win consensus. Again, the ATCPs adopted a less ambitious recommendation, which invited SCAR to offer scientific advice on "steps that possibly could be taken to improve the comparability and accessibility of scientific data on Antarctica."[33]

The environmental costs of not having impact assessments in the Antarctic Treaty System were revealed during construction of the French airfield at Dumont d'Urville on Point Geologie in 1985,[34] the Dry Valley Drilling Project (1973–76),[35] and the Ross Ice Shelf Project (1975–76).[36] These projects were undertaken without EIAs, and in each case notable damage was done to the local environment. Concern escalated sharply over the need for objective environmental impact assessment as the prospects for concluding a minerals regime crystallized. Recommendations and guidelines for such assessment existed, but these were mere voluntary codes of conduct whose interpretation, implementation, and enforcement were left to each government. By 1990 the need for a legally binding, comprehensive system of environmental impact assessment had been recognized by the Consultative Parties.

The first annex of the Protocol sets procedures for conducting EIAs.[37] The mandate for EIAs flows from the Protocol's Article 3, which affirms the principle that activities must be "planned and conducted on the basis of information sufficient to allow for prior assessments of, and informed judgments about, their possible impacts on the Antarctic environment." For assessing environmental impacts, human activities are divided into those having "less than a minor or transitory impact," those having "a minor or transitory impact," and those having "more than a minor or transitory impact."[38]

Annex I sets out a three-stage procedure for performing environmental impact assessment. First, preliminary assessments for proposed activities are conducted by parties "in accordance with appropriate national procedures."[39] Second, an Initial Environmental Evaluation is performed for activities "likely to have not more than a minor or transitory impact" by the party proposing the activity.[40] Third, the concerned government prepares a Comprehensive Environmental Evaluation (CEE) for activities deemed "likely to have more than a minor or transitory impact." The government is then obliged to circulate that CEE to all the Antarctic Treaty parties and to the public for comment.[41]

These procedures mark a significant step toward environmental protection. Even so, greater responsibility for environmental impact assessment could have been given to the Committee for Environmental Protection. More extensive CEP involvement would have ensured objectivity and consistency in the EIAs, improving the quality of the assessment process at each stage. Instead, the burden of assessment weighs mainly on the governments planning the activities.

Once a CEE is circulated, it is evaluated by the government concerned and a decision is made as to whether the proposed activity should take place. That decision on an activity goes as a CEE (under Article 3) to the Committee on Environmental Protection (Under Article 3[4]) and to other parties (under Articles 3[3] and 6). No final decision can be taken to proceed with a proposed activity until the draft evaluation has been considered by an Antarctic Treaty Consultative Party meeting on the advice of the CEP.[42] But neither the Committee nor the ATCM decides finally on a proposed activity; both merely give advice to the national government submitting the CEE. Thus, the ultimate arbiter of what will be done on the continent belongs to individual national governments. A government can proceed as it wishes, and this procedure contradicts what should be a comprehensive approach. The Protocol appears to place a great deal of faith in diplomatic pressure as an effective check against governments making irresponsible national decisions.

This annex also appears weakened by the ambiguity of critical terms in its provisions—for example, what is the distinction in Article 2(1) between "minor" and "transitory" impacts, and what is an "appropriate" national procedure? Regrettably, these terms are not precisely defined either in Article 8 of the Protocol or in Annex I. Hence interpretation and implementation of environmental impact assessment procedures are left primarily to the discretion of each party.

Annex II: Protection of Fauna and Flora

Annex II of the Protocol, consisting of only nine articles, strives to preserve Antarctic fauna and flora by updating the 1964 Agreed Measures.[43] In Annex II the parties agree to prohibit "the taking of any native mammal, bird, or plant" without a permit from their national governments.[44] Permits are to be issued conservatively and conditionally, when necessary for limited scientific studies and removal for zoos and museums,[45] and on condition that "no more native mammals or birds are taken from local populations than can . . . normally be replaced by natural reproduction in the following breeding season."[46] Parties are to refrain from wantonly and negligently interfering with indigenous plants and mammals,[47] and necessary takings "shall be done in the manner that involves the least degree of pain and suffering practicable."[48]

The annex plainly transforms the Agreed Measures into legally binding rules, an important improvement. Annex II, moreover, makes three notable advances in protecting the Antarctic environment. First, protection is extended to terrestrial and freshwater invertebrates;[49] second, dogs are prohibited in Antarctica after April 1, 1994;[50] and third, significant damage to native terrestrial plants is included within the definition of "harmful interference" to the Antarctic environment.[51]

Three brief appendixes to the second annex contribute even further to environmental protection in the Antarctic. Appendix A cites two species, the fur seal and the Ross seal, as being specially protected. Appendix B protects against the introduction of nonnative species, parasites, or diseases by regulating the importation of plants and animals through special permits under Article 4 of the annex. Last, Appendix C lays out special precautions to prevent the introduction of microorganisms, especially by banning importation of live poultry, other birds, and nonsterile soils into the Antarctic Treaty area.

Although this second annex contains little that seems new, it does integrate the conservation of Antarctic fauna and flora into a more comprehensive, comprehensible framework for environmental protection. Indeed, conservation of wildlife is integral to the system of Antarctic protected areas that is regulated by a fifth annex to the Protocol and is rooted in the idea of Antarctica as a world park. Annex II to the Protocol is a significant step toward attaining a comprehensive and compulsory system for protecting Antarctic flora and fauna.

Annex III: Waste Disposal and Waste Management

The Protocol's third annex, on waste disposal and waste management,[52] grew out of the 1975 Code of Conduct for Antarctic Expeditions and Stations Activities[53] and from ATCP Recommendation XV-3, which upgraded the 1975 Code.[54] Annex III notably improves on the 1975 Code by placing greater emphasis on retrograding waste materials from the continent and standardizing data collection and circulation of information on waste management.

Waste is classified under the third annex into five main groups: Group 1, sewage and domestic liquid wastes; Group 2, other liquids and chemicals, including fuels and lubricants; Group 3, solids to be combusted; Group 4, other solid wastes; and Group 5, radioactive materials.[55] The annex asserts that parties must remove all Group 2, 4, and 5 wastes from the region if they are generated after entry into force of the Protocol. Parties are obligated to remove Group 1 wastes "to the maximum extent possible" from the treaty area.

Annex III is not without flaws. For one, provisions often contain qualifiers, such as "to the maximum extent practicable" and "as far as practicable." Such vague parameters will make it difficult to hold operators (or governments) accountable for their actions. Environmentalists also object to the annex's acceptance of incineration as an environmentally safe form of waste disposal. In fact, incineration pollutes the air and produces contaminated, toxic ash that must be disposed of. Sewage and liquid waste present more problems. The annex relies on maceration (i.e., softening by soaking in a liquid over time) as a principal means for disposal of such waste products,[56] but this method fails to treat heavy metals, bacteria, viruses, and other contaminants in the waste matter. Moreover, the annex explicitly permits discharge of liquid wastes directly into the sea.[57] Environmentalists would prefer that such waste sludge be "retrograded" (i.e., removed) from the continent, rather than dumped at sea.[58]

Annex IV: Marine Pollution

The fourth annex concerns "Prevention of Marine Pollution"[59] and is directly linked to the International Convention for the Prevention on

Pollution from Ships, as amended by its 1978 Protocol (MARPOL 73/78).[60] This annex deals with ship discharges, particularly oil, noxious liquids, garbage, and sewage. Certain provisions of Annex IV highlight the need for improved vessel retention capacity, emergency response, and emergency preparedness among state parties to the ATS.

Concern over marine pollution is a recent arrival on the ATCP agenda. The Antarctic Treaty did not specifically address this problem, largely due to concerns over sovereignty complications that might arise from applying rules for maritime jurisdiction offshore the continent. No doubt the peculiar language of the high-seas exception in Article VI of the 1959 Treaty gave pause to the ATCPs in setting special standards for regions offshore. These difficulties were compounded by the 1982 UN Convention on the Law of the Sea and the significant revisions it made in the breadth and substance of jurisdiction in maritime zones offshore.

The importance of the Southern Ocean's ecosystem—given that nearly all living Antarctic resources are found in the circumpolar seas—made it inevitable that the ATCPs take up conservation and protection of the marine environment, including prevention of marine pollution. To that end, several ATCP recommendations were adopted during the 1970s.[61]

A turning point in the codification of marine pollution rules came in 1989, during discussions at the XVth ATCM, which culminated in the adoption of Recommendation XV-4 on marine pollution.[62] This instrument calls on governments to take measures that prohibit certain discharges from vessels and to comply with provisions of specified international conventions concerning pollution control and safety at sea.[63] The recommendation required parties to establish contingency plans for responding to marine pollution in the Antarctic area, especially by vessels carrying oil. ATCM Recommendation XV-4 laid out core obligations that are now enshrined in the Madrid Protocol's fourth annex.

Annex IV prohibits "any discharge of oil or oily mixture," except in circumstances permitted under the MARPOL 73/78 Convention.[64] The discharge "of any noxious liquid substance, and any other chemicals or other substances, in quantities or concentrations that are harmful to the marine environment" is also forbidden.[65] Article 5 of the Annex goes on to prohibit disposal into the sea of two other categories of substances: (1) plastics, "including but not limited to synthetic ropes, synthetic fishing nets, and plastic garbage bags . . ."; and (2) all forms of garbage, "including paper products, rags, glass, metal, bottles, crockery, dunnage, incineration ash, lining, and packing materials. . . ." Parties are further obligated under Article 6 to "eliminate all discharge of untreated sewage . . . within 12 nautical miles of land or ice shelves." Beyond that distance, any sewage discharge is to be made "at a moderate rate of speed, and where practicable, while the ship is en route at a speed of no less than 4 knots." An obvious loophole, however, could undermine this fiat. As the preface to paragraph 1 of Article 6 suggests, this prohibition applies, "[e]xcept where it would unduly impair Antarctic operations." Not only are the terms "unduly," "impair," and "Antarctic operations" left undefined, but determination of where and when those conditions exist apparently is left to the discretion of vessel operators. Such an open-ended provision might well be an invitation to abuse and neglect.

Compliance is left to each contracting party to enforce on ships flying that state's own flag or supporting its Antarctic operations.[66] The annex also obliges states to ensure that all their vessels are fitted with retention tanks sufficiently large to hold "all sludge, dirty ballast, tank washing water and other oily residues and mixtures" while operating in the region.[67] Contracting governments are responsible for ensuring that ships flying their flags have "sufficient capacity" to retain all their garbage while within the Antarctic Treaty area[68] and are provided with "adequate facilities" on shore to receive all sludge, dirty ballast, tank washing water, oily residues, and garbage from these ships.[69]

The marine pollution annex attempts to close gaps in enforcement due to sovereign immunity, gaps that were left in previous instruments. It does so, but with only partial success. Protection by reason of sovereign immunity is retained, as the annex "shall not apply to any warship, naval auxiliary, or other vessel owned or operated by a State. . . ."[70] Parties are obligated, though, to "ensure by the adoption of appropriate measures not impairing the operations or operational capabilities of such ships owned or operated by it, that such ships act in a manner consistent, so far as reasonable and practicable" with the annex. The problem here is obvious: Most vessels operating in circumpolar Antarctic waters are state-owned or -operated. Most vessels therefore will be exempted from the annex's requirements by reason of sovereign immunity. To the extent that determination of "appropriate measures" and "reasonable and practicable" conditions for compliance is left to the discretion of vessel operators, the opportunity for violations widens and the prospects for enforcement of compliance are narrowed. That situation is indeed regrettable, since it compromises the fundamental purposes of the annex.

One reasonable suggestion to improve monitoring and enforcement of antipollution regulations is to mandate the inspection of ships in gateway ports to the Antarctic. Common standards established by MARPOL 73/78 could be applied by national inspectors in Chile, Argentina, Australia, New Zealand, South Africa, and the United Kingdom (on the Falkland Islands and South Georgia) to ensure that ships bound for the Antarctic are in compliance with provisions in Annex IV of the Madrid Protocol. Port state control would thus be used to complement flag state control to preclude breaches of Annex IV.[71] Two key obstacles encumber this sensible suggestion, however. First, there is the expense of these inspections. Governments are not eager to incur additional financial burdens to protect against possible pollution of ocean waters hundreds of miles away in the frozen South. Second, there remains concern over the infringement of flag state sovereignty implicit in such vessel inspections, and governments are not particularly eager to entertain that political situation either.

Annex V: Area Protection and Management

In October 1991, at the XVIth ATCM in Bonn, the United States and the United Kingdom proposed a fifth annex to the Protocol that simplifies and expands the scope of the Antarctic protected area system.[72] As adopted, this annex supplies an integrated approach to the creation and management of these areas in the Antarctic.

Over the past three decades the ATCPs had developed a rather complex system for protected areas.[73] Eight types of specially protected areas and sites were designated (Specially Protected Areas, Sites of Special Scientific Interest, Marine Sites of Special Scientific Interest, Historic Sites and Monuments, Specially Reserved Areas, Multiple Use Planning Areas, Areas of Special Tourist Interest, and CCAMLR Environmental Monitoring Programme Sites), with different conservation regimes subjected to disparate management procedures, as formulated in a series of disconnected recommendations.[74] This situation generated conflicts of interest in environmental, scientific, and economic dimensions; prompted controversies among ATCPs;[75] and fostered general criticism of the Antarctic protected areas system.

In 1989 at the XVth ATCM in Paris, Consultative Parties discussed the issue of protected areas, in particular the designation of new categories for such areas. It was apparent that increased human activities in the Antarctic were likewise increasing the risks of cumulative environmental impacts, particularly in high-use areas such as the Antarctic Peninsula. But ATCPs were concerned that designating new protected areas might increasingly restrict access to parts of Antarctica and thus further curtail freedom of scientific research throughout the region.

At the XVIth ATCM in Bonn in October 1991, the debate focused on whether to rationalize existing categories of environmental management in accordance with the values to be protected (e.g., fauna and flora, geological, scientific, or wilderness) or in accordance with the means by which protection was to be managed. Annex V to the Protocol does both. Annex V consolidates the five existing categories of protected zones under the Antarctic Treaty into two types of protected areas. First are Antarctic Specially Protected Areas (ASPAs), which are to remain inviolate from human interference. ASPAs are subjected to protection because they are representative of major human ecosystems or are of outstanding environmental, scientific, historic, aesthetic, or wilderness value.[76] A second category, Antarctic Specially Managed Areas (ASMAs), coordinates multiple-use activities in the same area and thus reduce possibilities for conflicts.[77] Here attention falls on activities in the area. Access to ASPAs requires a permit; access to ASMAs does not. The protection mechanism for both ASPAs and ASMAs is a detailed management plan.[78] Annex V improves the previous minimum size requirements by designating that an area should be of "sufficient size to protect the values for which the special protection or management is required."[79] The annex also regulates tourist visits.[80] The presumption underpinning the fifth annex is that the Environment Committee and the Scientific Committee on Antarctic Research (SCAR) will play pivotal roles in advising the management plan process.

Negotiation of Annex V consolidated the unwieldy array of area protection and management schemes for the Antarctic commons into a more manageable, uniform system. It not only promotes better cooperative planning and coordination of activities in Antarctica, but also helps avoid environmental damage more easily and effectively.

THE BALANCE SHEET

Assets and Attributes

The greatest strengths of the Madrid Protocol emanate from its environmental principles, particularly as codified in Article 3 and in the prohibition on mining. Indeed, the language of Article 7 that bans mining or drilling provides powerful symbolic value. In addition, the accountability and foresight provided in Article 8 for planning is a welcome addition of elements that had been noticeably absent from the Antarctic Treaty process.

The Madrid Protocol is especially notable as a diplomatic achievement because it was negotiated in such a short time. That accomplishment demonstrated the political will of the ATCPs to protect the environment. The Protocol brought together political, public, and environmental forces to protect the environment and sped up the process of pulling the entire Treaty regime in the direction of environmental preservation.[81]

The Protocol brings the protected areas of the Antarctic commons into a new era. It organizes protected areas more regionally and places them under multinational cooperative management. ASPAs and ASMAs institutionalize ways and means for cooperation on science, waste management, and management planning. The Protocol systematizes environmental regulation for the continent and puts environmental protection on the international agenda by formalizing means to preserve the continent's delicate ecosystems. In this regard, the Protocol has consolidated several issues of environmental protection and preservation—the Agreed Measures, waste management, marine pollution, EIAs, and protected areas—into one document. New concepts for the southern polar region have also been introduced, among them aesthetics, wilderness values, and geomorphological values.[82]

The Protocol is thoroughly integrated into the ATS and its attendant international regimes. The Protocol reserves the rights and obligations under the Antarctic Treaty, Seals Convention, and CCAMLR.[83] And the Protocol consciously tries to avoid interference with their objectives or "any inconsistency between the implementation of those instruments and of this Protocol."[84] Other international instruments, in particular, the International Whaling Convention and the MARPOL 73/78 Convention, complement and bolster legal protection for the Antarctic.

The ATS has proven politically resilient and legally flexible in adapting to and accommodating shifting global demands. The most effective political position for international agreements usually is one of balance and compromise, and the Protocol strikes such a balance between environmental concerns and industrial interests. The Protocol supplies more breathing space for environmental protection of the polar South. Commercial interests, which are presently not concerned with pursuing minerals exploitation in Antarctica, can focus their extraction efforts elsewhere and develop more advanced mining and drilling techniques that one day might permit more measured control of Antarctic mineral exploitation that would be more consistent with environmental concerns. Any attempt to exploit minerals or hydrocarbons in the Antarctic appears at least several decades away.

The Protocol's drafters wisely avoided the sticky sovereignty issue. Moreover, the Protocol's prohibition on mining operations throughout Antarctica greatly reduces anxieties over the possibility of territorial disputes flaring up over conflicting minerals activities in claimed sectors. If no state is permitted to prospect for minerals, then conflicts over ownership of potentially exploitable resources become moot.

Another beneficial result of the Protocol is that the process of intense debate in its negotiations effectively canceled the need to review the Antarctic Treaty.[85] The treaty parties analyzed the ATS thoroughly and carefully in deliberating which way to go after CRAMRA and what environmental protection priorities were appropriate for the region. The conclusion was that the ATS was working well and that the Madrid Protocol and its annexes rounded out the regime. The Madrid Protocol, moreover, stemmed the international rush to accede to the Antarctic Treaty. Negotiations for the minerals treaty during the 1980s fueled a membership drive to the Antarctic Treaty.[86] With a minerals agreement no longer viable and the prospects darkened for any forthcoming revenues from minerals activities, international interest in Antarctica waned after 1990. The demise of CRAMRA, underscored by the Protocol's flat prohibition on mineral activities in the Antarctic commons, combined to temper interest among other states for joining the treaty regime.

Negotiation of the Madrid Protocol also decelerated calls for the conversion of Antarctica into a common heritage regime. Since 1991 criticism of the Antarctic Treaty System generally and the Consultative Parties activities in particular has softened markedly in the UN General Assembly. Now that opportunities for exploiting (unknown) mineral riches in the frozen continent have evaporated, the developing states that had hoped for shared profits from mining are content to allow the Antarctic Treaty System to manage the region, free from outside interference.

The Madrid Protocol also reunified the ATCPs. The frictions sparked by the defections of ATCP support for CRAMRA largely dissipated with the Madrid agreement. The Protocol apparently has produced a better outcome for all governments over the next several decades. But that reunification remains incomplete. A residue of resentment remains over the failure to consummate the CRAMRA process and over the manner in which the minerals agreement was brought down. That legacy of frustration and perceived unfairness seems likely to persist for a while longer.

In short, then, the Protocol contributes much by addressing issues unresolved in the 1959 Treaty and by bringing environmental protection for the Antarctic commons into the modern era. The instrument suggests a move toward greater international cooperation in the frozen South—not just among governments, but among national operators and nongovernmental environmental interest groups.

Deficiencies and Defects

The Madrid Protocol represents a tactical victory for the ATCPs and an impressive step toward the goal of sustaining wilderness values in the polar South. Even so, certain deficiencies of commission and omission are apparent in the agreement. One problem centers on the Protocol's geographical scope of application, which is confined to the area south of 60° south latitude. This demarcation is consistent with the 1959 Antarctic Treaty, but it represents an arbitrary political boundary. There is no ecological justification for an Antarctic perimeter set at 60° south, and it creates difficulties in sustaining the Protocol's avowed intent to protect Antarctica's "dependent and associated ecosystems" as well. A more ecologically relevant demarcation would be the area south of the Antarctic Convergence, which meanders around 40° to 50° south latitude and which was applied in CCAMLR. In addition, the Protocol does not apply to subantarctic islands outside the treaty area. In the case of CCAMLR, claimed island groups such as South Georgia, the Kerguélen Islands, and the South Shetlands are significant fishing grounds—and thus targets for CCAMLR conservation measures. That these island groups and others are omitted from environmental protection under the Protocol may become a notable impediment to that instrument's effectiveness in preserving and protecting the Antarctic marine ecosystem.

The instrument's key regulatory provision, Article 3, provides only for "regular" and "effective" monitoring of all activities. It does not create ways or means to police the region or sanctions to enforce the rules. While actual compliance with the Protocol by member states is assigned in Article 13 (which establishes a self-monitoring and notice program), there are scant deterrent provisions to intimidate potential violators.

Another defect lies in the procedure for conducting environmental impact assessment. A close reading of Annex I indicates that governments ultimately can do whatever they like after the EIA process. While assessments of the environmental impact of proposed activities are required, the government concerned makes the final decision to carry out the planned activity based on its own evaluation. This may be politically convenient, but it is hardly conducive to uniformity of behavior in a system of comprehensive environmental protection.

The Protocol establishes a dispute settlement mechanism and an intraregime Antarctic Arbitral Tribunal. Still, exactly where that panel's actual enforcement power lies in settling disputes remains uncertain. The Tribunal is authorized to resolve disputes but not to invoke punitive sanctions on violators of the protective regime. Were that tribunal to hand down a judgment on some dispute, it is still unclear what kind of force might be marshalled to ensure that the judgment is carried out by both parties.

The Mining Ban

Article 7 prohibits mineral resource activities other than scientific research; this fiat entails the thrust of the Protocol. When interpreted alone, the ban implies a permanent restraint on all mining activity in Antarctica, but when coupled with subsequent provisions in the Protocol, the ban is widely interpreted to constitute merely a fifty-year moratorium on mining and drilling, subject to review (and possible revision) at the end of that period. This interpretation came at the insistence of the United States, and the environmentalists argue that it may seriously threaten the integrity of the Protocol.

Controversy at the second session of the XIth ATSCM in Madrid in June 1991 arose over language proposed by the United States that would provide ways to lift the ban on mining in the future. The plenary in Madrid adopted all the provisions at the meeting except this one. The unwillingness to agree on this issue prompted the United States to leave the June meeting without approving the Protocol—it was the only ATCP government to do so. The United States favored including a provision that would make it considerably less difficult for a government to withdraw unilaterally from the Protocol and thereafter conduct practically unregulated mining operations in Antarctica. This U.S. language was eventually written into the final draft, whereupon the Protocol was adopted by all the ATCPs in October 1991.

The controversy centers around Article 25 in the Protocol. This article, comprised of five sections, outlines the modification and amendment procedures for the Protocol. Section 1 asserts that modifications and amendments may be made at any time in accordance with Article XII of the Antarctic Treaty. Section 2 provides that after the expiration of fifty years from the date of entry into force, any Consultative Party may convene a conference to review the operation of the Protocol.

Section 3 stipulates that any modification or amendment proposed at such a review conference must be adopted by a majority of the parties. This majority must include at least three-fourths (i.e., twenty) of those who were ATCP states when the Protocol was adopted in 1991. Section 4 posits that for any adopted modification or amendment to enter into force, it must be ratified by three-fourths of the Consultative Parties. This three-fourths majority must include all those states that were Consultative Parties at the time of the adoption of the Protocol. This section prompted concern for the United States, since it effectively gave to each of the twenty-six governments who were then Consultative Parties a veto over any amendment.

The U.S. alteration of section 5 counters the effect of this section. Section 5(a) specifies that the ban on minerals activity shall remain indefinitely. If, however, the parties do agree to change this policy, there must be established a binding legal regime that regulates at least three concerns: (1) answers whether mineral resource activities can take place; (2) sets conditions under which minerals activities can take place; and (3) provides safeguards to protect the interests of all states referred to in Article IV of the Antarctic Treaty.

Section 5(b) contains the so-called "walkout clause." This caveat was proposed by the United States to offset the impact of section 4 and was incorporated into the final draft. The subsection provides that "if any such modification or amendment has not entered into force within 3 years of the date of its adoption, any Party may at any time thereafter notify to the Depository of its withdrawal from this Protocol, and such withdrawal shall take effect two years after receipt of the notification by the Depository." This proviso supplies the means through which any party may walk away unilaterally from the mining ban after the fifty-year moratorium has concluded.

Article 25 would thus allow parties to withdraw from the Protocol if an amendment to lift the ban on mineral activities did not enter into force within three years of its adoption. The petitioning party could thereafter lawfully leave the Protocol, be unbound by its rules, and presumably go on to pursue minerals activities in the Antarctic. While complying with the strict letter of the Protocol's law, such a maneuver would clearly contravene the spirit of the Protocol and could prompt other governments to abandon the Protocol as well.

Certain implications of Article 25 should be kept in mind. For one, while the ban on minerals activities and mining in Article 7 is not made permanent, neither is an expiration date provided. The mining ban continues indefinitely unless actively ended by amendment to the Protocol. Second, while modification or amendment to the Protocol may be made at any time through consensus agreement by the ATCPs,[87] that option might not necessarily weaken the Protocol. It is equally possible that amendments could be adopted to strengthen the environmental protection provisions of the Protocol. Third, nothing in Article 25 mandates that a conference *must* be called to review the Protocol or the mining ban. Such a review conference *may* be called by a party after fifty years, but it does *not have* to be called. Nor would such a conference have to confront the decision to lift the ban on mining. Though that might occur, it only remains a possible option, not a necessary reality. Thus, absent efforts to overturn it by any Consultative Party, the mining ban could extend indefinitely.

Environmentalists remain concerned that Article 25 may contain the seeds of the Protocol's self-destruction and might over the long term contribute to the unraveling of the Antarctic Treaty System. The prospect that states might consider modifying the Protocol is viewed as a potential threat to the environmental integrity of the Antarctic commons. This fear may or may not be justified, but if past behavior of governments in the region is any guide, there is just cause for that concern.[88]

Another deficiency concerns the Committee on Environmental Protection. While important for the Protocol, this body lacks the authority to compel compliance. Yet the CEP will advance the consultative process. It will require that decisions affecting the environment be made by experts using science, rather than by diplomats acting on the basis of national interests or political advantage.

The CEP's effectiveness will be determined by the degree to which parties can separate that body's scientific functions from the world of diplomacy and politics. Scientific, technical experts must be kept from involvement in political and diplomatic functions. The CEP's advice must be given on the basis of scientific findings, not political perceptions. This model for decision-making clearly follows that of the Scientific Committee of CCAMLR.

Liability

Another concern is the issue of liability for violations of the Protocol. While the Protocol stipulates that liability rules and procedures are to be drafted, incorporated in an annex, and adopted in accordance with Article 9 of the Protocol,[89] no liability annex has yet been promulgated. Moreover, no timetable is set as to when liability rules should be fixed or when they should be put into force.

Liability assigns responsibility to a party for an act or event. Its core purpose can be to penalize and thus deter the commission of a criminal act, or to help allocate the cost of compensation and restitution for damage. In the case of damage to the environment, both purposes are well served.

The effectiveness of any system of liability depends upon the existence of some mechanism to enforce the legal obligation to compensate those who suffer harm as the result of someone's activities. For domestic legal systems, the enforcement agent is usually the government, supported by the courts. If the developer of some natural resource violates conditions regarding environmental preservation that were set when a development permit was granted, then that developer may be fined or have his permit revoked.

Extending liability to an international commons area complicates an already difficult situation on several counts. First, there is the critical need to provide a clear legal definition of damage, since that will be the basis for determining liability and the scope of any remedial action. Additionally, standards of liability must be fixed. Liability may be founded on fault or may not require fault. When no fault is required, "strict" liability is set. In addition, a number of fundamental issues must be resolved if a liability regime is to be devised for the Antarctic commons. What damages should be covered by a liability regime? Should a liability regime permit excuses? If so, which excuses would be acceptable? What means are appropriate for calculating the amount of compensation for damage to the Antarctic environment? Should limits be put on the amount of compensation owed? Who would be the proper plaintiff in a case of damage to the Antarctic environment, and who would be the appropriate debtor? How does one distinguish between state liability and operator liability in this context? If a viable liability annex is to be produced, these issues must all be addressed in time, to the political and legal satisfaction of every Consultative Party government.[90]

Certain elements are necessary for a liability annex to be viable. One is that the definition of damages must be clearly linked to the EIA process. Second, the process of assessing liability must be unambiguous, and standards adopted for liability must be strict and high. Third, once an annex is in place and operative, liability issues must be resolved expeditiously, since quick, resolute action to enforce liability claims is likely to be a stronger deterrent than actions that are mild, slow in coming, or indecisive. Fourth, a liability annex must apply to all factors in Antarctica, with residual liability falling on the appropriate state (i.e., that state which made the go-ahead decision on its EIA or whose nationals are responsible for causing the environmental damage for which liability is being sought), whether or not that government endorsed the form of activity taking place. Fifth, there must be an understanding of how to place a value on damage. In an ideal world, liability would extend beyond the costs of restoration, but it seems unlikely that a liability annex will codify that ambition. Sixth, who pays what to whom? For example, who would be responsible in the event that during the visit of a tourist group serious damage was done to the Antarctic environment? The tour operator alone? The government that approved that tour operator? The flag state of the vessel or aircraft ferrying in the tourists? The claimant country whose sector is being visited? Agreement is still needed on a procedure for determining which state should be held responsible for a liability action.

Various conflicts of jurisdiction and liability also need to be resolved. For example, were a government to assert its authority over an operation, it would inherit responsibility and incur liability for that operation. Claimants want to assert sovereign authority in their sectors. Accordingly, one could argue that the claimant government should be responsible for making the environmental impact assessment. But would the claimant government want to do so at the risk of incurring residual liability for operator's activities? One would think not.

The question also lingers as to what kind of liability should be imposed in the Antarctic. Should all operators be held fully accountable for all acts that damage the environment (i.e., under "absolute" liability)? Or are there certain conditions that might excuse such damage if it occurs, strengthening the case for strict liability? Absolute liability might be ideal, but for practical reasons of self-interest the ATCPs will more likely settle on some version of strict liability. There will always be grounds for excuses in Antarctica (be it climate, weather, terrain, wind, cold, or so forth). Attaining strict liability is more practicable and therefore more likely to be adopted by ATCPs. But even strict liability might be too high a standard for many Consultative Parties. ATCPs are reluctant to think in "green" terms about policy options in Antarctica. Governments look for pragmatic, reasonable options that are not too grand or ambitious. Strict liability appears more conducive to that mindset than the absolute variety.

The liability regime is still incomplete. Eight "informal drafts" of a liability annex have been prepared by Rüdiger Wolfrum, the chair of the Meeting of Legal Experts on Liability. Still, progress in negotiating the annex is slow and may not produce a final draft until late 1998, if then.[91] But a liability annex is taking shape. The Eighth Offering states the purpose of the annex as "to promote the prevention, minimization and containment of damage to the Antarctic environment and dependent and associated ecosystems, and to provide adequate compensation for damage"[92] within the Antarctic Treaty area.[93] "Damage" in the draft annex refers to "any harmful impact upon the Antarctic environment and dependent and associated ecosystems [if it] is a significant and lasting one."[94] "Unavoidable impacts" or procedures deemed "acceptable" under the environmental impact procedures in the Environmental Protocol (Article 8) or in its Annex I (Articles 2 or 3) would not be considered "damage."[95] Environmental groups interpret such exclusions from the definition of "damage" as a very serious weakening of the annex.[96] The requirement that "damage" must have "significant and lasting" adverse impacts is also viewed as unduly raising the burden of proof for damage.[97]

The draft offering sets the standard for liability as "strict," i.e., it will not be necessary to establish fault for damage,[98] with the possibility of extending joint liability to damage if the circumstances warrant.[99] States are obligated to impose liability on their nationals operating within the Antarctic,[100] and operators are obligated to be prepared for incidents that might have "harmful impacts," as well as to take "response actions" and "remedial measures," with the latter remaining contingent upon recommendation by the ATCPs upon the advice of the Committee on Environmental Protection.[101] An operator to whom damage is attributable must reimburse "the reasonable costs" incurred by other persons carrying out response actions or remedial measures to redress the situation created by the "damage."[102]

The draft liability annex provides that compensation for any "unrepaired damage" should be made in the form of a lump sum payment to an Environmental Protection Fund[103] that is established under the annex.[104] Any disputes over reimbursement of costs for liability will be decided by the Arbitral Tribunal established in the Schedule to the Protocol.[105] Finally, the draft annex would not impose liability on operators if damage were caused by some act of omission left uncovered in the Protocol or its annexes, or if by "a natural disaster of an exceptional character which could not have been reasonably foreseen, . . . [or] an armed conflict, should it occur notwithstanding the Antarctic Treaty, or an act of terrorism against which no reasonable measures could have been effective."[106]

The chairman's Eighth Offering represents sure but painfully slow progress toward a liability annex. Environmental groups seem generally supportive of the direction in which the annex is headed, although greater clarification of terms is wanted. What has become apparent in the five years since formulation of the liability annex began is that the main impediments to resolving difficulties in drafting the annex are more political than legal.

Omission of a liability regime arguably could be the most significant environmental threat left by the Madrid Protocol. An annex containing rules for binding liability supplies legal clout for the Protocol and also furnishes a tangible mechanism for converting the Protocol into a real regulatory instrument. So long as no such annex exists, the risk remains that liability might be deferred. That situation would undermine the credibility of the Protocol, since the threat of imposing liability would deter harmful activities from being committed by governments or private operators in the frozen South. Delay in negotiating and implementing a liability annex could be detrimental to effective environmental protection in the Antarctic commons.

The Protocol thus remains unfinished business and, aside from issues of interpretation and practice, is not yet complete. Rules and procedures "relating to liability for damage arising from activities taking place in the Antarctic" still need to be adopted.[107] The Protocol thus remains lawmaking in progress. But formulating a liability annex has been prolonged and protracted. Completing negotiations on a liability annex could take even longer, since ATCPs are not able (or willing) to push hard because diplomatic and political resources are still needed to implement the Protocol. Genuine consensus is required to make a liability annex viable, and that consensus only appears willing to accept a strict liability regime. While perhaps more environmentally desirable, absolute liability is not a practical option for most governments.

Balance Sheet

There is a real need to convert international commitment to environmental protection into national law. This is a special challenge for many governments, especially when standards agreed to internationally have no parallel under domestic legislation. Several ATS states have only rudimentary environmental legislation and no experience with critical processes such as environmental impact statements. Sharing the experience of national models could facilitate and expedite broader acceptance of such standards at the international level.

The Protocol provides a framework for directing national behavior toward genuine environmental protection in the Antarctic commons. Led by the mining ban, the Protocol and its annexes set much-needed limits on waste disposal and marine pollution, and establish new regulations for protecting wildlife and conducting environmental impact assessments. Perhaps most significant, the Protocol has revitalized the Antarctic Treaty System as the operative means for devising acceptable solutions to highly complex international problems. In the aftermath of CRAMRA's demise, that is a salient accomplishment.

The Madrid Environmental Protocol entered into force in 1998. The final stage of the ratification process involved three states—Japan, Russia, and the United States—and the United States proved to be the key. Once the United States deposited its instrument of ratification on April 17, 1997, Russia followed suit. The process had been delayed for the United States since October 2, 1996, when the legislation implementing the Protocol into U.S. law was signed by President Clinton.[108]

Lingering concern by the Department of State hinged on the belief that the United States might be accused of not being in compliance with the Protocol because all the domestic rules and relevant regulations were not yet in place. The United States, therefore, should not deposit its instrument of ratification.[109] Interagency coordination involving the Department of State, Environmental Protection Agency, National Science Foundation, the Coast Guard, and Antarctic tour operators produced a workable compromise and opened the door for U.S. deposit.[110] Japan ratified in late 1997, allowing the Protocol to enter into force on January 14, 1998.

While the Madrid Protocol's entry into force is a notable achievement, for an Antarctic protection strategy to be effective, gaps left by the Madrid Protocol and other ATS instruments must be bridged, especially by reviewing and upgrading agreements. There is still a critical need to develop and implement in practice a proactive and precautionary approach to activities in the Antarctic commons. The evolution of a "world park mindset" contributes toward that end.

A World Park?

The Madrid Protocol consolidates environmental measures into a single instrument under the Antarctic Treaty. Before this agreement, environmental rules for Antarctic Treaty states were negotiated on an ad hoc, piecemeal basis, with little linkage or substantive integration. The Madrid Protocol transformed that patchwork of rules into a more comprehensive approach to environmental protection in Antarctica. In the process, the Protocol enabled revision and improvement of detailed measures as circumstances evolve.

But does this set of comprehensive protective commitments mean that Antarctica has actually been transformed *de jure* into a world park? What exactly is meant by an "Antarctic world park"? The concept of "World Park Antarctica" has given rise to misconceptions over the past decade. One image of the world park suggests erection of a legal "fence" around the continent to eliminate all human activities there. Others have implied that a world park involves an elaborate scheme to promote tourism in Antarctica. Scientists have suggested that such world park status would impinge upon their freedom to conduct research. Certain ATCP governments have presumed that "World Park Antarctica" means dissolution of territorial claims to the continent, thus inviting destabilization of the coalition of Antarctic Treaty parties and perhaps even undermining the entire ATS. And non–Antarctic Treaty states in the Third World seem inclined to view a world park scheme as synonymous with the "common heritage of mankind" notion, such that all peoples would be allowed to share in benefits derived from developing Antarctica.[111] According to environmental groups, all these impressions are faulty and misguided.[112]

Environmentalists have suggested that several criteria are implicit in the Antarctica-as-world-park concept. First, priority should be given to maintaining Antarctica's wilderness values. Second, scientific and tourist activities should continue but within strict environmental guidelines. Third, areas should be zoned to supply special conditions for special purposes, e.g., scientific bases and tourism. Fourth, zones should be governed by special management conditions, with management plans provided for each area. Fifth, all mineral activities should be prohibited. Sixth, a special institution should be established to supervise activities, development proposals, and environmental impact assessments. Seventh, the limits for the world park should extend beyond the continent to encompass the entire "Antarctic region," meaning either south of 60° south latitude or, better yet, to the Antarctic Convergence.[113]

In the view of environmentalists, protection and conservation are the hallmarks of the Antarctic world park. Within the ATS measures to protect the fragile Antarctic environment have always enjoyed considerable support. The conservation issue was even raised at the first ATCM in 1961 when the British delegation advocated recognizing Antarctica as a "natural reserve."[114] The first noteworthy suggestion for declaring Antarctica a world park, however, came from outside the Antarctic Treaty System—at the Second World Conference on National Parks held in the United States at Yellowstone Park in 1972. Sponsored by the International Union for the Conservation of Nature and Natural Resources (IUCN), the Conference agreed to a resolution that acknowledged "the great scientific and aesthetic value of the unaltered natural ecosystems of the Antarctic . . .," and unanimously recommended that the Antarctic continent and its circumpolar waters be established as the first world park, under the auspices of the United Nations.[115] At the Eighth ATCM in 1975, New Zealand proposed the establishment of a world park for Antarctica that would not alter the existing treaty regime. While Chile supported the concept, the issue was never formally placed on the agenda, and no reference to the New Zealand initiative appears in the official published records of the meeting.[116] As noted in earlier chapters, this suggests that the proposal met with opposition among other state delegations.

Throughout the 1970s and 1980s ATCP governments rejected a world park status for Antarctica because the notion of "world park" was viewed as conceptually fuzzy, legally undefined, and internationally unenforceable. Contentious debate during the 1980s between governments and environmentalists over the minerals regime, however, served to sharpen the legal earmarks and environmental implications of designating Antarctica as a world park.

As the world park concept emerged during the 1980s, certain aspirations and goal values of the environmental community became apparent. For conservation groups, governance of Antarctica as a world park would be guided by certain fundamental principles. Among these were the following:

1. The Antarctic should be an area where wilderness values are paramount.
2. The Antarctic should be an area where there is comprehensive conservation of flora and fauna (terrestrial and marine) and the environment (including atmosphere).
3. The Antarctic should be an area of limited scientific research which encourages cooperation between scientists of all nations.
4. The Antarctic should be an area of peace, free of nuclear and other weapons and all military activities.[117]

Environmentalists contended that these world park principles should be incorporated into a special, legally binding international conservation instrument. Further, basic obligations should be fixed for member states, among them the need to: (1) protect the Antarctic environment and its dependent and associated ecosystems; (2) respect Antarctica's significance for, and influence on, the global environment; (3) respect all legitimate uses of Antarctica; (4) respect Antarctica's scientific value and aesthetic and wilderness qualities; (5) ensure the safety of operations in Antarctica; and (6) take into account the interests of the international community as a whole.[118] If governments truly abided by these duties, environmentalists argued, Antarctica would perforce become a world park.

The most recent vision of World Park Antarctica takes account of the Madrid Environmental Protocol as an instrument environmentalists hold worthy of protection. Under the status of a world park,

> Antarctica would be maintained as a peaceful, demilitarized, nuclear-free region. The wilderness qualities of the continent and the Southern Ocean would be preserved, and conservation would be the paramount consideration when judging the acceptability of any and all human activities in the region. International scientific cooperation would continue to be fostered. Indeed, science should be the primary reason for human activity on the continent. All commercial minerals activities would be banned as inherently too damaging to the environment and other qualities of Antarctica. There would also be a ban on the storage, discharge or incineration of toxic or radioactive waste, and the use of nuclear reactors for any purpose would be forbidden. The ecosystem approach to marine living resources management conceived under the Convention for the Conservation of Antarctic Marine Living Resources would be sustained. A management structure would be established to ensure that all activities undertaken in the Antarctic are managed according to a consistent set of standards, and to provide for uniform enforcement of rules, regulations and measures. Juridical arrangements made under the Antarctic Treaty with regard to territorial claims would remain in place.[119]

How does this concept of World Park Antarctica square with the legal attributes of the ATS, especially as manifested in the protections afforded by the Madrid Environmental Protocol? Strong links among the agreements in the Antarctic Treaty System suggest some congruence. For one, the Agreed Measures define the Antarctic as a Special Conservation Area. Its provisions animate this designation and demonstrate that states can devise and agree on strict conservation and protection rules. Specific procedures can be designed to ensure that any activity undertaken in the region will not cause adverse impacts upon Antarctic fauna and flora. These commitments lie at the foundation of environmental protection.

A second connection is found in the Seals Convention. The Seals Convention was the first Antarctic-related marine resource agreement to be negotiated and signed prior to any significant contemporary commercial exploitation of the species targeted for protection. The thrust of the Seals Convention aims at conservation, and it stresses protective measures such as quotas, closed seasons, sealing reserves, and total protection for some species, with strict reporting requirements imposed for all activities.

A third link is between world park principles and the purpose and intentions of CCAMLR. CCAMLR's unique ecosystem approach to managing Antarctic marine resources is compatible with and reenforces the environmental protections in the Protocol. Article II of CCAMLR plainly asserts that "The objective of this Convention is the conservation of Antarctic marine living resources." This provision then sets out special principles for "harvesting and associated activities" which generally complement basic principles for protection and preservation contained in the Madrid Protocol.

Perhaps most significant, however, rejection by the ATCPs of the Wellington Minerals Convention signaled a clear refocusing of Antarctic resource policy. Whereas the minerals regime indicated the intention to *regulate against* environmental degradation should Antarctic mineral resource activities occur, the Madrid Environmental Protocol revealed a commitment by states to *protect and prevent* any such degradation before it occurred. This strategy is one of preclusive protection. The ATCPs opted to preempt and prevent degradation of the Antarctic commons, rather than to engage in reactive policies to repair damages already done. That change in policy attitude no doubt is welcomed by Antarctic environmentalists and international conservationists.[120]

Logical deduction suggests that the Madrid Environmental Protocol is philosophically compatible with principles inherent in the ATS and may help realize Antarctica as a world park. But that observation does not translate into a valid legal conclusion. The Antarctic remains a commons area, not a region recognized as a world park.

The Madrid Protocol and the Antarctic Treaty regime, generally, establish a broad framework for environmental protection principles. But the Madrid Protocol cannot ensure the "permanent protection" for Antarctica that seems implicit in the idea of a world park. Because of its amendment provisions, the Protocol remains incapable of guaranteeing "the implementation of legal mechanisms, whether they are new legal structures, existing international conventions, or an evolution of the Antarctic Treaty system itself, which would ensure that the natural environment of the Antarctic is forever protected, free from the destruction wrought by humans on every other continent on Earth."[121] It is true that the Environmental Protocol furnishes a legal design with obligations and lays the foundation for compliance and enforcement for its member governments. Still, Antarctica remains open and accessible to persons from any state, whether it is legally obligated to the Antarctic Treaty System or not. Conservation restrictions or environmental restraints legally pertain only to nationals of party states. Consequently, while the Madrid Protocol may have moved the status of Antarctica closer to a world park *de facto*, that instrument falls far short of converting the region into a world park *de jure*.

CONCLUSION

The Antarctic Treaty Consultative Parties have, for three decades, increasingly applied international law to protect the Antarctic from environmentally degrading activities. Not only have they reinforced international environmental law to prohibit the continent's degradation, but Antarctic Treaty governments have also negotiated specific instruments that regulate pollution activities directly threatening the Antarctic marine ecosystem. The Agreed Measures, the Seals Convention, CCAMLR, and the promulgation of a special regulatory regime for mineral resources activities clearly attest to this concern. The recent Madrid Environmental Protocol, with its five annexes, ties these regulations together into a neater, tighter, and more manageable legal package.

The Madrid Protocol represents a significant achievement for the Antarctic Treaty regime because of its global perspective. It responds to a global concern—protecting the Antarctic environment. The Antarctic Treaty System had been isolated from world affairs, without apparent accountability. The Protocol brings the ATS into world affairs by imposing public responsibilities and legal obligations upon the ATCPs to preserve and protect the Antarctic, so as not to exploit the area for private gain. The Protocol, in sum, compels the Consultative Parties seriously to consider how best to use, manage, and protect the Antarctic commons.

The Madrid Environmental Protocol represents a profound redirection in ATCP policy. In 1989 the Antarctic Treaty states were headed toward a regime that could have permitted development of Antarctic mineral resources. By 1991 that course had been reversed in favor of a legal commitment to protect and preserve the Antarctic environment, lending the region a status akin to a world park. That policy shift was indeed profound, as it contributed mightily to the international movement toward global environmental governance for the Antarctic commons.

Chapter 7

SCIENCE AND TOURISM

The Antarctic commons is a valuable natural scientific laboratory. Scientific research continues to be the predominant activity in the polar South, and the continent is now recognized as vital for understanding global phenomena. Scientific activity in the Antarctic makes possible monitoring of global changes that affect the planet's condition, as well as acquisition of new knowledge that enables more informed judgments about the environmental consequences of those changes.

The Antarctic commons is removed from direct, intensive human interference. The region affords scientists a near-pristine natural laboratory that is remote from large human populations and persistent environmental pollution. Being relatively undisturbed, Antarctica and its circumpolar ocean can serve as benchmarks against which other ecosystems around the globe may be compared.[1] Put another way, pollution levels in Antarctica may serve as standards for the global minimum. Benchmark monitoring may also assist in assessing perturbations in other global ecosystems.

Notwithstanding the major role for science, tourism has also emerged since 1985 as an important activity in the Antarctic. As increasing numbers of tourists visit the polar South, more human pressures are placed on that delicate environment and on the scientific enterprise in the region. It is therefore increasingly necessary for scientists to determine what areas of Antarctica should be investigated before they are visited by tourists. This situation is made even more urgent by the relative lack of knowledge about either unperturbed Antarctic ecosystems or about how nonindigenous factors impact upon those environments.

This chapter thus undertakes two purposes. It first seeks to examine the role of science as a pervasive activity in the Antarctic commons. In this respect, the chapter outlines the policy objectives of scientific research and the wide-ranging nature of scientific activity there. Second, the chapter critically explores the nature of tourism as an activity in the Antarctic. The special attention given tourism by the Antarctic Treaty System, the environmental consequences posed by tourist visits to the continent, and the possible conflict between tourism and scientific activity are assessed. Finally, some conclusions are suggested concerning the symbiotic role that science and tourism must play if the Antarctic commons is to be managed for the good of both endeavors.

Science under the Antarctic Treaty System

The exact scope of "science" has never been precisely defined within Antarctic Treaty documents. Even so, the meaning of scientific activity appears intuitively clear.[2] Science may be defined as the systematic study of an object to gain knowledge about it, or generally to acquire knowledge through study so as to obtain general truths about that object. Science has played a critical role in Antarctic affairs since the International Geophysical Year in 1957/58 and has since anchored the legal management of Antarctic Treaty System (ATS). Each agreement adopted as part of the ATS, including the now-moribund minerals treaty, hails Antarctica as the continent of science and widely acknowledges science as the "currency of credibility" within the Antarctic international community.[3]

Science underpins the Antarctic Treaty.[4] The second substantive paragraph of the preamble acknowledges "the substantial contributions to scientific knowledge resulting from international co-operation in scientific investigation in Antarctica" during the IGY. Article I mandates that Antarctica shall be used "for peaceful purposes only," a condition that promotes the conduct of scientific operations in the region. Article II links scientific activity closely to the fulfillment of the 1959 Treaty. It asserts that "Freedom of scientific investigation in Antarctica and co-operation toward that end, as applied during the International Geophysical Year, shall continue, subject to provisions of the present Treaty." Scientific activity, then, is deemed essential to the purposes of the treaty and especially to promoting international cooperation toward that end.

The main provision in the Antarctic Treaty regarding science is Article III, which stipulates that scientific cooperation should be promoted "to the greatest extent feasible and practicable" in three ways. First, "information regarding plans for scientific programs in Antarctica shall be exchanged to permit maximum economy and efficacy of operations."[5] Free exchange of information among parties is thus called for to ensure that opportunities for cooperation can be fostered and improved. Second, "scientific personnel shall be exchanged in Antarctica between expeditions and stations."[6] This provision provides a practical way to promote international cooperation through collaboration on projects between like-minded scientists from various countries. Finally, Article III states that "scientific observations and results from Antarctica shall be exchanged and made freely available."[7] Scientific research in the Antarctic, therefore, is not the private province of one or a few governments who desire to use that information for national security or other purposes. Rather, information from scientific research in the Antarctic commons is considered an international product, to be shared and exchanged freely in the interest of bettering the human condition.[8]

Not surprisingly, guarantees stipulating the secure right to pursue scientific activities have evolved as critical components in every instrument comprising the Antarctic Treaty System (ATS). The very premise of the Seals Convention (i.e., that regulation can conserve seals in the Antarctic) requires that adequate scientific information will be available about the status of seal species. As recognized in its preamble, "in order to improve scientific knowledge and so place exploitation on a rational basis, every effort should be made both to encourage biological and other research on Antarctic seal populations and to gain information from such research. . . ."[9] Indeed, the Scientific Committee on Antarctic Research (SCAR) is assigned critical tasks in the Convention. In particular, SCAR serves as a depository for the exchange of scientific information and advice on seals for the Contracting Parties, as a repository of biological information on seals—including reproductive data and statistical information on seals killed—and as an official commentator on methods used for killing and capturing seals.[10] Without scientific research, then, the Seals Convention would have little effect.

Science also undergirds the 1980 Convention on the Conservation of Antarctic Marine Living Resources (CCAMLR).[11] In fact, scientific research remains the staple ingredient for making the Convention viable as an international legal instrument. The various functions of the Commission to effect conservation of Antarctic marine living resources can only be fulfilled thorough research and comprehensive studies of living resources and their interrelationships with the Antarctic marine ecosystem.[12] Moreover, a special Scientific Committee is established by CCAMLR to serve as a "forum for consultation and co-operation concerning the collection, study and exchange of information" regarding marine living resources in the Antarctic commons.[13] The Committee's essential work is to set criteria and methods for scientific research in the Antarctic seas, as well as to assess the ecological impacts of harvesting living marine resources. As made clear throughout the Convention, if conservation of living resources is to be accomplished effectively for Antarctic ocean space, continuous scientific research is essential. Science, then, becomes the vital element on which the success of CCAMLR depends.

Science is no less salient to the regime negotiated to regulate mineral resource development in the Antarctic. The Convention on the Regulation of Antarctic Mineral Activities (CRAMRA)[14] included among its chief objectives and principles the need to assess possible impacts of mineral activities on the Antarctic environment, determine the acceptability of minerals activities, govern the conduct of acceptable minerals activities, and ensure that all mineral resource activities "are undertaken in strict conformity" with the Convention.[15] Each of these objectives demanded constant, careful scientific analysis. Similarly, scientific assessment was required to obtain information needed to make informed decisions on the impact of a proposed activity on the environment,[16] and to determine what degree of response might be needed or liability assessed should an accident occur.[17]

Science obviously would have had an integral decision-making role in both CRAMRA's Commission and in any Regulatory Committees established for areas identified for possible exploration and development. The functions of the special Scientific, Technical and Environmental Advisory Committee plainly attests to that.[18] In sum, the success of the Antarctic minerals regime would have pivoted on the availability of hard scientific data. Ongoing scientific activity in the region thus would have been essential.

Finally, science permeates the purpose and functions of the 1991 Madrid Environmental Protocol as well.[19] The central objective of the Protocol commits its parties "to the comprehensive protection of the Antarctic environment and dependent and associated ecosystems and hereby designate[s] Antarctica as a natural reserve, devoted to peace and science."[20] Among the values chiefly embraced in the Protocol are Antarctica's wilderness and aesthetic qualities and "its value as an area for the conduct of scientific research, in particular research essential to understanding the global environment."[21] Importantly, these values are stated as fundamental considerations in the planning and conduct of all activities in the Antarctic Treaty area.

As expected, science is a prerequisite for achieving the Protocol's purpose of protecting the Antarctic environment and its dependent and associated ecosystems. Careful, unbiased scientific assessment is essential for planning activities in the region; for obtaining sufficient information on which to make decisions regarding possible environmental impacts; for performing environmental impact assessment; for determining the effectiveness of measures taken pursuant to the Protocol; for carrying out environmentally related inspections; and for enabling the Committee for Environmental Protection (CEP) to formulate sound advice for the Consultative Parties on environmental measures, impact assessment, and response actions. Scientific activity and analysis are also essential for determining liability for any damage arising from activities within the Antarctic Treaty area.

Science is also the glue that binds together the Protocol's five annexes. It is indispensable for making a comprehensive environmental evaluation of a proposed activity's possible impact, as well as for monitoring activities. Science is necessary for sustaining protection of native fauna and flora. Scientific analysis is essential for waste management, as well as for assessing benign levels of incineration and waste disposal both on land and at sea. Likewise, constant scientific observation is fundamental to ensuring compliance with provisions prohibiting pollution of the marine environment. Special scientific activities must focus on analyzing the discharge levels of oil, noxious liquid substances, garbage, and sewage into circumpolar waters in order to ensure that procedures are carried out in accordance with the 1973/78 International Convention for the Prevention of Pollution from Ships.[22] Finally, scientific appraisals are needed to determine areas that require special protection and management. Scientific data is necessary to determine the conditions required for granting visitation permits, designating appropriate codes of conduct, preventing harmful interference with fauna and flora, and disposing of wastes.

Science, then, permeates the family of Antarctic Treaty agreements. Without pervasive scientific activity investigating the Antarctic commons, these international instruments could not obtain the knowledge necessary to attain their legal mandate.

POLICY OBJECTIVES FOR ANTARCTIC SCIENCE

Why has science become so central to human activity and international governance in the Antarctic? For one thing, science is necessary if states are to qualify for consultative status under the Antarctic Treaty.[23] For another, intellectual curiosity remains a driving force of humans. A third reason is highly pragmatic: The polar regions furnish vast resources of worldwide interest—krill, fish, whales, and even ice. For environmentalists, research provides the essential basis for rational resource management and conservation. Moreover, Antarctica provides valuable opportunities for studying global environmental problems, especially sea-level change, weather and climate patterns, and atmospheric cycles of important constituents such as ozone.[24]

Scientific activity supports at least four main policy objectives of the states that jointly govern the Antarctic. These objectives should be viewed against the broader background of national policy interests in Antarctica, which vary according to perceptions of the region's scientific, environmental, and economic importance to governments. In this regard, support for the Antarctic Treaty System, with its emphasis on science, remains fundamental to meeting policy interests of Consultative Parties. One principle fundamental to Antarctic affairs is keeping the area immune from political confrontation and armed conflict. The Antarctic Treaty System has been extraordinarily successful in preventing military or political confrontation in the region for nearly four decades, and the central role of freedom of scientific investigation and international cooperation contributes toward that end. By focusing national efforts on science, and by emphasizing programs for international cooperation in science, governments demonstrate their mutual commitment to avoid political confrontation in Antarctica,[25] just as they did before the treaty's inception in the 1957/58 IGY.

It is not possible to quantify how much international scientific cooperation has contributed to keeping the Antarctic commons free from political tension. There is no doubt, though, that when coupled with the treaty's provisions on nonmilitarization (Article I) and accommodation of sovereignty (Article IV), scientific cooperation has done much to secure that end. The provision in Article VII that guarantees the right of inspection by any party, and which is used regularly by various Antarctic Treaty Consultative Parties, supplies tangible assurance to states that peaceful uses and other provisions of the treaty are being observed.[26]

A second policy objective furthered by Antarctic science is protection of the Antarctic environment, with particular regard for the special impacts the region has on global climate. The negotiation of the Madrid Protocol in 1991 illustrates how protection of the environment has been advanced through the ATS. The resolve of all ATCP governments to follow through with this environmental initiative, launched in 1989 by Australia and France, demonstrates national commitment to this outcome. So, too, does the raft of scientific work that led to the various conservation measures progressively developed at ATCMs. The fruits of these efforts are contained in the protection provisions of the Environmental Protection Protocol and its annexes.

Scientific information remains essential for implementing the Protocol's provisions on environmental impact assessment, environmental monitoring, and verification of activities. Scientific advice is also essential for the Committee on Environmental Protection to do its work efficiently and with any degree of accuracy. Likewise, scientific information remains the critical ingredient for decision-making in CCAMLR, which has adopted nearly 120 conservation measures to manage, preserve, and protect living resources in the Southern Ocean.

A third policy objective of states in the Antarctic is maximizing advantage of the unique opportunities that the Antarctic provides for scientific research, opportunities that cannot be duplicated anywhere else in the world. Maintaining the pristine nature of the Antarctic and protecting the unique species that live there are essential for sustaining the continent's value for scientific studies. Especially important are factors relating to global climate change, alterations in stratospheric ozone levels, and the impacts that anthropogenic pollutants such as DDT and chlorofluorocarbons have on the globe's environment.[27]

Antarctica serves as a geophysical platform for scientific observations that cannot be made at all, much less properly, from other locations on Earth. Investigation of the Earth's magnetosphere and unobstructed astronomical viewing are possible only on the high Antarctic plateau. Such unique platform studies furnish knowledge about the continent's surface geology, variations in upper atmospheric cosmic rays, and cosmic events, as well as the performance of humans in isolated environments. Relatedly, atmospheric and oceanographic observations may be undertaken to determine the dynamics of climate processes. When linked with studies of sea ice and dynamics of the ice cap, such research findings reveal information on long-range climatic trends. Simi-

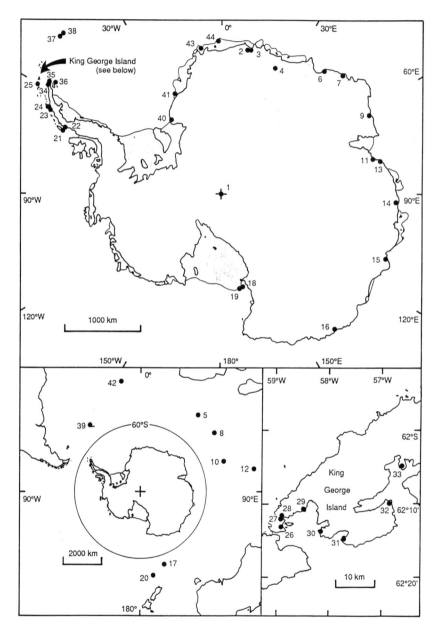

Figure 7.1
Scientific Stations in the Antarctic

Stations of SCAR Nations Operating in the Antarctic

Stations are numbered clockwise from the Greenwich Meridian.
*Stations north of 60 °S; †Stations on King George Island

1	Amundsen-Scott	United States	90 °S	
2	Maitri	India	70 °46'S	11 °44'E
3	Novolazarevskaya	Russia	70 °46'S	11 °50'E
4	Asuka	Japan	71 °32'S	24 °08'E
5	*Marion Island	South Africa	46 °52'S	37 °51'E
6	Syowa	Japan	69 °00'S	39 °35'E
7	Molodezhnaya	Russia	67 °40'S	45 °51'E
8	*Alfred Faure, Is Crozet	France	46 °26'S	51 °52'E
9	Mawson	Australia	67 °36'S	62 °52'E
10	*Port aux Français, Is Kerguelen	France	49 °21'S	70 °12'E
11	Zhongshan	China	69 °22'S	76 °23'E
12	*Martin de Viviès, I Amsterdam	France	37 °50'S	77 °34'E
13	Davis	Australia	68 °36'S	77 °58'E
14	Mirny	Russia	66 °33'S	93 °01'E
15	Casey	Australia	66 °18'S	110 °32'E
16	Dumont d'Urville	France	66 °40'S	140 °01'E
17	*Macquarie Island	Australia	54 °30'S	158 °57'E
18	McMurdo	United States	77 °51'S	166 °40'E
19	Scott Base	New Zealand	77 °51'S	166 °45'E
20	*Campbell Island	New Zealand	52 °33'S	169 °09'E
21	Rothera	United Kingdom	67 °34'S	68 °07'W
22	San Martin	Argentina	68 °08'S	67 °06'W
23	Faraday	United Kingdom	65 °15'S	64 °16'W
24	Palmer	United States	64 °46'S	64 °03'W
25	Capitan Arturo Prat	Chile	62 °30'S	59 °41'W
26	†Great Wall	China	62 °13'S	58 °58'W
27	†Teniente Rodolfo Marsh	Chile	62 °12'S	58 °58'W
28	†Bellingshausen	Russia	62 °12'S	58 °58'W
29	†Artigas	Uruguay	62 °11'S	58 °51'W
30	†King Sejong	Korea	62 °13'S	58 °47'W
31	†Jubany	Argentina	62 °14'S	58 °40'W
32	†Arctowski	Poland	62 °09'S	58 °28'W
33	†Commandte Ferraz	Brazil	62 °05'S	58 °24'W
34	General Bernardo O'Higgins	Chile	63 °19'S	57 °54'W
35	Esperanza	Argentina	63 °24'S	57 °00'W
36	Marambio	Argentina	64 °14'S	56 °37'W
37	Signy	United Kingdom	60 °43'S	45 °36'W
38	Orcadas	Argentina	60 °44'S	44 °44'W
39	*Bird Island	United Kingdom	54 °00'S	38 °03'W
40	Belgrano II	Argentina	77 °52'S	34 °37'W
41	Halley	United Kingdom	75 °35'S	26 °15'W
42	*Gough Island	South Africa	40 °21'S	09 °52'W
43	Neumayer	Germany	70 °39'S	08 °15'W
44	SANAE	South Africa	70 °18'S	02 °25'W

Figure 7.1 (chart)
Scientific Stations in the Antarctic

larly, information obtained from ice cores and sediments helps reveal the historical framework against which climate fluctuations might be better understood and even predicted.

A fourth policy objective furthered by Antarctic science is deriving reasonable economic benefits from living and nonliving resources of the Antarctic, albeit excluding extraction of minerals by mining or hydrocarbons by drilling. One economic benefit derived largely from Antarctic scientific activities is the enhancement of agriculture from improved weather and climate prediction services that use Antarctic data in computer prediction models. In addition, in the future, Southern Ocean fisheries might greatly supplement the world's growing need for protein. However, such economic development depends upon the scientifically accurate assessment of resources and the capacity of those fisheries to withstand intensified harvesting. More and better data from the Southern Ocean should greatly improve these services in coming years.

Science is, therefore, essential for responsible stewardship in the Antarctic. Over the past four decades Antarctic science has thrived, expanded in scope, and taken on new responsibilities. Science has become the means for making "reasoned, forward-looking decisions based on scientific knowledge for the preservation, protection, and conservation of Antarctica for current and future generations, and for Earth as a system."[28]

While scientific research is the main activity in the Antarctic commons, its mission has recently taken on a broader purpose. Antarctic science has become more globally directed not only because of scientific imperatives. Rather, the critical place of the polar South in global affairs has given added dimension to Antarctic science. A convergence of interests has emerged among scientific researchers, environmental groups, and the general public asserting that the Antarctic commons, including its circumpolar seas, must be preserved and protected as a means to and a model of global environmental protection. Science is the linchpin to promoting that responsible stewardship. See figure 7.1.

ANTARCTIC SCIENCE'S MULTIPLE FACETS

Several characteristics set Antarctic science apart from science in general. For one, while polar science is principally regional in character (e.g., there is Antarctic geology, Antarctic biology, Antarctic ecology, Antarctic meteorology), it poses global implications for climate change, sea-level fluctuations, and availability of world food supply. Thus, the continent acts as a platformed scientific observatory that permits a detailed view of certain aspects of nature that are not observable anywhere else on the planet.

Another distinguishing feature is that Antarctic scientific programs of global significance (e.g., climate modification and biological resources) are usually coordinated in collaboration with international research programs. This is usually not the case with national scientific studies. Many programs generally involve collecting extensive sets of environmental data on a continual basis. For example, the Experiment of the International Joint Global Flux Study (JGOFS) will examine flow of carbon from fossil-fuel burning on land into the atmosphere as carbon dioxide to its ultimate burial into the floor of the southern ocean. Relatedly, the Global Ocean Ecosystems Dynamics (GLOBEC) program will assess how environmental change affects the abundance and production of marine animals.[29] Most scientific work performed in Antarctica is such that it is planned well in advance and is integrated into long-term cooperative programs.[30]

Logistical facets of Antarctic science also merit mention. The harsh environment and long distances create distinctions between Antarctic science and other science. In addition, Antarctic science is highly seasonal. While some programs operate year-round (e.g., monitoring programs in geophysics, upper atmospherics, meteorology, medical studies, and cosmic ray analyses), most Antarctic programs are conducted only during the austral summer months (December through March).[31] Most scientists and technical personnel working in Antarctica work on short-term contracts for fewer than three years, and senior, experienced scientists make only brief visits. Finally, Antarctic science is far more expensive to carry out than are the programs of national science agencies of ATCP states.[32]

Scientific priority has traditionally been given to Antarctica's geophysical environment, highlighting research on glaciology, oceanography, continental and marine geology, atmospheric physics, and chemistry. Support research for these studies involves remote sensing, geodesy, and cartography of the Antarctic commons. Satellite imagery allows study of Earth's surface from space, supplying data on rock outcrops, shelf ice, and sea ice distribution throughout the Antarctic.[33]

But Antarctic science yields information on human biology as well.

Scientists investigate the impacts of isolation on human metabolism, nutrition, psychology, physiology, and virology in cold climes. Research is done on how frigid environmental conditions and changes in light and darkness affect work performance. Research on how humans react to the Antarctic environment and are able to adapt to isolation, cold, and photoperiodicity has implications for medical research and long-term space voyages.[34] Antarctic science helps us to understand more clearly how cold places stress on the body, as well as the impacts of confined space on human factors, e.g., behavioral adaptation, nutrition, and stress on the human condition.[35] Studies already suggest that personnel in Antarctica are subject to significant disturbances in physiology and psychology.

Terrestrial Geology

Greater (or East) Antarctica is comprised mainly of complex Precambrian shield structure, which makes very old parts of the Earth's crust accessible to geologists.[36] The main rock exposure in Antarctica is in the Transantarctic Mountains, which form a natural geographical divide between Greater Antarctica and Lesser (or West) Antarctica. Lesser Antarctica consists of massive archipelagiclike rock formations separated by subglacial basins, all overlaid together by the continental ice sheet. To examine these features, Antarctic geologic research focuses on plate tectonics, sedimentology, paleontology, marine geology, radiometric dating, magnetometry, seismic sounding, and gravity surveys.[37]

Several geological questions of global significance are being investigated in the Antarctic. The break-up of Gondwana (the supercontinent that existed 200 million years ago) ranks high, as does studying the nature of the junction between Greater and Lesser Antarctica,[38] since debate persists over the structure and geological history of the two parts. Further studies of the geology of the intervening basins in Lesser Antarctica could also reveal their potential as reservoirs for hydrocarbons. In addition, considerable attention is now being focused on the discovery of fossils in Antarctica, which could yield valuable clues about the geological history of the planet.[39]

Meteorology and Climatology

Antarctic research is heavily focused on understanding the profound influences of the massive Antarctic ice cap and circumpolar sea ice on meteorological processes affecting global weather patterns and climate. Cores from the Antarctic ice sheet and offshore marine sediments offer unique opportunities to study past changes of climate. Such data may also prove useful for improving weather analysis and forecasting.[40]

The Antarctic is a major heat sink for the world's climate system. The circumpolar pack-ice zone significantly influences the global albedo by enlarging the reflective surface area of the planet. This condition can alter the Earth's entire heat balance. All synoptic weather systems that affect southern regions—and Antarctica itself—are ultimately driven by this massive, heat-induced turning over of the atmosphere. Climate research seeks to understand these processes by explaining long-term data for meteorological and oceanic observation systems.[41]

Variations in sea ice also affect moisture and heat exchange between the ocean and the atmosphere. Given that 10 percent of the world's ocean lies south of the Antarctic Convergence, the Antarctic marine commons is a major factor in the planet's carbon dioxide cycle. Scientists estimate that 30 percent of the CO_2 emitted into the atmosphere is absorbed by the Southern Ocean, a fact with important implications for the greenhouse effect. Other climatic phenomena to be analyzed include ice-melt rates, radiation balance, freezing processes, water circulation, and the exchange process between moisture and gas.[42]

The energy source for atmospheric circulations is solar radiation, which strikes at lower intensity near the poles. The continent's high-domed ice sheet and the surrounding ice pack act as strong reflectors of incoming solar radiation, thereby contributing to a substantial radiation deficit in the Antarctic. This situation, in turn, affects global atmospheric circulation. Scientists can assess the cooling character of the atmosphere in the southern hemisphere, the influence that it exerts as a vortex in global wind flows, and how temperature variations affect the seasonal rise and fall of stratospheric ozone levels over Antarctica.[43]

Due to its vast area, elevation, asymmetry, and location in an oceanic hemisphere, the Antarctic ice cap profoundly influences the daily meteorology in southern lands, as well as variations in the geographical and temporal variability of the Earth's climate. In turn, the behavior of the Antarctic ice sheet may respond to changes in global atmospheric and ocean circulations on timescales measured from years to millennia.

Much Antarctic climate research focuses on sea ice in the region. When circumpolar sea ice becomes fixed during the winter and spring seasons, that ice zone effectively doubles the size of the continent. But in summer the sea ice shrinks back to the continent's margin. This situation clearly affects local weather conditions and may well affect global climate.[44] International sea ice studies using satellites and ship-based observations can provide new data on heat exchange between the atmosphere and the ocean and hence about global climate change. The presence of sea ice strongly alters the radiation balance and the heat exchange between the ocean and atmosphere over most of the Southern Hemisphere. While varying in extent, concentration, thickness, and physical characteristics from year to year and season to season, these conditions affect and are affected by the circulation of the ocean. Considerable research data on these phenomena come from drifting buoy fleets and ship-based expeditions into the Weddell Sea.[45]

Antarctica's vital place in major planetary environmental systems was spotlighted in 1985 by the discovery of springtime depletion of stratospheric ozone in Antarctica.[46] Popularly known as the ozone hole, this phenomenon ranks among the most crucial scientific discoveries of the twentieth century.[47] At the same time, it underscores the critical importance of science in Antarctica.[48]

International interest has recently arisen over the possible climatic effects of increasing levels of so-called greenhouse gases (carbon dioxide, ozone, methane, and nitrogen oxides) and the predicted increase in the Earth's atmospheric temperature with unknown impacts on climate, sea level, terrestrial and aquatic biology, agricultural activity, and national economies. Such interest has underscored the salience of atmospheric-ocean gas exchange to climatic conditions and has revealed the rather poor knowledge about that relationship. Continued analysis of trace gases in the Antarctic atmosphere, which is far from pollution sources, might also contribute to the predictability of future climatic conditions.[49]

Ice cores taken from drilling deep into the Antarctic ice cap supply a paleoclimatic record of temperature (by measuring oxygen isotopes of the ice at different depths) and atmospheric contents (through chemical analysis of trapped air bubbles).[50] Such records, complemented by sedimentary studies drawn from glacial geomorphology, can furnish clearer impressions of what Earth's atmosphere was like millions of years ago and the extent to which industrialization processes have adversely affected global atmospheric conditions during the past two centuries.[51]

The size and attributes of the great ice sheet overlaying Antarctica are controlled by global climate conditions. Consequently, the stability of the Antarctic ice sheet attracts much scientific interest. If the ice sheet were to melt completely, the world's sea level would rise some sixty meters, enough to flood many world cities and most islands. That scenario suggests the need to study the mass balance of the ice sheet and interactions between ice shelves, the ice sheet, and the ocean.[52] Such investigations of ice-mass balance and thermal dynamics in the Antarctic remain important for understanding and predicting mass changes at the continent's edge, which might produce considerable alterations in global sea level and important consequences for the global climate.[53] No less important is research into the potential impacts of climate change on Antarctic marine life.[54]

Study of the physical and chemical oceanography of the southern polar seas clarifies the interaction between the world ocean with the atmosphere. The Southern Ocean joins with the southern reaches of the Atlantic, Pacific, and Indian Oceans, and their circulation patterns mix. The colder Antarctic seas absorb atmospheric gases and transport them to deep water for recirculation. The interaction of carbon dioxide and sink-bottom water could be a crucial consideration in future global climate change, and in this regard, much oceanographic data remains to be collected. Chemical and physical oceanography can be analyzed by remote sensing, particularly by focusing on iceberg behavior, current movement, water temperature, chemistry, density and distribution, surface topography, and ice distribution throughout the southern seas.[55] There is no question that understanding oceanography is vital for understanding the nuances of Antarctic marine environment and therefore becomes critical for CCAMLR's management of the Southern Ocean's ecosystem.[56]

Glaciology

Glaciology examines characteristics and dynamics of the Antarctic ice sheet, glaciers, ice streams and ice shelves, sea ice, and pack ice. Such research requires not only fieldwork on the Antarctic ice cap but also deployment of automatic weather stations, airborne radar ice surveys, and remote sensing from satellites. Antarctic glaciological studies secure data on the distribution and depletion of the ice cap and the rates at which ice structures are formed; the potential hazards to ice formation posed by human activities on the continent and along its margins; and the cumulative atmospheric impacts of the greenhouse effect set in historical perspective over millennia.[57]

Antarctic glacier studies supply data on the mass balance of the ice sheet, which enables better evaluation of its influence on sea-level change over a timescale of decades, centuries, and millennia. Studies of iceberg melting can indicate melting rates for Antarctic ice shelves as a consequence of global warming. Such glacial research will undoubtedly also be useful in determining whether, when, and where calved icebergs might be harvested as a potential source of fresh water.[58]

Antarctica supplies a unique laboratory for studying continental glaciation and the formation and influence of Antarctic bottom water on world climate. The Antarctic ice sheet, because of its remoteness, contains records of the atmosphere's overall composition and its levels of pollution. The concentration of meteorites and cosmic dust in areas of the ice sheet holds great interest for cosmologists as well.[59]

Marine Geology

Research into the geology and geophysics of the Southern Ocean's sea floor can yield insights into oceanographic and paleoclimatic change in sedimentary rocks on Antarctica's continental margins and in the deep circumpolar ocean basins. The evidence on the continental margins was left by the advance and retreat of Antarctica's massive continental ice sheet. Research by international ocean drilling programs, which recover rock cores and obtain sediments and fossil samples, can help explain the geological evolution of circumpolar ocean basins and continental margins.

These studies provide valuable clues to the evolution of the Antarctic environment and the organisms living in it over time. Such science uses techniques of gravity, seismology, and magnetics to reveal characteristics of the Earth's deep crust, mantle movements, and continent formation. Airborne-conducted magnetic, gravity, and ice radar surveys assist in learning more about geological composition, structure, and evolution of the continent, as well as the structure and dynamics of the great ice sheet.[60]

Cosmology

Antarctica holds importance for outer space studies as well. Cosmic rays are particles from space that enter Earth's atmosphere and are influenced by its magnetic field. Because of special attributes of Earth's magnetic field, the polar regions are particularly well suited for observing cosmic rays. Cosmic rays are the only material source of information from the universe outside our own galaxy. Hence, their study is significant for astronomy.[61]

Features in the upper atmosphere (ranging from 70 to 250 kilometers) and the ionosphere (from 80 to 450 kilometers) can also be more readily analyzed in the Antarctic. The effects of solar winds, the global magnetic field, and electrical field dynamics make polar research on the upper atmosphere especially valuable. The ionosphere, important for high frequency radio communication, is strongly influenced by solar disturbances that produce auroras and other electrical phenomena. Antarctic science might yield clues to the nature of solar-terrestrial relations and natural plasmas, as well as clarify the character of atmospheric circulation patterns and global temperature distribution.[62] In addition, more than one-third of the meteorites available for study have been discovered on Antarctica's inland ice plateau, where the movement of glaciers has pushed rock ridges containing this prehistoric spacefall to the surface.[63]

THE ANTARCTIC MARINE ECOSYSTEM

The world ocean's ecosystem is strongly influenced by the Antarctic marine biosphere, the balance of which already has been disturbed by past exploitation of whales and seals. Marine biological research yielding information on the Southern Ocean's ecosystem can be used by CCAMLR and other international agencies to improve their stewardship of the Antarctic commons.

True Antarctic biota are found south of the Antarctic Convergence (or Polar Front). This biological boundary runs circumpolar about 50° south latitude where cold, northward flowing surface waters meet warmer, southward flowing waters of the Atlantic, Pacific, and Indian Oceans. Herein lies a paradox of the Antarctic seas. On the one hand, the Southern Ocean contains the world's windiest and most turbulent waters; because of this, key primary phytoplankon producers are not able to make optimal use of solar energy. Consequently, levels of primary production are not much higher than in other oceans. On the other hand, despite this, higher levels of marine life—especially seabirds, whales, and seals—are found in profuse concentrations. This contradictory situation may be explained in part by the Antarctic Convergence's influence in nutrient cycling. That is, the Convergence creates a tremendous upwelling of nutrients, so that primary producers are able to proliferate and create greater food supplies, especially krill, for higher species.[64]

The marine biology of the Southern Ocean is the focus of much scientific research today, and for good reason. Krill is the principal prey species in the Southern Ocean ecosystem, and squid, fish, seabirds, seals, and whales are dependent on krill stocks. More study of the Antarctic marine ecosystem is necessary in order to learn more about krill stocks and their relationships to krill consumers. These assessments must be performed not only to appreciate the biology of the Southern Ocean but also to help CCAMLR in its effort to conserve and manage the Southern Ocean's ecosystem. More research is needed on the behavior, ecology, physiology, and biochemistry of krill, as well as on the impact that ozone depletion is having on the krill-based food chain, so that the distribution, abundance, reproduction, and swarming behavior of this building-block species can be better understood.[65]

Krill consumers likewise merit more scientific attention. Research should be conducted on how fish have adapted physiologically and biochemically to Antarctic conditions, as well as the ecological place of seabirds as predators of Antarctic marine resources, especially krill. Similar studies on seals, especially their population structure and dynamics, social organizations, and feeding behavior, would also be useful.[66]

Science permeates CCAMLR's research program, which ultimately seeks to obtain data necessary for adopting policies that can ensure the long-term well-being of living resources within the Convention area. Toward this ambition, scientists strive to improve knowledge about the structure and functioning of the marine ecosystem. They aim to develop techniques and procedures that can more closely examine different harvest levels and management strategies. Plainly put, CCAMLR requires that the basic biology of key species in the Antarctic ecosystem be carefully and constantly examined, and certain questions answered. The existence, abundance, and distribution of key prey species (i.e., krill and seals) likely to be harvested must be determined and annual variations in these categories estimated. The behavioral relationships between prey and predators and between species competing for the same food source must be clarified. Science supplies the only means for answering all these questions.

Alternative methods of managing the southern marine ecosystem must also be considered by governments interested in the Antarctic. In this regard, scientists are studying and developing techniques for monitoring the effects of harvesting on dependent and related species. Key research seeks to determine if relationships exist between the ocean's composition and the distribution of krill and phytoplankton. These studies are focusing on the internal structure of krill swarms, the winter distribution of krill and their larvae, the behavioral ecology of krill larvae, the life cycle of krill, the foraging ranges of major predators, the detailed distribution of prey species within range of those foragers, the role of fish in the ecosystem as predators of krill, and the population dynamics and stock assessment of krill and fish.[67]

As noted earlier, three international legal agreements regulate the management of marine living resources in Antarctic waters: (1) the International Whaling Convention, which applies to whaling activities worldwide; (2) the Seals Convention, which applies to all seals found south of 60° south latitude; and (3) the Convention on Antarctic Marine Living Resources (CCAMLR), which applies to all finfish, mollusca, crustacea, and other species of living organisms, including birds, found south of the Antarctic Convergence. Of these, CCAMLR retains the most pervasive significance for biological science in the Antarctic marine commons.

Several international programs are relevant for marine biology under CCAMLR. The SCAR Working Group on Biology coordinates CCAMLR programs with other SCAR biology activities. SCAR, along with the Scientific Committee on Oceanographic Research (SCOR), has established a group of Specialists on Southern Ocean Ecology to identify important topics in Antarctic marine ecology for cooperative, interdisciplinary study. The Antarctic Sea Ice Zone Project (ASIZP) was formed by SCOR and cosponsored by SCAR to study the ecology of sea ice. This research group reviews sea-ice biology and the chemical and physical properties of sea ice in the Antarctic. Finally, the World Ocean Circulation Experiment, the main international program studying dynamics of the marine environment, assists CCAMLR by linking the implications of biological activities in the Southern Ocean to the global context.[68]

Considerable scientific effort is devoted to realizing CCAMLR's fundamental objectives, namely: to prevent the decrease of any harvested population below a level which can ensure the greatest net annual increment (i.e., to maintain maximum sustainable yield); to maintain the ecological relationships between harvested, dependent, and related populations of Antarctic marine living resources and to restore depleted populations to acceptable levels as defined above; and to prevent, or minimize the risk of, changes in the marine ecosystem that are not potentially reversible in two or three decades, with the aim of making possible sustained development and conservation of Antarctic marine living resources.[69]

Estimates of krill abundance and annual variations in population numbers are thus critical to CCAMLR's operation. But the swarming nature of krill and special techniques developed for harvesting make traditional methods of stock assessment inapplicable. The Scientific Committee has launched long-term plans for monitoring the marine ecosystem. A program is under way to monitor predator species in order to assess their variability over time and space. The Working Group for the CCAMLR Ecosystem Monitoring Program (WG-CEMP) focuses on key species in that part of the food chain most dependent on krill (i.e., crabeater seals and penguins). This Working Group has also decided on subareas around Antarctica which qualify as more discrete research sites. The gyre around Pridtz Bay (55°–85° east latitude) is designated the priority study site. The CEMP program intends to detect and record significant changes in critical components of that local ecosystem. That information can then be used as the basis for formulating more effective strategies and measures to conserve Antarctic marine living resources. This is a microcosm of CCAMLR's ecosystem approach to marine environmental management.[70]

Science and Environmental Management

Effective management and protection of the Antarctic environment are not possible without the understanding lent by Antarctic science. But the growth in human activities that can disturb or damage the Antarctic environment presents science with a new challenge in environmental management. Human disturbance is caused by the exploitation of resources and impacts caused by the human presence, especially when concentrated in small areas.

Human activities in Antarctica bring potential environmental problems. Such problems may be magnified as more scientific activities increase pressures on the continent. An appropriate response to these developments thus requires greater scientific analysis of the Antarctic environment. To this end, priority research objectives for environmental management might include: developing an effective baseline monitoring system; establishing key sites and species conserved within an enhanced protected areas network; developing regional environmental plans and implementation for major station areas; adopting improved environmental impact statement procedures for scientific sites and operations; introducing an effective code of conduct for regulating tourism and private expeditions; and improving training of personnel and deployment of environmental officers at main stations and field sites.[71]

The most serious environmental threats within the Antarctic Treaty area come from the logistical activities that support scientific research. Transportation, handling and use of fuels, and waste disposal are essential for the logistics system, but they constitute environmental hazards. Containment against spills and leak protection for fuel stored in drums or tanks are particularly difficult. The introduction of standardized steel tanks can reduce the number of refillings and reloading, thus decreasing the risks of accidents and leaks. Less harmful fuels with lower sulphur and particulate content might also reduce the toxic severity of spills. Waste management today in the polar South ultimately aims to: (1) remove solid wastes from Antarctica; (2) phase out open-air burning and dumping of wastes; and (3) end the disposal of empty fuel drums.[72]

Scientific research not only eases the impact of human activity in Antarctica, it also permits the human presence on the continent to be maintained in a more cost-effective manner. In most cases the Antarctic Treaty mandates the free exchange of scientific information. Difficulties can arise, however, when data obtained are not merely of scientific value but also have potential economic value. For instance, in the case of CCAMLR scientific advances and applications for conservation management measures were sometimes frustrated during the 1980s when a few fishing governments refused to release data on the distribution of their fishing fleets and the scientific details of krill and fish catches. Such obstructions frustrated the work of the CCAMLR's Scientific Committee for nearly a decade. Another example where the exchange of scientific data was less than fully achieved concerned marine seismic geophysical data. During the 1980s some governments conducted surveys of sedimentary basins that might hold potential value for hydrocarbon exploration. While these surveys were carried out under the guise of scientific research, their findings have yet to be freely released.

TOURISM

Tourists are visitors not associated officially with any national Antarctic program. Most are fare-paying passengers traveling with tour operators, although some are private expedition members.[73] Tourism has not yet greatly affected Antarctica, though it has recently grown considerably. Over the past thirty-five years nearly one hundred thousand tourists have visited Antarctica,[74] either by air—by overflying the continent or landing at various sites—or by cruise ship and private vessels.[75]

Airborne tourism involves "flightseeing," in which sightseers are flown in groups over the continent. On select occasions independent adventurers make brief visits in light aircraft and land-based tourists are flown in on group tours. From 1977 to 1980 Quantas and Air New Zealand carried some 11,000 passengers on forty-four Antarctic overflight tours.[76] These air tours became less popular after the crash of an Air New Zealand DC-10 on Mount Erebus in November 1979, which killed all 257 passengers and crew on board.[77] Currently the Chileans provide the only regular tourist air link with Antarctica, flying from Punta Arenas to Teninete Rodolfo Marsh base on King George Island. This link uses C-130 aircraft, which typically carry some forty tourists on each trip.[78]

Shipborne tourism is currently the most popular way to visit Antarctica, and most tourists sailing to Antarctica depart from ports in South America or New Zealand. Since 1957 more than 70,000 tourists have come by ship.[79] Since the early 1980s seaborne visitors have accounted for more than 95 percent of all visitors.[80] Since 1991, interestingly enough, the number of tourists has exceeded the number of personnel involved in scientific activities on the continent.[81] In 1995/96, 9,200 tourists visited the Antarctic,[82] but the estimate for 1996/97 is upwards of 11,000, the largest number ever.[83]

The region in Antarctica most frequently visited is the Antarctic Peninsula. The popularity of this area can be explained by its closeness to South American ports, its relatively milder summer climate, the abundance of diverse wildlife there, the relative freedom from pack-ice conditions along the coast, and its having the largest concentration of Antarctic research stations, which most tourists visit.[84]

REGULATION OF TOURISM

No legally binding rules exist to ensure that all tour operators will take steps to protect the Antarctic environment from potential harm. As world tourism grows, tour operators must focus greater attention on Antarctica, particularly on devising strategies to protect the environment. The Antarctic Treaty System supplies the logical legal forum for meeting this need. The Antarctic Treaty implicitly distinguishes between two groups of persons in the Antarctic. The first group includes observers, scientific personnel, and staff members accompanying these people.[85] The second group includes all "other persons" in Antarctica.[86] This "others" category would cover visiting family members, journalists, nongovernmental expeditions, VIP visitors, and, of course, tourists.

There are no universally sanctioned enforcement measures in any provisions of the ATS agreements. Further, tourism is not mentioned specifically in the Antarctic Treaty text, and no instrument within the ATS contains rules precluding the entry of tourists, or any other visitors, into the treaty area. Thus, the ATS might appear deficient as regards tourism. One might infer that tourism requires specialized regulation to prevent its having any impacts upon scientific activity or the Antarctic environment. But that would be a rash conclusion. Tourist activities in the Antarctic have not escaped regulation under the Antarctic Treaty System. A number of ATCM recommendations have been adopted concerning tourism in the region and the need to set out rules and guidelines to ensure safe conservation practices on land and at sea.

Early ATCM recommendations expressed concern that the effects of tourist activities might "prejudice the conduct of scientific research, conservation of fauna and flora and the operation of scientific stations."[87] Accordingly, the recommendations required that notice of tourist and nongovernmental expedition activities be given in advance to government stations that might be visited and that permission be secured from those governments for such visits.[88] More specific attention to tourism came from the ATCPs in 1970, largely prompted by concern that visitors "can have lasting and harmful effects on scientific programmes, on the Antarctic environment, particularly in Specially Protected Areas, and on historic monuments."[89] Recommendation VI-7 stipulated that governments should "exert appropriate efforts" to ensure that tourists and other visitors do not engage in acts contrary to the principles and purposes of the Antarctic Treaty.[90] Concern over "self sufficiency and prior notification" by visitors to stations, as well as their possible harmful effects on Antarctic environment, led the ATCPs in 1972 to adopt Recommendation VII-4. This measure advocated that the ATCPs consult on a statement of accepted practices for tourists and designate "an adequate number of areas of interest" as prospective visitation sites.[91] The ATCPs for the first time in this recommendation asserted that provisions in the Antarctic Treaty and in the Agreed Measures apply "in practice to visitors who are not sponsored by Consultative Parties, as well as to tourists."[92]

The threshold regulatory ATCP action on tourism came in 1975. Recommendation VIII-9 requested that all tourist group organizers visit only stations where permission had been granted beforehand and land only within Areas of Special Tourist Interests, which were designated in an appended list. The recommendation also required that tourist operators report to their governments their activities within the treaty area.[93]

The most significant aspect of this ATCM recommendation, however, was its attachment of three annexes: Annex A is a "Statement of accepted principles and the relevant provisions of the Antarctic Treaty" that stipulates guidelines for visitors to the Antarctic. It provides general explanations for why the Antarctic commons environment should be protected and the wildlife there conserved, asserts the need to protect historic monuments and sites of specific scientific interest, and enumerates the various responsibilities of tour group organizers planning to visit scientific stations. Five additional annexes attached to Annex A lay out specially protected areas, a code of conduct for Antarctic expeditions and station activities relating to waste disposal, a list of historic monuments, sites of selected scientific interest, and the standard format for reporting annual exchange of information, respectively. In addition, an attached statement of "Guidance for Visitors to the Antarctic" lists dos and don'ts that contribute to preserving the unique Antarctic environment.[94] Annex B announces the ATCPs' intention to list Areas of Special Tourist Interest (albeit none have yet been designated), and Annex C lists items to be reported by tour organizers (e.g., name and nationality of ship, name of captain, number of tourists, sites and dates of landing, and number of persons landed on each occasion).

Recommendation VIII-9 sets out the framework for tourist activities in the Antarctic. The ATCPs have the fundamental obligation to ensure that their nationals observe the provisions of the ATS agreements. Treaty parties are responsible for making visitors and tour operators aware of relevant Antarctic Treaty provisions and recommendations and for ensuring that tourists do not commit actions contrary to measures adopted by the ATCPs. Visitors are not to prejudice scientific research activities, and permission is required for visits to scientific bases. The concern of the ATCPs is to make tourism compatible with conservation of the environment, protection of fauna and flora, and preservation of specially protected areas, specially protected species, and historic monuments.

ATCM recommendations on tourism do respond to tourist activity in the Antarctic commons, but only in an ad hoc fashion. Yet, taken in the aggregate, these recommendations carry legal weight tantamount to a comprehensive set of agreed measures on tourist activities. If such an instrument explicitly restated this set of principles, it would consolidate ATS policies on tourism that are now scattered within the system, facilitating their comprehension and accessibility. This would permit a more comprehensive regulatory regime covering all aspects of tourism.

TOURISM AND THE MADRID PROTOCOL

The Madrid Protocol designates Antarctica as a natural reserve, devoted to peace and science. It establishes environmental principles for the conduct of all activities, prohibits all activity relating to mineral resources other than scientific research, and subjects all activities to prior assessment of potential environmental impacts. For these reasons, the Madrid Protocol marks an important step toward regulation of tourism in the Antarctic, although it stops short of doing so directly. Under the Protocol tourism is not treated as a special issue but rather as one of many challenges to the region's environment.[95] The ATS provides the forum for developing strategies to protect Antarctica from the effects of human activity, and cooperation between tour operators and ATCPs is thus essential to the development of measures aimed at regulating the Antarctic tourist industry.

Although the Madrid Protocol covers all human activity in Antarctica, not just tourist activities, Article 3 sets out environmental principles that can be applied to Antarctic tourism.[96] The principles on cooperation in Article 6 (which include provision of relevant information on potential environmental risks and assistance to minimize accidents that might damage the ecosystem) are likewise applicable to tourism. Provisions regarding inspection ("to promote protection of the Antarctic environment . . . and ensure compliance with this Protocol") and emergency response action ("to such emergencies which might arise in the performance of scientific research programmes, tourism, and all other governmental and non-governmental activities in the Antarctic Treaty area for which advance notice is required under Article VII(5) of the Antarctic Treaty") are also applicable to tourist activities.[97]

All of the Protocol's annexes as well can be applied to tourist activities in the Antarctic Treaty area. Each ATCP government is obligated to ensure that environmental assessment procedures in the Protocol's Annex I are applied to tourism and to all other nongovernmental activities in the treaty area. The Committee on Environmental Protection has functions regulating tourism, including furnishing advice on the "means of minimising or mitigating environmental impacts of activities in the Antarctic Treaty area" and "the operation and elaboration of the Antarctic Protected Area System."[98] All activities in the Antarctic, including tourism, should be assessed for their possible effects on the environment.[99]

Annex II, which restates and strengthens the Agreed Measures on Antarctic Flora and Fauna, particularly affects tourist activities through those provisions that concern harmful interference and the introduction of nonindigenous species. Tourists are prohibited from killing, handling, molesting, or capturing native birds and seals or damaging plant life,[100] and certain "Specially Protected Species" of seals are accorded extra protection by the ATCPs.[101] Also relevant for tourists are strict prohibitions on introducing nonnative species of animals or plants into the Antarctic Treaty area. In addition, precautions are required to ensure that tourists do not introduce any foreign microorganisms (i.e., viruses, bacteria, parasites, yeasts, or fungi) into the area.[102]

Annex III deals with waste disposal and management. This annex imposes on parties the duty "to reduce as far as practicable" the amount of waste produced or disposed of in the Antarctic so as to minimize impacts on the environment. It concomitantly asserts the obligation on governments to remove from Antarctica, "to the maximum extent possible," any wastes that they may produce.[103] This annex, too, applies to tourist activities, particularly to ship-based tourism where waste management becomes essential. But weaknesses in this annex are the key qualifying phrases "to reduce as far as practicable" and "to the maximum extent possible." No specification, regrettably, is provided to indicate when or how tourist vessels are to determine when those two critical thresholds are reached. Nor is any special body assigned to assess or monitor whether provisions are being obeyed by tourist agencies registered to an ATCP government.

Annex IV on the Prevention of Marine Pollution applies to each state party, to ships flying its flag, and to any other ship engaged in or supporting its Antarctic operations in the Antarctica Treaty area.[104] Tourist vessels registered in ATCP states are legally affected by Annex IV in several ways. For one, this annex prohibits tourist vessels from discharging into the sea oil or oily mixtures, except as permitted by MARPOL.

Second, tourist vessels may not discharge into the sea any noxious liquid substance, or any other chemical or other substances, in quantities that are harmful to the marine environment, and they may not dispose into the sea any garbage or plastics.[105] Third, all parties are required to take into account the objectives of the annex in the design, construction, manning, and equipment of ships engaged in or supporting Antarctic operations.[106] Tourist ships would fall under this stipulation.

Annex V on area protection and management was added to the Protocol to reorganize and improve the system of Antarctic protected areas. The rapid growth of tourism during the 1980s undoubtedly contributed to the need for these provisions. Accordingly, Annex V permits any area in Antarctica, inclusive of marine areas, to be designated an Antarctic Specially Protected Area (ASPA) or an Antarctic Specially Managed Area (ASMA). Activities by tourists in these areas may be prohibited, restricted, or managed in accordance with management plans under the annex. Tourist access to various areas may also be restricted or forbidden in accordance with specific regulations in the annex.

Annex V highlights several concerns. Among them are needs for regulating tourist activities on land, registration and licensing of shipping, the availability of emergency rescue services, creation of special tourist areas, and the integration of existing regulations into a single code. Under the Protocol, special tourist sites could be treated as Antarctic Specially Managed Areas to ensure tight control over activities there. Management plans would have to be drafted that stipulate tourism as the principal objective of setting a particular area aside.

The Madrid Protocol stands out as the most comprehensive regulatory regime for protecting the Antarctic environment yet adopted by the ATS. Even so, some aspects of tourism remain insufficiently addressed by the Protocol and its annexes. The Protocol contains gaps pertaining to safety, search and rescue expenses, insurance and liability, and disruption of scientific programs. Serious consideration was, therefore, given by the ATCPs throughout 1992 and 1993 to the possible need for a special annex on tourism to supplement the Protocol.[107] After careful deliberation, however, the ATCPs opted not to adopt such an annex.

In April 1994, at the XVIIIth ATCM in Kyoto, Japan, it was decided that the Protocol explicitly applied to all activities in Antarctica, both governmental and nongovernmental. The agreement does not distinguish between types of operators, but rather establishes a system in which the acceptability of activities is evaluated based on their potential for causing environmental harm. The ATCPs concluded that no special provisions in an annex should single out any one group. Hence, tourism would be treated as an Antarctic activity, subject to the broad body of rules and regulations in the Protocol and other ATS instruments.[108]

In addition, the ATCPs in Kyoto adopted Recommendation XVIII-1, which acknowledged the increasing development of tourist activities in the Antarctic and the concomitant need to provide practical guidance on planning and making visits to the area. The measure simply recommended that ATCP governments circulate "widely and as quickly as possible" the Guidance to Visitors to the Antarctic and the Guidance for Those Organising and Conducting Tourism and Non-governmental Activities in the Antarctic, both of which had also been agreed upon in Kyoto. Governments also were to urge their visitors and tour operators "to act in accordance with the annexed guidelines consistent with the relevant provisions of their applicable law."[109] Recommendation XVIII-I sets out key obligations and procedures to be followed by tour operators, which have subsequently been adopted by most tour companies as essential guidelines for their operations in the Antarctic.[110]

SAFETY ISSUES

Antarctica is a hazardous place to visit. Given the harsh conditions, accidents and mechanical problems are practically inevitable. Airborne tourism proved fatal in the 1979 Mount Erebus air disaster, as previously mentioned. More than fifty U.S. aircraft have been destroyed since 1960, and in 1988 eight American tourists were killed while attempting to land at Chile's Teniente Rodolfo Marsh base.

Mechanical breakdowns, strandings, and groundings of ships have also occurred—thus far, fortunately, with little loss of life. In 1968 the *Magga Dan*, under tourist charter, ran aground on a shoal off Ross Island and had to be towed off by the U.S. icebreaker *Westwind*.[111] The next year the Chilean naval transport *Aquiles* attempted to place passengers ashore on a small island off Palmer Station, but after quickly rising winds forced the operation to be abandoned, a U.S. boat had to take the tourists to their base.[112] The *Lindblad Explorer* ran aground in Admiralty Bay, King George Island in 1972, and passengers had to be transported to Punta Arenas by the Chilean navy.[113]

The grounding in 1989 of the Argentine naval supply ship *Bahia Paraiso*, which was carrying 81 fare-paying passengers, might well have been more costly in lives lost had not considerable resources of the U.S.

Antarctic Program at Palmer Station been mobilized for the immediate rescue, feeding, and sheltering of 300 passengers and crew. This emergency relief operation came at the expense of ongoing research projects, and a 250,000-gallon slick of diesel oil inflicted high mortality rates on bird colonies at the peak breeding season.[114] Cruise ships have suffered occasional damage, but no cruise vessel has yet been lost.

The safety of ships raises several issues. Tour groups need to be entirely self-sufficient, since safety remains the chief responsibility of the tour operator. Any search-and-rescue mission conducted by ATCPs on behalf of tourists endangers personnel from the Antarctic station providing emergency assistance, as well as putting rescue team members at risk. Consultative Party governments do not assume legal responsibility or liability for accidents or injuries sustained by visitors and nongovernmental expeditions to Antarctica. A government might incur responsibility, however, if it failed to provide humanitarian assistance to visitors in distress when aid was reasonably possible under the circumstances. In any event, Antarctica remains a continent of vastly dispersed human populations. Unless an accident occurs relatively near a station, search-and-rescue operations cannot reach stranded parties without exorbitant expenditures in time and resources.

Some accidents can result from using vessels not designed or suitable for Antarctic conditions. Antarctic tourist vessels are presently not required by any registration body to be ice-rated for operations in Antarctic waters. Ice-rating is often obtained without strict controls from various shipping societies for insurance and other purposes,[115] a pattern that can lead to unsafe practices. Many different rating authorities exist, with disparate rating standards. There is no international body to ensure that all Antarctic tour operators have access to the same information, much less to guarantee that uniform standards are applied to all tourist vessels sailing in Antarctic waters. The point must be made, however, that the tourist ship industry has maintained a remarkable safety record in the Antarctic. To date, no vessel solely dedicated to tourism has been lost or caused serious environmental damage while visiting the region.

DISRUPTION OF SCIENTIFIC PROGRAMS

Tourism is often perceived as a threat to Antarctica's role as a continent for science, particularly as tourist visits to bases persist in interrupting research programs. Base personnel must take the time to show tourists around the station; additionally, emergency assistance to tourists or vessels can disrupt carefully planned logistical programs. Tour operators can reduce their intrusion by keeping communication lines open, coordinating station visits well in advance, and notifying ATCP governments of any change in their visitation plans. Uncontrolled tourist activities could diminish the scientific value of certain areas and damage specific sites used for prolonged scientific studies.

Access to a station remains subject to permission of the government concerned. During visits to a station all persons, regardless of nationality, come under the authority of the station commander. Antarctic Treaty governments are also obliged to withhold permission to visit unless the tour organizer gives assurance of compliance with the rules and regulations of ATS.[116]

ENVIRONMENTAL ISSUES

Antarctic tourists are only a small group of "commercial visitors" to Antarctica. Even so, their numbers have increased so dramatically within the past decade that their presence warrants special attention. Moreover, with advances in polar technology and a demonstrated public desire to visit the cold continent, more commercial tourist entrepreneurs have been drawn to the area's tourism market.[117] With more visitors coming to the Antarctic, greater impacts will be felt on indigenous ecosystems.

Antarctic tourism has both positive and negative ramifications for the region's environment. On the positive side, continued tourism publicly highlights the need for continued protection of the region. Visitors who experience the area's magnificent scenery and wildlife gain profound appreciation for Antarctica's global importance. Tourism also fosters public awareness about the Antarctic commons. Visitors can become public relations ambassadors who can advocate conservation of the Antarctic commons and bolster political support for the ATS regime and for conducting scientific activities there. The presence of tourist vessels also improves transportation and communication capabilities throughout the south polar region.

Certain negative effects accompany tourists as well. For example, shipborne tourism poses serious environmental risks to the Antarctic commons, and at present cruise ships rank as the most popular means for visiting the area.[118] Cruise travel in south polar waters puts pressure on the environment, since it coincides with peak breeding seasons for much of Antarctica's wildlife, a period when disturbances can have serious consequences. In addition, visitors bring along general pollution, as cruise ships introduce sewage, waste, oil, fuels, and noise into the environment. Nonindigenous soils, microbes, plants, and animals also accompany visitors. Other serious costs of tourism include tramping of vegetation, uncontrolled dumping of solid and liquid wastes in inshore waters, unscientific collection of materials, and disruption of scientific programs and routines at stations. There is also the potential for environmental hazards from accidents, requiring cleanup and perhaps even search-and-rescue operations, which can be costly and time-consuming.[119] Ship-based tourism remains heavily reliant upon support from national science programs in the event of accidents or the need for search-and-rescue assistance.

Tourism usually causes environmental harm via one of three activities: (1) shipboard observation, which involves cruising or anchoring at various sites and looking for whales, seals, and seabirds; (2) small-boat operations, such as ferrying groups ashore in zodiacs; and (3) land excursions, such as visits to research stations and wildlife areas not inhabited by humans. The first two are not likely to perpetrate much environmental damage, other than disposal of wastes. Provided no disaster occurs, such as with the *Bahia Paraiso,* the severest environmental impacts are usually felt when tourists go ashore. During the past decade the Antarctic Treaty Consultative Parties have sensibly sought to create a regulatory regime for tour operators before major problems occur.

Overflights seem to put only little pressure on the environment, since aircraft operate at fairly high altitudes and tend not to disturb wildlife.[120] While the number of overflight passengers is not significant, however, the number of flights is.[121] Increased numbers of tourists arriving at scientific stations on airborne flights could pose considerable problems, since landing on the ice involves serious risks and dangers. The lack of any international air traffic control and the availability of only a few navigational aids make Antarctic landings more unpredictable and hazardous than those on other continents.[122] The major environmental impacts from landing flights include exhaust from engines, disturbance and panic of wildlife from the noise of aircraft, and accidents and spills from fuel dumps and storage of fuel supplies on the continent.[123]

The prospect of Antarctic tourism generates frightening images of environmental damage, including littering and careless disposal of wastes. In actuality, however, these problems are more accurately attributed to ATCP-contracted supply ships than to tourist vessels.[124]

Tourists in the Antarctic tend to be responsible, though enthusiastic cleanup activities on beaches by visitors can inadvertently remove valuable artifacts as well as waste debris.[125] In addition, tourists may disturb and disrupt Antarctic fauna. Nesting birds and basking seals are especially vulnerable. When groups of tourists intrude upon small colonies of animals, exciting and confusing them, the result can be increased anxiety (usually among penguins) and disruption of whole breeding colonies.[126] In fact, tourists and other visitors have deliberately disturbed nesting penguins in order to get "action" photographs.[127]

Tourism also potentially threatens the health and diversity of fragile Antarctic flora. The scarcity of ice-free areas in Antarctica, coupled with the difficulty of protecting Antarctica flora, means that where vegetation has arisen it comes under considerable pressure from human visitors. A footprint on a delicate moss bed may still be visible ten years later, and the moss may take a century to regenerate. Or that footprint may be further accentuated by wind, leading to destruction of the entire plant community.[128] Indeed, damage to moss mats and hummocks from trampling can already be seen in areas of the Antarctic Peninsula.[129]

Maintaining biological and geophysical processes without disturbance is critical for preserving a wilderness. In Antarctica such protection is essential to ensure local ecological stability and to provide scientific opportunities that are not available elsewhere. The remoteness, the dearth of human interference, the intensely pristine nature of the Antarctic—these wilderness values are likely to become more important for humans in the foreseeable future. Degradation of such wilderness qualities due to human activities could adversely impact science and tourism alike.[130]

NON-ATS TOURIST REMEDIES

Concern over possible harmful effects in the Antarctic by tourist activities has fostered noteworthy efforts at self-policing within the tourist industry. In August 1991 the International Association of Antarctica Tour Operators (IAATO) was formed by the seven commercial tour operators that were responsible for carrying most tourists to Antarctica. The purpose of IAATO is "to advocate, promote and practice safe and environmentally responsible private sector travel to the Antarctic" and to promote closer industry cooperation.[131] By 1997 membership in IAATO had grown to twelve full and nine associate members in the United States, Germany, the United Kingdom, Australia, Canada, New Zealand, Japan, Chile, and the Netherlands.[132]

IAATO members are expected to abide by a mutually agreed upon set of environmental standards and a code of conduct for Antarctic tourist visits.[133] In addition, these tour operators are supposed to observe regulations in MARPOL, SOLAS, and other national and international instruments. IAATO members publicly proclaim that their tourist operations in Antarctica promote environmental education, public support for Antarctica, and scientific research.[134] The organized tour industry has, in fact, acknowledged that environmental responsibility is essential as a commercial asset for sustaining an Antarctic tourism industry.

IAATO's "Guidelines of Conduct for Antarctica Visitors" is a model of straightforward, simple rules for tourist behavior in the polar South. Broad rules are stated, with specific examples given to make those rules effective. For instance, "Do Not Disturb, Harass, or Interfere with the Wildlife" lists among its subrules never to touch the animals, to maintain a distance of at least fifteen feet from penguins and nesting birds (and fifty feet from fur seals), to give the animals right-of-way, to keep noise to a minimum, and not to feed the animals. Other examples of major headings include "Do Not Walk on or Otherwise Damage the Fragile Plants, i.e., Lichens, Mosses, and Grasses"; "Leave Nothing Behind, and Take Only Memories and Photographs"; "Do Not Interfere with Protected Areas or Scientific Research"; and "Do Not Smoke during Shore Excursions."[135]

IAATO has adopted ATCM Recommendation XVIII-I (approved at the 1994 Kyoto Meeting) as its "Guidance for those Organising and Conducting Tourism and Non-Governmental Activities in the Antarctic." This pamphlet, intended to serve as the framework for Antarctic tour operators, directs members to comply with all requirements of agreements in the Antarctic Treaty System, especially the 1991 Madrid Protocol.[136] Key obligations of tour organizers and operators include prior notification of and reports on their activities to competent authorities of the ATCPs, assessment of potential environmental impact of their activities, provision of effective emergency response in the event of marine pollution, and prevention of the disposal and discharge of prohibited waste.[137] Other guidelines assert the need to educate the crew and passengers on specific ATS conservation requirements, to ensure the safety of tourist passengers, to give proper notice to all research stations, and to respect the work of scientists, as well as historic huts, markers, and monitoring devices. Responsibility is fixed on the tour operator "to ensure that no evidence of our visits remains behind. This includes garbage (of any kind), marine pollution, vandalism, etc. Litter must never be left ashore."[138]

SCAR performs a principal advisory role for tourist companies by offering expert advice on specially protected areas (SPAs) and sites of special scientific interest (SSSIs). One special contribution of SCAR to regulating tourism is its *Visitor's Introduction to the Antarctic*.[139] The Group of Specialists on Environmental Affairs and Conservation (GOSEAC), affiliated with SCAR, advises SCAR on scientific and other matters concerning conservation within SCAR's ambit of interest,[140] including tourism.

In 1988 the heads of National Antarctic Agencies established a Council of Managers of National Antarctic Programs (COMNAP) that is affiliated with SCAR.[141] The Council regularly reviews operations, exchanges information, and provides a forum to consider more timely and efficient responses to common issues affecting national Antarctic operators.[142] COMNAP has a Standing Committee on Antarctic Logistics and Operations (SCALOP), also founded in 1988, comprised of the operations and logistics managers of the ATCPs' national programs. SCALOP provides SCAR with advice on Antarctic operations and logistics, and also sponsors symposia that review and assess technological advances.[143] Such activities could furnish information and insights on questions affecting the tourism industry, particularly how tourists can travel more safely in the Antarctic.[144] In fact, COMNAP/SCALOP were directly linked with IAATO in mid-1992 so that detailed information exchanges could be made on various issues, including relations between scientific agencies and tourism.

The issue of state responsibility for tourism must still be resolved. Closer supervision of tourist activities by ATCP governments is necessary, and every tour operator with expert observers should be encouraged to report on its trips. ATCPs must work with tour operators and rely on their commitment to do the right thing. COMNAP might be used as a vehicle to maintain good will and foster cooperation. Representatives from IAATO might also be invited to attend sessions of ATCMs in which tourism policies are being discussed.

The ATCPs opted wisely in promoting a recommendation on tourism instead of a special annex on tourism. The activity was already generally covered by the Madrid Environmental Protocol, and it was neither practical nor prudent to separate tourism's effects from those of other human activities on the environment. A key weakness now, however, is that no agreed means are available by which to identify which government is responsible for monitoring and reporting on which tourist activities being conducted in the Antarctic. To rectify this situation, COMNAP could instigate planning for tourist activities, and GOSEAC and SCAR could help interpret the provisions relevant to tourism in all the Madrid Protocol's annexes. While no panacea, these arrangements would improve present uncertainties about tourist activities in the Antarctic.

The tourist industry is reluctant to accept international, or national, regulations, but the IAATO code of conduct only suggests and urges. The code is a list of *guidelines* for operations in the Antarctic that neither aggregates enforceable fiats nor furnishes binding obligations with punitive costs attached. Such guidelines are blanket recommendations, neither site-specific nor "inflexible to changing conditions."[145] Moreover, not every operator of tours to Antarctica is a member of IAATO. For example, during 1993 five tour companies that were not IAATO members carried nearly 1,950 passengers on twelve cruises to the Antarctic.[146]

Another problem concerns how to calculate the cumulative environmental impact of tourist activities in the Antarctic. Baseline information must be acquired before a comparative assessment can be made. The tourist industry, unfortunately, is not in the business of conducting baseline assessments.

Science and Tourism

The relationship between science and tourism in the Antarctic, as the preceding discussion suggests, has three dimensions. First, these activities can be in conflict. Confrontation occurs when tourist activities are detrimental to scientists and their programs. For example, tourists might disrupt and distract scientific personnel, place growing pressures on the Antarctic environment by increased visits to historic sites, contribute to the degradation of wilderness values, compromise the integrity of scientific research and monitoring operations, divert resources from scientific activities to accommodate interests of tourists, or redirect to assist tourists those logistical needs usually used by scientists.

Second, tourism and science can merely coexist. Coexistence occurs when tourists and scientists encounter one another in a restricted fashion that limits disruption. Given the remote, isolated, barren conditions in the Antarctic, tourists are sure to find scientists, and vice versa. And third, tourism and science can experience symbiosis. A symbiotic situation occurs when tourism and science are organized such that each activity derives benefits from the relationship. This is the preferred alternative because such integrated activities could have far-reaching benefits. Tourism can aid science, and scientists can generate good tourism. High among the positives are promotion of environmental awareness and support for Antarctic issues; political support for scientific activities; government cooperation in the regulation of tourism; coordinated environmental monitoring; and cooperation among governments, tour operators, and scientists on logistical needs.[147]

Environmental monitoring has become fundamental to both science and conservation in the Antarctic. Interestingly enough, up to now, monitoring suggests that scientific activities have caused considerably more disturbances to the Antarctic environment than have tourists. Degradation from scientific activities is often justified or overlooked as an inevitable consequence of an activity, or considered as acceptable because of the greater value of the science being conducted.[148] But the permissibility of such degradation by scientists in the Antarctic should narrow considerably once the Madrid Environmental Protocol enters into force.

Integrated management of organized tourism and government-sponsored science can benefit both activities. Antarctic tourism permits scientists to show nonscientists (on whom they depend for political and financial support) how worthwhile the work is that they do. By the same token, revenues from tourism and political influence from environmentally sensitive tourists may furnish useful media for promoting the cause of conservation in the Antarctic commons. There is a salient political dimension to tourism. The political basis for costly Antarctic science is widely recognized and often explicitly acknowledged in national program policies.[149] But herein lies an intriguing pair of paradoxes. First, tourism can bolster the political motivation to pursue science in Antarctica, and yet tourism might also jeopardize the very integrity of scientific investigation in the region. Second, science retains the capacity to answer many questions posed by tourists, but science can be so obtuse that it offends tourists. Each paradox can undercut the value of both science and tourism in the Antarctic. The plain hope is that science and tourism work symbiotically to educate and improve knowledge. In the Antarctic both activities can go forward, with neither suffering at the hands of the other.

THE BALANCE SHEET

All humans in the Antarctic, be they scientists or tourists, are visitors. Tourists are attracted to Antarctica for various reasons—the scenic beauty of the frozen landscape, the untouched quality of the environment, the abundant wildlife, historic interest, or personal ambition of visiting a place rarely seen. They may also have an interest in the operation of national stations and working conditions of scientists in Antarctica.

Like all tourism, the special opportunities available for visiting the Antarctic have evolved in response to customer demand, tour operator investment, improvements in technology, and changes in the tourism industry itself.[150] When compared to tourist flows elsewhere, Antarctic tourism represents but a tiny fraction. Still, tourism in the polar South is unique because of the region's environment, the legal framework for its administration, and the physical conditions that affect it.

As a wilderness area, Antarctica must not become overrun or overwhelmed by tourists. But at the same time, Antarctica as a global commons cannot be kept free from all human activities. Visitors are going to keep coming to Antarctica, and the question of wilderness management must be addressed. The rapid, unplanned, uncontrolled growth of tourism has already deteriorated wilderness values in other parts of the world, as tourists tend to destroy the very values that brought them to a spot in the first place.[151] That must not be permitted in the Antarctic.

Tourists become Antarctic ambassadors. These Antarctic visitors are often affluent and possibly politically influential, and they help create incentives for governments to maintain support for scientific efforts and conservation measures in Antarctica. Tourism promotes greater understanding of and appreciation for Antarctica's global importance and can promote the development of environmentally sensitive values and a more pervasive respect for nature and the place humans have in it.[152]

Antarctic tourism is thus a form of ecotourism. Ecotourism involves traveling to relatively undisturbed natural areas for purposes of admiring, studying, and enjoying scenery, flora, and fauna as well as cultural features in the area. Such tourist activity strives to promote greater understanding of cultural and natural history, while safeguarding the integrity of the ecosystem where it occurs and producing economic benefits that encourage conservation.[153] Antarctic ecotourists acquire an active and informed interest in the region's history, science, and natural setting. They acquire environmental consciousness and conscientiousness, attributes that are critical to preserving the environmental integrity of any global commons.[154]

CONCLUSION

Over four decades science has continued to motivate international cooperation among governments working in Antarctica. Scientific research remains the only means to attain Consultative Party status among Antarctic Treaty states and involvement in the Antarctic Treaty System. To date, science remains the only publicly acceptable basis for occupation (i.e., establishing a base or station) on the continent.

Scientific research for Antarctica benefits from the unique political situation there. The absence of national boundaries under the Antarctic Treaty facilitates large-scale cooperation in scientific programs. The exorbitant costs of supporting research in the harshest, coldest, remotest, most inhospitable region on Earth creates basic needs to share logistical support and to collaborate through interdisciplinary programs. The Antarctic Treaty with its family of agreements supplies the legal conduits through which these programs can be planned and carried out in an environmentally acceptable manner.

The Antarctic Treaty System is the dominant legal force in the Antarctic and affects all persons associated with states party to the treaty. Article I of that instrument, by recognizing the use of Antarctica for exclusively peaceful purposes, implicitly guarantees freedom of tourism. Article II assures freedom of scientific investigation, thereby securing freedom of movement throughout the Antarctic for nongovernmental expeditions of scientists and explorers, as well as for official government scientists. The bottom line is this: science remains the preeminent human activity on Antarctica, and tourism is viewed as an acceptable activity.

Any human activity might compromise the integrity of an environment unless special measures are taken to minimize its possible harmful impacts on atmospheric, terrestrial, and marine ecosystems. While Antarctic tourism is not wholly unmanaged, it represents an emerging concern. More attention to regulating tourist activities seems likely, given the growth of the industry in a pristine commons region earmarked by so many natural uncertainties and complexities. Such attention will require active contributions from Antarctic science to make regulation work well.

Chapter 8

COMMON HERITAGE

INTRODUCTION

Among the main sources of international law are "general principles of law recognized by civilized nations."[1] These principles suggest the transformation of broad, universally applicable precepts into specific international legal rules. A general principle of law entails some legal proposition that is so fundamental as to be found in virtually every legal system and thus merits inclusion in international law as well. For regimes affecting global common spaces, including Antarctica, certain governments have touted the doctrine of common heritage of mankind as having the status of a general principle of international law. Notwithstanding that assertion, the common heritage of mankind (CHM) remains inadequately defined as a legal construct in international relations. Moreover, the profound ramifications of CHM's application in the real world have more often been dressed up in ideological rhetoric than exposed to politico-economic reality.

This chapter strives to clarify the common heritage of mankind as a legal concept, with a view to gauging what relevance it holds for the Antarctic commons. The analysis examines the attraction of CHM as a legal device for facilitating management of global common spaces. In this way, clearer insight might be gained into the political and economic capacity that CHM holds as a policy instrument for managing the polar South. Likewise, a better idea can be gleaned of CHM's authority to challenge the legitimacy of the Antarctic Treaty System to set rules governing activities in the region.

Historical Background

As a philosophical construct, the common heritage of mankind is a recent development in international legal thought. Its intellectual history has been intense, however. This legacy has thus produced a notable corpus of international materials that supply visible underpinnings for the common heritage of mankind concept under international law.

The notion of CHM was suggested as early as June 1967, in discussions before the Legal Subcommittee of the Committee on the Peaceful Use of Outer Space.[2] But the critical impetus to the concept was generated by Malta's ambassador to the United Nations, Arvid Pardo, in his now famous address before the First Committee of the General Assembly. On November 1, 1967, Pardo declared that a novel concept, "the common heritage of mankind," should replace the traditional notion of freedom of the sea. Pardo stressed the ecological unity and commonality of interactions between uses and areas of ocean space. He then posited that the common heritage of mankind contained five fundamental principles: (1) the commons area is not subject to national appropriation in any manner whatsoever; (2) the commons area is reserved exclusively for peaceful purposes; (3) scientific research conducted in the commons area is freely permissible, and its results are to be made available to all; (4) resources of the commons, if exploited, must be done in the interest of mankind, with particular regard to the needs of the developing countries; and (5) exploration and exploitation of commons should be conducted in a manner consistent with the principles and purposes of the UN Charter and in such a manner that no serious damage is caused to the environment.[3] These principles, Pardo contended, should serve as the legal pillars upon which a new order for using ocean space is built.

The "principles" Pardo set out were little more than theoretical constructs. Over the past three decades, however, CHM has evolved from being merely a theoretical aspiration to becoming progressively accepted as a principle in international treaty law. This impressive progress proved to be the catalyst for applying the CHM notion elsewhere on Earth, including Antarctica.

The "Commons" in Common Heritage

The definition of "a commons" is critical for determining the legal character of the common heritage of mankind concept. What does the notion of "global commons" mean? What is the nature of a commons area? As determined in chapter 2, a number of requirements seem necessary for some space to be considered a commons area: A commons area must (1) exist within the legal framework of available international law or accepted customary practices; (2) be identifiable through rules that distinguish it from a noncommons area; (3) be open for community access and public use and closed to exclusive appropriation or individual use; and (4) exist in such a condition that its use by some agent does not preclude, impinge upon, or interfere with use by others.

Drawing from these preconditions, a global commons space may be defined as an area situated beyond the limits of national jurisdiction that is open to use by the community but closed to exclusive appropriation. The commons area is managed such that free exploration and reasonable use are combined with shared respect and equal access rights in order to provide the potential for shared benefits. The inference here suggests that areas which qualify as common spaces are susceptible to the legal application of common heritage of mankind. The Antarctic may qualify as such an area. Even so, the fact that seven national sovereignty claims are asserted to portions of the continent clearly complicates the purity of that qualification.

CHARACTERISTICS OF COMMON HERITAGE

The evolution of CHM over the last three decades has been driven by the aim of becoming a general legal principle embodying fundamental community aspirations. The notion of common heritage has developed markedly since its original proposition during the 1960s. In this regard, a number of prominent attributes now earmark the contemporary concept of common heritage of mankind.

First, there is *nonappropriation*. Under CHM common space areas are not subject to appropriation of any kind, either public or private, national or corporate. Common space areas legally belong to no one. Hypothetically they are to be managed by everyone. Sovereignty and its ramifications of possession, title, and authoritative control are absent. This quality of nonproprietorship rejects the traditional legal argument that a commons territory is *res nullius*, i.e., land which belongs to no one and hence could be subject to sovereignty and jurisdiction if appropriate means for territorial acquisition and claims to title were performed.[4] Under CHM the chief consideration pertaining to a common space area is not ownership; rather it is open access and free use of the area.[5]

A second element of common heritage is *shared management*. Under the CHM doctrine all people are expected to share in the management of a commons area. National governments are precluded from assuming that role, except as the representatives of all humankind. This quality of shared management aims to eliminate national interest and sovereignty considerations from the process of administrative decision-making that pertains to the common space. The logic here runs as follows: A commons area is literally considered to be space that belongs to all persons in the international community. That space therefore should be managed by all persons, for all their corporate interests. Since all persons cannot possibly participate in the management operation of commons spaces, a special agency to coordinate shared management policies must be designed and implemented. Such an international authority would administer the common space in the name of all humankind.[6]

This attribute of shared management invites the establishment of an international regulatory mechanism to manage and administer a common space area in the interest and for the benefit of all humankind. Such international regulatory machinery sets CHM apart from the general precept of *res communis*, which mandates that the commons would be territory owned by no one but available for use by everyone. The *res communis* notion does exclude possession of and sovereign control over an area by any polity or person and also forbids sovereign claims by any state over an area. But it still permits everyone to use the area freely, without undue restraint.[7] Such an open access situation obviously works to the greater advantage of technologically developed states over the majority of developing countries. As a consequence, the common heritage concept advocates creation of a special international institution to administer policies and regulate activities in the area.

Shared benefits are a third modern characteristic of common heritage. The CHM doctrine espouses that benefits derived from the commons area are to be shared by humankind as a whole. If natural resources are exploited, economic benefits from that exploitation should be shared internationally. Under a common heritage regime, private corporate agents that engage in commercial profits or gains would be denied access to the commons area for exploitation purposes, save for their performing operations that enhance the common benefits for all humankind.

CHM endorses the principle of equitable sharing. Benefits derived from activities in the area should be equitably apportioned among all humankind. This notion of equitable sharing of benefits remains essential to CHM, though with critical points left ambiguous. How will such equitable sharing be carried out? Who will administer that sharing? Who determines what is equitable? Who decides who gets what, when, and where? Who determines which benefits are worth how much? These are all key considerations that must be calculated into any international equitable sharing arrangement. Presumably these responsibilities would devolve to the managing international authority, though at present that situation remains more hypothetical than real for any common space area. The tendency under CHM, however, has been to concentrate on sharing of economic benefits (i.e., redistribution) to the diminution of other benefits (e.g., peace, scientific research, aesthetic, and wilderness values).[8] Of special concern in this regard has been the lesser priority given to conservation of the environment under a common heritage regime.

The priority of resource exploitation over environmental protection and conservation under a CHM regime mirrors aspirations by developing countries for a changed world economic order. Also evident here is that international common spaces and their natural resources are supposed to be inherited from generation to generation. This reflects the intent behind the "heritage" facet of CHM. Thus, not only are interests of the present generation at stake, but unrestricted use of the commons may put at risk future generations as well.[9]

A fourth element of common heritage is *peaceful purposes only* of the area. Common space areas under CHM are reserved exclusively for peaceful purposes. No military bases are permitted, no weapons can be tested, no maneuvers can be conducted, and no weapons systems can be installed. The area of the common space should be totally demilitarized, such that any activity of a military character is excluded. In this way conflict and discord are discouraged and peaceful uses of the commons can be ensured.

A regime that fails to stipulate that a commons area must be used exclusively for peaceful purposes as it is administered under a shared management system fails to uphold the CHM concept. Shared management by an international regime should enhance prospects for compliance by national governments since all states would hold vested stakes in the regime. The regime for shared management should also contribute to maintaining nonmilitarization of the commons, and all activities conducted in the commons should be peaceful and nonmilitary. Under those conditions the sanctity of the commons can be preserved more effectively, and inclinations by governments to use military force can be dissuaded more easily.[10]

A final defining trait of the CHM principle is *conservation of resources and preservation of environmental quality in the commons area for future generations.* The concept of CHM advocates that as part of the world heritage, global common spaces should be preserved for use and appreciation by future generations. Freedom of access to the region is guaranteed without discrimination or obstruction so long as activities do not seriously impair the environment. Once the environment is threatened, impaired, or degraded, the common heritage element may be severely compromised. This risk, CHM advocates assert, should not be tolerated under international law. Future generations would pay the price for imprudent exploitation in the present.

If common heritage of mankind is to be converted into policy for a given global area, protection of that commons' environment becomes fundamentally necessary. A rational system of resource development must be put in place that protects the commons from excessive resource depletion and environmental contamination. Protection through deliberate pollution control and prudent conservation measures remains critical. Unless preservation of the environment can be assured—and ecological degradation prevented—the commons area and its resources might not be available for use by succeeding generations.

Importantly, the concept of CHM often tends not to emphasize economic costs. Common heritage should be viewed from a more balanced perspective. That is, under the common heritage of mankind not only might gains be realized in the exploitation and redistribution of certain resources, but losses are also incurred. Resources are depleted and the quality of the environment is affected, often in ways that diminish it. This fact is hardly surprising and should not be left out of the CHM equation. In the same vein, all persons are supposed to share in benefits derived from a commons by a management system grounded in common heritage of mankind precepts. Likewise, all persons should expect to share in any deficits and losses incurred by that system. This point underscores the critical role that equity supposedly plays in the CHM notion. Yet it receives only little attention. The focus of CHM advocates remains concentrated on the redistribution of benefits, rather than on considerations of reallocating costs that might be caused by a CHM regime.

International Dimensions of CHM

Economics, law, and ecology are intimately integrated into the complex of modern international relations. Each force converges to commingle with the others and form an interactive nexus. This situation holds explicitly true for the common heritage as it impacts upon contemporary international affairs. The various elements of CHM—nonappropriation, shared management, shared benefits, peaceful purposes only, and conservation for future generations—all combine to generate shared attributes. Viewed holistically, these attributes assume three salient dimensions affecting international activities: the economic, the legal, and the ecological. These dimensions define the unique role of CHM in international politics and point up its particular relevance for the Antarctic commons.

The Economic Dimension

The economic dimension of CHM stresses nonownership of the heritage. CHM connotes reserving global areas for public use. Thus, in terms of property relationships, the common heritage of mankind can be defined as a common property having a common sovereignty. Put another way, the notion of CHM fosters the right to use certain property but not the right to own it. This entails the need to manage that commons property, with a concomitant obligation by the international community to transmit this common heritage to succeeding generations.

The CHM principle does require management, but not only over resources; management applies to all uses of the area. As a result, common heritage means benefit sharing. These needs for shared management and derived benefits that are implicit in the CHM notion underscore the prerequisite necessity for international cooperation in decision-making. Such cooperation also involves international sharing in any benefits that might accrue from management decisions affecting exploitation of the commons area.

As regards economic theory, the essence of the CHM doctrine concerns property rights (i.e., the privileges to own and use scarce economic resources). The key consideration turns on whether all or only a select group of the international community should be given jurisdiction to administer or develop certain unique global resources, be they on the deep seabed, in outer space, or around Antarctica. Important in this connection, property rights are not exclusively economic in character. They are interdisciplinary and involve law, politics, culture, and philosophy. Assignment of international property rights relies, moreover, on a mix of domestic governmental decisions as well as international decisions. Supranational property rights are, of course, ratified and enforced by national government decisions. Consequently, much debate over common heritage focuses on how decisions involving distribution of resources and benefits should be made in an international setting.

The CHM concept also connotes a form of social property and a process that ascribes new relationships between people and resources. Under a true common heritage system, both natural resources and technology would become nonproperty and devolve to the world community as a whole. As communal social property, all ownership rights, including rights of possession by those with the means to exploit and use particular resources for their own purposes, are negated. These conditions point up a key presumption behind the common heritage concept: International socialization of a commons area as property and the area's concomitant global management are intended to combine and transform relationships of inequality and domination into relationships of equity and parity. To the degree that these conditions can be attained, the ambitions of common heritage will be well served.

Importantly, however, the common heritage notion can carry with it profound intentions for resource exploitation. CHM became closely associated with the politico-economic movement of the 1970s called the New International Economic Order (NIEO), which sought more equitable distribution of resources and income between developed industrial states and developing countries.[11] The common heritage of mankind embraces a theory of international property rights, spurred on by the quest for a changed world economic situation. This aspiration for world economic security asserted that nonsovereign resources in the global commons are perforce the common heritage of mankind. Accordingly, property rights or sovereignty over these resources ought to accrue to all peoples of the world. This notion of world property ownership in turn suggested global sharing in the economic use of such resources, be it as preservation under a world park or through exploitation of common resources.

The assignment of property rights affecting CHM prompts a fundamental question: How do governments obtain sovereignty over territory and economic resources? International law has determined that national sovereignty may be obtained over land and resources under the principle of *res nullius*. This doctrine holds that a government may lawfully acquire property rights to unclaimed territory and resources through discovery, exploration, and effective occupation, usually defined as "permanent settlement."[12] This principle of international law has supplied the legal means through which territories have been claimed, settled, and developed into recognized state polities. The NIEO reflected an effort by developing countries to set aside these international legal tenets as they might apply to certain special commons areas. These designated areas—the moon, the seabed, and Antarctica—should be reserved as commons spaces in which all peoples share property rights to resources. Accordingly, these commons could be exploited for everyone's benefit, albeit priority in receiving benefits would go to the neediest nations.[13]

The economic dimension reveals a basic problem in CHM: Economic growth and economic development are not the same thing. Development does not merely imply a range of values broader than growth; it also necessarily invokes the notion of sustainability, which recalls the possibility that a tragedy of the commons could unfold. The tragedy of the commons, as Garrett Hardin posited, suggests that market forces naturally will make it economically more attractive for landowners to retract these common rights of use and enclose the land for public use.[14]

Even so, the translation of a profound environmental ethic from philosophical musing into political reality rarely occurs naturally or easily. While proper words and sensible logic may be there, political will and economic commitment by governments often are not. The political and economic implications of common heritage, moreover, detract from the moral compulsion and psychological cohesion necessary to attract wide international legal acceptance. Different developing countries argue differently according to their own national interests and priorities in CHM-related issues. As for having Antarctica declared a lawful part of the common heritage, the efforts of developing countries fell short. Their strength in numbers could not compel a legal metamorphosis of the status of Antarctica through a UN General Assembly voting system in which resolutions adopted by the majority are mere recommendations, without the force of law binding the entire membership.[15] Ideological assertions and economic aspirations gave way to the realities of international law and politics.

The Legal Dimension

The historical evolution of the CHM concept reveals a legal dimension as well. The medieval period in European history introduced the notion of what today is recognized and designated as "common space." Medieval commons were designated areas of untilled pasture and forest lands where everyone was permitted to graze animals, gather firewood, and hunt. This open access regime was in contrast with estates and private lands, appropriately labeled the "close." As settlements grew in the early Middle Ages, agriculture expanded and populations increased. These commons—though often located on waste ground or woodlands—accordingly appreciated in value.[16] The right price for agricultural produce created incentives to "enclose" the commons by fence or hedge. By way of analog, the present situation with the global commons is not far different. States today effectively serve as a "fence" of sovereignty for bounding commons areas, which have as their legal fundament the absence of sovereign ownership. Common spaces have essentially become areas enclosed within walls of sovereign polities.

The common heritage notion furnishes an alternative to the *res nullius* approach for determining property rights among states. The concept of *res nullius* refers to a thing that is the property of no one but remains susceptible to appropriation by anyone. This doctrine was used by Europeans to justify assertions of sovereignty over uninhabited territory, usually in the New World. When applied to some space, the legal precept of *res nullius* holds that land and natural resources belong to no state until particular activities such as discovery, exploration, and occupation through permanent settlement establish widely recognized national sovereignty over them. Under *res nullius* the prior distribution of economic, military, and political power largely determines actual or subsequent distribution of property rights and sovereign status.

In legal situations where a thing cannot be possessed, the concept of *res communis* has been generally applied. The regime of *res communis* permits open access to the area by everyone, and anyone has unrestricted access to explore the area and use it. Those who make use of the area receive benefits, and those who do not cannot complain. *Res communis* status applied to something generates two legal attributes. First, the thing may not be appropriated; it is not susceptible to private ownership. Second, the thing belongs equally to all people; everyone has a stake in its ownership. International law thus permits states to use common space areas, including the right to appropriate certain natural resources from those areas.

Res communis furnishes the interpretation of property rights often associated with common heritage status. This legal notion asserts that rights to certain unique areas and global resources transcend national political boundaries. Ownership rights accrue to all nations as common property resources, which are not subject to appropriation by any person or polity, regardless of the ability to appropriate them. Consequently, the common heritage of mankind notion is often viewed as resembling the *res communis* concept. Still, a notable distinction stands out. As a philosophical precept, common heritage projects a legal reach farther than *res communis* by embracing the quality of being *territorium commune humanitatis*. By this concept the common heritage of mankind applies to commonly held spaces whose management, exploitation, and distribution of natural resources would be determined by the international community, rather than left to the sole discretion of individual governments, corporations, or persons. Decisions affecting allocations and exploitation of common spaces under *territorium commune humanitatis* are to be made by the international community as a whole.

In the real world, however, neither *res nullius* nor *res communis* as legal constructs can ensure equal access for developing countries to the global commons. Certainly neither concept can ensure equal distribution of benefits derived from those areas by developed states. Such dissemination of economic benefits can only come with the genuine commitment of governments to make it happen as foreign policy.

To what extent can it be said that CHM has evolved to the status of a legal norm? For CHM to qualify as a norm of international law, certain minimum requirements for its conceptual development must be realized. First, the concept it embodies must be separate, distinct, and unique from other norms of international law. Second, the concept must reflect the substantial practice of states in their international relations. Third, the concept must be undergirded by an international commitment of *opinio juris*, a sense of legal obligation by states to accept and abide by that concept.

As to the requirement of being distinct, CHM may be considered from several vantage points. That is, common heritage involves: (1) the right to use a space beyond national jurisdiction, without the concomitant customary right to exercise claims of sovereignty or ownership; (2) the assertion that the world community is title holder to the common space; (3) the obligation to share benefits deriving from the exploitation of that common space; and (4) the establishment of multilateral institutions for controlling the management of resources that fall within common space areas. Given these perspectives, CHM clearly is not wholly unique to common space land areas. Similar commons jurisdiction also pertains to principles upholding freedom of the high seas and the freedom of airspace beyond the limits of national jurisdiction. Such principles already exclude extension of ownership, appropriation, or sovereignty to those spaces. But regarding considerations of world title holder, shared benefits, and international institutions, the idea of CHM does generate unique considerations. Indeed, if applied in the real world, such a concept would be revolutionary in its international economic implications and legal responsibilities.

On the other hand, the notion of a collective title that accrues to the international community and is coupled with obligations to share benefits and manage resources internationally radically departs from the classic practice of international law. International rights and duties are traditionally viewed as being vested in sovereign states. International norms are similarly supposed to preserve or limit the exercise of such sovereign power in the international system. The theme of international socialistic solidarity marks a departure from these traditional premises in the law of nations. Moreover, it dovetails with the notion of "New Solidarity Human Rights" for certain global problems (e.g., maintaining environmental integrity, humanitarian disaster relief, and international peace) that elude solution by an individual sovereign state.[17]

The concept of common heritage presents innovative implications for international law and international political economy. As a construct, moreover, its content and intent appear distinguishable from traditional norms of international law. Yet, whether CHM has evolved beyond the threshold of acceptance to become an international norm remains open to question. For a rule of international law to be binding, it must be premised on the voluntary consent and collective will of states. Restrictions on the sovereignty and independence of states should not be presumed and must be verified by state practice. The record for CHM evidences but modest achievements in that direction.

The common heritage of mankind notion found legal expression first by the General Assembly in its Declaration on Principles Governing the Seabed.[18] Adopted in late 1970, this General Assembly resolution averred that "The sea-bed and ocean floor, and the subsoil thereof, beyond the limits of national jurisdiction (hereinafter referred to as the area), as well as the resources of the area, are the common heritage of mankind."[19] It is true that General Assembly resolutions are in and of themselves devoid of legally binding force.[20] Even so, the fact remains that adoption of this resolution mirrored a general international consensus on the merits and substance of its contents. No state voted in opposition to this resolution. Moreover, many industrialized states, including some who later adamantly opposed the system of seabed management in Part XI of the 1982 Convention on the Law of the Sea (UNCLOS), supported the measure.[21] CHM as a concept of international law formally was deemed applicable to the deep seabed.

As a recognized principle of law, however, the common heritage of mankind has acquired binding force only in two relatively recent international legal instruments. The first is the so-called Moon Treaty of 1979, which entered into force in 1984[22] and asserts in its Article XI that "The moon and its natural resources are the common heritage of mankind. . . ."[23] Yet, the significance of this agreement for substantiating the viability of CHM as a principle of international law, never mind as a pillar of outer space law, is only minimal. Only nine states thus far have ratified the Moon Treaty, and not one of them can be called a spacefarer.[24]

CHM found more prominent legal expression in the second instrument, the 1982 United Nations Convention on the Law of the Sea.[25] Explicit expression of the common heritage of mankind principle is stated in Article 136 of the ocean law convention, which in reference to the deep seabed directly asserts that "The Area and its resources are the common heritage of mankind." Importantly, the Implementation Agreement of July 29, 1994, which modified the seabed portion of the 1982 LOS Convention and thereby made possible widespread international adherence to that instrument, does not tamper with either the declared provision or the legal implications associated with the seabed's common heritage status. International objections to provisions in the convention concerning the deep seabed appeared aimed more toward the institutional machinery for administering that area than on legal or philosophical grounds opposing the CHM concept per se.[26]

The history of United States participation in the Third Conference on the Law of the Sea tends to support this conclusion. The United States government, before becoming the preeminent critic of the deep seabed mining portions of the convention, had actually indicated a willingness to accept CHM as a legal principle applicable to deep seabed resources. As early as July 1966 President Lyndon Johnson had declared that the deep seabed should be considered "the legacy of all human beings." Toward this end Johnson advocated that the area should be protected from open exploitation and from unilateral appropriation that could perpetuate forms of colonialism from which developing countries were only now emerging.[27] Significant to note, this suggestion preceded Arvid

Pardo's call in 1967 for international acceptance of the common heritage of mankind concept.

In 1970 President Nixon formally proposed to the United Nations that common heritage be applied to all resources of the seabed beyond the limit then applied to the continental shelf (i.e., to a depth of 200 meters pursuant to the 1958 Geneva Convention on the Continental Shelf), with an international authority that would administer a system of revenue sharing to assist developing countries.[28] A similar position was later endorsed by the Ford and Carter administrations during the Third Law of the Sea Conference negotiations, up to the policy review undertaken in 1980 by the Reagan Administration. Importantly, however, the Reagan reappraisal of the U.S. position on the deep seabed was not a fundamental rejection of CHM as a legal principle. Rather, objections were focused more on the mechanics underlying the competence of the International Seabed Authority and the monopolistic decision-making structure in Part XI of UNCLOS that was accorded to the proposed institution. Though of concern, the critical problem fell not so much on common heritage of mankind as a legal principle but rather on the nature of the regime proposed for mining the deep seabed.[29]

Since 1982 the concept of common heritage has been subjected to international tests regarding its legal relevance for the deep seabed and Antarctica. In both cases state practice has failed to substantiate wholesale legitimacy of common heritage as a legal principle being applied to common spaces. As regards deep seabed mining, several industrialized states undertook national efforts to set up their own "mini-mining" regimes outside the ambit of the 1982 law of the sea instrument. During the 1980s the United States, the United Kingdom, the Federal Republic of Germany, France, Japan, Italy, Belgium, and the Netherlands engaged amongst themselves in various intergovernmental negotiations aimed at producing certain "reciprocating state agreements" among their various mining consortia for coordinating national policies for mining the deep seabed.[30] These efforts hardly affirmed international recognition of or respect for the legitimacy of the common heritage status of the deep ocean floor and its resources by the most important industrialized mining governments. Similarly, as will be discussed later, the Antarctic Treaty Consultative Parties (ATCPs)—inclusive of these same governments—were less than enthusiastic about replacing the Antarctic Treaty System (ATS) with the application of CHM to the south polar region.

The common heritage of mankind thus appears a paradox. On the one hand, CHM has been accepted in specific international treaties as a legal principle applicable to certain global commons. The precept is legally binding on governments who become parties to those particular international instruments, with effects on those specific common space areas. On the other hand, common heritage has yet to obtain the status of a universal principle of international law. Less than sufficient *opinio juris* has been demonstrated in state practice to merit the concept being confirmed as a principle of customary international law.

Put bluntly, the common heritage concept has not been openly or tacitly embraced as a binding principle of international law by those governments having the technology to make exploitation of the commons possible for the benefit of all mankind. CHM likewise lacks sufficient consensus among developing countries to compel some accommodation with developed states on the concept as a rule of customary international law. Consensus demonstrated in United Nations resolutions and at international conferences might be seen as evidence of state practice, but this may be misleading. Positions taken in suck force by governments might be motivated by considerations of politics or national expediency rather than any devotion to abiding by a universal legal duty. While common heritage has become an acknowledged principle of international treaty law, it has not yet attained the status of a norm of customary international law. At best, CHM remains in the evolutionary dynamic toward that end.

Environmental Dimension

There is also an environmental dimension to the common heritage of mankind. Generations have a right to use and enjoy the planet's legacy of resource wealth but at same time have a paramount obligation to conserve those rights for the future. Each generation is permitted to use the Earth's natural resource wealth but is also obliged to conserve and husband that wealth to ensure that succeeding generations inherit sufficient natural resources to sustain their needs. Generations must be mindful of the future as they consume finite resources. They must preserve, conserve, and protect the natural bounty for the future. They must prudently manage the environment of the commons, so as to assure that the needs of succeeding generations are met. That is the critical essence of the "heritage" element in the common heritage of mankind.[31]

CHM connotes peaceful uses, freedom of access, and open availability to those having stakes in the heritage. CHM also implies regulation of use to conserve the heritage and the need to avoid infringement upon the rights of others. In addition, equal distribution of benefits should come from exploitation of the heritage. This situation, the common heritage philosophy asserts, entails certain fundamental rights of mankind.

But the rights of humankind must be distinguished from the corpus of international law concerned with human rights. They are not the same. The rights of humankind suggest certain entitlements.[32] Human rights embrace those civil rights and liberties that should be guaranteed by governments. Economic rights by entitlement suggest rights owed the individual by the state. CHM implies basic human rights to which persons are entitled by virtue of being human beings on the planet. Those rights do not flow from the state but rather stem from considerations that wealth derived from common space areas should be reallocated to persons in need of international assistance and public welfare. In addition, the notion of "common" implies belonging to the people at large and involves a public heritage property or cultural tradition that can be inherited and handed down from generation to generation.[33]

COMMON HERITAGE, ANTARCTICA, AND THE UNITED NATIONS

The Antarctic as a commons area cannot be appropriated. Still, a key consideration turns on who can or should administer the area so as to ensure the maintenance of peace and sustainable use of resources most compatible with the interests of future generations. As previously discussed, the Antarctic Treaty System furnishes a unique situation in international law and politics. An entire continent is governed by treaty arrangement rather than by individual sovereign states. During the 1980s, however, an international challenge was mounted to the legitimacy of purpose and lawful authority of the ATS to perform that role. The forum for that challenge was the United Nations General Assembly. The crux of that debate focused on the common heritage of mankind as a more appropriate regime for managing Antarctica in the interest of the international community.

Background

In 1976 Ambassador Shirley Hamilton Amerasinghe of Sri Lanka, then chair of the Third Conference on the Law of the Sea, presaged the debate over Antarctica as part of the common heritage of mankind when he observed that:

> There are still areas of this planet where opportunities remain for constructive and peaceful cooperation on the part of the international community for the common good of all rather than for the benefit of a few. Such an area is the Antarctic continent . . . Antarctica is an area where the now widely accepted ideas and concepts relating to international economic cooperation, with their special stress on the principle of equitable sharing of the world's resources, can find ample scope for application, given the cooperation and goodwill of those who have so far been active in the area.[34]

The resounding international silence over the legal status of Antarctica in the postcolonial era had been broken.

Six years later the Malaysian government emerged as the leading critic of the Antarctic Treaty System and chief advocate of common heritage status for Antarctica. The Malaysian prime minister, Dr. Mahathir-bin Mohammad, suggested as much on September 29, 1982, in a speech before the General Assembly. He proposed that the United Nations should administer the Antarctic area, or that the "present occupants" should act as trustees for the rest of the world. As Mahathir averred, "Uninhabited lands . . . the largest of which is the continent of Antarctica . . . do not legally belong to the discoverers as much as the colonial territories do not belong to the colonial powers."[35] He went on to criticize the Antarctic Treaty as an agreement among a select few privileged states which in no way represented the true aspirations of the United Nations membership, and he demanded that a new international treaty be negotiated.[36] Malaysia's intentions became clearer in December 1982 at the signing of the UN Convention on the Law of the Sea in Montego Bay, Jamaica. At that occasion the Malaysian delegate declared, "It is now time to focus our attention on Antarctica where immense potentialities exist for the benefit of mankind."[37] The debate in the United Nations General Assembly over the international legal status of the frozen continent had begun.

Malaysia, acting through the United Nations and the Non-Aligned Movement, then sought to broaden international decision-making on Antarctic affairs beyond the select group of treaty powers. It was Malaysia who in 1983 called for the question of Antarctica to be placed on the General Assembly agenda, and it was Malaysia who repeatedly attempted to link Antarctica to the 1982 Convention on the Law of the Sea.[38]

In the latter effort Malaysia justified its Antarctic policy position in terms of the new political and legal concepts embodied in the 1982 ocean law treaty. The legal logic here became clear. No government in the world (except for the seven claimants themselves) recognized the lawfulness of national claims made to the Antarctic. If legal grounds for territorial claims to Antarctica were thus deemed illegitimate, then what should preclude the continent and its resources from being made available to the entire international community? If claims to the continent were not recognized as valid, what legal reason is there not to designate Antarctica as a common heritage area and entrust it thereafter as a public trust to the United Nations? As determined by Malaysia in particular and the developing world in general, no acceptable reason could be found. Consequently, critics of the ATS led by Malaysia came strongly to advocate that the "international community" should take "collective actions under the auspices of the United Nations for an open, accountable and equitable framework for Antarctica for the benefit of mankind as a whole."[39]

At the Non-Aligned Summit in New Delhi in March 1983, Prime Minister Mahathir succeeded in gaining support from the Non-Aligned Movement. He sought a comprehensive study by the United Nations of the Antarctic question as an initial step toward the emergence of an alternative to the ATS, a view endorsed by an "Economic Declaration" adopted at the end of the conference.[40]

Malaysia thus sought to mobilize the Non-Aligned Movement as the conduit for securing international support for its CHM position on Antarctica. By September 1983 Malaysia, Antigua and Barbuda, joined by Algeria, Pakistan, and Singapore, succeeded in having the question of Antarctica placed on the agenda of the General Assembly. This opened the door for the First Committee of the General Assembly to pass a resolution on Antarctica that requested the secretary-general to prepare and place before the next General Assembly session "a comprehensive factual study of all aspects of Antarctica, taking into account the Antarctic Treaty System and other relevant factors."[41] The plenary of the UN General Assembly adopted that resolution on December 15, 1983.[42] It was this act that initiated formal concern by the United Nations with Antarctic affairs and that also substantiated the key role that Malaysia would play in having Antarctica considered part of the common heritage of mankind.[43]

In November 1984 the secretary-general submitted his *Study on the Question of Antarctica*.[44] Part I of the study provided a relatively straightforward and balanced analysis of the continent's geographical profile and the legal, political, scientific, and economic implications of national activities in Antarctica and the Antarctica Treaty System in practice. Part II consisted of statements and opinions submitted to the secretary-general from fifty-four member states.

Significant in the secretary-general's study is pervasive recognition that the Antarctic Treaty had contributed positively to stabilizing the political situation in the region. This was particularly so as the treaty has functioned to ensure "the peaceful use of Antarctica":

> For nearly two and a half decades, Antarctica and its surrounding maritime areas have been free from militarisation of any kind, including nuclear weapons. No armed conflict has taken place in the area. Peace on the continent has been maintained to a large extent through the agreements embodied in the Antarctic Treaty. The Treaty has provided a frame-work for the parties to the Treaty to carry out peaceful activities related to scientific research, exploitation of marine resources, and protection of the environment.[45]

Furthermore, the study recognized the treaty's contribution to establishing conservation measures for the region: "It would appear that no major danger has so far occurred to the Antarctic eco-system. Human activities in Antarctica remain very limited . . . and are being carried out in accordance with the strict rules and regulations imposed by such activities by the Antarctic Treaty Consultative Parties."[46] The statement submitted in May 1984 by Malaysia for the secretary-general's study foreshadowed the diplomatic offensive in the General Assembly against the ATS. Malaysia argued that the proposed study should examine the present attitudes of states toward the Treaty System in order to obtain a "broader basis and firmer foundation for international co-operation in Antarctica acceptable to, and in the interest of, the international community as a whole."[47] The study should evaluate the growing significance of Antarctica for the international community as regards international peace and security as well as economic opportunities for developing countries, with special reference to Antarctic marine and possibly mineral resources. Regarding the claims issue, Malaysia contended that if nonclaimant ATS governments could assert that the continent was available for their use, then "Why should such an assertion not be made applicable to the entire international community?" Moreover, the validity of the claims was highly suspect under international law. "If such claims to sovereignty have not been so recognized, why should Antarctica not be a 'common heritage' and invested in the United Nations?"[48]

The legal status of Antarctica was not the only deficiency found in the ATS. Another issue criticized by Malaysia concerned the status of South Africa as a Consultative Party among the treaty parties: "Antarctica as the common heritage of mankind requires a regime that is truly universal in character and committed to serving the interest of the entire international community. In this respect, the exploration of Antarctica and its resources must be carried out for the benefit of mankind."[49] The white-minority apartheid government in South Africa was hardly considered representative of that ambition. It should be pointed out that Malaysia was not alone in these efforts in the United Nations. Steadfast allies in the First Committee debates were Sri Lanka,[50] Pakistan,[51] Bangladesh,[52] and Indonesia,[53] with support also offered at times by Bhutan,[54] Nepal,[55] and the Philippines.[56]

Common Heritage and the General Assembly

Led by the critics, certain fundamental attitudes came to underpin political perspectives by most developing countries toward Antarctica during the 1980s. These attitudes were most acutely expressed during the debates on Antarctica in the First Committee and were formally demonstrated in votes cast in the General Assembly from 1983 to 1989 on the question of Antarctica. Predictably, many governments not party to the Antarctic Treaty tended to view Antarctica politically and legally through the lens of developing countries, particularly on issues that affected their own socio-economic concerns.

It was during the 1980s in the General Assembly that a common heritage status for Antarctica was given political impetus and formal endorsement by developing countries not party to the Antarctic Treaty.

Each of the concerns above about Antarctica became formally registered in special General Assembly resolutions on the question of
Antarctica. While such resolutions by the General Assembly are not
legally binding, they do suggest international public opinion on community issues. They can even indicate the direction in which
international law may be heading. For these reasons, as well as because resolutions were generally aimed at promoting common
heritage attributes in Antarctica, some detailed attention to their
content is warranted.

In 1983 and 1984 the first two General Assembly debates on the
question of Antarctica in the First Committee resulted in consensus
agreement on resolutions. Hence, no votes were taken.[57] After that,
however, consensus in the General Assembly eluded sponsors of
various resolutions—often Malaysia and Pakistan—as well as the
parties to the Antarctic Treaty. It is especially significant to note that
on every General Assembly resolution, nearly all Antarctic Treaty
parties refused to participate in the voting. This strategy was intentional, designed to demonstrate solidarity and support by those
governments for the Antarctic Treaty System.

Themes of Criticism

Seven fundamental themes emerged about Antarctica in the General Assembly debates during the 1980s, and each carried implications
for the legal status of Antarctica. The gnawing assumption fundamental
to these criticisms was that the present Antarctic Treaty System was
flawed, fatally so. It was therefore necessary that the deficient ATS be
replaced with an international, more equitable common heritage of
mankind regime.

Environmental Stakes
The first theme centered on the great global environmental stakes
associated with the Antarctic commons. Accepting the premise that Antarctica was the last frontier for humankind, developing governments
posited that the continent contains vast amounts of natural resources,
including minerals and a superabundance of fresh water, the availability of which continues to diminish on other continents as world
population grows. Antarctica's ecosystem was aptly viewed as fragile,
and the continent was recognized for its profound influence on global
ecology and environmental conditions worldwide.

Legal Status

A second theme raised in the UN debate focused on the legal status of the continent. Developing countries contended that Antarctica today was *terra nullius*, no-man's-land. Claims of sovereignty to the continent had neither been politically accepted nor legally recognized by the international community. As seen by developing countries, the legal argument on the sovereignty question was quite straightforward: Permanent human settlement on the continent had not occurred. Effective occupation, the necessary ingredient to acquire a valid claim to title, had not been fulfilled. As a result, the question of sovereignty on Antarctica remained at best arguable and legally unresolved, notwithstanding assertion during this century of seven national claims to the continent.[58]

Exclusivity

A third theme of criticism targeted the nature of the Antarctic Treaty. During the UN debates the Antarctic Treaty group was denounced for being a self-designated exclusive club, without any clear legal authority to manage Antarctica for the rest of mankind. In the mid-1980s developing states also condemned the "secretive" character of Antarctic Treaty meetings and the dearth of public information then available about those proceedings and the substance of decisions taken by the Antarctic Treaty Consultative Parties.

To address exclusivity in the Antarctic Treaty System, three General Assembly Resolutions were adopted during the 1980s. The first, G.A. Resolution 40/156 A, was introduced in 1985 by Malaysia and requested the ATCPs to make information generally available to the United Nations.[59] Resolution A called for an additional study to be produced by the secretary-general on three questions: (1) the availability of information to the United Nations from the ATCPs on their activities and deliberations regarding Antarctica; (2) the involvement of relevant specialized and intergovernmental organizations in the Antarctic Treaty System; and (3) the significance of the 1982 UN Convention on the Law of the Sea for the Southern Ocean.

The theme of a more open Antarctic Treaty arrangement was continued. In 1986 G.A. Resolution 41/88 A promoted the role of the United Nations as a central repository for information on all aspects of Antarctica and called for an updated report by the secretary-general to be prepared for the 1987 General Assembly session.[60] In 1987 G.A. Resolution 42/46 B called upon the ATCPs to invite the secretary-general to all meetings of the Antarctic Treaty parties, ATCP meetings, and the minerals negotiations. This resolution also reiterated the call for the ATCPs to impose a moratorium on the minerals regime negotiations "until such time as all members of the international community can participate fully in such negotiations."[61]

Inequity

A fourth alleged deficiency related to the "two-tiered" character of the Antarctic Treaty System in the early 1980s. That is, there existed a select group of principal decision-makers, the Antarctic Treaty Consultative Parties, who made policy decisions by themselves, in their own closed forum, for the entire treaty membership and purportedly for the rest of mankind as well. A second group of states, the Non-Consultative Parties, played little formal role in the decision-making process and were not even permitted to attend ATCP meetings. No less objectionable to the critics was that admission of a government into the Consultative Party group could be obtained only through unanimous consent of current ATCP members. That kind of arrangement was viewed as inequitable, discriminatory, and unfair to disadvantaged developing countries.[62]

Government by Minority

As a fifth concern, critics observed that only a few states had opted to become parties to the Antarctic Treaty. In 1986 there were only eighteen Consultative Parties and fifteen Non-Consultative Parties, for a total of thirty-three treaty members. This amounted to less than one quarter of the United Nations membership. Of these, it was noted that industrialized states remained predominant. Only six developing countries from Asia and Latin America were included among the Consultative Parties.[63] That disparity in the composition of the treaty's membership vexed developing states. Given the Antarctic Treaty's decision-making procedure, the vast majority of UN member states could never participate in the management of Antarctic affairs, even if they opted to become parties to the Antarctic Treaty. Absent Consultative Party membership, developing states could never be privy to decisions taken by that group. Such inequities, developing countries averred, were considered counter to contemporary norms of democratic rule and international majoritarianism.

South Africa

A sixth theme for developing countries centered on South Africa's inclusion as a full Consultative Party to the Antarctic Treaty. Practically every state viewed the minority white government in South Africa as manifestly illegitimate on account of its racist apartheid policy. Such an outlaw regime, developing states asserted, should not be permitted to participate in managing Antarctic affairs "in the interest of all mankind." Accordingly, critics demanded throughout the UN debates that the Consultative Parties should expel South Africa from their membership until a democratically elected representative majority government was empowered in Pretoria.[64]

In 1985 G.A. Resolution 40/156 C directly expressed concern about South Africa's involvement in the Antarctic Treaty System.[65] Resolution C accordingly urged that the ATCPs exclude "the racist *apartheid* regime of South Africa" from participation in Consultative Party meetings "at the earliest possible date" and keep the secretary-general informed of developments.

In December 1986 the General Assembly adopted Resolution 41/88 C, which reiterated its appeal to the ATCPs to expel South Africa from Consultative Party meetings. It also requested that the secretary-general submit a report on this issue to the 1987 General Assembly session.[66] The outcome of the General Assembly's vote on this resolution was considerably more impressive than on previous Antarctic-related measures: 119 in favor, none opposed, and 8 abstentions.

In 1987 G.A. Resolution 42/46 A reiterated the appeal to ATCPs that they exclude South Africa from their meetings and invite the secretary-general to report back to the General Assembly.[67] Resolution A again generated impressive support among the General Assembly membership in the roll call voting: 122 states in favor, none opposed, with 9 abstaining. The antiapartheid theme carried over to 1988, as G.A. Resolution 43/83 B reasserted the General Assembly's call to the Consultative Parties to exclude South Africa from their meetings and to inform the secretary-general of their action.[68]

Minerals Negotiations

The minerals issue, exacerbated by the Consultative Parties' rush to complete a treaty regime for regulating minerals development in Antarctica, became the most catalytic theme for international action. During the 1980s developing countries grew increasingly wary and perturbed

over the urgency being exercised by the Consultative Parties to negotiate a minerals regime for Antarctica. Governments of developing
countries were hardly mollified by ATCP assertions that no minerals
bonanza existed in Antarctica and that even if minerals exploitation occurred, it would only be far off in the future. Many Third World states
believed that as the negotiations for a minerals regime were proceeding,
exploration for minerals was actually going on by the ATCPs under the
guise of scientific research. The minerals negotiations during 1985–86
had become politically protracted as respective interests had to be satisfied between claimant and nonclaimant states, developed and developing
states, and Consultative and Non-Consultative Parties.[69] Hence, developing countries grew increasingly alarmed when the mineral
negotiations accelerated during 1987–88. States outside the ATS perceived
the quickened effort to conclude negotiations on a minerals agreement
as an attempt by the Consultative Parties to preempt contrary initiatives in the United Nations and in other international bodies.

Predictably, the minerals issue received considerable attention in
Antarctic-related resolutions adopted by the General Assembly. In 1985
G.A. Resolution 40/156 B, introduced by Pakistan, expressed specific
concern over the negotiations to conclude a regime governing possible
minerals development in Antarctica.[70] Resolution B also reflected ap-
prehension by developing countries about the secretive, unrepresentative
nature of the mineral negotiations and called upon the ATCPs to make
information on these negotiations available to the United Nations.

In 1986 G.A. Resolution 41/88 B affirmed that any Antarctic resource
exploitation should ensure the maintenance of international peace and
security in Antarctica, the protection of the Antarctic environment,
nonappropriation and conservation of Antarctic resources, and international management and equitable sharing of benefits from exploitation
of resources.[71] Importantly, it added a demand that the ATCPs should
impose a moratorium on the minerals negotiations "until such time as
all members of the international community can participate fully in such
negotiations." These attributes reflected core features of the common
heritage concept as applied to the deep seabed and the moon, and the
measure passed in the General Assembly by a vote of 96–0–12.

In December 1988 G.A. Resolution 43/83 A expressed the General
Assembly's "conviction" that any minerals regime for Antarctica should
be negotiated with the full participation of the international community, as well as its "deep regret" that the ATCPs had proceeded with

adopting the Wellington minerals treaty rather than accepting imposition of a moratorium on negotiations as had been urged by the General Assembly in 1986 and 1987.[72]

The motivations of the Consultative Parties in establishing a minerals regime came to be perceived with acute suspicion from the southern vantage point. An ATCP-created minerals treaty was viewed as a selfish, contrived instrument principally intended to deny most of the international community rightful access to mineral wealth in Antarctica. Such a situation, the critics contended, hardly contributed to international peace and security, enhanced cooperation in the global economy, or added to preservation of the world environment. Nor would a new ATS minerals regime for Antarctica represent the inherent rights of states that had been excluded from participating in its negotiation. The principal recourse taken by developing states was to address these criticisms through the United Nations. This strategy was done by publicly debating the issues in the First Committee of the General Assembly and then adopting plenary resolutions that affirmed the views of the ATS critics.[73] These UN efforts, however, had little dissuasive impact on priorities pursued by the Consultative Parties.

The Waning of Common Heritage

In 1989 a shift occurred in the General Assembly regarding the status of Antarctica. A new Antarctic ethic emerged in the United Nations, one which emphasized the environmental quality of the continent rather than the status of exploitable resources there. The focus of debate shifted in this session of the assembly such that the economic facet of common heritage was detached from and made subordinate to the environmental element. This UN redirection no doubt came as a spin-off generated by the defection of Australia and France from the Antarctic Minerals Convention, leading to collapse of ATCP support for that agreement.

During the General Assembly debates governments had often expressed concern for conservation of the Antarctic environment. This was done, however, with the implicit assumption that Antarctic mineral resources could be exploited for the benefit of all humankind. Incredibly, the UN discussions failed to observe that the two notions of conservation and exploitation in the Antarctic were inherently incompatible and likely even mutually exclusive.

In 1989 Malaysia reversed this course by arguing that a world park status should be adopted for Antarctica. This position became formally realized in G.A. Resolution 44/124 Part B, which articulated that a new environmental ethic be adopted for Antarctic matters, one that discarded resource exploitation.[74] Resolution B expressed the conviction that any Antarctic regime established for the protection and conservation of the Antarctic environment and its associated and dependent ecosystems must be negotiated with the "full participation of all members of the international community." More importantly, this resolution urged that all states support a ban on prospecting and mining in and around Antarctica and ensure that all activities be used exclusively for peaceful scientific investigation. Resolution 44/124 B also advocated that Antarctica be established as a "nature reserve or a world park" that would ensure the protection and conservation of the region's environment "for the benefit of all mankind." The General Assembly also revisited the South African question in 1989. Part A of G.A. Resolution 44/124 reappealed to the ATCPs "to take urgent measures" to exclude South Africa from their meetings and requested the secretary-general to make a report on this issue to the forty-fifth General Assembly session.[75]

The forty-fifth session of the General Assembly produced two more resolutions on Antarctica in December 1990. In G.A. Resolution 45/78 A the General Assembly expressed its conviction that negotiation of a comprehensive environmental protection convention for Antarctica, as well as establishment of a nature reserve or world park, should be pursued within the context of the United Nations system.[76] In addition, Resolution A urged all states to support a ban on prospecting and mining in and around Antarctica and advocated that all activities associated with scientific investigation be carried out so as to ensure the maintenance of international peace and security in Antarctica and the protection of its environment "for the benefit of all mankind." The measure also requested that the secretary-general prepare a study on the establishment of a United Nations–sponsored station in Antarctica that would promote scientific research on the importance of Antarctica for the global environment and climate change. The General Assembly approved Resolution 45/78 A by a vote of 98–0–7.

G.A. Resolution 45/78 B repeated the General Assembly's concern over South Africa's minority white government as a participant in Consultative Party affairs.[77] Resolution B reiterated the appeal to the ATCPs to exclude the "racist *apartheid* regime" from participation in their meetings and requested the secretary-general to report back on this matter to the General Assembly at its forty-sixth session. The measure was adopted by a margin of 107–0–7.

General Assembly resolutions adopted since 1991 have repeatedly emphasized three themes in their action clauses. They have: (1) supported establishment of Antarctica as a "nature reserve or world park" through an international convention negotiated "with the full participation of the international community"; (2) urged treaty parties to establish monitoring and implementation mechanisms for ensuring compliance with the Protocol on Environmental Protection, while reiterating calls for a permanent mining ban; and (3) urged Antarctic Treaty parties to reduce the number of scientific bases through international cooperation.

Two resolutions were adopted by the General Assembly in 1991. G.A. Resolution A/46/41 A was concerned with the Antarctic Treaty System. Among its provisions was to advocate creation of a world park; to welcome the Protocol but identify its deficiencies (i.e., the need to ensure compliance and to adopt a permanent ban on mining, and the failure to include the entire international community in the negotiations); and to urge the ATCPs to reduce the number of scientific bases by consolidation into internationally coordinated stations.[78] The second resolution adopted in 1991, A/46/41 B, continued the attack on South Africa's minority white regime by advocating exclusion of South Africa from the treaty meetings.[79] Subsequent resolutions in 1992 and 1993 consolidated these demands, reiterating the call on the ATCPs to "prevent South Africa from participating fully in [Consultative Party] meetings pending the attainment of non-racial democratic government in that country."[80]

The attainment of black majority rule in 1994 diminished the General Assembly's concern over South Africa's presence in the ATCP group and returned the UN's focus more squarely to the management and use of Antarctica. While applauding the constructive cooperation furnished by the Antarctic Treaty and its contributions to international peace and scientific cooperation as well as the Madrid Environmental Protocol for its devotion to peace and protection of the Antarctic environment, the most salient provision in the General Assembly's 1994 resolution was a call for the secretary-general to prepare a report on the question of Antarctica.[81] The question of Antarctica was not placed on the agenda of the 1995 General Assembly, although it again appeared in 1996. The content of the 1996 resolution is impressive for its appreciation of Antarctic-related developments. G.A. Resolution A/51/390 is more welcoming and procedurally approving of the status quo in the Antarctic than critical or substantive of ATCP actions. The tone of the 1996 recommendation is one of recognition and highlighting of international achievements pertaining to maintaining peace and security in the region, facilitating exchange of scientific information, and encouraging environmental protection in the Antarctic Treaty area, rather than condemning the ATCPs for political and economic aspirations left undone.[82] The secretary-general was requested to prepare a report on developments in the Antarctic for the General Assembly's fifty-fourth session in 1999.

Thus, removal of the minerals regime and apartheid issues from the UN General Assembly debates has permitted a growing willingness by member states to accept the continued existence of the Antarctic Treaty System and suppressed calls for adopting common heritage of mankind as the legal principle for governing the frozen commons. At the same time, the political atmosphere has cleared such that some conclusions can be crystallized from the UN experience about the lawfulness of applying common heritage to Antarctica.

During the 1980s the developing countries used the UN General Assembly, in which they held a substantial voting majority, as the world forum in which to promote application of CHM to Antarctica. The prevalent theme from these UN discussions was that of participation. Several governments advocated the right to participate in making policy for the Antarctic without having to become a member of the Consultative Party group. Indeed, participation became the essential quality in the Third World's perception of CHM. In any event, the bottom line by 1989 was clear: While common heritage might be a doctrine possessed of considerable philosophical merit, the established political and legal order governing Antarctica refused to credit the economic element with substantial legitimate status. CHM was deemed not acceptable as an international regime by the very states that mattered most in the region. The Antarctic Treaty System was left preeminent as the governing authority for the Antarctic commons.

In response to the challenge in the United Nations, Antarctic Treaty parties reasserted the point that if developing countries want to participate in Antarctic matters, they are welcome to do so. But participation must come in accordance with the rules of the Antarctic Treaty regime. Indeed, the Treaty System is not a static creature: it is evolving. And the ATS has progressively become more environmentally concerned. But the ATS remains *res inter alios acta*—it is only binding on those states which have acceded to it, thereby submitting to its regime. Nothing legally prevents any state or group of states from lawfully conducting their own scientific expeditions to Antarctica. Antarctica legally is not the exclusive domain of the Antarctic Treaty parties, and any state may explore the polar South on its own.

CHM, Environmentalism, and Links to the Protocol

Criticism of the Antarctic Treaty and its regime for managing Antarctica came during the 1980s from developing countries, largely as part of a general movement toward a new international economic order. Criticism has come more recently in response to an emerging global environmental ethic. Interestingly enough, when common heritage is applied to Antarctica, two of its cardinal elements—economics and environmentalism—are now seen as being mutually exclusive. The upshot has been to discredit the whole concept of common heritage as applied to Antarctica, a development that may well have retarded CHM's general acceptability into international law.

The critical development came in 1991 with the adoption of the Madrid Environmental Protection Protocol by the Consultative Parties.[83] This addition to the Antarctic Treaty implicitly stemmed from an assumption that global environmental considerations now retain overarching priority for the Consultative Parties. Such priority devolves from the belief that common responsibility is required for preserving the environment and that such a common responsibility implies common rights. In line with the common heritage philosophy, the Protocol was expressly designed to protect Antarctica's environment and preserve its resources for succeeding generations. Yet, this intention again highlights the intriguing paradox in managing the Antarctic commons: While common responsibility is sought from all states to preserve the Antarctic environment, common rights to use Antarctica are fashioned for use only by those states participating in the Antarctic Treaty System. The Protocol implies standards for the entire international community, but its jurisdictional reach only goes as far as the ATCPs.

Still, the Madrid Protocol breaks fresh legal ground. It contains twenty-seven articles; a schedule on arbitration; and annexes dealing with environmental impact assessment, conservation of Antarctic fauna and flora, waste disposal and waste management, prevention of marine pollution, and area protection and management. The Protocol aims to ensure comprehensive environmental protection for the Antarctic commons by regulating all human activities there. The Protocol's general principles and more detailed rules supply a legally binding instrument that, once in force, can be used by the ATCPs to redress inconsistencies and close loopholes in earlier recommendations on conduct and behavior affecting the environment.

The fact remains, however, that even when ratified and implemented the Protocol will only be as good as practicality permits and will only be as effective as the party ATCP governments are willing to make it.

Explicit links nonetheless can be found between conservation qualities embraced by common heritage and stipulations in the Madrid Environmental Protocol. For example, in the Protocol, Antarctica is designated as a "natural reserve"[84] and specific environmental principles are articulated for that commons area, one being the promotion of wilderness and aesthetic values.[85] Such values support a world park in principle if not in name. The criticality of Antarctica is fixed, then, by affirming the region's wilderness status and by restricting access by humans who might disturb Antarctica's environment and its dependent and associated ecosystems.

Other connections can be found between the Madrid Environmental Protocol and the CHM doctrine. Protection of the environment is proposed minimally for the span of two generations, i.e., for at least fifty years given the Protocol's amendment process.[86] Several references are cited throughout the Protocol that suggest greater public availability of information. Activities of the Committee for Environmental Protection (Article 11), inspection reports (Article 14), annual reports by parties (Article 17), draft comprehensive evaluations (Annex 1, Article 3), and designated data (Annex 1, Article 6) are all intended to promote better understanding of Antarctic issues and to facilitate more prudent decision-making about that commons region. Similarly, the freedom to exchange scientific information fosters the common heritage notion and could provide the means for challenging ATCPs in public or governmental forums for some failure to comply with the Protocol or one of its annexes.

The Balance Sheet

The demise of the minerals regime in 1989–90, coupled with the shift of attention since 1991 to an environmental protection protocol, has led interest over Antarctica to wane among developing states in the United Nations. At the same time, the clamor by Malaysia and other governments to push for conversion of the legal status of Antarctica to common heritage of mankind has also faded away. Even so, a number of conclusions can be crystallized from the UN experience about the lawful applicability of common heritage to Antarctica.

Deficiencies

One conclusion is that deficiencies in the General Assembly movement eroded arguments for application of CHM to Antarctica. That is, the Third World majority in the United Nations was unable to come together into a cohesive, united coalition to promote the CHM concept. Instead various governments tended to support those subissues about which they were most concerned. Another real impediment was that Antarctic Treaty states publicly ignored the debate process and generally refused to participate in votes on General Assembly resolutions. In effect, the treaty parties demonstrated public discredit of the challenge to the ATS in general and the common heritage issue in particular by consistently refusing to vote in the General Assembly. Worth reiterating here is that General Assembly resolutions are not legally binding on Antarctic Treaty states (or on any state, for that matter). They are only recommendations for action. Though General Assembly resolutions may reflect a majority of international public opinion, they lack the force of a legal fiat. Hence, whatever prescriptions the General Assembly might propose for the Antarctic could only be suggestions, not legal mandates for action or change.

Disparities

A second general conclusion is that certain difficulties and differences complicate application of CHM to Antarctica. For example, some states assert claims of sovereignty to Antarctica, unlike outer space and the deep seabed. Granted, those claims are contentious and their legal validity is arguable. Even so, the claims are real, and they are taken quite seriously by the seven claimant governments. Hence, while the lawfulness of such claims may not be recognized by the international community—and effective national practices through the claims have been set aside by the Antarctic Treaty—assertions of sovereign title to Antarctica do persist. The outcome here is plain: A fundamental presumption of CHM turns on disavowal of national sovereignty in a commons area, and that situation has not happened in the Antarctic.

Still another difference concerns the human presence. In contrast to the deep seabed and outer space, in Antarctica considerable human activity regularly occurs. Although human presence in Antarctica is limited mainly to scientific operations and logistical support, humans live there year round. As many as five thousand scientists have worked there in an austral summer. Furthermore, the sovereign claims to Antarctica—and indeed the treaty-based legal regime governing that region as well—existed long before the concept of CHM was even introduced. It therefore seems surrealistic at best to have expected that the concept of CHM might have been received enthusiastically and applied willingly by ATCPs to Antarctica.[87] It, of course, was not.

Sovereignty

A third conclusion confirms that the status of sovereignty and jurisdiction in Antarctica remains unsettled in Antarctic affairs. Since the claims to Antarctic territory are not viewed as being perfected under international law—and are presently neutralized by Article IV of the 1959 Treaty—concern within the Consultative Party group over sovereignty remains muted. Thus, the General Assembly debate over common heritage failed to resolve the sovereignty situation on the continent. But, significantly, it did not further complicate the question either.

The unresolved sovereignty issue has not produced divisive effects on the ATS. In fact, criticism of the regime in the United Nations and other Third World forums during the 1980s apparently fostered even greater political cohesion among Antarctic Treaty parties. States party to Antarctic Treaty instruments comply with principles and rules of agreements largely out of national self-interest. Their decision to comply is hardly a simple yes or no proposition. Other considerations certainly enter into that calculus, such as what benefits might be accrued (from joint scientific activities), political expediency, potential trade-offs on other questions, and so forth. Internal rivalry and resentment are kept in check through processes of political maneuvering, bilateral suasion, and mutual accommodation—an equilibrium that eventually permits consensus decisions to be taken by the ATCPs.[88]

Congruencies

A fourth conclusion is paradoxical. That is, as the Antarctic Treaty System evolved over the past decade, its adopted policies increasingly appeared to converge toward attributes associated with the common heritage doctrine. In fact, the UN General Assembly debates over the status of Antarctica spotlighted and reaffirmed legal and functional analogs between facets of the Antarctic Treaty System and the philosophical aspirations of common heritage of mankind. Certain points in this connection merit mention.

Clearly, a commons area designated as common heritage may not be appropriated. Both the area and its resources are immune from sovereign appropriation. The common heritage theory on nonappropriation holds that the area and its resources shall not be annexed by way of sovereignty or exercise of sovereign rights or by way of the free access regime of the commons. The obligation is to refrain from appropriating what is common to all. Resource exploitation and use of the area should occur only under a common management system.

Under common heritage, the Antarctic regime would be expected to forgo sovereignty claims and disavow any bases for those claims. Since sovereignty claims are rendered nonoperative under Article IV of the Antarctic Treaty, the condition that ownership rights not be actively exercised is satisfied in part. Put another way, under the Antarctic Treaty System neither the continent nor its circumpolar waters are owned by anyone but are effectively managed by all treaty parties. While neither sovereignty nor ownership rights are actively evinced by state practice under the Antarctic Treaty System, the rights and duties for such resource use and exploitation are separately set out in appendage resource regimes. As a consequence, the Antarctic Treaty System has evolved more as a free access regime than as a regime predicated on ownership rights. This situation made it easier to appropriate resources in the Antarctic area without appropriating the entire commons space.

Noteworthy also is that certain collectively consumed international public goods have emerged under the Antarctic Treaty System. Scientific research, bolstered by the free exchange of research information guaranteed under the treaty, has become the primary industry of the continent. Antarctica has been declared a zone of peace, with military activities and nuclear testing explicitly prohibited. A treaty-imposed moratorium on sovereignty and the claims issue has defused potential conflict over who owns what territory on the continent. The Antarctic environment and its dependent and associated ecosystems have been protected by the treaty's ban on nuclear waste disposal, as well as by limitations in other ATS agreements on the harvesting of seals, conservation of marine living resources, and an indefinite ban on minerals development and mining.[89]

Another facet of the CHM doctrine would put the area under a commons management system, with an institutional framework capable of effecting global benefits sharing. Through such a commons management system a truly international regime presumably would be operationalized. An international structure with universal participation to assist in the protection of the interests of all humankind would be established, with the aim of ultimately attaining a global forum for democratic decision-making.

The Antarctic Treaty System does provide for common management. That process is far from the scheme of universal participation envisioned under a CHM regime, however. The Antarctic Treaty and its constellation of agreements are generally open to accession by any state wanting to become party to an agreement. Even so, mere accession cannot guarantee participation in the regime's decision-making capacity. Management under the ATS occurs through the Consultative Party process. Policies are negotiated, adopted, and implemented by those governments that have demonstrated through substantial scientific activity their interest in Antarctica. These are the Consultative Parties, as provided for in Article IX of the Antarctic Treaty. This qualification clause precludes universal participation and thus ensures that the common management system will remain influenced only by a select group of states.

In substantial part, the Antarctic Treaty System generates an international regime that gives effect to most common heritage objectives. Excluded from these objectives, though, is active and equitable sharing of benefits derived from exploitation of the common heritage area and its resources. In the ATS there is no equitable sharing of economic benefits with the international community. A commons regime based on equitable sharing does not permit wholesale appropriation by the exploiter. Antarctic resource conservation regimes thus conflict with this aspiration in a CHM regime. The Antarctic Treaty's family of agreements rests on free access and open opportunity under a regulated system. Even so, equitable sharing with the remainder of the international community is not mandated for any treaty member, or the ATCP group as a whole.

Future Considerations

A final conclusion points to the future. The UN debate over application of common heritage to Antarctica underscores the vital need to preserve and protect that area for succeeding generations. The Antarctic commons must not be exploited merely for present gain but rather should be preserved for future appreciation. This means that policies of environmental protection must be realistically fashioned and effectively enforced by the Consultative Parties throughout the region. If eventually deemed permissible, a rational system of resource development must be devised to protect the Antarctic commons from depletion and contamination. In addition, environmental protection through pollution control and prudent conservation remains essential. Unless environmental protection and resource conservation can be enforced, future generations will inherit an Antarctic commons whose pristine quality has been contaminated and despoiled.[90]

Critical, too, for sustaining the Antarctic for future generations is strict observance of peaceful uses only of the area. The last half-century demonstrated that commonality and exclusivity are conflicting concepts and may not always be easily reconciled among governments involved in Antarctic affairs. Some parties retain hidden agendas (e.g., sovereignty considerations of the claimants); some governments may have aspirations for political leadership (e.g., Malaysia); others appear paranoid over the prospects of greater international bureaucracy (hence Argentina's argument persistently to oppose creation of an ATS Secretariat); and still others resent being dictated to (viz., the United States and Russia). The point here seems plain: The quest for national political aggrandizement and self-interest could aggravate tensions that would undermine international cooperation in the Antarctic. Overt tendencies toward such lapses into nationalism could prove risky to political stability in the region. In any event, the Antarctic commons must not be allowed to become the object of conflict or discord between states having interests in that region.

CONCLUSION

Common heritage as a concept is multidimensional. There is a philosophical dimension, in which the moral grounds for the common heritage are measured and set out. An economic dimension deals with fixing nonownership of the heritage, with shared benefits accruing to the international community. There is also an environmental dimension, in which conservation is mandated for all humanity, including future generations. A political and security dimension advocates shared management, with the prescribed area to be used for peaceful purposes only. Finally, there is a legal dimension, in which no sovereignty is exercised or rights of claim to title are permitted.

Common heritage spaces refer to regions beyond the limits of national jurisdiction that are not subject to national appropriation by sovereignty, by means of use or occupation, or by any other means. CHM areas are to be managed for the benefit of humankind as a whole. Their domain and resources are to be used exclusively for peaceful purposes, in order that the heritage might be conserved as an entrustment to future generations.

Under the common heritage of mankind, states agree to suspend national rights to jurisdiction so as to benefit the whole community and promote the common interest of humankind. Herein operates the principle of nonappropriation. CHM becomes the instrument of peaceful use and prudent management in the interest of all mankind. Common heritage essentially contains a trust underpinned by a duty to ensure integrity, protection, conservation, and transmission to future generations of that heritage. To attain those ambitions involves rational management and conservation of a commons area and its natural resources. Thus, CHM remains guided mainly by long-term objectives, with few if any immediate advantages to the international community. The operative obligation attains common acceptance by virtue of treaty relationships, rather than the slower, more ambiguous formulation of customary law through state practice.

Antarctica enjoys a unique status in international law. The Antarctic Treaty provides the most comprehensive and widely accepted statement of international legal principles considered applicable to Antarctica. Certain principles in the treaty intimate that Antarctica is earmarked by the status of being a global common space. Core precepts in the Antarctic Treaty furnish credence to that instrument's functioning as an effective regime for managing the commons area of the polar South. Among these are the following: First, the treaty provides for nonappropriation of the area, which is administered by parties through a consultative governance mechanism. The treaty extends no form of positive recognition of claims to territorial sovereignty in Antarctica, though neither does it deny that such claims may rightfully exist. Second, the treaty provides for common rights of access and does not deny access to any state or person. No restrictions in the treaty are placed on any person to move freely and establish settlements on continent. Third, the treaty allocates no exclusive rights to resources; it does so by establishing means of common governance and free, open access to all. Fourth, the treaty imposes shared rights on decision-making. Equal participation is provided for

ATCPs on all deliberations concerning Antarctica, and decisions by consensus (and in effect, rule by unanimity) ensure that each state retains equal power in making policy. Fifth, the treaty endorses the need for environmental protection. Nuclear explosions and the disposal of radioactive materials are expressly banned in Antarctica. The 1959 Treaty also identifies "preservation and conservation of living resources" as a topic appropriate for future ATCP discussions, which, of course, it has become. And sixth, the treaty aims to ensure that scientific information be shared and peace on the continent be maintained. Antarctica under the treaty may be used for peaceful purposes only; this is in the interest of all humankind and is supportive of principles in the UN Charter.

The reform program implicit in CHM aimed at restructuring the legal regime for managing areas beyond the limits of national jurisdiction, inclusive of the Antarctic. Such restructuring would furnish the means to reshape the existing economic system and facilitate redistribution of wealth to needy countries so as to promote their national development. Arvid Pardo's proposal of common heritage of mankind covered issues of jurisdiction, peace, freedom of scientific research, equitable distribution of benefits, and environmental cognizance. But the essential element of nonownership remained: CHM areas would be situated beyond the limits of national jurisdiction and available for use by any state. They would not be susceptible, though, to ownership by any state.

The common heritage of mankind has not received express recognition as a concept legally applicable to the Antarctic. A reformed international economic order was seen by developing states as a panacea for remedying socio-economic inequities. Such was the case advanced for the New International Economic Order (NIEO) during the 1970s. The NIEO contained essential ingredients of "equality" and "justice" which could be pursued through channels of reversing biases in the free trade system.

Predictably, serious resentment and strong objection by the Consultative Parties erupted during the 1980s over the attempt to apply the NIEO variety of common heritage to Antarctica. Much of this objection centered on the notion of equitable benefits sharing, which purportedly would come from economic revenues derived from exploitation of natural resources in Antarctica. While, at the same time, ATCPs were willing to share aesthetic, wilderness, cultural, and scientific benefits, among others, strong insistence by claimant states on retaining sovereign rights over sector territories surfaced. Much attention on Antarctica now focuses on preserving and conserving Antarctica's resource base, not exploiting it.

The Antarctic, with some qualification, comprises part of the global commons. Antarctica may be treated legally as a common space area, and it is subject to certain international legal regimes that have been negotiated over the last four decades by interested parties. That said, a fundamental distinction between the Antarctic and other common space areas still turns on sovereignty considerations. Antarctica remains the only common space area subject to sovereignty claims. One might argue, then, that because seven states assert national claims to portions of the continent, Antarctica does not lie beyond the limits of national jurisdiction. Even so, those claims are not accepted as valid title by the international community. Not one of those national claims is recognized as legitimate territory by any other government, and three of the claimants—Argentina, Chile, and the United Kingdom—refuse to recognize the validity of each other's claims.

Antarctica thus remains unique as a common space area. It is the only global commons where ownership claims are disputed and where the status of asserted sovereignty claims are considered manifestly unperfected under international law. While the complex sovereignty situation in the Antarctic may therefore seem inviting for a common heritage regime, it cannot be so, at least for the foreseeable future. International law must evolve and progress to reflect the demands of modern society, especially its prevalent political interests and developmental aspirations. Within that legal system, the common heritage of mankind inculcates a form of trust, the primary objectives of which are rational use, good management, and transmission to future generations. But the complex interdependencies among politics, economics, and law affecting the Antarctic commons make difficult the processes of change.

So long as the Antarctic Treaty regime well serves the common interests of humankind, neither its lawfulness nor its purposes seem likely to be effectively challenged. Nor is the ATS likely to be replaced by any other regime resembling the common heritage of mankind. Hence, for the foreseeable future, the Consultative Parties will continue to manage Antarctica in trust for the international community. And whatever common heritagelike benefits accrue for the Antarctic commons, they will be the deliberative products from those governments' cooperative policies and programs effected through the Antarctic Treaty System.

Chapter 9

CONCLUSION

The Antarctic commons is an awesome wilderness. Of the seven continents, only Antarctica remains free of significant human habitation and intervention. It is the coldest, driest, wettest, windiest, highest, remotest, most inhospitable place on Earth. The vast land and its surrounding seas are dominated by nature, by cold and wind, by ice and snow. The continent is barren. There are no trees, flowers, butterflies, worms, reptiles, or amphibians. Antarctic wildlife depends on food from the ocean. Humans can exist there only with outside support.

Yet Antarctica exerts tremendous impacts on geophysical processes affecting the planet. Its ice cap and circumpolar seas are major factors in long-term climate change. Variation in stratospheric ozone above Antarctica holds global significance for the level of ultraviolet radiation that reaches Earth. The Southern Ocean, in particular the influence of its main circumpolar current, drives the circulation of the entire world ocean. Antarctic seas also contain a superabundance of living marine resources and potential food to feed the world's hungry.

The nature of the Antarctic is without peer. As such, understanding its environment can only be advanced by close study. The role of the Southern Ocean and the Antarctic ice cap are now being appreciated as central influences on the global environment. The geology of Antarctica holds clues to how the Earth's continents were at one time melded together into a giant supercontinent. Deep cores drawn from this ice mantle, supplemented by marine sediment data, reveal much about climate variation over many millennia. The biology of terrestrial and marine organisms in the Antarctic commons requires careful scrutiny both for understanding those species' populations and for their impacts on other species in the same ecosystem.

Research into how the Antarctic affects global weather patterns and climate offers insight into polar climate processes, including the mass and energy budgets of the Antarctic region. This is essential for understanding the nature and evolution of the Antarctic continent itself. Comprehending the mechanisms of the global climate remains prerequisite to understanding the circulation patterns and geophysics of the Southern Ocean as well.

Antarctica, keystone to the prehistoric supercontinent called Gondwana, remains integral for the study of paleotectonics. The white continent is the strongest cooling center of the global system and accordingly generates impacts for meteorological and climatic studies. The isolation of Antarctica by a wide and deep circumpolar ocean allows it to be relatively unaffected by human activities, and such a relatively pristine condition permits a natural baseline for studies in global pollution of various kinds. Many biological problems peculiar to the Antarctic commons are studied as well.

The value of scientific information from the Antarctic is immense. Scientific study in the polar South generates greater knowledge and better comprehension of the region's natural environment, improves our understanding of global processes, and permits the bases for assessing consequences of human activities worldwide. Research enables compilation of an inventory of biological, glaciological, and geological attributes of the Antarctic, scientific investigations of which can lead to designs for regional conservation measures. Science activities also document the geophysical condition of Antarctica and point out unique features there as contrasts for better understanding other places on the Earth's surface. Special, directed scientific research increases knowledge about those physical, chemical, geological, and biological processes that have formed and now sustain the unique natural environment of the Antarctic commons.

A chief advantage of Antarctica for scientific research is the unique political situation there. The absence of national boundaries under the Antarctic Treaty facilitates large-scale cooperation in scientific programs. But the extremely high costs of supporting research in the harshest, coldest, most remote and inhospitable region on Earth creates the basic need to share logistic support and collaborate more through interdisciplinary programs. The Antarctic Treaty and its family of legal agreements supply the conduits through which these programs are planned and carried out in an environmentally acceptable manner.

The Antarctic commons likewise enjoys a unique status in international law. The Antarctic Treaty provides the most comprehensive and widely accepted statement of international legal principles applicable to Antarctica. Principles in the treaty intimate that the Antarctic merits the status of a global commons space. In this regard, six core precepts undergird the Antarctic Treaty's credibility for functioning as an effective regime for managing the polar South. First, the treaty provides that the area must not be appropriated and should be administered by parties through a consultative governance mechanism. It extends no form of positive recognition of claims to territorial sovereignty in Antarctica, though neither does it deny that such claims may rightfully exist. Second, the treaty provides for common rights of access and does not deny access to any state or individual. No restrictions are placed on any person to move freely and establish settlements on the continent. Third, the treaty allocates no exclusive rights to resources. It does so by establishing means of common governance and free, open access to all. Fourth, the treaty imposes shared rights on decision-making. Equal participation is provided for every Consultative Party (ATCP) on all deliberations concerning the Antarctic. Decision by consensus (and, in effect, rule by unanimity) ensures that each state retains equal power in making policy. Fifth, the treaty endorses the need for environmental protection. Nuclear explosions and the disposal of radioactive materials are expressly banned in Antarctica. The agreement also identifies "preservation and conservation of living resources" as a topic appropriate for future ATCP discussions, which, of course, has been carried through. Sixth and finally, the treaty aims to ensure that scientific information is shared and peace on the continent is maintained. The treaty stipulates that, in the interest of all humankind and supportive of principles in the UN Charter, the Antarctic may be used for peaceful purposes only.

These core precepts have been integrated into a constellation of supplementary agreements—the Antarctic Treaty System (ATS)— specifically designed for managing the Antarctic commons. Indeed, this system supplies an integrated approach for governing the Antarctic area. The ATS provides the structure through which to manage and, if necessary, make policy decisions about the values affecting the frozen South. The ATS constitutes the international legal regime for managing and administering the activities of at least forty-three governments and their nationals in the polar South.

It must be remembered, though, that vital national interests guide each government's Antarctic policy positions. In this regard, four universal interests can be posited as being preeminent among the ATCPs' foreign policies. First, all ATCPs want to maintain the Antarctic as a region free from military or geopolitical confrontation. Second, they intend to protect the Antarctic environment. Third, they aim to ensure freedom for scientific research there. And fourth, they hope to derive reasonable economic benefits from the region. Still, any list of national interests does not entail a national strategy for attaining them. Such a national strategy requires integration of various elements of national interests, inclusive of environmental protection, national security, resource use, and scientific inquiry,

Each ATCP government administers the activities of its own nationals in the Antarctic through its own domestic legislation. Oversight regulation of some activities, including fishing in the Southern Ocean, is performed under international agreements to which the most important fishing states have given their consent.

Indeed, all fisheries in Antarctic waters are now controlled for ATCP nationals by regulations contained in the Convention on the Conservation of Antarctic Marine Living Resources (CCAMLR). This includes designation of prohibited areas and protected species and the imposition of closed seasons and catch limits. Regulations are based on scientific assessments conducted annually on data acquired directly from fisheries and research surveys. The CCAMLR Commission has also adopted measures that require members to provide specific information before engaging in new fisheries.[1]

The critical policy-making component of the Antarctic Treaty System finds expression in the Antarctic Treaty Consultative Party Meetings (ATCMs). Power in Consultative Meetings is keyed to a number of factors. One is the influence of personalities. The force of a diplomat's personality and/or reputation as well as how effective he or she is at making things happen during a meeting carry considerable clout among delegates. In addition, the ability to communicate in English is fundamental to speaking and being heard at ATCMs, since English is the common language, the "default" language in diplomatic parlance. Other factors also contribute to perceptions of a government's special prominence among the ATCPs. A state's status as a claimant, its degree of scientific investment in Antarctic activities, and its level of technological expertise—all of these add to the political clout of a government in Antarctic affairs. Thus, the outcome of an ATCM actually depends on how many levers are pulled in which direction by whom. In short, the legal products of Consultative Meetings do not necessarily flow from the quality or quantity of debate. Rather, policies adopted derive more from the power of personalities, the personal deals struck, and the language used to consolidate an agreement.

It comes as little surprise, then, that effectiveness in compliance often evolves in an indirect manner. Compliance relates to the degree of publicizing and documenting a decision's objective, which is made scientifically unfettered by political considerations. Enforcement often is done through diplomatic pressure at ATCMs, which often occurs more informally than formally. Considerable pressure is also applied internationally between sessions. Intercessional pressure on ATCPs usually comes through diplomatic channels as communications and correspondence, although sometimes pressure can stem from nongovernmental organizations as well.

ATCM recommendations comprise significant aspects of the Antarctic Treaty System's regime structure and supply the legal sinews that bind together the cluster of Antarctic subregimes produced by ATS agreements. Yet, while consensus on a recommendation might be obtained from all delegates at a Consultative Meeting, that recommendation is not binding until it has been approved domestically by Consultative Party governments. Although voluntary compliance is encouraged during this interim period, it is not mandatory and certainly not enforceable. Many recommendations take years to get approved, and some are still pending. These delays reveal limitations of the ATCPs' real authority to implement policy for the Antarctic.

The inability of the ATS to enforce international adherence to all its provisions is a deficiency evident for environmental safeguards, particularly in three areas. First, as just noted, there has been a lack of timely approval of ATCM recommendations by contracting parties. Second, there is inconsistent compliance with recommendations that are approved. Third, there is the lack of any enforcement mechanism against governments that are not contracting parties to the Antarctic Treaty.[2] In this regard, it remains important to realize that the ATS agreements apply only to those governments that decide to become parties. Absent any mechanism for formal restraint, nonmember governments or their nationals are free to establish bases and conduct minerals operations anywhere on the continent. While this scenario appears unlikely to occur, it should not be wholly discounted.

International law must evolve and progress to reflect the demands of modern society, especially its prevalent political interests and developmental aspirations. Within that legal system the common heritage of mankind inculcates a form of trust, the primary objectives of which are rational use, good management, and transmission to future generations. But the complex interdependencies among politics, economics, and law affecting the Antarctic commons make change difficult.

Developing states have asserted that they have a stake in, or the right to derive benefits from, the Antarctic commons. Nonparties to the Antarctic Treaty System have no assurance that one day the more powerful, self-regulating ATS member states might decide to embark on exploitation of the continent and usurp the benefits deemed to belong to all mankind. The Antarctic commons, developing countries have maintained, should legally become part of the common heritage of mankind (CHM). The developing countries' arguments are straightforward. Under this common heritage doctrine states would agree to suspend national rights to jurisdiction so as to benefit the whole community and promote the common interest of humankind. Herein operates the principle of nonappropriation. CHM becomes the instrument of peaceful use and prudent management in the interest of all mankind. Common heritage essentially contains a trust underpinned by a duty to ensure integrity, protection, conservation, and transmission to future generations of that heritage. To attain those ambitions involves rational management and conservation of a commons area and its natural resources. Thus, CHM remains guided mainly by long-term objectives, with few if any immediate advantages to the international community. Operative obligations attain common acceptance by virtue of treaty relationships rather than the slower, more ambiguous formulation of customary law through state practice.

Furthermore, no binding liability mechanism yet exists for damage caused by activities in the Antarctic. Since most developing states played no part in negotiating the Protocol, nor presently participate in administering activities on the continent, these governments voice concern over the degree of liability to be imposed on ATCPs that do violate the rules. Until a formal annex on liability is agreed to and put in place, self-policing of the ATCPs' adherence to the Protocol will remain suspect in the eyes of non-ATS governments.

These developing countries' views are understandable. Yet so long as the Antarctic Treaty regime well serves the common interests of humankind, neither its lawfulness nor its purposes are likely to be challenged. Nor is the ATS likely to be replaced by another regime resembling the common heritage of mankind. The situation is profoundly complicated by the seven sovereignty claims to the continent. While the Antarctic Treaty does not resolve this legal conundrum, it does provide a practical means for setting those claims aside so that peaceful activities, especially scientific ones, may go forward in the Antarctic. Hence, for the foreseeable future, the Consultative Parties will continue to manage Antarctica in trust for the international community. And whatever common-heritage-like benefits accrue for the Antarctic commons, they will be the deliberative products from those ATCP governments' cooperative policies and programs effected through the Antarctic Treaty System.

The Madrid Environmental Protocol, promulgated legally as an integral part of the Antarctic Treaty, dedicates Antarctica to be a natural reserve devoted to peace and science. The Protocol establishes a comprehensive, legally binding regime for ensuring that all activities undertaken in Antarctica are consistent with protection of the environment and its dependent and associated ecosystems. As such, it represents the most recent addition to the Antarctic environmental regime and the culmination of ATCP efforts to protect the Antarctic commons from human-inflicted harm.

The greatest strengths of the Protocol lie in its environmental protection regime, the recognized need for environmental impact assessment, and the setting of higher standards for waste management practices. Implicit in the Protocol is the recognition that past practices were not good enough. Indeed, the success of the Madrid Protocol may come down to how effectively and efficiently its five annexes are operationalized by each ATCP government. The Madrid Environmental Protocol represents a significant achievement. Not only does it reaffirm the norms, principles, and values in the Antarctic Treaty regime, it also imbues the treaty parties with a new commitment to conservation and the recognition that the Antarctic is critical to the Earth's environmental condition.

But entry into force of the Madrid Protocol will not alleviate international concerns about the Antarctic environment. The area of the Protocol is limited: its jurisdiction only extends to 60° south latitude. Moreover, the Protocol—even with its annexes—falls short of integrating all existing international environmental agreements under the ATS. The need for more extensive coordination of national policies for international management of the Antarctic commons appears real and vital.

The Consultative Parties have made certain rules to be adhered to without creating adequate power to enforce them. A gap remains between provisions in the Protocol and the means to be used for ensuring compliance by governments or their operators. Other salient problems must also be addressed if the Protocol is to work effectively and expeditiously. For one, more efficient collaboration must be effected within the ATS. Key to that is the establishment of a Treaty System secretariat with the ability to disseminate information to all ATCPs on Antarctic-related issues and policies. Regrettably, prospects for adoption of a centralized ATS secretariat seem far off.[3] In addition, the ATCPs must allocate resources for more inspections—for example, to investigate whether scientific bases and stations remain in compliance with the Protocol's provisions. Policies and decisions must also be made regarding the problem of minerals prospecting being done under the guise of scientific research, though national inspections might offer some control in that regard.

Another limitation of the Protocol, especially from the viewpoint of conservationists, is that the ban on minerals activities in the Antarctic commons may not necessarily be permanent. After fifty years an amendment to lift prohibitions can be proposed at a review conference. Adoption of such an amendment would require only a majority of ATCPs, including three-fourths of the current Consultative Parties. The threshold for ratification of such an amendment is admittedly higher. Three-fourths of the ATCPs, including all current ATCP governments, would have to vote in favor. Furthermore, a legally binding regime for regulating minerals activities must also be implemented. Nonetheless, the fact remains that the much-heralded prohibition against mining and drilling in the Antarctic *could* eventually be lifted.

A related concern turns on the polemical "walkout" clause in the Protocol that could undermine the traditional ATS principles of consensus and unanimity.[4] Indeed, the Antarctic Treaty has been sustained and strengthened since 1961 by these principles. While the substantive impact of the "walkout" clause may not be realized for at least fifty years, the psychological effects may already be taking root in the political agendas of the most powerful ATCP governments. The United States insistence on inserting the "walkout" provision was viewed by many as a serious deviation from the spirit of international cooperation in order to pursue a domestic agenda. In the extreme, the "walkout" clause openly implies that each treaty party may pursue its own national priorities for the Antarctic, perhaps even at the expense of the entire Antarctic Treaty System. No less significant, the Protocol provides no incentives during the next five decades for member governments not to develop technologies that might permit them to exploit the Antarctic commons in the future for their own domestic gain.

Is there any place for the Convention on the Regulation of Antarctic Mineral Resource Activities (CRAMRA) to act as a safety net in the event the Protocol fails? Is it possible that CRAMRA could be resurrected and used if necessary? The Wellington Treaty is not going anywhere. CRAMRA represents a tremendous investment in time, energy, political accommodation, and intellect. The minerals agreement should not be forgotten for its valuable contribution to influencing the composition of the Madrid Protocol's environmental protection provisions, most notably Articles 3 and 4.[5] Yet, while this view seems eminently practical, the belief persists among many governments that CRAMRA today is dead. Technically, CRAMRA may be a treaty caught in legal limbo, waiting eventually to be ratified. But, the argument runs, it has no life. CRAMRA is no longer seen as the ugly duckling of the Antarctic Treaty System, waiting to grow someday into a beautiful regulatory swan. It is now regarded as just a dead duck.[6]

The reality, though, is that should mining ever appear in the offing, a return to the Wellington Minerals Convention would be quite reasonable as a starting point for a regulatory regime. Perhaps CRAMRA as such would not be resurrected, but it could be reincarnated in some other legal instrument. The bottom line, however, remains the same: It will be far more difficult to negotiate an effective instrument for regulating resource development *after* minerals have been discovered than to do so before anything of immense value is found, as was the case for CRAMRA. That fact should not be lost in the decision to conclude any future regime for overseeing minerals development in the Antarctic commons.

In spite of all this, the Antarctic Treaty System is working. The ATS has sought to deal with a wide range of issues, from conflicts over political sovereignty, to environmental conservation and protection safeguards, to preservation of scientific research and concerns over regulating tourism. Such a breadth of scope in an international treaty forum is a formidable ambition. Yet that effort has produced a complex international regime for governing the Antarctic commons. Norms, principles, and rules have been explicitly adopted by the ATCP governments to protect core values gleaned from the Antarctic situation. Special legal agreements have been promulgated and implemented that establish institutions, procedures, and processes to give effect to those norms, principles, and rules. To this extent, the Antarctic Treaty System functions as a multifaceted international regime for environmental governance in the polar South.

Nevertheless, the Antarctic Treaty System must still operate through an ongoing balancing act that presently involves twenty-six ATCP domestic agendas against the greater global needs of all states. For instance, the compromise in the Protocol on mineral resource exploitation may not be the ideal solution for environmentalists. Indeed, the argument can be made that it provides little more than a fifty-year moratorium on minerals activities—a period during which Antarctica's mineral resources might become more commercially lucrative and when industrialists will have perfected technologies that can exploit ice-infested regions more efficiently. Yet a deal was struck that ensures a legal obligation among ATCPs to protect the Antarctic environment against mining or drilling for at least half a century. Although compromise may not always lead to the best solution, it usually does produce the most workable one.

The Antarctic Treaty System can furnish substantial protection for the Antarctic environment against exploitation of mineral resources there over the next half-century. The ATS regime can also provide the international legal framework for managing the conservation of living resources throughout the Antarctic commons. Even so, permanent environmental security is not assured. The Antarctic commons is not an internationally protected world park. The region is still managed by governments, for governments, with policy-makers who make choices according to their states' own political agendas and national interest priorities. So long as each government's national interest is considered best served by participation in the ATS, then governments will observe the common good of ATS.

States are sovereign polities, organized and directed by governments. But governments are people, too. The real efficacy, then, of environmental protection policies must rest with the degree of genuine commitment by policy-makers in national governments. Governments participating in the Antarctic Treaty System process have made international laws protecting the Antarctic environment, and those governments must enforce their laws against nationals who violate them.

In the final analysis, the fault for degradation of the Antarctic commons will not lie in frail law. The law is present and plain. Moreover, an international regime has been established for administering that law throughout the polar South. If the past is prologue, additional environmental law will be created by the Consultative Parties as various new needs are perceived. The fault for violations instead can be found in the lack of political will among the Consultative Parties to monitor activities, enforce compliance, and compel compensation for liability. For in truth, the instruments in the Antarctic Treaty System can be only as strong as the participating governments are willing to make them. If the Antarctic commons is to be preserved and conserved as a de facto world park for future generations, then exercising and sustaining the necessary political will to accomplish that goal ranks as the critical consideration. That task undoubtedly cannot help but remain a preeminent challenge for Antarctic Treaty governments in the coming decades.

EPILOGUE

The Antarctic Treaty regime progressively developed in 1998. The XXIInd ATCM convened from May 25–June 5 in Tromso, Norway, and approved Bulgaria as the twenty-seventh Consultative Party. Several instruments were adopted: four decisions, including the rules of procedure for the Committee for Environmental Protection; two measures on the Antarctic Protected Area System; and six resolutions (concerning protected areas, a safety code for ships in polar waters, Antarctic data management, and emergency response action). The corpus of ATS policy instruments was thus enlarged to 203 recommendations (through 1995), and twenty-three resolutions, eight decisions, and fourteen measures (1996–1998). Many governments, moreover, have implemented the Madrid Environmental Protocol into their domestic law. But serious problems remain. Negotiation of an annex on liability for environmental damage remains stalled over the extent of liability and types of damage to be covered. The seven-year deadlock over the location of a secretariat persists. Global warming threatens near-term collapse of the Larsen B ice shelf, potentially the greatest disintegration of ice in history. Antarctic tourism grows steadily, enticing suggestions of other corporate ventures moving into the Antarctic. It is ironic indeed, given the Environmental Protocol's entry into force in January 1998, that globalization activities aimed at commercialization in the Antarctic could threaten grave degradation of its pristine environment. Successful resolution of these problematic trends will be critical to protecting and conserving the frozen commons in the twenty-first century.

NOTES

CHAPTER 1: INTRODUCTION

1. While the Antarctic commons is best delimited by the Antarctic Convergence, the Subtropical/Subantarctic Convergence appears the most appropriate natural boundary for designating the northern periphery of the Southern Ocean, which exceeds the bounds of the Antarctic. This subantarctic oceanic zone marks the point where northern, warmer surface waters initially meet southern, colder surface waters, around 40° south latitude. The area south of the Subantarctic Convergence is extensive: The combined ocean and land space covers some 52 million square kilometers (20 million square miles), more than one-tenth of the Earth's surface. This figure is derived from the composite sum of the area of ocean space (36 million square kilometers), the area of continental land and ice shelves (14.5 million square kilometers), and the area of all islands within the circumference of the Southern Ocean (approximately 1.5 million square kilometers).

2. IUCN—World Conservation Union, *A Strategy for Antarctic Conservation*, 9.

3. "Antarctica," in *New Encyclopaedia Britannica (Macropaedia)*, vol. 13 (Chicago: Encyclopaedia Britannica Inc., 1993), 788.

4. See C. S. M. Doake, "Keystone to Gondwana," in Walton, ed., *Antarctic Science*, 174, 178–88; and Central Intelligence Agency, *Polar Regions Atlas*, 35.

5. See generally David J. Drewry, "The Response of the Antarctic Ice Sheet to Climatic Change," in Harris and Stonehouse, eds., *Antarctica and Global Climate Change*, 90–106.

6. CIA, *Polar Regions Atlas*, 35;

7. "Antarctica," in *New Encyclopaedia Britannica*, 792.

8. CIA, *Polar Regions Atlas*, 35 (Map: Mean Air Temperature). See generally H. R. Phillpot, "Physical Geography—Climate," in Bonner and Walton, *Key Environments: Antarctica*, 23–38.

9. "Antarctica," in *New Encyclopaedia Britannica*, 792.

10. CIA, *Polar Regions Atlas*, 37; Anthony J. Gow, "The Ice Sheet," in Trevor Hatherton, ed., *Antarctica* (New York: Praeger, 1965), 225; J. R. Dudeney, "The Antarctic Climate Today," in Walton, ed., *Antarctic Science*, 209, 216.

11. "Antarctica," in *New Encyclopaedia Britannica*, 795; IUCN, *A Strategy for Antarctic Conservation*, 14. For a comprehensive examination of Antarctic terrestrial botany, see R. I. Lewis Smith, "Terrestrial Plant Biology of the Sub-Antarctic and Antarctic," in Laws, ed., *Antarctic Ecology*, vol. 1,61–162. See also "The Terrestrial Environment," in Ibid., 1–61; and R. E. Longton, "Terrestrial Habitats—Vegetation," in Bonner and Walton, *Key Environments: Antarctica*, 73–105.

12. See L. Somme, "Terrestrial Habitats—Invertebrates," in Bonner and Walton, *Key Environments: Antarctica*, 106–17; J. Linsley Gressett, "Terrestrial Animals," in Hatherton, ed., *Antarctica*, 351–71; IUCN, *A Strategy for Antarctic Conservation*, 15.

13. "Antarctica," *New Encyclopaedia Britannica*, 788; CIA, *Polar Regions Atlas*, 35. The ice sheet is estimated to cover some 13.5 million square kilometers in area. Gow, "The Ice Sheet," 222.

14. "Antarctica," *New Encyclopaedia Britannica*, 788. Anthony Gow has estimated that the volume of ice would compute to around 27 million cubic kilometers, or the equivalent of 24.5 million cubic kilometers of water. This is approximately 2 percent of the world's water budget, or 90 percent of the total ice in the world. If this ice mass were suddenly to melt into the Southern Ocean, the mean sea level would be raised by approximately 60 meters (200 feet). Gow, "The Ice Sheet," 229.

15. IUCN, *A Strategy for Antarctic Conservation*, 11.

16. "Warm Weather Aids Onyx River Flow," *Antarctic* 9(2) (1980): 49. Inland water bodies are few in Antarctica, though both freshwater and saline lakes can be found in coastal areas. See Julian Priddle, "Terrestrial Habitats—Inland Waters," in Bonner and Walton, *Key Environments: Antarctica*, 118–32.

17. T. D. Foster, "The Marine Environment," in Laws, ed., *Antarctic Ecology*, vol. 2, 353.

18. See C. Swithinbank, P. McClain, and P. Little, "Drift Tracks of Antarctic Icebergs," *Polar Record* 18 (1977): 495–501; and U. Radok, N. Streten, and G. E. Weller, "Atmosphere and Ice," *Oceanus* 18 (1975): 16–27.

19. See generally Jane Ellen Stevens, "Exploring Antarctic Ice," *National Geographic* 189 (May 1996): 36–553.

20. Richard M. Laws, "The Ecology of the Southern Ocean," *American Scientist* 73 (January–February 1985): 28.

21. Foster, "The Marine Environment," 351–52.

22. S. El-Sayed, "On the Productivity of the Southwest Atlantic Ocean and the Waters West of the Antarctic Peninsula," in *Biology of the Antarctic Seas* (American Geophysical Union Antarctic Research Series, Vol. 11, 1968), 15, 46. See generally I. Everson, "Antarctic Food Webs," in Walton, ed., *Antarctic Science*, 113–24.

23. J. W. S. Marr, "The Natural History and Geography of the Antarctic Krill (*Euphausia superba*)," *Discovery Report* 32 (1962): 33–464; Inigo Everson, *The Living Resources of the Southern Ocean* (UNDP/FAO Southern Ocean Fisheries Survey Programme), GLO/SO/77/8 (1977), at sec. 8. Also see N. A. Mackintosh,

"Distribution of Post-Larval Krill in the Antarctic," *Discovery Report* 36 (1973): 157–78; and map illustrating krill distribution in CIA, *Polar Regions Atlas*, 54.

24. Estimates of the krill stock vary widely, from 500 million to 5 billion metric tons. A more reasonable estimate may be the total krill biomass in the Southern Ocean put at 600 million metric tons, which may comprise 50 percent of the biomass of Antarctic animal plankton. IUCN, *A Strategy for Antarctic Conservation*, 17.

25. Knox, "The Living Resources of the Southern Ocean," 34–36; Karl-Hermann Kock, "Marine Habitats—Antarctic Fish," in Bonner and Walton, *Key Environments: Antarctica*, 171–92; I. Everson, "Fish," in El-Sayed, ed., *Biological Investigations of Marine Antarctic Systems and Stocks. Vol. II*, 31–46.

26. See generally I. Everson, "Fish," in Laws, ed., *Antarctic Ecology*, vol. 2, 491–532; P. Andriasev, "A General Review of the Antarctic Fish Fauna," in P. van Oye and J. van Miegham, eds., *Biogeography and Ecology of Antarctica* (The Hague: Dr. W. Junk, 1985), 491–550.

27. See generally Malcolm R. Clarke, "Marine Habitats—Antarctic Cephalopods," in Bonner and Walton, *Key Environments: Antarctica*, 193–200; and M. R. Clark, "Cephalopod Biomass—Estimation from Predation," *Memorial National Museum of Victoria*, no. 44 (1983): 95–107; Group of Specialists on Living Resources of the Southern Ocean, Scientific Committee on Antarctic Research and Scientific Committee on Oceanic Research, *Biological Investigations of Marine Antarctic Systems and Stocks (BIOMASS)* 1 (1977): 28–37.

28. Laws, "The Ecology of the Southern Ocean," 33. See generally W. R. Siegfried, "Birds and Mammals—Oceanic Birds of the Antarctic," in Bonner and Walton, *Key Environments: Antarctica*, 242–65; and J. P. Croxall, "Seabirds," in Laws, ed., *Antarctic Ecology*, 533–616.

29. IUCN, *A Strategy for Antarctic Conservation*, 17 (Table 4). Compare generally Bernard Stonehouse, "Birds and Mammals—Penguins," in Bonner and Walton, *Key Environments: Antarctica*, 266–92; J. W. H. Conroy, "Recent Increases in Penguin Populations in the Antarctic and Sub-antarctic," in B. Stonehouse, ed., *The Biology of Penguins* (Baltimore: University Park Press, 1975), 321–36; and G. J. Wilson, *Distribution and Abundance of Antarctic and Sub-Antarctic Penguins: A Synthesis of Current Knowledge* (Cambridge: SCAR and SCOR, 1983).

30. For the ecosystemic implications of these interdependent relationships, see the discussion of the CCAMLR Ecosystem Monitoring Program (CEMP) in chapter 5 *infra*.

31. See generally W. Nigel Bonner, "Birds and Mammals—Antarctic Seals," in Bonner and Walton, *Key Environments: Antarctica*, 202–22; and R. M. Laws, "Seals," in Laws, ed., *Antarctic Ecology*, 621–716.

32. IUCN, *A Strategy for Antarctic Conservation*, 18 and Table 5. Estimates on the crabeater population vary significantly, however. El-Sayed estimates the total at 30 million individuals. Sayed El-Sayed, "Biology of the Southern Ocean,"

Oceanus 18(4) (1975): 44. The BIOMASS study puts the number at 15 million (pp. 20–21, Table), while Green suggests a range of from 15 to 70 million individuals. Katherine A. Green, "The Role of Krill in the Antarctic Marine Ecosystem" (1977), p. 19, reprinted in U.S. Department of State, *Final Environmental Impact Statement for a Possible Regime for Conservation of Antarctic Marine Living Resources* (Washington, D.C.: Bureau of Ocean Affairs, 1978), Appendix C, 1–34.

33. Green, "The Role of Krill in the Antarctic Marine Ecosystem," 21.

34. Figures are from IUCN, *A Strategy for Antarctic Conservation*, 18.

35. Laws, "The Ecology of the Southern Ocean," 37; Laws, "Seals and Whales of the Southern Ocean," *Philosophical Transactions of the Royal Society*, London 279 (1977): 81–96.

36. See generally Ray Gambell, "Birds and Mammals—Antarctic Whales," in Bonner and Walton, *Key Environments: Antarctica*, 223–41; S. G. Brown and C. H. Lockyer, "Whales," in Laws, ed., *Antarctic Ecology*, 717–81; J. Gulland, "Antarctic Baleen Whales: History and Prospects," *Polar Record* 18 (1976): 5–13; and Laws, "Seals and Whales of the Southern Ocean," 81–96.

37. IUCN, *A Strategy for Antarctic Conservation*, 19. Figures are drawn from the IUCN discussion.

38. "British Letters Patent appointing the Governor of the Colony of the Falkland Islands to be Governor of the South Georgia, the South Orkneys, the South Shetlands, the Sandwich Islands, and Graham's lands, and providing for the Government thereof as Dependencies of the Colonies—Westminster, July 21, 1908," United Kingdom, *British Foreign and State Papers* 101 (1909): 76.

39. "British Letters Patent, passed under the Great Seal of the United Kingdom, providing for the further Definition and Administration of certain Islands and Territories as Dependencies of the Colony of the Falkland Islands—Westminster, March 28, 1917," United Kingdom, *British Foreign and State Papers* 111 (1919): 16.

40. These assertions to discovery by English explorers were formally set out in defense of the British claim when the United Kingdom attempted to bring Argentina and Chile to the International Court of Justice in 1956 to adjudicate the question of sovereign title to their overlapping Antarctic claims. Neither of the Latin American states opted to accept the United Kingdom's petition. See *Antarctica Cases* (United Kingdom v. Argentina) (United Kingdom v. Chile) International Court of Justice *Pleadings* (1956), 11 ff.

41. "Order in Council under the British Settlements Act, 1887 (50 & 51 Vict. C. 54) Providing for the Government of the Ross Dependency," New Zealand *Government Gazette* 2 (Wellington, 1923), 2211 (August 16, 1923), reprinted in W. Bush, *Antarctica and International Law*, vol. 3 (Dobbs Ferry, N.Y.: Oceana Pub., 1988), 44.

42. Title to Antarctica was officially accepted through the Australian Antarctic Territory Acceptance Act 1933, Act no. 8 of 1933, in Australia, *Commonwealth Acts 1901–1950* vol.1 (Sydney: Law Book Co., 1952–55), 221.

43. "Proclamation by the Governor-General Fixing the Date upon which the Order in Council Placing the Australian Antarctic Territory under the Authority of the Commonwealth Shall Come into Operation," Australia, *Commonwealth of Australia Gazette* No. 70 (August 24, 1936), 1,553, reprinted in W. Bush, *Antarctica and International Law*, vol. 2 (Dobbs Ferry, N.Y.: Oceana Pub., 1982), 151–52.

44. "Decree Attaching French Antarctic Territories to the Government General of Madagascar (21 November 1924)," in France, *Journal officiel de la Republique fracaise; lois et decrets* (Paris, November 27, 1924), 10,452–53, reprinted in Bush, *Antarctica and International Law*, vol. 2, 494.

45. "Decree Defining the Limits of Adelie Land (1 April 1938)," in France, *Journal Officiel*, April 6, 1938, 4,098–99, reprinted in Bush, *Antarctica and International Law*, vol. 2, 505–6.

46. "National Sovereignty in the Antarctic (Proclamation of King Haakon of Norway, January 14, 1939)," reprinted in *American Journal of International Law* 34 (Supplement 1940): 83. The motivation for Norway's claim being asserted in 1939 was to preclude possible German claims in the region. See International Institute for Environment and Development, *The Future of Antarctica* (Earthscan Press Briefing Doc. No. 5 1978), reprinted in U.S. Congress, Senate, *Exploitation of Antarctic Resources, Hearings* before the Subcommittee on Arms Control, Oceans and the International Environment, Senate Committee on Foreign Relations, 95th Cong., 2d Sess. (1978), 197.

47. See, respectively, "Royal Decree Approving a Proposal of the Ministry of Foreign Affairs that Bouvet Island be Placed under Norwegian Sovereignty (23 January 1928)," reprinted in U.S. Naval War College, *International Law Documents, 1948–49* 46 (Washington, D.C., 1950), 238 and "Royal Proclamation Placing Peter I Island under Norwegian Sovereignty (1 May 1931)," in Ibid., 239.

48. As Amundsen himself put it in raising the Norwegian flag over the South Pole, "Thus we plant thee, beloved flag, at the South Pole, and give to the plain on which it lies the name of King Haakon VII's Plateau." Amundsen, *The South Pole*, 121–22.

49. See Donat Pharand, *Canada's Arctic Waters in International Law* (Cambridge: Cambridge University Press, 1988), 78.

50. See CIA, *Polar Regions Atlas*, 43.

51. "Decree No. 1,747 Declaring the Limits of the Chilean Antarctic Territory (6 November 1940)," in Chile, *Boletin de los leyes; de los ordenes; decretos del Gobierno, 1940* 109 (1940): 2,440–41; reprinted in Bush, *Antarctica and International Law*, vol. 2, 311.

52. For discussion, see Pinochet de la Barra, *Chilean Sovereignty in Antarctica*, 63–67.

53. For an analysis of Chile's Antarctic activities since 1947, see Joyner and Ewing, "Antarctica and the Latin American States," 17–23, 33–34, 43.

54. See "Report of a Chilean Memorandum to Argentina Reserving Chilean

Rights with Regard to an Argentine Map Delimiting Argentine Claims to an Antarctic Sector," in W. Bush, ed., *Antarctica and International Law,* vol. 1 (Dobbs Ferry, N.Y.: Oceana Pub., 1982), 627–31.

55. Of this area, approximately 1 million square kilometers is considered "firm land." Jorge A. Fraga, *El Mar y La Antartida en la Geopolitica Argentina* (Buenos Aires: Instituto de Publicaciones Navales del Centro Naval de Nuevos Aires, 1980), 215–16.

56. See P. de Mones Ruiz, *Antartida Argentina, Islas Oceanicas, Mar Argentino* (Buenos Aires: Libreria del Colegio, 1948), 44.

57. See Joyner, "Anglo-Argentine Rivalry After the Falklands/Malvinas War, 474–75.

58. *Uti possidetis* has been formally defined as a "species of interdict for the purpose of retaining possession of a thing granted to one who, at the time of contesting suit, was in possession of an immovable thing, in order that he might be declared legal possessor." Black, *Black's Law Dictionary,* 1546. See Waldock, "Disputed Sovereignty in the Falkland Islands Dependencies," 319–25.

59. See the discussions in Daniel, "Conflict of Sovereignties in the Antarctic," 262–66; Bernhardt, "Sovereignty in Antarctica," 345–47; Hayton, "The 'American' Antarctic," 583, 585; and Joyner, "Anglo-Argentine Rivalry," 476–78.

60. See Bernhardt, "Sovereignty in Antarctica," 339–42.

61. F. A. Mila, *La Atlantartida in Espacio Geopolitico* (Buenos Aires: Ediciones Pleamar, 1978), 248. See Joyner, "Anglo-Argentine Rivalry," 479–80. For an analysis of Argentina's Antarctic activities since 1945, see Joyner and Ewing, "Antarctica and the Latin American States," 4–17.

62. D. P. O'Connell, *International Law,* Dobbs Ferry, NY: Oceana Publishers (2nd ed. 1970), 408. Also see Van der Heydte, "Discovery, Symbolic Annexation and Virtual Effectiveness in International Law," 448.

63. Lassa Oppenheim, *International Law* (Hersh Lauterpacht ed., 8th ed., London: Longmans Green, 1955), 509–10.

64. For discussion of the legal particulars, see *Island of Palmas Case* (U.S. v. Netherlands), Permanent Court of Arbitration, *U.N. Report of International Arbitration Awards* 2 (1928): 884; *Legal Status of Eastern Greenland Case* (Denmark vs. Norway), Permanent Court of International Justice, Series A/B, No. 53 (1933). 3 Hudson, *World Court Reports* 148. See also M. F. Lindley, *The Acquisition and Government of Backward Territory in International Law* (London: Longmans, Green and Co., 1926), 141.

65. See Oppenheim, *International Law,* 509–510; O'Connell, *International Law,* 409–18; and Smedal, *Acquisition of Sovereignty Over Polar Areas,* 38.

66. Interestingly enough, both Argentina and Chile have sponsored national "colonies" as demonstrable evidence that settlers are inhabiting their claimed sectors. The Argentine colony is located at Esperanza Bay, on Trinity Peninsula, and some 60 colonists live there. There is a bank, a hotel, a post office, and living quarters. Chile's national colony is Lt. Adolopo Marsh/Presidente Frei Base,

located on King George Island, populated by 70 "settlers." While perhaps symbolically interesting, the legal weight attached to these bases is slight at best, principally because these "colonies" are peripheral to the entire continent. Personal communication from Ricardo Roura, April 9, 1997.

67. Normally in international law, effective occupation of uninhabited territory requires demonstration of effective, exclusive authority through an administration capable of securing respect for sovereign rights. Two cases involving disputed claims to title over territory cast conflicting views over this standard.

First, in 1932, France and Mexico submitted their dispute over Clipperton Island, a small unpopulated guano island in the Pacific about 670 miles southwest of Mexico, to arbitration by King Victor Emmanuel III of Italy. The French claim was based on discovery of the island by a French naval officer in 1858, who had proclaimed French sovereignty and published a declaration to that effect in a Honolulu journal. He had, however, left no signs of sovereignty on the island. Mexico claimed it had inherited sovereignty by virtue of Spanish discovery. The arbitrator ruled in favor of France, holding that France had fulfilled the requirement for effective occupation of Clipperton Island sufficiently, despite that it had remained uninhabited and that the administrative details of sovereignty—e.g., post offices, currency services, and police forces—were absent. In effect, then, symbols of administration were not necessary to fix valid claim to title over an unpopulated region. France had demonstrated *animus occupandi*, the will to act as sovereign, when it need be. See *Clipperton Island Arbitration, U.N. Reports of the International Arbitration Awards* 2 (1931): 1105.

The second case involved a decision by the Permanent Court of International Justice in 1933 concerning the legal status of Eastern Greenland. A Norwegian proclamation of 1931 purported to place portions of Eastern Greenland under Norwegian sovereignty on the premise that that territory had never been occupied by its claimant, Denmark, and was therefore *terra nullius*. The court ruled against Norway's contention, concluding that Denmark had shown a "continued display of authority," with the intention and will of acting as sovereign. Denmark had exercised sufficient sovereignty over all the island, not just over the colonized areas. The failure to colonize was not due to will so much as the relatively inaccessible, inhospitable nature of Greenland given its severe climatic conditions. See *Legal Status of Greenland Case* (Denmark v. Norway), Permanent Court of International Justice, Permanent Court of International Justice Series, A/B, No. 53 (1933), 3 Hudson, *World Court Reports,* 148. The law of occupation interpreted from these cases emerges as neither black nor white, but rather as a murky hue of gray.

68. See Joyner and Theis, *Eagle Over the Ice,* 150–52; and Rothwell, *The Polar Regions and the Development of International Law,* 65–66.

69. Antarctic Treaty, Article VI.

70. The Antarctic Treaty Consultative Parties, which possess full voting membership among the Antarctic Treaty parties, presently count twenty-six states as members. The twelve original parties to the Antarctic Treaty (viz., Argentina, Australia, Belgium, Chile, France, Japan, New Zealand, Norway, South Africa, the Soviet Union [Russia], the Union Kingdom, and the United States) comprised the initial group of Consultative Party states. Since the Antarctic Treaty's entry into force in 1961, Consultative Party status has been granted to certain states that have "demonstrated scientific research activity" in and around the continent. The Antarctic Treaty, done Dec. 1, 1959, 12 U.S.T. 794, T.I.A.S. No. 4780, 402 U.N.T.S. 71, art. IX, para. 2. As of 1997 the following additional states have been admitted to the Consultative Party group: Brazil, China, Ecuador, Finland, Germany, India, Italy, South Korea, the Netherlands, Peru, Poland, Spain, Sweden, and Uruguay. These ATCPs work in annual meetings to set recommended policy for the Antarctic.

Seventeen other contracting states have ratified the Antarctic Treaty but have not opted to become ATCPs. Included in this group of Non-Consultative Parties in 1998 are: Austria, Bulgaria, Canada, Colombia, Cuba, the Czech Republic, Denmark, Greece, Guatemala, Hungary, the Democratic People's Republic of Korea, Papua New Guinea, Romania, the Slovak Republic, Switzerland, Turkey, and the Ukraine. U.S. Department of State, *Treaties in Force: A List of Treaties and Other International Agreements of the United States in Force on January 1, 1997* (Washington, D.C.: Department of State, 1997): 321–22.

71. Done at Brussels, June 2–13, 1964, 17 U.S.T. 996, 998, T.I.A.S. No. 6058, modified in 24 U.S.T. 1802, T.I.A.S. No. 7693 (1973).

72. Done at London, June 1, 1972, entered into force March 11, 1978. 27 U.S.T. 441, T.I.A.S. No. 8826.

73. Done May 20, 1980, 33 U.S.T. 3476, T.I.A.S. No. 10,240.

74. Ibid., Article I.

75. Done at Wellington, June 2, 1988, opened for signature November 25, 1988. Document AMR/SCM/88/78 (June 2, 1988), reprinted in *International Legal Materials* 27 (July 1988): 859–900. For discussion of the negotiations that produced this agreement, see Joyner, "The Antarctic Minerals Negotiating Process," 888–905; and Franciso Orrego Vicuña, *Antarctic Mineral Exploitation: The Emerging Framework* (Cambridge: Cambridge University Press, 1988).

76. Protocol on Environmental Protection to the Antarctic Treaty, XIth Special Consultative Meeting in Madrid, Doc. XI ATSCM/2, June 21, 1991, adopted October 4, 1991. [Hereinafter Madrid Environmental Protocol]. The protocol was then signed by twenty-three of twenty-six Antarctic Treaty Consultative Parties and by eight Non-Consultative Parties. "Statement of James Neil Barnes and Beth Claudia Marks to the Committee on Foreign Relations of the U.S. Senate on the Antarctic Environmental Protection Protocol," Hearings before the Senate Foreign Relations Committee, 102nd Cong., 2nd sess., at 7 (May 4, 1992) (mimeograph). The Protocol entered into force on January 14, 1998.

CHAPTER 2: THE FROZEN COMMONS

1. Declaration of the United Nations Conference on the Human Environment (Stockholm Declaration), U.N. Doc. A/Conf. 48/14/Rev.1 (1973), U.N. Pub. No. E.73.IIa.14 (1974), also reprinted in *International Legal Materials* 11 (1972): 1416.

2. World Commission on Environment and Development, *Our Common Future*, 263. The present study emphasizes the "global" aspects of the commons concept, as distinct from many thousands of so-called commons areas in less-developed countries, such as small lakes, wells, grazing areas, and fields, where local management regimes somehow govern use. The problems facing such localized commons areas are detailed in "Whose Common Future: A Special Issue," *The Ecologist* 22 (July/August 1992): 125 and *World Development* 19 (1991) (a special issue addressing commons issues).

3. See generally Kish, *The Law of International Spaces*.

4. Compare, e.g., Ostrom, *Governing the Commons* and Sir Arthur Watts, *International law and the Antarctic Treaty System*.

5. This is a definition of the early English commons. See discussion in the text *infra* accompanying notes 28–30.

6. Neva R. Goodwin, "Introduction," *World Development* 19 (1991): 1.

7. Stone, *The Gnat Is Older Than Man*, 34.

8. See Ostrom, *Governing the Commons* and note 50 *infra*.

9. Christy and Scott, *The Common Wealth in Ocean Fisheries*, 6. Put another way, one individual or state cannot appropriate the full yield of a common property resource. See also "The Commons: Neither Public Nor Private," *The Ecologist* 22 (July/August 1992): 125, which explains that commons are "'resources for which exclusion is difficult' and boundary-setting not worthwhile, or which 'are needed by all by whose productivity is diffuse rather than concentrated, low or unpredictable in yield, and low in unit value.'"

10. Wijkman, "Managing the Global Commons," 511, 512.

11. The concept of indivisibility of a good or resource can be construed as purely economic. As one scholar has observed: "A good is indivisible if either of the following two sufficient but not necessary conditions are met: 1) It is not possible to divide or partition the consumption among different individuals; the good is a nonexcludable public good or externality. 2) The technology by which the good is produced involves such a significant indivisibility that, when a Pareto-efficient quantity of the good is produced, marginal cost is less than average cost." Olson, "Environmental Indivisibilities and Information Costs," 262, 264.

12. The oceans provide a number of examples of regional management regimes in the form of the Regional Seas Programme sponsored by the United Nations. See Peter H. Sands, *Marine Environment Law in the United Nations Environmental Programme*, Natural Resources and the Environment Series, vol. 24

(London: Tycooly, 1988). For a specific application of this regional approach to a pollution problem, see Christopher C. Joyner and Scot Frew, "Plastic Pollution in the Marine Environment," *Ocean Development and International Law* 22 (1991): 33, 47–53.

13. Wijkman, "Managing the Global Commons," 7, noting that common pool resources will have differing economic characteristics relating to their use.

14. Levin, "Regulating the Global Commons," 252.

15. Harlan Cleveland, "The Global Commons," *The Futurist* 10 (May/June 1993). See also Seyom Brown, Nina A. Cornell, Larry L. Fabian, and Edith Brown Weiss, *Regimes for the Ocean, Outer Space and Weather* (Washington, D.C.: Brookings Institution, 1977).

16. For a general discussion of ocean issues, see generally World Commission on Environment and Development, *Our Common Future*, 262–74.

17. See Christopher C. Joyner, "Introduction," in Joyner and Chopra, eds., *The Antarctic Legal Regime*, 1–6; and Oran R. Young, "Global Commons: The Arctic in World Affairs," *Technology Review* 93 (February/March 1990): 54.

18. I am grateful to Marvin S. Soroos for noting this point. For discussion on the atmosphere as a global commons area, see his *The Changing Atmosphere: The Quest for Global Environmental Security* (Columbia, S.C.: University of South Carolina Press, 1997).

19. Malcolm N. Shaw, *International Law* (Cambridge: Cambridge University Press, 1994), 328. Some have suggested 110 kilometers. Ibid., 329, at note 31.

20. Agreement Governing the Activities on the Moon and Other Celestial Bodies, text annexed to U.N.G.A. Res. 34/68, 34 U.N. GAOR Supp. (No. 46) at 77, U.N. Doc. A/Res/34/68 (1979) [hereinafter Moon Treaty]. See Stephen D. Mau, "Equity, the Third World, and the Moon Treaty," *Suffolk Transnational Law Journal* 8 (1984): 221; and Christol, "The Common Heritage of Mankind Provisions in the 1979 Agreement Governing the Activities on the Moon and Other Celestial Bodies," 429.

21. Treaty on Principles Governing the Activities of States in the Exploration and Use of Outer Space, Including the Moon and Other Celestial Bodies, 18 U.S.T. 2411, T.I.A.S. No. 6347, 610 U.N.T.S. 205 (1967).

22. Levin, "Regulating the Global Commons," 254 (defining orbit spectrum as a commons but noting that usage affects its "globalness"); Stephen Gorove, "Geostationary Orbit: Issues of Law and Policy," *American Journal of International Law* 73 (1979): 445; Soroos, "The Commons in the Sky," 665. The geostationary orbit exists 22,300 miles above the Earth's equator, where communications satellites can park and appear to remain over one spot on the globe as they orbit. This promotes efficient global coverage. Owing to interference between satellites, a certain distance must be maintained between "parking spots," hence the limitation on the resource.

23. See Levin, "Regulating the Global Commons," 254; and Soroos, "The Commons in the Sky," 665.

24. Gareth Branwyn and Peter Sugarman, "Computer Networks as an 'Information Commons,'" *The Futurist* 24 (July/August 1990): 46.

25. Most important among these were Brazil, Indonesia, and Malaysia. James Brooke, "On Amazon, Foes Are Reptiles and Environmentalists," *New York Times*, June 13, 1992, p. A4. For discussion, see Christopher C. Joyner, "Deforestation in Amazonia: Policies, Politics, and Global Implications," *International Studies Notes* 16 (Winter 1991): 24–30.

26. That the world's forests with their biological richness are a commons resource remains a contentious point. These resources are in fact enclosed within the territory of sovereign states and are subject to those states' jurisdiction. See Stone, *The Gnat Is Older Than Man*, 203, who asserts that biodiversity would not qualify as part of the common heritage of mankind or as part of his global trusteeship.

The U.S.-sponsored effort during 1991–92 to negotiate an international convention for the protection of tropical forestry resources, however, failed to generate sufficient support among states having tropical forests. As a result, the only relevant product of the Rio Summit was a nonbinding statement of forestry principles.

27. United Nations, *Global Outlook 2000: An Economic, Social, and Environmental Perspective* (1990): 79, U.N. Doc. ST/ESA/215/Rev. 1 (1990) ("The maintenance of biological diversity is a precondition for sustainable development.") See also Michael McCarthy, "North and South Bicker Over Value of Wildlife," *The Times* (London), June 3, 1992, p. 12.

28. "Biodegradable Treaty," *The Times* (London), June 3, 1992, p. 15. The United States refused at that time to sign because of problems with the patent protection provisions for genetic research. See "Excerpts From Speech By Bush on 'Action Plan,'" *New York Times*, June 13, 1992, p. A5: "[The] proposed agreement threatens to retard biotechnology and undermine the protection of ideas."

29. The "commons" aspect of forests and biomass lies neither in their situation nor ownership; it turns on the globally common effect that is created by their destruction. In addition to these "conventional" commons, one commentator has suggested that the global economy be regarded as a commons, because it is subject to similar abuses, and the effects of abuse are universal. See Hilary F. French, *After the Earth Summit: The Future of Environmental Governance* (Washington, D.C.: Worldwatch Institute, Worldwatch Paper 107, March 1992), 21.

30. See generally the selections in Hardin and Baden, eds., *Managing the Commons*.

31. Hardin, "The Tragedy of the Commons," 1243–48.

32. Some commentators draw a distinction between Hardin's conceptualization of the commons, arguing that it is an "open access" regime over which no one has authority, and that of a true commons, over which the community has ultimate authority. See "The Commons: Where the Community

Has Authority," *The Ecologist* 22 (July/August 1992): 127. Compare also Beryl L. Crowe, "The Tragedy of the Commons Revisited," *Science* 166 (1969): 1103–7, reprinted in Hardin and Baden, eds., *Managing the Commons*, 53–65; and Elinor Ostrom, "Collective Action and the Tragedy of the Commons," in Ibid., 173–81.

33. For discussion, see generally Ostrom, *Governing the Commons*; D. W. Bromley, ed., *Making the Commons Work: Theory, Practice and Policy* (San Francisco: Institute for Contemporary Studies, 1992); and D. W. Bromley, *Environment and Economy: Property Rights and Public Policy* (Oxford: Basil Blackwell, 1991).

34. See Ophuls, *Ecology and the Politics of Scarcity*, 148–49; and Ostrom, *Governing the Commons*.

35. See generally Bromley, *Making the Commons Work*; Young, *International Cooperation*; and Oran R. Young, *International Governance: Protecting the Environment in a Stateless Society* (Ithaca, N.Y.: Cornell University Press, 1994).

36. As defined by an authoritative source, *res nullius* is "[t]he property of nobody. A thing which has no owner, either because a former owner has finally abandoned it, or because it has never been appropriated by any person, or because (in the Roman Law) it is not susceptible to private ownership." *Black's Law Dictionary*, 6th ed. (1992), 1306.

37. See von Glahn, *Law Among Nations*, 296–348; and Sudhir K. Chopra, "Antarctica as a Commons Regime: A Conceptual Framework for Cooperation and Coexistence," in Joyner and Chopra, eds., *The Antarctic Legal Regime*, 165.

38. As *Black's Law Dictionary* states, *res communes* means, "In the civil law, things common to all; that is, those things which are used and enjoyed by everyone, even in single parts, but can never be exclusively required as a whole, e.g. light and air." *Black's Law Dictionary*, 1304.

39. See Joyner, "Legal Implications of the Concept of the Common Heritage of Mankind," 190–99. For a more detailed analysis of the history of the CHM principle, see Anthony Dolman, "The Common Heritage of Mankind and Global Reform," in his *Resources, Regimes, and World Order* (New York: Pergamon Press, 1981), 223–67; and Larschan and Brennan, "The Common Heritage of Mankind Principle in International Law," 305.

40. The concept of common heritage was introduced by Ambassador Arvid Pardo of Malta in 1967 to the United Nations in his famous speech concerning ocean space. See "Declaration and Treaty Concerning the Reservation Exclusively for Peaceful Purposes of the Seabed and of the Ocean Floor, Underlying the Seas Beyond the Limits of Present National Jurisdiction, and the Use of Their Resources in the Interests of Mankind," U.N. Doc. A/AC.105/C.2/SR.75 (August 17, 1967). Six years later this led to convening the Third United Nations Conference on the Law of the Sea and culminated in 1982 with the United Nations Convention on the Law of the Sea. This instrument, as it specifically applies to the deep seabed, remains the primary embodiment of the common heritage doctrine in international law. See the discussion in chapter 8 *infra*.

41. These are drawn from Arvid Pardo, "The Common Heritage: Selected

Papers on Oceans and World Order 1967–1974," International Ocean Institute Occasional Paper No. 3, 1975.

42. In this respect, CHM resembles *res nullius* and *res communis*. All humankind, not merely states, share rights and responsibilities in the area.

43. In this connection, a distinction must be drawn for the commons area between freedom for military training and rights of passage as opposed to offensive military considerations and preparations for war. Whereas the former may be permissible, the latter clearly are not.

44. Unlike common heritage, benefits may be directly accrued by the user under a *res communis* regime.

45. For a balanced, insightful assessment of the need to consider the impacts of policies on future generations, see Edith Brown Weiss, *In Fairness to Future Generations: International Law, Common Patrimony, and Intergenerational Equity* (Dobbs Ferry, N.Y.: Transnational Press, 1989).

46. Joyner, "Legal Implications of Common Heritage," 192–93.

47. For the powers and functions of this structure, the International Seabed Authority, see 1982 LOS Convention, Articles 156–83. Controversy over the nature of the Authority led to the eventual modification of its structure, powers, and functions in order to make the convention acceptable to developed states as a whole. For discussion see Joyner, "The United States and the New Law of the Sea," 41–58.

48. See The Moon Treaty, Article XI.

49. See the discussion in chapter 8 *infra*.

50. Not surprisingly, common heritage became an integral feature undergirding the so-called New International Economic Order, in which economic equity among states would be sought in part through redistribution of benefits from developing global commons resources. See the discussion in chapter 8 *infra*.

51. Suter, *Antarctica*, 169–81.

52. Sudhir K. Chopra, "Antarctica as a Commons Regime: A Conceptual Framework for Cooperation and Coexistence," in Joyner and Chopra, eds., *The Antarctic Legal Regime*, 167–69.

53. See Suter, *Antarctica*, 169–81. Increasingly this form of regime has been advocated for Antarctica, in part because it accords well with the current Antarctic Treaty System. By making conservation and protection primary concerns, the public regime accords well with duties and obligations for use of commons in international law.

54. See "Enclosure in Britain," *The Ecologist* 22 (July/August 1992): 132–33.

55. See generally B. J. McCay and J. M. Acheson, eds., *The Question of the Commons: The Culture and Ecology of Communal Resources* (Tucson: University of Arizona Press, 1987).

56. See Goldwin, "Common Sense vs. The Common Heritage," 59–78.

57. For relevant discussion, see J. Samuel Barkin and George E. Shambaugh, eds., *Anarchy and the Environment: The International Relations of Common Pool Resources* (SUNY Press, forthcoming 1998).

58. The NIEO was formalized in 1974 with the Declaration on the Establishment of a New International Economic Order, U.N.G.A. Res. 3201, S-6 U.N. GAOR Supp. (No. 1) at 3, U.N. Doc. A/9559 (1974). This document called for "equity, sovereign equality, interdependence, common interest, and cooperation among all States." The NIEO was theoretically implemented by the "Programme of Action on the Establishment of a New International Economic Order," U.N.G.A. Res. 3202, S-6 U/.N. GAOR Supp. (No. 1) at 5, U.N. Doc. A/9559 (1974). See generally K. Sauvant and H. Hasenpflug, eds., *The New International Economic Order: Confrontation or Cooperation Between North and South* (Boulder, Colo.: Westview, 1977); and Pradip K. Ghosh, *The New International Economic Order: A Third World Perspective* (Westport, Conn.: Greenwood Press, 1984).

59. Developing countries have maintained that wealthy industrialized states have already experienced the "dirty phase" of economic development and further contended that the countries of the developing South are also unable to develop industrially without damaging the environment. At the same time, northern developed countries assert that economic development must not damage the world's environment, especially the global commons areas. Poorer developing countries assert in rejoinder that such "green" development is possible only if richer developed states provide substantial financial assistance, mostly as direct aid and technology transfer.

60. Article 136 of the 1982 LOS Convention flats asserts that: "The Area [i.e., deep seabed] and its resources are the common heritiage of mankind." By February 1998 at least 158 states had signed and 123 had ratified the 1982 LOS Convention, thereby becoming legally obligated to treating the deep seabed as the common heritage of mankind.

61. See World Commission on Environment and Development, *Our Common Future*, 43–66.

62. Cleveland, "The Global Commons," 21.

63. "The Earth Summit Debacle," *The Ecologist* 22 (July/August 1992): 122.

64. See Todd Sandler, "After the Cold War, Secure the Global Commons," *Challenge* (July–August 1992): 16–23.

65. See generally Fikret Berkes, "Social Systems, Ecological Systems, and Property Rights," in Susan S. Hanna, Carl Folke, and Karl-Goran Maler, eds., *Rights to Nature: Ecological, Economic, Cultural, and Political Principles of Institutions for the Environment* (Washington, D.C.: Island Press, 1996), 87–107; and the selections in D. W. Bromley, ed., *Making the Commons Work: Theory, Practice and Policy* (San Francisco: Institute for Contemporary Studies, 1992); and Fikret Berkes, ed., *Common Property Resources: Ecology and Community-Based Sustainable Development* (London: Belhaven, 1989).

66. See generally Bonnie J. McCay, "Common and Private Concerns," in Hanna et al., *Rights to Nature,* 111–26.

67. Stone, *The Gnat Is Older Than Man,* 149 and generally 122–52.

68. Ibid., 129–32. See Particia W. Birnie and Alan E. Boyle, *International Law and the Environment* (Oxford: Oxford University Press, 1994), 109–11 (paperback ed.).

69. Stone, *The Gnat Is Older Than Man,* 132–34.

70. See Jessica Tuchman Mathews, "Redefining Security," *Foreign Affairs* 68 (Spring 1989): 162. Mathews argues that traditional concepts of "national security" must be broadened to incorporate the reality that the planet is threatened and that national security will be seriously undermined if irreversible harm is done to the planet on which the nation is situated.

71. "Reclaiming the Commons," *The Ecologist* 22 (July/August 1992): 195–204.

72. See generally French, *After the Earth Summit.*

73. Stone, *The Gant Is Older Than Man,* 117.

74. Convention on Long-Range Transboundary Air Pollution, done in Geneva on November 13, 1979, entered into force March 16, 1983, reprinted in *International Legal Materials* 18 (1979): 1442.

75. Entered into force September 22, 1988, reprinted in *International Legal Materials* 26 (1987): 1516.

76. Protocol on Substances that Deplete the Ozone Layer, done at Montreal, September 16, 1987, entered into force January 1, 1989, reprinted in *International Legal Materials* 26 (1987): 154.

77. United Nations Framework Convention on Climate Change, done May 9, 1992, entered into force March 24, 1994, reprinted in *International Legal Materials* 31 (1992): 849.

78. See William K. Stevens, "Lessons of Rio: A New Prominence and an Effective Blandness," *New York Times,* June 14, 1992, p. A10. General agreement among the European Community, for example, was to stabilize emissions at 1990 levels by the year 2000. William K. Stevens, "With Climate Treaty Signed, All Say They'll Do Even More," *New York Times,* June 13, 1992, p. A1.

79. Frederick R. Anderson, "Of Herdsmen and Nation States: The Global Environmental Commons," *American University Journal of International Law and Policy* 5 (1990): 217, 218. Satellites, for example, enhance global monitoring of ocean dumping and driftnetting activities and can dramatically indicate rates of desertification.

80. See Stone, *The Gnat Is Older Than Man,* 91–95,

81. French, *After the Earth Summit,* 23.

82. Stone, *The Gnat Is Older Than Man,* 117.

83. See Stone, *The Gnat Is Older Than Man,* 89–90, and French, *After the Earth Summit,* 30.

84. "Global Management," *The Ecologist* 22 (July/August 1992): 181. See also U. E. Simonis et al., "The Crisis of Global Environment: Demands for Global Politics," *Interdependz* 3 (1989): 9.

85. Economic actions taken by the United States against Mexico for that government's failure to protect dolphins from being taken with domestic tuna catches were declared discriminatory in 1993 by a GATT panel. See GATT Panel Report, "The United States—Restrictions on Imports of Tuna," No. DS21/R, reprinted in *International Legal Materials* 30 (1993): 1594–1623. For a critical assessment of the implications this case holds for international trade, see McLaughlin, "UNCLOS and the Demise of the United States' Use of Trade Sanctions To Protect Dolphins, Sea Turtles, Whales, and Other International Marine Living Resources," 1–78.

86. French, *After the Earth Summit*, 31.

87. Similarly, it was better to get a minerals agreement in Antarctica before any exploitable minerals were actually discovered. See generally Joyner, "Fragile Ecosystems," 879–904.

88. Cleveland, "The Global Commons," 10.

89. Wijkman, "Managing the Global Commons," 511, 532.

90. See generally Chopra, "Antarctica as a Commons Regime," 165–86; and John Warren Kindt, "Ice-Covered Areas and the Law of the Sea," in Joyner and Chopra, eds., *The Antarctic Legal Regime*, 187–217.

91. For discussion, see Joyner, *Antarctica and the Law of the Sea*, 195–201.

92. Chopra, "Antarctica as a Commons Regime," 165; Herbert W. Briggs, *The Law of Nations*, 2nd ed. (1952), New York: Appleton-Century-Crofts, 239–40; von Glahn, *Law Among Nations*, 296–316.

93. See Chopra, "Antarctica as a Commons Regime," 166–67. By way of legal argument on this point, Chopra distinguishes between the concept of *dominium* and *imperium* in Roman law, attributing to the latter a higher standard of sovereignty. Given the intensely severe environmental conditions in the Antarctic, neither condition has been adequately satisfied by claimant states.

94. Kish, *The Law of International Spaces*, 70–81; Kindt, "Ice-Covered Areas," 194–96.

95. Antarctic Treaty, Article IV. Article IV states that nothing in the Treaty renounces or diminishes a claim and then goes on to assert that "No acts or activities taking place while the present Treaty is in force shall constitute a basis for asserting, supporting, or denying a claim to territorial sovereignty in Antarctica or create any rights of sovereignty in Antarctica. No new claim, or enlargement of an existing claim, shall be asserted while the present Treaty is in force." Ibid., paragraph 2.

96. Ibid., Article IV, paragraph 1(c).

97. A plausible argument can be made that the "common rights" approach fits reality in Antarctica better than either *res nullius* or common heritage of

mankind. Chopra, "Antarctica as a Commons Regime," 169–74.

98. Antarctic Treaty, Article IX.

99. Antarctic Treaty, Article XIII. While most countries are UN members, there is additional provision for exceptions for those that are not.

100. See Kindt, "Ice–Covered Regions," 204-5 (suggesting that the Antartic Treaty states might serve as a "collective sovereign").

101. Suter, *Antarctica*, 173–81.

102. Canmann, "Antarctic Oil Spills of 1989," 211, 220 (noting that over seventy states have their own environmental agencies). Such an "Antarctic EPA" would investigate, monitor, report, and prepare recommendations. Serious concern exists, however, that such an agency would become highly politicized.

103. Kindt, "Ice-Covered Regions," 205 (hypothesizing on the inception of an International Common Enterprise [ICE]).

104. Ibid. Note, however, that such a suggestion suffers from the inapplicability of Article 76 of the UN Charter, which stipulates that UN Trusteeships are to be designed to promote the independence of a trusteeship's inhabitants. Canmann, "Antarctic Oil Spills," 220.

105. Cleveland, "The Global Commons," 10.

106. Kindt, "Ice-Covered Areas," 206–8; Canmann, "Antarctic Oil Spills," 220–21; J. R. Rowland, "Whither Antarctica? Alternative Strategies," in Triggs, ed., *The Antarctic Treaty Regime,* 218–26. See the discussion in chapter 8.

107. See Christopher C. Joyner, "The 1991 Antarctic Environmental Protection Protocol: What Prospects for Antarctica as a World Park?," *Review of European Community and International Environmental Law* 1 (1992): 328–39.

108. See Jonathan I. Charney, "The Antarctic Treaty System and Customary International Law," in Francioni and Scovazzi, eds., *International Law for Antarctica,* 51–101.

109. See Lee Kimball, "The Role of Non-Governmental Organizations in Antarctic Affairs," in Joyner and Chopra, eds., *The Antarctic Legal Regime,* 33–64.

110. See Bill Dietrich, "Special Report: Antarctica the Coldest Laboratory," *Seattle Times,* January 29–February 1, 1995, pp. 7–13; Usha Lee McFarling, "The Frozen Continent," "Life on the Edge: Antarctica," and "An Uncertain Future: Antarctica," *Boston Globe,* February 26, 27, 28, 1995 (series).

CHAPTER 3: GOVERNANCE STRUCTURES

1. Bush, ed., *Antarctica and International Law,* vol. 3, 461–68.

2. Bush, *Antarctica and International Law,* vol. 2, 385.

3. See Hanessian, "The Antarctic Treaty 1959," 436, 449.

4. U.N. Doc A/38852, July 15, 1958.

5. This claim was based on the voyage of Adm. Thaddeus von Bellingshausen between 1819 and 1821 and the activities of Russian whalers in subantarctic waters during the late 1940s.

6. See generally Christopher C. Joyner, "U.S.-Soviet Cooperative Diplomacy: The Case of Antarctica," in Nish Jamgotch, ed., *United States–Soviet Cooperation: A New Future* (New York: Praeger, 1989), 39–61.

7. Antarctic Treaty, Dec. 1, 1959, 12 U.S.T. 794, 402 U.N.T.S. 71, Article IX, paragraph (1)(f).

8. Ibid., Preamble.

9. Antarctic Treaty, Article I.

10. Antarctic Treaty, Article III, paragraphs (1)(a),(b), and (c).

11. This comes in accordance with Article III in the Antarctic Treaty. See the discussion and exchanges in Counsellor Sergei Karev, "Relations with International Organisations—UNEP, IMO, FAO, WMO, ICAO, and UNGA," in Andrew Jackson, ed., *On the Antarctic Horizon: Proceedings of the International Symposium on the Future of the Antarctic Treaty System* (Australian Antarctic Foundation, 1995), 43–56.

12. Antarctic Treaty, Article IV, paragraph 1.

13. Antarctic Treaty, Article IV, paragraph 2.

14. Triggs, "The Antarctic Treaty Regime," 195–228.

15. The United States exercised this caveat when it constructed a nuclear power facility at McMurdo station in 1968. The facility was removed in 1978, along with the radioactive debris that had been accumulated. See Wilkes and Mann, "The Story of Nukey Poo," 32, 34; and "McMurdo Station Reactor Site Released for Unrestricted Use," *Antarctic Journal* 15(1) (1980): 1–3. See also Auburn, *Antarctic Law and Politics*, 146.

16. On the relevance of this provision for the high seas freedom of marine scientific research, see Patricia Birnie, "Effect of Article VI of the Antarctic Treaty on Scientific Research," in Wolfrum, ed., *Antarctic Challenge III*, 105–20.

17. For discussion of the legal implications presented by waters offshore Antarctica, see Joyner, *Antarctica and the Law of the Sea*, 75–106.

18. Ibid., 76–87.

19. Antarctic Treaty, Article VII, paragraph 3.

20. "Annex H: Inspections by Year, Nationality and Location Carried out under Article VII of the Antarctic Treaty," in Antarctic Treaty, *Final Report of Nineteenth Antarctic Treaty Consultative Meeting, Seoul, 8–9 May 1995* (1996), 299–303. See also United States, "Final Report of the 1995 United States Antarctic Inspection Team, February 9–March 1, 1995," in Ant. Doc. XX ATCM/INF 129 (May 1996). This was the tenth inspection carried out by the United States since 1963, more than any other government. See also Pietro Giuliani, "Inspections under the Antarctic Treaty," in Francioni and Scovazzi, eds., *International Law for Antarctica*, 459–74.

21. Antarctic Treaty, Article VII, paragraph 5.

22. See, e.g., Antarctic Treaty Consultative Meeting Recommendations I-VI (1961), II-II (1962), V-2 (1968), VI-7 (1970), VIII-9 (1975), XII-1 (1985), XIV-10 (1987).

23. Antarctic Treaty, Article VIII, paragraph 1.

24. Ibid., Article VIII, paragraph 2.

25. During that time, however, no Consultative Meeting was ever hosted in the Soviet Union or South Africa.

26. "Extract from the Report of XVIth ATCM," in John Heap, ed., *Handbook of the Antarctic Treaty System*, 8th ed. (Washington, D.C.: U.S. Department of State, April 1994), 31.

27. The chief obstacle to establishing a central secretariat has been concern by Argentina and Chile that any administrative arrangement not prejudice their sovereignty and jurisdiction over Antarctic sectors.

28. Antarctic Treaty, Article IX, paragraphs 1 and 2.

29. Heap, *Handbook of the Antarctic Treaty System*, 18–19. Czechoslovakia initially joined the treaty as a Non-Consultative Party on June 14, 1962. The Czech Republic and Slovak Republic succeeded to the treaty as parts of Czechoslovakia, which separated into two republics on January 1, 1993. Ibid., 19.

30. Antarctic Treaty, Article IX, paragraph 1.

31. Antarctic Treaty, Article IX, paragraph 4.

32. Ibid., Article IX, paragraph (1) (a)–(f).

33. Rule 24, "Rules of Procedure of Antarctic Treaty Consultative Meetings," as revised in 1992, but similar in substance to Rule 23 as originally adopted and amended in 1983, reprinted in Heap, *Handbook of the Antarctic Treaty System*, at 282.

34. Antarctic Treaty, Article IX, paragraph 1.

35. Antarctic Treaty, Article X.

36. Antarctic Treaty, Article XI.

37. Ibid., Article XII. The 1991 Madrid Protocol represents the first such modification to the Antarctic Treaty. If such ratification is not received from any Consultative Party within two years of the entry into force of the modification or amendment, then that party shall be deemed to have withdrawn from the treaty. Ibid., paragraph 1(b).

38. Ibid., Article XII, paragraph 2(a).

39. Ibid., Article XII, paragraph 2(c).

40. Ibid., Article I.

41. Ibid., Article V.

42. Ibid., Article VII.

43. Ibid., Articles II and III.

44. Ibid., Articles II and III.

45. See the discussion in chapter 7 *infra*.

46. Antarctic Treaty, Article IX, paragraph (1)(f).

47. Recommendation III–VIII, approved (1964), 17 U.S.T. 996, T.I.A.S. No. 6058 (1965), as modified in 24 U.S.T. 992, T.I.A.S. 7692 (1973). The Agreed Measures will in substantial part be superseded by Annex II to the 1991 Protocol on Environmental Protection to the Antarctic Treaty once that protocol enters into force.

48. Agreed Measures, Article IV.

49. As provided for in Article III, "Each Participating Government shall take appropriate action to carry out these Agreed Measures."

50. Agreed Measures, Article VI.

51. Ibid., Article VIII.

52. Ibid., Article IX.

53. Ibid., Article XII.

54. Recommendation VI-9, "Data on the Conservation of Fauna and Flora," reprinted in Heap, *Handbook of the Antarctic Treaty System*, 2055.

55. The Agreed Measures apply to the "same area to which Antarctic Treaty is applicable . . . namely the area south of 60° South Latitude, including ice shelves." Agreed Measures, Article I, paragraph 1.

56. Agreed Measures, Article I, paragraph 2.

57. Agreed Measures, Article XIV, paragraphs 1 and 2.

58. Agreed Measures, Article XIV, paragraph 2.

59. "Extract from report of VIth ATCM," in Heap, *Handbook of the Antarctic Treaty System*, 154.

60. 29 U.S.T. 441, T.I.A.S. No. 8826, entered into force March 11, 1978. States party to the Seals Convention in 1997 include Argentina, Australia, Belgium, Brazil, Canada, Chile, France, Germany, Japan, Norway, Poland, South Africa, Russia, the United Kingdom, and the United States.

61. Seals Convention, Article 5, paragraph 7.

62. Ibid., Article 5.

63. See Seals Convention, Articles 4 and 5, paragraphs 1, 2, and 7.

64. Seals Convention, Annex, paragraphs 6(a)–(d) and 7(b).

65. Ibid., Article 5, paragraph 5.

66. Ibid., Article 1, paragraph 1.

67. SCAR's role vis-à-vis the Antarctic Treaty was fixed early on by ATCP Recommendations I-I and I-IV. For discussion of the role of SCAR and the Antarctic Treaty, see Auburn, *Antarctic Law and Politics*, 171–83.

68. Antarctic Seals Convention, Annex, paragraph 4.

69. Convention on the Conservation of Antarctic Marine Living Resources, done at Canberra, May 7–20, 1980, 33 U.S.T. 3476, T.I.A.S. No. 10240, reprinted in *International Legal Materials* 19 (1980), 837.

70. For more detailed discussion on the role of CCAMLR in Antarctic marine conservation, see chapter 5 *infra* and Elliott, *International Environmental Politics*, 82–102.

71. The International Convention on Regulation of Whaling is not restricted to the Southern Ocean, though for the Southern Ocean 40° south is imposed as the northernmost boundary permissible for factory ships. See generally Maria Clara Maffei, "The Protection of Whales in Antarctica," in Francioni and Scovazzi, *International Law for Antarctica*, 171–224.

72. CCAMLR, Article VIII.

73. CCAMLR, Article IX, paragraph (1)(f). According to CCAMLR, conservation measures should be based on the best scientific information available. Ibid. Decisions on matters of substance, e.g., conservation measures, require consensus in the Commission. CCAMLR, Article XII, paragraph 1.

74. CCAMLR, Article XII.

75. Countries that have acceded to CCAMLR but are not members of the Commission include Bulgaria, Canada, Finland, Greece, the Netherlands, and Peru. Commission for the Conservation of Antarctic Marine Living Resources, *The Schedule of Conservation Measures in Force 1996/97* (Hobart: CAMLR, 1996), inside front cover.

76. CCAMLR, Article XII, paragraph 1.

77. CCAMLR, Article XV, paragraph 1.

78. CCAMLR, Article VII.

79. CCAMLR, Article XXIII, paragraph 3.

80. As provided for in Article I, paragraph 2, "the populations of finfish, molluscs, crustaceans and all other species of living organisms, including birds, south of the Antarctic Convergence."

81. Compare the Antarctic Treaty, Article VI and the Seals, Convention, Article I.

82. Article VI of CCAMLR provides in full: "Nothing in this Convention shall derogate from the rights and obligations of Contracting Parties under the International Convention for the Regulation of Whaling and the Convention for the Conservation of Antarctic Seals."

83. See CCAMLR, Final Act, paragraphs 1, 2, 3, 4, and 5.

84. Ibid., fifth preambular paragraph.

85. Ibid., sixth preambular paragraph.

86. Ibid., seventh preambular paragraph.

87. Ibid., Article III. Article I of the Antarctic Treaty guarantees peaceful uses only of Antarctica. Article V prohibits nuclear explosions and disposal of radioactive waste.

88. CCAMLR, Article V, paragraph 1.

89. Ibid., Article V, paragraph 2.

90. International Convention for the Regulation of Whaling with Schedule of Whaling Regulations, done in Washington, D.C., on December 2, 1946, entered into force November 10, 1948, T.I.A.S. No. 1849, 4 Bevans 248, 161 U.N.T.S. 72.

91. CCAMLR, Article VI.

92. Ibid., Article XV, paragraph 3.

93. Ibid., Article XXIII, paragraph 1.

94. The following states were Antarctic Treaty Consultative Parties that participated in negotiating CRAMRA's promulgation: Argentina, Australia, Belgium, Brazil, Chile, China, France, German Democratic Republic, Federal Republic of Germany, India, Italy, Japan, New Zealand, Norway, Poland, South Africa, So-

viet Union, United Kingdom, United States, and Uruguay. Final Act of the Fourth Special Antarctic Treaty Consultative Meeting on Antarctic Mineral Resources, reprinted in Heap, *Handbook of the Antarctic Treaty System*, 201. For discussion of CRAMRA's evolution, see generally Wolfrum, *The Convention on the Regulation of Antarctic Mineral Resource Activities* and Vicuña, *Antarctic Mineral Exploitation*.

95. For the progressive development of the minerals regime, see Joyner, "The Evolving Antarctic Minerals Regime," 73–95; and Joyner, "The Antarctic Minerals Negotiating Process," 888–905.

96. CRAMRA, Articles 18–22.

97. Ibid., Article 28.

98. Ibid., Articles 23–27.

99. Ibid., Article 29.

100. Ibid., Article 31.

101. Ibid., Article 33. For comparative assessments of the entire mineral regime's operation, see Joyner, "1988 Antarctic Minerals Convention," 69–85; and Beck, "Convention on the Regulation of Antarctic Mineral Resource Activities," 19–32.

102. For an analysis of the minerals treaty and its operational provisions, see generally Joyner, "1988 Antarctic Minerals Convention," 69–85; and Wolfrum, *The Convention on the Regulation of Antarctic Mineral Resource Activities*.

103. See Joyner, "The Legitimacy of CRAMRA," 246–68.

104. See CRAMRA, Article 29, paragraph (2)(a) and note 94 *supra*.

105. CRAMRA, Preamble.

106. Ibid., Article 2, paragraph 1.

107. Ibid., paragraph 2.

108. Ibid., Article 2, paragraph 3.

109. Ibid., Article 2, paragraph 3(a).

110. Ibid., Article 5, paragraph 2. The minerals convention would regulate mineral resource activities on the continent and on all Antarctic islands, including all ice shelves, and on the seabed and subsoil of adjacent offshore areas up to the deep seabed. This scope of jurisdiction was purposefully designed so as not to conflict with deep seabed mining provisions in the 1982 Law of the Sea Convention. For discussion, see Joyner, *Antarctica and the Law of the Sea*, 127–30.

111. CRAMRA, Article 6.

112. Ibid., Article 7, paragraph 9.

113. Ibid., Article 9.

114. See Joyner, "The Effectiveness of CRAMRA," 152–73.

115. Ibid., Article 13, paragraph 1.

116. Ibid., Article 13, paragraph 6.

117. Ibid., Article 18, paragraph 2(a).

118. Ibid., paragraphs 2(b) and (c).

119. Ibid., Article 18, paragraph 3.

120. Ibid., Article 18, paragraph 6.

121. Ibid., Article 23.

122. Ibid., Article 28.

123. Ibid., Article 29, paragraph 2.

124. Ibid.

125. Ibid., Article 2.

126. "Press Release from the Prime Minister for Australia: Joint Statement with the Minister for Foreign Affairs and Trade, Senator Gareth Evans QC, and the Minister for Arts, Sport, the Environment, Tourism & Territories, Senator the Hon. Graham Richardson," May 22, 1989. See Scott, "Australia Advocates Wilderness Status for Antarctica," 4; and Malcolm W. Browne, "France and Australia Kill Pact on Limited Antarctic Mining and Oil Drilling," *New York Times,* September 25, 1989, p. A10.

Under Article 62 of the Wellington Convention, all seven states that have claims to the continent would have to sign and ratify the convention for it to enter into force. Both Australia and France are claimant states. Thus, by their refusal even to sign the treaty, those governments effectively precluded the possibility of the agreement's entry into force.

127. Protocol on Environmental Protection to the Antarctic Treaty, XIth Special Consultative Meeting in Madrid, Doc. XI ATSCM/2, June 21, 1991, adopted October 4, 1991. [Hereinafter Madrid Environmental Protocol]. The final ratification for the Protocol was deposited by Japan on December 15, 1997, and thirty days later, on January 14, 1998, the Madrid Protocol entered into force. "The Antartic Environmental Protocol Enters into Force!!!," *The Antartic Project,* vol. 6:4 (December 1997), 1.

128. See Francisco Orrego Vicuña, "The Legitimacy of the Protocol on Environmental Protection to the Antarctic Treaty," in Stokke and Vidas, *Governing the Antarctic,* 268–93.

129. Madrid Environmental Protocol, Article 25. However, pursuant to a U.S. proposal, any state has the right to withdraw from the provisions of the protocol (presumably giving it the right to mine without regulation) if an amendment lifting the ban is enacted but not ratified within five years of its proposal. Ibid., paragraph 6.

130. Ibid., Article 11.

131. Ibid., Articles 11 and 12. Specifically in this regard, the Committee is to furnish advice on:

    (a) the effectiveness of measures taken pursuant to this Protocol;

    (b) the need to update, strengthen or otherwise improve such measures;

    (c) the need for additional measures, including the need for additional Annexes, where appropriate;

(d) the application and implementation of the environmental impact assessment procedures set out in Article 8 and Annex I;

(e) means of minimizing or mitigating environmental impacts of activities in the Antarctic Treaty area;

(f) procedures for situations requiring urgent action, including response action in environmental emergencies;

(g) the operation and further elaboration of the Antarctic Protected Area system;

(h) inspection procedures, including formats for inspection reports and checklists for the conduct of inspections;

(i) the collection, archiving, exchange and evaluation of information related to environmental protection;

(j) the state of the Antarctic environment; and

(k) the need for scientific research, including environmental monitoring, related to the implementation of this Protocol.

Ibid., Article 12, paragraph 1.

132. Madrid Environmental Protocol, Article, art. 13.

133. Annex I to the Protocol on Environmental Protection to the Antarctic Treaty: Environmental Impact Assessment, XI ATSCM/2, June 21, 1991, in Heap, *Handbook of the Antarctic Treaty System*, 2040.

134. Annex II to the Protocol on Environmental Protection to the Antarctic Treaty: Conservation of Antarctic Fauna and Flora, XI ATSCM/2, June 21, 1991, in Heap, *Handbook of the Antarctic Treaty System*, 2056.

135. Annex III to the Protocol on Environmental Protection to the Antarctic Treaty: Waste Disposal and Waste Management, XI ATSCM/2, June 21, 1991, in Heap, *Handbook of the Antarctic Treaty System*, 2068.

136. Recommendation XII-4, "Man's Impact on the Antarctic Environment, Code of Conduct for Antarctic Expeditions and Station Activities," reprinted in Heap, *Handbook of the Antarctic Treaty System*, 2062.

137. "Recommendation XV-3, Human Impact on the Antarctic Environment: Waste Disposal," reprinted in Heap, *Handbook of the Antarctic Treaty System*, 2063.

138. Annex IV to the Protocol on Environmental Protection to the Antarctic Treaty: Prevention of Marine Pollution, XI ATSCM/2, June 21, 1991, in Heap, *Handbook of the Antarctic Treaty System*, 2077.

139. International Convention for Preventing Pollution from Ships, done at London, November 2, 1973, I.M.C.O. Doc. MP/CONF/WP.35, amended by Protocol of 1978 Relating to the International Convention for the Prevention of Pollution from Ships, done at London, February 17, 1978, entered into force October 2, 1983, I.M.C.O. Doc. TSPP/CONF/11.

140. Annex to Recommendation XVI: Annex V to the Protocol on Environmental Protection to the Antarctic Treaty: Area and Management, in Heap, *Handbook of the Antarctic Treaty System*, 2125.

141. Ibid., Article 9.
142. Madrid Environmental Protocol, Article 5.
143. Ibid., Article 3.

CHAPTER 4: REGIME DYNAMICS

1. Stephen Krasner in "Structural Causes and Consequences, 1.

2. See generally Young, *International Cooperation;* Tony Evans and Peter Wilson, "Regime Theory and the English School of International Relations: A Comparison," *Millennium: Journal of International Relations* 21 (Winter 1992): 329–51; Marc A. Levy, Oran R. Young, and M. Zuern, "The Study of International Regimes," *European Journal of International Relations* 1 (1995): 267–330; Stephen Haggard and Beth A. Simmons, "Theories of International Regimes," *International Organization* 41 (Summer 1987): 491–515; and Helen Milner, "International Theories of Cooperation Among Nations," *World Politics* 44 (April 1992): 466–96.

3. For the theoretical underpinnings of such a strategy, see Robert Axelrod and Robert O. Keohane, "Achieving Cooperation under Anarchy: Strategies and Institutions," in Kenneth A. Oye, ed., *Cooperation Under Anarchy* (Princeton: Princeton University Press, 1986), 226–54.

4. See generally L. F. E. Goldie, "Special Regimes and Pre-Emptive Activities in International Law," *International and Comparative Law Quarterly* 11 (July 1962): 670–700. Compare Peter M. Haas, Robert O. Keohane, and Marc A. Levy, "The Effectiveness of International Environmental Institutions," in Peter M. Haas, Robert O. Keohane, and Marc A. Levy, eds., *Institutions for the Earth* (Cambridge: MIT Press, 1993), 3–24.

5. Keohane, *After Hegemony,* 51–52.

6. Krasner, "Structural Causes and Consequences," 11.

7. Goldie, "Special Regimes," 698; Haas, Khohane, and Levy, "Effectiveness of International Environmental Institutions," 16–17.

8. See Young, "International Regimes," 106.

9. See Oran Young's *Resource Regimes,* 20; *Compliance and Public Authority* (Washington, D.C.: Resources for the Future, 1979); and "International Regimes," 331–35.

10. Values are generally accepted judgments of what has intrinsic worth, of what is worthy of esteem for its own sake. Values are standards or qualities considered desirable in life.

11. Norms are shared standards regarding what is and what is not acceptable behavior. Norms carry moral and ethical imperatives concerning what ought to be done in various situations.

12. As Rosalyn Higgins posited, a norm "is an authoritative provision of law that continues to command significant community expectations as to its contemporary validity and which may be appropriately invoked and applied in

the particular factual context." Rosalyn Higgins, "The Role of Resolutions of International Organizations in the Process of Creating Norms in the International System," in William E. Butler, ed., *International Law and the International System* (Dordrecht: Martinus Nijhoff, 1987), 2.

13. Within Krasner's framework, rules are "specific prescriptions or proscriptions for action." Krasner, "Structural Causes and Consequences," 2. For Higgins, a rule "is an obligation of law that can not be gainsaid." Higgins, "Role of Resolutions in International Organizations," 2.

14. Krasner, "Structural Causes and Consequences," 2. Principles are fundamental tenets or truths generally believed and which serve as a rule of action or as basis for a system.

15. Procedures are manners of proceeding and effecting affairs; procedures furnish a set of established means or forms for conducting affairs or for setting a course of action.

16. See Snidal, "Limits of Hegemonic Stability Theory," 579–614.

17. Thomas Gehring, "International Environmental Regimes: Dynamic Sectoral Legal Systems," *Yearbook of International Environmental Law* 1 (1990): 35–56.

18. Such regime cohesion, however, cannot ensure that an association of states will be able to preserve its unity and viability over time, especially as it encounters external stresses or internal strains that might threaten its stability or existence.

19. The success of regime cohesion depends upon the effectiveness of regime formation and the ability of the regime to impose its decision upon its members. See Ernst B. Haas, "Regime Decay: Conflict Management and International Organization, 1945–1981," *International Organization* 37 (1983): 189, 193. See also Rothwell, *The Polar Regions and the Development of International Law,* 9–20.

20. See Peterson, *Managing the Frozen South,* 123–42.

21. See generally Oran R. Young, "Rights, Rules and Resources in International Society," in Susan S. Hanna, Carl Folke, and Karl-Goran Maler, eds., *Rights to Nature: Ecological, Economic, Cultural, and Political Principles of Institutions for the Environment* (Washington, D.C.: Island Press, 1996), 245–63; and Oran R. Young, *International Goverance: Protecting the Environment in a Stateless Society* (Ithaca: Cornell University Press, 1993). M. J. Peterson refers to a similar process as "regime amendment." See Peterson, *Managing the Frozen South,* 143–74.

22. See Arthur A. Stein, "Coordination and Collaboration: Regimes in an Anarchic World," in Stephen A. Krasner, ed., *International Regimes* (Ithaca: Cornell University Press, 1983), 115–40.

23. Richardson L. Williamson, Jr., "Building the International Environmental Regime," *University of Miami Inter-American Law Review,* 30 (Summer): 743.

24. Young, "Rights, Rules and Resources," 256–59.

25. See Peterson, *Managing the Frozen South,* 123–42.

26. Antarctic Treaty, done at Washington, D.C., December 1, 1959, entered into force June 23, 1961, 12 U.S.T. 794, T.I.A.S. No. 4780, 402 U.N.T.S. 71.

27. As the Antarctic Treaty provides, the Consultative Parties shall meet "at suitable intervals and places, for the purpose of exchanging information, consulting together on matters of common interest pertaining to Antarctica, and formulating and considering, and recommending to their Governments, measures in furtherance of the principles and objectives of the Treaty. . . ." Antarctic Treaty, Article IX, paragraph 1a.

28. Recommendations are adopted by the ATCPs through unanimous agreement of their governments. Ibid., Article IX, paragraph 4. By 1998, 228 recommendations had been adopted through the Consultative Party process. For elaborabtion, see Christopher C. Joyner, "Recommended Measures under the Antartic Treaty: Hardening Compliance with Soft International Law," *Michigan Journal of Internatinal Law* 19 (Winter 1998).

29. Recommendation III-VIII, approved 1964, 17 U.S.T. 996, T.I.A.S. No. 6058 (1965), as modified in 24 U.S.T. 992, T.I.A.S. No. 7692 (1973). See the discussion in chapter 5 *infra*.

30. Convention for the Conservation of Antarctic Seals, done in London, June 1, 1972, 29 U.S.T. 441, T.I.A.S. No. 8826, entered into force March 11, 1978.

31. See the discussion in chapter 5 *supra*.

32. Convention on the Conservation of Antarctic Marine Living Resources, done at Canberra, May 7–20, 1980, 33 U.S.T. 3476, T.I.A.S. No. 10240.

33. See the discussion in chapter 5 *supra*.

34. Protocol on Environmental Protection to the Antarctic Treaty, done October 3, 1991, reprinted in *International Legal Materials* 30 (1991), 1455 and in Heap, *Handbook of the Antarctic Treaty System*, 2018.

35. The annexes to Environmental Protocol are reprinted in Heap ed., *Handbook of the Antarctic Treaty System*, 2031–2262.

36. Done at Wellington, June 2, 1988, opened for signature November 25, 1988. Document AMR/SCM/88/78 (June 2, 1978), reprinted in Heap ed., *Handbook of the Antarctic Treaty System*, 203.

37. Antarctic Treaty, Article IX, para. 1(a)–(f).

38. See Heap, *Handbook of the Antarctic Treaty System*, 35–36.

39. See the discussion concerning the United Nations debates over the status of Antarctica in chapter 8 *supra*.

40. Interview with Andrew Jackson, May 7, 1994, Australian Antarctic Division Headquarters, Kingston, Tasmania; Interview with R. Tucker Scully, U.S. Department of State, Washington, D.C., February 14, 1997.

41. In 1982 a major threat with the potential to disrupt the Antarctic Treaty regime was the Falklands/Malvinas War, which involved two key claimant states, Argentina and the United Kingdom. Preservation of the Antarctic Treaty and the then-ongoing minerals regime's negotiations was seen by both governments as paramount to the conflict between them, and ATCP meetings proceeded during the spring of 1982 without incident by either government. In 1989 a second

key threat to the regime occurred when Australia and France refused to sign, or ratify, the Wellington agreement on minerals regulation. As a result, eight years of negotiations on an Antarctic minerals treaty came to naught, leaving bitterness and a sense of betrayal for some ATCPs. Successful completion in 1991 of the consensus negotiations that produced a comprehensive environmental regime for the region did much to heal that schism, however.

42. For example, strong disagreements over the past decade have affected ATS members' policies and attitudes in both the International Whaling Commission and the Food and Agriculture Organization.

43. Regimes such as those for regulating Antarctica, as well as for ensuring the law of the sea, preventing ozone depletion, halting transboundary air pollution, preserving biological diversity, and preventing global warming all have as their hub a central, binding international agreement. Some commentators have suggested that such core conventions are essential to the formation and maintenance of these regimes. See, e.g., Eckart Klein, "International Regimes," *Encyclopedia of Public International Law* 9 (The Netherlands: Amsterdam: North-Holland Publishing Company, 1986), 202; Winfried Lang, "Diplomacy and International Environmental Law-Making: Some Observations," *Yearbook of International Environmental Law* 3 (1992): 120; Gehring, "International Environmental Regimes," 37.

44. International Convention for the Regulation of Whaling with Schedule of Whaling Regulations, done in Washington, D.C., on December 2, 1946, entered into force November 10, 1948, T.I.A.S. No. 1849, 4 Bevans 248, 161 U.N.T.S. 72.

45. For an authoritative account of the international regime for managing whale resources, see Birnie, *International Regulation of Whaling*.

46. United Nations Convention on the Law of the Sea, done at Montego Bay, December 10, 1982, entered into force November 16, 1994, U.N. Doc. A/CONF.62/122, reprinted in United Nations, The Law of the Seas: Official Text of the Convention on the Law of the Sea with Annexes and Index, U.N. Sales No. E.83.V.5 (1983) [hereinafter cited as 1982 LOS Convention]. As of March 1997, 110 ratifications had been deposited.

47. Insightful treatments of the new convention for the law of the sea are provided in "The New Law of the Sea," *Ocean Development and International Law* (Special Double Issue) 27(1&2) (January–June 1996) and "The Law of the Sea Convention: Unfinished Agendas and Future Challenges," *International Journal of Marine and Coastal Law* (Special Issue) 10(2) (May 1995). Among the ATCPs, the following states are parties to the 1982 LOS Convention: Argentina, Australia, Brazil, China, Finland, France, Germany, India, Italy, Japan, the Netherlands, New Zealand, Norway, Republic of Korea, Russia, Sweden, and Uruguay. United Nations Treaty Collection, Multilateral Treaties Deposited with the Secretary-General, http://www.un.org./Depts/Treaty/final/ts2/newfiles/part_boo/xxi_boo/xxi-6.html (Web site visited April 1, 1997).

48. International Convention for the Prevention of Pollution from Ships, 1973, done November 2, 1973. I.M.C.O. Doc. MP/CPNF.WP.35/ (1973), reprinted in *International Legal Materials* 12 (1973): 1319 and Protocol of 1978 Relating to the International Convention for the Prevention of Pollution from Ships, 1973, done February 17, 1978, entered into force October 2, 1983. I.M.C.O. Doc. TSPP/CONF/11 (1978), reprinted in *International Legal Materials* 17 (1978): 546. The 1973 MARPOL Convention was not intended to enter into force or be applied on its own. The regime to be used by states party to the 1978 Protocol is that contained in the 1973 Convention, as modified by the 1978 Protocol.

49. See Joyner, "The 1991 Madrid Environmental Protection Protocol," 183–97.

50. Convention on the Prevention of Marine Pollution by Dumping of Wastes and Other Matter, done at London, December 29, 1972, 26 U.S.T. 2403, T.I.A.S. No. 8165, 1046 U.N.T.S. 120 (entered into force August 30, 1975). [Hereinafter referred to as London Dumping Convention].

51. See Joyner, *Antarctica and the Law of the Sea*, 148–49.

52. Done at London, October 20, 1972, entered into force July 15, 1977, 28 U.S.T. 3459, T.I.A.S. No. 8587.

53. Framework Convention on Climate Change, United Nations Conference on Environment and Development, opened for signature June 4, 1992, reprinted in *International Legal Materials* 31 (1992): 849. For an analysis see Barratt-Brown, Hajost, and Stearne, "A Forum for Action on Global Warming," 103.

54. United Nations Conference on Environment and Development; Convention on Biological Diversity, done June 5, 1992, reprinted in *International Legal Materials* 31 (1992): 818 (entered into force December 29, 1993) [hereinafter Biodiversity Convention]. For a useful analysis, see Bell, "The 1992 Convention on Biological Diversity," 479; and Chandler, "The Biodiversity Convention," 141.

55. See Christopher C. Joyner, "Biodiversity in the Marine Environment: Resource Implications for the Law of the Sea," *Vanderbilt Journal of Transnational Law* 28 (October 1995): 635, 680–82.

56. Vienna Convention for the Protection of the Ozone Layer, opened for signature March 22, 1985, S. Treaty Doc. No. 99–9, reprinted in *International Legal Materials* 26 (1987): 1516.

57. Montreal Protocol on Substances that Deplete the Ozone Layer, reprinted in *International Legal Materials* 26 (1987): 1541.

58. Basel Convention on the Control of Transboundary Movements of Hazardous Wastes and Their Disposal, opened for signature March 22, 1989, U.N. Environmental Programme, Agenda Item 3, U.N. Doc. UNEP/IG.80/3 (1989), reprinted in *International Legal Materials* 28 (1989): 657.

59. For discussion on how individuals are socialized to norms, see Robert D. Putnam, *Making Democracy Work: Civic Traditions in Italy* (Princeton: Princeton University Press, 1993), 171–76.

60. Interview with Andrew Jackson, May 7, 1994, Australian Antarctic Division Headquarters, Kingston, Tasmania.

61. See generally Olav Schram Stokke and Davor Vidas, eds., *Governing the Antarctic: the Effectiveness and Legitimacy of the Antarctic Treaty System* (Cambridge: Cambridge University Press, 1996).

62. Stokke and Vidas, "Effectiveness and Legitimacy of International Regimes," 15–20.

63. Olav Schram Stokke and Davor Vidas, "Conclusions," in Stokke and Vidas, eds., *Governing the Antarctic*, 451–53.

64. Stokke and Vidas, "Effectiveness and Legitimacy of International Regimes," 20–26.

65. Stokke and Vidas, "Conclusions," 454–56.

66. See Stokke and Vidas, "¡and Legitimacy of International Regimes," 26–28.

67. Namely, West Germany (1981), Brazil and India (1983), China and Uruguay (1985), Italy (1987), Spain and Sweden (1988), East Germany (1987), Peru, Finland, and the Republic of Korea (1989). The Netherlands and Ecuador became Consultative Parties in November 1990. U.S. Department of State, Bureau of Oceans, International Environment and Scientific Affairs, "Ratifications or Accessions to the Antarctic Treaty" dated June 1996 (fax communication to the author, July 11, 1996.

68. This overture to Pakistan was made during a conference on "Asia in Antarctica," which convened in Hobart Tasmania, in late 1991. See Sir Ninian Stephen, "Opening Address," in Herr and Davis, eds., *Asia in Antarctica*, 3; and M. M. Rabbani, "Pakistan's Interest in Antarctica," in Ibid., 119–22.

69. Interview with Andrew Jackson, May 7, 1994, Australian Antarctic Division Headquarters, Kingston, Tasmania.

70. See Joyner, "Protection of the Antarctic Environment," 259–74.

71. Interview with David Agnew, May 12, 1994, CCAMLR Headquarters, Hobart, Tasmaina; Interview with Andrew Jackson, May 7, 1994, Australian Antarctic Division Headquarters, Kingston, Tasmania.

72. See Commission for the Conservation of Antarctic Marine Living Resources, *Schedule of Conservation Measures in Force 1996/97* (Hobart: CAMLR, 1996), i–iii (Table of Contents).

73. Interview with David Agnew, May 12, 1994, CCAMLR Headquarters, Hobart, Tasmaina.

74. The role of informal diplomacy often is critical for making communications clearer and the negotiating process work more efficiently. See Joyner, "The Antarctic Minerals Negotiating Process," 898–901.

75. This situation is aptly illustrated by the Prisoner's Dilemma game, where the values of each actor's options are clearly specified. See generally Robert Axelrod, *The Evolution of Cooperation* (New York: Basic Books, 1984).

76. Axelrod and Keohane, "Achieving Cooperation under Anarchy," 234–38.

77. Interview with Andrew Jackson, May 7, 1994, Australian Antarctic Division Headquarters, Kingston, Tasmania.

78. See, e.g., Joyner, "Security Issues and the Law of the Sea," 171, 189–91.

79. See generally Axelrod, *The Evolution of Cooperation*. As noted by Axelrod and Keohane, effective reciprocity in international relations often depends on three salient conditions: (1) the ability of players to identify defectors; (2) the ability of players to focus retaliation on defectors; and (3) the long-term political will ("incentive") to punish defectors. See Axelrod and Keohane, "Achieving Cooperation under Anarchy," 235.

80. Interview with Andrew Jackson, May 7, 1994, Australian Antarctic Division Headquarters, Kingston, Tasmania. On the theoretical merits of this observation generally, see Donald J. Puchala and Raymond F. Hopkins, "International Regimes: Lessons from Inductive Analysis," in Krasner, ed., *International Regimes*, 61–91.

CHAPTER 5: RESOURCE CONSERVATION AND MANAGEMENT

1. See Nicholas D. Kristof, "In Pacific, Growing Fear of Paradise Engulfed," *New York Times*, March 2, 1997, p. 1. A 1996 study by the Intergovernmental Panel on Climate Change suggested a possible sea-level rise of eighteen inches by the year 2100, which would have serious implications for most Pacific island countries. Ibid., 16.

2. See ATCM Recommendation VI-4 (1970); ATCM Recommendation VII-1 (1972); ATCM Recommendation VIII-1 (1975); ATCM Recommendation IX-5 (1977); ATCM Recommendations X-4 and 5 (1985); and ATCM Recommendations XIV-2 and 3 (1987), all of which are entitled "Man's Impact on the Antarctic Environment." See also ATCM Recommendation VIII-13 (1975), which is entitled "The Antarctic Environment."

3. Agreed Measures for the Conservation of Antarctic Fauna and Flora, [ATCM Recommendation III-VIII (1964)], June 2–3, 1964, 17 U.S.T. 996, 998, T.I.A.S. No. 6058 (1966), modified in 24 U.S.T. 1802, T.I.A.S. No. 7692 (1973) [hereinafter Agreed Measures]. The Agreed Measures grew out of two recommendations, ATCM Recommendation I-VIII (1961) and ATCM Recommendation II-II (1962). These recommendations, both of which are entitled "Conservation of Antarctic Fauna and Flora," urged, *inter alia*, that the Consultative Party governments formulate and implement measures as soon as possible for the long-term conservation and protection of living resources in the Antarctic.

4. Agreed Measures, Article VI.

5. Ibid., Article IX.

6. Ibid., Article VIII. As of 1997 at least twenty-four such SPAs had been established by the Consultative Parties. For detailed descriptions, see Heap, ed., *Handbook of the Antarctic Treaty System*, 2131–83. See also Antarctic Treaty, *Final Report of the Twentieth Antarctic Treaty Consultative Meeting, Utrecht 29 April-10*

May 1996 (1997), 44–45 (Proposed Renumbering of Antarctic Protected Areas).

7. By 1998 at least thirty-six SSSIs had been created by the ATCPs in the Antarctic commons, including among them two specially designated marine sites. Heap, *Handbook of the Antarctic Treaty System*, 2184–2243. Most SSSIs are located in Antarctica's coastal regions. See also Antarctic Treaty, *Final Report of the Twentieth Antarctic Treaty Consultative Meeting*, 44–45.

8. By 1998 at least sixty such historic sites and monuments had been identified by the Consultative Parties. For the list of these locations, see Heap, *Handbook of the Antarctic Treaty System*, 2253–61; and National Science Foundation, *Antarctic Conservation Act of 1978 (Public Law 95–541* (Arlington, Va.: NSF, October 1995), 157–62.

9. Recommendation XV-10, "Antarctic Protected Area System: Establishment of Specially Reserved Areas (SRAs)," reprinted in Heap, *Handbook of the Antarctic Treaty System*, 2108–09. The Dufek Massif in the Pensacola Mountains has been designated as a SRA. Ibid., 2244–45.

10. Recommendation XV-11: "Antarctic Protected Area System: Establishment of Multiple Use Planning Areas (MPAs)," (1989), in Heap, *Handbook of the Antarctic Treaty System*, 2109–10. At least one such area, Southwest Anvers Island offshore the Antarctic peninsula, was proposed in 1991 by the Consultative Parties. Ibid., 2245–53.

11. Agreed Measures, Article XII.

12. The Agreed Measures apply to the "same area to which Antarctic Treaty is applicable . . . namely the area south of 60° South Latitude, including ice shelves." Agreed Measures, Article I, paragraph 1.

13. Agreed Measures, Article I, paragraph 2.

14. ATCM Recommendation VIII-11 (1975): "Man's impact on the Antarctic environment," reproduced seriatim in Heap, *Handbook of the Antarctic Treaty System*, 2003, 2031, 2061.

15. Annex A: "Statement of accepted principles and the relevant provision of the Antarctic Treaty," attached to ATCM Recommendation X-8: "Effects of Tourists and Non-government Expeditions in the Antarctic Treaty Area" (1979), in Heap, *Handbook of the Antarctic Treaty System*, 2290–92.

16. Done June 1, 1972, 27 U.S.T. 441, T.I.A.S. No. 8826, entered into force March 11, 1978.

17. Seals Convention, Article 1, paragraph 2.

18. Ibid., Annex I.

19. Ibid., Preamble.

20. Ibid., Article 3.

21. Ibid., Article 12. for example New Zealand, a claimant ATCP, is still not party to the Seals Convention.

22. ATCM Recommendation VIII-10, "Antarctic Marine Living Resources."

23. ATCM Recommendation IX-2: Antarctic Marine Living Resources, Part II, paragraph 1.

24. Ibid., Part III.

25. Article II, paragraph 1 of CCAMLR asserts its principal objective to be "the conservation of Antarctic marine living resources."

26. CCAMLR, Article II, paragraph 2.

27. CCAMLR, Article II, paragraph 2.

28. As provided for in CCAMLR's Article I, paragraph 2, "the populations of finfish, molluscs, crustaceans and all other species of living organisms, including birds, south of the Antarctic Convergence."

29. Compare Article VI in the Antarctic Treaty with Article I in the Seals Convention.

30. CCAMLR, Article VI.

31. CCAMLR, Article IV, paragraph (2)(b).

32. See CCAMLR, Final Act, paragraphs 1, 2, 3, 4 and 5.

33. CCAMLR, Article VIII.

34. CCAMLR, Article IX, paragraph (1)(f) and Article XII.

35. CCAMLR, Article XV, paragraph 1.

36. CCAMLR, Article XXIX, paragraph 1. See note 69 *infra* and accompanying text.

37. CCAMLR, Article IX, paragraph 1. Interesting to note is that this principle is also contained in Article 119 of 1982 UN Convention on the Law of the Sea.

38. As stipulated by CCAMLR, Article IX.

39. Conservation Measure 7–V, in CCAMLR, *Schedule of Conservation Measures in Force*, 1996/97 (Hobart: CAMLR, 1996), 4.

40. CCAMLR, Article II.

41. See CCAMLR, Article II, paragraph 3 (b).

42. *Report of the Fourth Meeting of the Scientific Committee*, SC-CCAMLR-IV, (1985) para. 7.2, p. 34.

43. Croxall, "Use of Indices of Predator Status and Performance in CCAMLR Fishery Management," 355–65.

44. See Conservation Measure 62/XI, reprinted in CAMLR, *Schedule of Conservation Measures in Force 1996/97*, 37.

45. CCAMLR, "CCAMLR Ecosystem Monitoring Program," (1991) (pamphlet).

46. The Commission has adopted three special Conservation Measures relating to the protection of CEMP sites: CM 18/XIII calls for protection of CEMP sites generally; CM 62/XI aims to protect seals island sites; and CM 82/XIII calls for protection of the Cape Shirreff CEMP site. See CAMLR, *Schedule of Conservation Measures in Force 1996/97*, 37.

47. See W. K. de la Mare, "Factors To Consider in Developing Management Measures for Krill," in *Selected Scientific Papers, 1991 (SC- CAMLR-SSP/7)* (Hobart: CCAMLR, 1991), 175–88.

48. See Constable, "CCAMLR Ecosystem Monitoring and a Feedback Management Procedure for Krill," 345–50.

49. Croxall, "Use of Indices of Predator Status and Performance in CCAMLR Fishery Management," 356.

50. See Kock, "Fishing and Conservation in Southern Waters," 4–5; and the discussion in Darry Powell, "Antarctic Fishing and its Likely Development," in Handmer and Wilder, eds., *Towards a Conservation Strategy for the Australian Antarctic Territory*, 75–89.

51. Antarctica and Southern Ocean Coalition, "ASOC Report on the XVth Meeting of the Convention on the Conservation of Antarctic Marine Living Resources" (January 1997), 4–5.

52. Kock, "Fishing and Conservation in Southern Waters," 8.

53. During 1996 at least 2,300 birds were reported caught in longlines fisheries, with 1,600 found dead. ASOC, "ASOC Report on XVth Meeting of CCAMLR," 12–13. Australia recently listed longlining as a major threatening process under its Endangered Species Act. Ibid., 12. Also see P. Jouventin and H. Weimerskirch, "Changes in Population Size and Demography of Northern Seabirds: Management Implications," in C. M. Perrins, D. Lebrton, and G. J. M. Hirons, eds., *Bird Population Studies: Their Relevance to Conservation and Management* (Oxford: Oxford University Press, 1991), 297–314.

54. ASOC, "ASOC Report on XVth Meeting of CCAMLR," 12–13.

55. Kock, "Fishing and Conservation in Southern Waters," 5.

56. Ibid., 5.

57. Beth Marks Clark, "Current Issues in Southern Ocean Fisheries" (Antarctica Project Statement, February 1997), 1–2.

58. Ibid., 1. See also "The XVth Meeting of the Convention on the Conservation of Antarctic Marine Living Resources (CCAMLR)," *Antarctica Project* 5(4) (November 1996): 2.

59. ASOC, "ASOC Report on XVth Meeting of CCAMLR," 10.

60. "Illegal Fishing Threatens CCAMLR's Ability to Manage Antarctica's Fisheries," *Antarctica Project* 5(2) (June 1996): 2.

61. Miller, "Commercial Krill Fisheries in the Antarctic, 1973 to 1988," 231.

62. CCAMLR, *Statistical Bulletin*, vol. 5 (1983–92) (Hobart: CCAMLR, 1992).

63. Kock, "Fishing and Conservation in Southern Waters," 5. See Figure 6, "Nominal Catch of Antarctic Krill," in Ibid., 9.

64. CCAMLR, *Statistical Bulletin*, vol. 5.

65. "ASOC Report on XVth Meeting of CCAMLR," 2; Antarctic and Southern Ocean Coalition, "ASOC Report on the XIVth Meeting of the Convention on the Conservation of Antarctic Marine Living Resources" (January 26, 1996), 2.

66. Kock, "Fishing and Conservation in Southern Waters," 5–6; and Powell, "Antarctic Fishing," 82–85.

67. CCAMLR, *Report of the Tenth Meeting of the Commission (CCAMLR-X)* (Hobart: CCAMLR, 1991), 7.

68. "ASOC Report on XVth Meeting of CCAMLR," 2. Also see CCAMLR, "Report of the Fifth Meeting of the Working Group on Krill," in *Report of the Twelfth Meeting of the Scientific Committee,* SC-CAMLR-XII, Annex 4 (Hobart: CAMLR, 1993), 4.

69. Ibid., 2. By early 1997 Panama had not yet responded to the CAMLR request.

70. Ibid., 2; Kock, "Fishing and Conservation in Southern Waters," 5.

71. Powell, "Antarctic Fishing," 82.

72. CCAMLR, *Report of the Tenth Meeting of the Commission,* 29.

73. SC-CAMLR, "Report of the Fifth Meeting of the Working Group on Krill," in *Report of the Twelfth Meeting of the Scientific Committee,* annex 4 (Hobart: CAMLR, 1993), 130 [Figure 1].

74. See Agnew, "Distribution of Krill," 287–303; and Kock, "Fishing and Conservation in Southern Waters," 6–9.

75. Kock, "Fishing and Conservation in Southern Waters," 7.

76. Ibid., 7–8.

77. ASOC, "ASOC Report on the XVth Meeting of CCAMLR," 9. Convention Measure 104/XV was adopted in 1996 to ensure use of the experimental harvest regime report as a monitoring device for exploratory fisheries. Ibid.

78. CCAMLR, *Report of the Eleventh Meeting of the Commission* (Hobart: CCAMLR, 1992), 19–20.

79. For origins of the map adopted by a CCAMLR Working Group in 1983/84, see *3rd Meeting of Scientific Committee* (Hobart: CAMLR, 1983), 7.

80. See *FAO Classification of Major Fishing Areas for Statistical Purposes,* in *FAO Fisheries Circular* No. 420 (Rome, December 1972).

81. See FAO Species Identification Sheets for Fishery Purposes, *Southern Ocean CCAMLR Convention Area Fishing Areas 48, 58 and 88* (Rome: FAO, 1985).

82. Inigo Everson, *The Living Resources of the Southern Ocean,* Food and Agriculture Organization of the United Nations, United Nations Development Programme, GLO/SO/77 (Rome: Southern Ocean Fisheries Programme, September 1977), 134.

83. See "Catches and Landings," in *FAO Yearbook of Fishery Statistics* (Rome: FAO, 1976), 40.

84. Interview with David Agnew, CCAMLR Research Scientist, May 12, 1994, CCAMLR Headquarters, Hobart, Tasmania.

85. Ibid.

86. See Resolution 7/IX, "Driftnet Fishing in the Convention Area," CCAMLR, 1990 *Report of the Ninth Meeting of the Commission* (CCAMLR-IX) (Hobart: CAMLR, 1990), 19.

87. International Convention for the Prevention of Pollution from Ships, Annex V: Regulations for the Prevention of Pollution by Garbage from Ships, I.M.C.O. Doc. MP/CONF/WP.21/Add.3 (1973), Article 2, para. 3(b)(i). For relevant discussion, see Joyner and Frew, "Plastic Pollution in the Marine Environment," 33–69.

88. Conservation Measure 31–X, CCAMLR, *Report of the Tenth Meeting of the Commission*, 27–28.

89. See Ibid., paragraph 4, p. 27.

90. CCAMLR, *Report of the Eleventh Meeting of the Commission*, 19–20.

91. See "CCAMLR System of Inspection," adopted at CCAMLR VII (para. 124), amended at CCAMLR XII (paras. 6.4 and 6.8), CCAMLR XIII (para 5.26), CCAMLR XIV (paras. 7.22, 7.26, and 7.28) and CCAMLR XV (para. 7.24), reprinted in CAMLR, *Schedule of Conservation Measures in Force 1996/97*, 67–70. For a national perspective of this system, see "Enforcement of International Maritime Conventions and Domestic Standards for the Inspection of Ships that Operate in the Antarctic," Ant. Doc. XX ATCM WP17 (April 1996) (submitted by Chile).

92. Kock, "Fishing and Conservation in Southern Waters," 23.

93. CCAMLR, *Report of the Tenth Meeting of the Commission*, 18.

94. "ASOC Report on the XVth Meeting of CCAMLR," 10–11.

95. Commission for the Conservation of Antarctic Marine Living Resources, *Schedule of Conservation Measures in Force, 1996/97*, i–iii (Table of Contents).

96. See Conservation Measure 72/XII and Conservation Measure 73/XII, in CCAMLR, *Schedule of Conservation Measures in Force 1996/97*, 18.

97. See CAMLR, *Schedule of Conservation Measures in Force, 1996/97*, 12–35.

98. ASOC, "ASOC Report on XVth Meeting of CCAMLR," 9–10.

99. Ibid., 10.

100. Clark, "Current Issues in Southern Ocean Fisheries," 2–3.

101. Contributing factors likely may be that this had been the first major fishery to be exploited in 1970 and that the region had been well mapped by whalers earlier in the century. Interview with David Agnew, May 12, 1994, CCAMLR Headquarters, Hobart, Tasmania.

102. Interview with David Agnew, May 12, 1994, CCAMLR Headquarters, Hobart, Tasmania.

103. Ibid. Ukraine joined CCAMLR in 1995, but Panama has yet to respond to the Commission's request.

104. CAMLR Resolution 10/XII, "Resolution on the Harvesting of Stocks Occurring Within and Outside the Convention Area" (1993).

105. Agreement for the Implementation of the Provisions of the United Nations Convention on the Law of the Sea of December 10, 1982, Relating to the Conservation and Management of Straddling Fish Stocks and Highly Migratory Species, UNGA A/CONF.164/33, August 3, 1995. While not yet in force, as of early 1997 the following Antarctic Treaty states have signed or ratified the Straddling Stocks Convention: Argentina (ratified), Australia, Belgium, Brazil, Canada, Denmark, the European Community, Finland, France, Germany, Italy, Japan, the Netherlands, New Zealand, Norway (ratified), Republic of Korea, Sweden, Russia, Ukraine, United Kingdom, United States (ratified), and Uruguay. Web site: http://www.un.orgs/Depts/Treaty/final/ts2/newfiles/part_boo/xxi_boo/xxi (visited on April 2, 1997). For treatment of a recent seri-

ous international dispute involving the issue of straddling stocks, see Christopher C. Joyner and Alejandro Alvarez von Gustedt, "The 1995 Turbot War: Lessons for the Law of the Sea," *International Journal of Marine and Coastal Law* 11 (November 1996): 425–58.

106. See Laws, "The Ecology of the Southern Ocean," 38–39.

107. Hempel, "Antarctic Marine Food Webs," 270.

108. For example, the availability of plankton can be measured by volume, net weight, dry weight, or carbon content. Or primary production can be measured in terms of oxygen production or carbon intake. Of these which is the more accurate or precise? Obviously, the relation between the calculations remains dependent upon the physical conditions of the phytoplankton and the corresponding environment in which they live.

109. Hempel, "Antarctic Marine Food Webs," 270.

CHAPTER 6: ENVIRONMENTAL PROTECTION AND PRESERVATION

1. The jurisdictional scope of the Antarctic Treaty is set at 60° south latitude. The Antarctic Treaty, done December 1, 1959, 12 U.S.T. 794, T.I.A.S. No. 4780, 402 U.N.T.S. 71, Article VI.

2. See generally Sir Arthur Watts, *International Law and the Antarctic Treaty System* (Cambridge: Grotius Publications, 1992), 253–90; and Laura Pineschi, "The Madrid Protocol on the Protection of the Antarctic Environment and Its Effectiveness," in Francioni and Scovazzi, eds., *International Law for Antarctica*, 2nd ed., 261–91.

3. Protocol on Environmental Protection to the Antarctic Treaty, XIth Special Consultative Meeting in Madrid, Doc. XI ATSCM/2, June 21, 1991, adopted October 4, 1991, reprinted in Heap, ed., *Handbook of the Antarctic Treaty System*, 2018–29. [Hereinafter Madrid Environmental Protocol]. By 1997 the Protocol had been signed by all twenty-six Antarctic Treaty Consultative Parties and by ten Non-Consultative Parties. Ibid., 2029–30 (List of states).

4. See generally Lorraine M. Elliott, *International Environmental Politics: Protecting the Antarctic* (New York: St. Martin's Press, 1994), 162–95.

5. Done at Wellington, June 2, 1988, opened for signature November 25, 1988. Document AMR/SCM/88/78 (June 2, 1988), reprinted in *International Legal Materials* 27 (July 1988), 859–900 and in Heap, *Handbook of the Antarctic Treaty System*, 203–38. For discussion of the negotiations that produced this agreement, see Joyner, "The Antarctic Minerals Negotiating Process," 888–905; and Vicuña, *Antarctic Mineral Exploitation*.

6. For discussion of the principal objections to CRAMRA, see Joyner, "CRAMRA: The Ugly Duckling of the Antarctic Treaty System?," 161, 170–73.

7. See Scott, "Australia Advocates Wilderness Status for Antarctica," 4 and Browne, "France and Australia Kill Pact on Limited Antarctic Mining and Oil Drilling," A10. Under Article 62 of the Wellington Convention, all seven states

that have claims to the continent would have to sign and ratify the convention for it to enter into force. Both Australia and France are claimant states. Thus, by their refusal even to sign the treaty, those governments effectively precluded the possibility of the agreement's entry into force.

8. See "Implications of Alaskan Oil Spill for the Antarctic," Antarctic & Southern Ocean Coalition (ASOC) Information Paper No. 1, PREP ATCM XV/ASOC INF.1 (May 9, 1989).

9. See XV ATCM/WP/2 and XV ATCM/WP/3, in *Final Report of Fifteenth Antarctic Treaty Consultative Meeting* (1989), 202–13.

10. See Antarctic Treaty Docs. XV ATCM/WP/7 (Chile), in Ibid, 227; XV ATCM/WP/4 (New Zealand), in Ibid., 214; XV ATCM/WP/8 (United States), in Ibid., 237; and XV ATCM/WP/14 (Sweden), in Ibid., 243.

11. For discussion of policy positions and negotiations during the Viña del Mar meeting, see Joyner and Ewing, "Antarctica and the Latin American States," 1, 33–41.

12. Ibid., Article 2.

13. Ibid., Article 3, paragraph 1.

14. Ibid., Article 3.

15. Importantly, much of this substance is borrowed from Article 4 in the Wellington Minerals Convention, save for the significant difference that Article 3 in the Protocol strives to apply uniform standards in a comprehensive fashion for all human activities in the Antarctic, not just those that might be related to minerals development. Compare CRAMRA, Article 4. For discussion, see Joyner, "CRAMRA's Legacy of Legitimacy," 20–23.

16. Madrid Environmental Protocol, Article 7.

17. Ibid., Article 25. In addition, fifty years after the Protocol enters into force, the prohibition on mining activity may be lifted if that decision is adopted at a Review Conference by a majority of all ATCPs, including three-fourths of current ATCPs, and then ratified by three-fourths of the ATCPs, "including the ratifications of all States that were Consultative Parties at the time of the adoption of this Protocol." Ibid., Article 25, paragraph 4. See discussion in the text.

18. Madrid Protocol, Articles 11 and 12.

19. Ibid., Article 12, paragraph 1.

20. Antarctic and Southern Ocean Coalition, "A Critique of the Protocol to the Antarctic Treaty on Environmental Protection," ASOC Information Paper No. 1, XVI ATCM (October 8, 1991), 4. [Hereinafter cited as ASOC Critique].

21. Madrid Protocol, Article 13.

22. Madrid Protocol, Article 14.

23. Ibid., Articles 18, 19, and 20. Arbitral tribunals had been previously included in the CCAMLR and CRAMRA instruments.

24. Ibid., Article 8.

25. Ibid., Article 15.

26. Ibid., Article 17.

27. Ibid., Article 13.

28. Ibid., Article 15.

29. Ibid., Article 9.

30. SCAR had proposed adoption in 1973 of "a comprehensive statement of anticipated short-term and long-term effects on the environment and its intimately associated macro- and micro-biota, together with their primary, secondary and tertiary consequences (and) delimitation of all probable and unavoidable adverse environmental effects, with suggestions for minimizing them." See *SCAR Bulletin* 43 (1973): 913. See also Barnes, "Legal Aspects of Environmental Protection in Antarctica," 241–43.

31. See ATCM Recommendation VIII-11 (1975): Man's Impact on the Environment including the Code of Conduct for Antarctic Expeditions and Station Activities, reprinted in Heap, *Handbook of the Antarctic Treaty System*, 2003, 2031, 2061.

32. See W. S. Benninghoff and W. N. Bonner, *Man's Impact on the Antarctic Environment: A Procedure for Evaluating Impacts from Scientific and Logistic Activities* (Cambridge: SCAR, 1985), 32–35. See Table 46 for a list of those activities that should require preparation of assessments.

33. ATCM Recommendation XIII-5: Man's Impact on the Antarctic environment: additional protective arrangements, reprinted in Heap, *Handbook of the Antarctic Treaty System*, 137 (italics omitted).

34. See ASOC, "Background Paper on the French Airfield at Point Geologie, Antarctica," March 1, 1985, and Antarctica Briefing No. 9, "The French Airstrip— A Breach of Antarctic Treaty Rules?," July 30, 1986.

35. See B. C. Parker, M. G. Mudrey, K. Cartwright, and L. D. McGinnis et al., "Environmental Appraisal for the Dry Valley Drilling Project, Phases III, IV, (1973–74, 1974–75, and 1975–76," in Parker and Holliman, eds., *Environmental Impact in Antarctica*, 37–143.

36. See B. C. Parker, M. A. McWhinnie, D. Elliott, S. Reed, and R. H. Rutland, "Ross Ice Shelf Project Environmental Impact Statement," in Parker and Holliman, eds., *Environmental Impact in Antarctica*, 7–36.

37. Annex I to the Protocol on Environmental Protection to the Antarctic Treaty: Environmental Impact Assessment, XI ATSCM/2, June 21, 1991, in Heap, *Handbook of the Antarctic Treaty System*, 2040. For an insightful analysis, see Lyons, "Environmental Impact Assessment in Antarctica under the Protocol on Environmental Protection," 111–20.

38. Annex I, Articles 1, 2, and 3.

39. Ibid., Article 1.

40. Ibid., Article 2.

41. Ibid., Article 3.

42. Ibid., Article 3, paragraph 5.

43. Annex II to the Protocol on Environmental Protection to the Antarctic

Treaty: Conservation of Antarctic Fauna and Flora, XI ATSCM/2, June 21, 1991, reprinted in Heap, *Handbook of the Antarctic Treaty System,* 2056. This annex on the conserving of Antarctic fauna and flora was proposed by the United States, ostensibly to ensure that, with treaty status, plant and animal life in Antarctica could be protected and preserved through enforceable means under international law. See "International Environment: 1991 Offers Chance to Set Global Agenda," Daily Report for Executives (BNA) (DER No. 12) (Jan. 17, 1991), S-18.

44. Annex II, Article 5, paragraph 1.

45. Ibid., Article 5, paragraph 2(a)–(e).

46. Ibid., Article 3, paragraph 3; Agreed Measures, Article 5, paragraph 3(b).

47. Ibid., Article 6.

48. Ibid., Article 3, paragraph 6.

49. Ibid., Article 6.

50. Ibid., Article 4, paragraph 2.

51. Ibid., Article 1, paragraph (h)(v).

52. Annex III to the Protocol on Environmental Protection to the Antarctic Treaty: Waste Disposal and Waste Management, XI ATSCM/2, June 21, 1991, reprinted in Heap, *Handbook of the Antarctic Treaty System,* 2068.

53. Recommendation XII-4, "Man's Impact on the Antarctic Environment, Code of Conduct for Antarctic Expeditions and Station Activities," reprinted in Heap, *Handbook of the Antarctic Treaty System,* 2062.

54. "Recommendation XV-3, Human Impact on the Antarctic Environment: Waste Disposal," reprinted in Heap, *Handbook of the Antarctic Treaty System,* 22063.

55. Annex III, Article 8.

56. See Ibid., Article 5, paragraph 1 (b) (Disposal of Waste in the Sea).

57. Ibid., Article 5, paragraph 1.

58. ASOC Critique, 8.

59. Annex IV to the Protocol on Environmental Protection to the Antarctic Treaty: Prevention of Marine Pollution, XI ATSCM/2, June 21, 1991, reprinted in Heap, *Handbook of the Antarctic Treaty System,* 2077.

60. International Convention for Preventing Pollution from Ships, done at London, November 2, 1973, I.M.C.O. Doc. MP/CONF/WP.35, amended by Protocol of 1978 Relating to the International Convention for the Prevention of Pollution from Ships, done at London, February 17, 1978, entered into force October 2, 1983, I.M.C.O. Doc. TSPP/CONF/11.

61. See ATCM Recommendation VIII-10 (1975) Antarctic Marine Living Resources, reprinted in Heap, *Handbook of the Antarctic Treaty System,* 170; ATCM Recommendation IX-2 (1977) Antarctic Marine Living Resources, in Ibid., 171; ATCM Recommendation XI-2 (1981) Antarctic Marine Living Resources, in Ibid., 173; ATCM Recommendation IX-6 (1977): Oil Contamination of the Antarctic Marine Environment, in Ibid., 2273; and ATCM Recommendation X-7 (1979): Oil Contamination of the Antarctic Marine Environment, in Ibid., 2273.

62. ATCM Recommendation XV-4 (1989), reprinted in Heap, *Handbook of the Antarctic Treaty System*, 2073–74.

63. Compliance with the following five conventions was cited as especially important for operations in the Antarctic: The Convention on the Prevention of Marine Pollution by Dumping of Wastes and Other Matter, 1972 (the London Dumping Convention); the International Convention for the Prevention of Pollution from Ships, 1973, and the Protocol of 1978 relating thereto, with Annexes I, II, III, and V (MARPOL); the International Convention on Standards of Training, Certification and Watchkeeping for Seafarers with Annex, 1978 (the STCW Convention); the International Convention for the safety of Life at Sea, 1974, and the Protocol of 1978 relating thereto (SOLAS); the International Convention on Load Lines, 1966 (the Load Lines Convention); and the Convention on the International Regulations for Preventing Collisions at Sea, 1972 (COLREGS).

64. Annex IV, Article 3.

65. Ibid., Article 4.

66. Annex IV, Article 2.

67. Ibid., Article 9.

68. Ibid., Article 9, paragraph 1.

69. Ibid., Article 9, paragraph 2.

70. Ibid., Article 11.

71. See, e.g., "Inspection of Ships in Gateway Ports to Antarctica, on the Basis of MARPOL 73/78 and in Antarctic Ports under the Environmental Protocol (Annex IV) to the Antarctic Treaty," Ant. Doc. XX ATCM/WP 9 (March 1996) (submitted by the Netherlands).

72. Annex to Recommendation XVI: Annex V to the Protocol on Environmental Protection to the Antarctic Treaty: Area and Management, in Heap, *Handbook of the Antarctic Treaty System*, 2125.

73. See generally Boczek, "Specially Protected Areas as an Instrument for the Conservation of Antarctic Nature," 65–102; and Beth Marks Clark and Karen Perry, "The Protection of Special Areas in Antarctica," in Francioni and Scovazzi, eds., *International Law for Antarctica*, 293–316.

74. ATCM Recommendations III-VIII (1964): Specially Protected Areas (SPA) and Special Conservation Areas (SCA); ATCM Recommendation VII-3 (1972): Sites of Special Scientific Interest (SSSI); ATCM Recommendation XIV-6 (1987): Marine Sites of Special Scientific Interest (MSSSI); ATCM Recommendation VIII-9 (1975): Areas of Special Tourist Interest (ASTI); ATCM Recommendations I-IX (1961), V-4 (1968), and VI-14 (1970): Historic Sites and Monuments (HSM); and ATCM Recommendation XV-10 (1989): Multiple Use Planning Areas (MPA).

75. See Auburn, *Antarctic Law and Politics*, 273–77; and Boczek, "Specially Protected Areas as an Instrument for the Conservation of the Antarctic Nature," 65–101.

76. Annex V, Article 3.

77. Ibid., Article 4.

78. Ibid., Article 5.

79. Ibid., Article 5, paragraph 2.

80. Ibid., Article 5.

81. Interview with David Lyons, Institute for Antarctic and Southern Ocean Studies, University of Tasmania, May 25, 1994.

82. Interview with Lorne Kriwoken, Institute for Antarctic and Southern Ocean Studies, University of Tasmania, May 30, 1994.

83. Madrid Environmental Protocol, Article 4.

84. Ibid., Article 5.

85. As provided for in the Antarctic Treaty, thirty years after that instrument enters into force (i.e., June 23, 1991), any ATCP may request that a conference be convened "to review operation of the Treaty." Antarctic Treaty, Article XII, paragraph 2(a).

86. During the course of the ATCP discussions on a mineral regime, from 1981 though 1990, eighteen states acceded to the Antarctic Treaty. Of these, fourteen applied for and were granted consultative status. Not only did the number of parties to the Antarctic Treaty increase twofold, the number of Consultative Parties also doubled.

87. Madrid Environmental Protocol, Article 25. In addition, fifty years after the Protocol enters into force, the prohibition on mining activity may be lifted if that decision is adopted at a Review Conference by a majority of all ATCPs, including three-fourths of current ATCPs, and then ratified by three-fourths of the ATCPs, "including the ratifications of all States that were Consultative Parties at the time of the adoption of this Protocol." Ibid., Article 25, paragraph 4. See discussion in the text at pp. 167–69 *supra*.

88. See, e.g., Bruce Manheim, "On Thin Ice: The Failure of the National Science Foundation to Protect Antarctica," Report for the Environmental Defense Fund Wildlife Program, August 17, 1988; and Congressional Research Service, *Effects of Recent Activities in Antarctica*. Report for Congress prepared by M. Lynne Corn, Marjorie Browne, Eugene H. Buck, and James E. Mielke. Report 88–439 SPR, June 15, 1988.

89. Madrid Environmental Protocol, Article 16.

90. These questions are drawn from "Liability Annex to the Protocol on Environmental Protection to the Antarctic Treaty," Agenda Item 6c (Submitted by Germany), ATCM Doc. XVIII ATCM/WP 2 (April 10, 1994), 1–6. The author of this paper and the chairman of the ATCP working group to produce a liability annex is Professor Rüdiger Wolfrum of Germany.

91. Rüdiger Wolfrum, "Chairman's *Draft* Eighth Offering," Annex on Environmental Liability" (26 June 1997). For a critique of this document, see Antarctic and Southern Ocean Coalition (ASOC), "Commentary on Chairman's Eighth Offering, Annex on Environmental Liability" (17 September 1997).

92. Chairman's *Draft* Eighth Offering, Article 1 or Preamble, at 1.

93. Ibid., Article 2.

94. Ibid., Article 3, para. (a).

95. Ibid., Article 3 (aa) and (bb).

96. ASOC, "Commentary on Chairman's Eighth Offering," 2.

97. Ibid.

98. Chairman's *Draft* Eighth Offering, Article 3 bis, at 3.

99. Ibid., Article 3 ter.

100. Ibid., Article 3 quater.

101. Ibid., Article 4. These terms embrace key concepts within a putative liability annex, though they lack precise definition or threshold designation. "Preparedness" implies prevention of "incidents," which may be defined as "any sudden occurrence or continuous or any series of occurrences having the same origin, which causes damage or creates a grave or imminent threat of causing damage." Article 2.11, Convention on Civil Liability for Damage Resulting from Activities Dangerous to the Environment. Finally "restoration" appears to imply a return to the status quo ante for the environment before damage was inflicted. But precisely how that situation is to be determined remains unclear. Alan D. Hemmings, "On the Terms 'Preparedness,' 'Response Action' and 'Remedial Measures' Employed in the Liability Discussion" (March 25, 1996) (Fax to the Antarctica Project, on file with the author).

102. Chairman's *Draft* Eighth Offering, Article 5.

103. Ibid., Article 5 bis.

104. Ibid., Article 10.

105. Ibid., Article 11.

106. Ibid., Article 6, para. 2.

107. Madrid Environmental Protocol, Article 16.

108. "President Signs Implementing Legislation—But U.S. Ratification Still Remains Elusive," *Antarctic Project* 5(4) (November 1996): 1.

109. The implementing legislation allows the EPA two years to promulgate the regulations for environmental impact assessment for nongovernment activities, i.e., tourism). The Coast Guard has three years to promulgate regulations to enforce marine pollution provisions of Annex IV of the Protocol, while NSF is given two years to promulgate regulations for waste disposal. "President Signs Implementing Legislation," 1.

110. See "U.S. Ratifies Protocol. . . ," *Antarctica Project* Vol. 6: 2 (June 1997), 1.

111. See "Remarks by Christopher C. Joyner," *Proceedings of the 79th Annual Meeting of the American Society of International Law* (Washington, D.C.: ASIL, 1987), 62–67.

112. "Statement of Greenpeace before the Foreign Relations Committee of the United States Senate at a Hearing on the Ratification of the Protocol to the Antarctic Treaty on Environmental Protection," 102nd Cong, 2nd sess. (May 4, 1992), 2–3 (mimeographed).

113. Mosley, *Antarctica*, 46–50.

114. See Myhre, *The Antarctic Treaty System*, 46.

115. See Appendix G in Barnes, *Let's Save Antarctica!*, 59.

116. See "Report and Recommendations of the Eighth Antarctic Treaty Consultative Party Meeting, Oslo," in Bush, *Antarctica and International Law,* vol. 2, 292–331.

117. Antarctic and Southern Ocean Coalition, "Permanent Protection for Antarctica; A Conservation Convention Is Urgently Needed," ASOC Information Paper No. 2, PREP ATCM XV/INF. 2 (May 11, 1989), 3. These points are virtually identical to the "World Park principles" set out by Greenpeace as a "code" for all human activities conducted south of 60° south latitude. See "Statement of Greenpeace," 4.

118. ASOC Paper No. 2, 3–4.

119. "Statement of Greenpeace," 4.

120. Compare Francisco Orrego Vicuña, "The Effectiveness of the Protocol on Environmental Protection to the Antarctic Treaty," in Stokke and Vidas, eds., *Governing the Antarctic,* 174–201 and Vicuña, "The Legitimacy of the Protocol on Environmental Protection to the Antarctic Treaty," in Ibid., 268–92.

121. "Statement of Greenpeace," 3.

CHAPTER 7: SCIENCE AND TOURISM

1. See generally S. B. Abbott and W. S. Benninghoff, "Orientation of Environmental Change Studies to the Conservation of Antarctic Ecosystems," in Kerry and Hempel, *Antarctic Ecosystems: Ecological Change and Conservation,* 394–402.

2. One expert commentator defines science as "pure and applied scholarly investigation . . . comprising activities in the realm of natural and social sciences . . . and encompassing the training of young scientists." Lucius Caflisch, "The Interaction of Science and Politics in the Field of International Relations: The Case of Antarctica," *Polar Record* 28(169) (1991): 159. Also see generally Patrizia de Cesari, "Scientific Research in Antarctica: New Developments," in Francioni and Scovazzi, eds., *International Law for Antarctica,* 2nd ed., 459–73.

3. See generally Tore Gjelsvik, "Scientific Research and Cooperation in Antarctica," in Wolfrum, ed., *Antarctic Challenge,* 41–52; Frank Wong and Felicity Newman, "Restrictions of Scientific Research through Environmental Protection," in Wolfrum, ed., *Antarctic Challenge II,* 103–9; and Patrick Quilty, "Cooperation in Antarctica in Scientific and Logistic Matters: Status and Mans of Improvement," in Wolfrum, ed., *Antarctic Challenge III,* 65–78.

4. Antarctic Treaty, done December 1, 1959, 12 U.S.T 794, 402 U.N.T.S. 71. See the Preamble and Articles I, II, III, and IX.

5. Ibid., Article III, paragraph 1(a).

6. Ibid., Article III, paragraph 1(b).

7. Ibid., Article III, paragraph 1(c).

8. See generally Mike Richardson, "Directions of Scientific Research," in Andrew Jackson, ed., *On the Antarctic Horizon*, 33–36.

9. Convention on the Conservation of Antarctic Seals, June 1, 1972, 29 U.S.T. 441, T.I.A.S. No. 8826 (entered into force March 11, 1978), reprinted in Heap, ed., *Handbook of the Antarctic Treaty System*, 156, fifth preambular paragraph.

10. See Ibid., Annex, Paragraphs 6 and 7. In 1995 the full members of SCAR included all the ATCP governments, save for Peru, which has associate membership. Heap, *Handbook of the Antarctic Treaty System*, 260.

11. Conservation on the Conservation of Antarctic Marine Living Resources, done May 20, 1980, 33 U.S.T. 3476, T.I.A.S. No. 10240 (entered into force April 7, 1982), reprinted in Heap, *Handbook of the Antarctic Treaty System*, 178.

12. Ibid., Article IX.

13. Ibid., Articles XIV and XV.

14. Convention on the Regulation of Antarctic Mineral Resource Activities, opened for signature November 25, 1988, reprinted in *International Legal Materials* 27 (1988): 859 and in Heap, *Handbook of the Antarctic Treaty System*, 203.

15. Ibid., Article 2.

16. Ibid., Article 4.

17. Ibid., Article 8.

18. Ibid., Articles 23, 43, 45, 47, 51, 52, and 54.

19. Protocol on Environmental Protection to the Antarctic Treaty, October 3, 1991, reprinted in *International Legal Materials* 30 1455 (1991) and in Heap, *Handbook of the Antarctic Treaty System*, 2018.

20. Ibid., Article 2.

21. Ibid., Article 3, paragraph 1.

22. International Convention for Preventing Pollution from Ships, done at London, November 2, 1973, I.M.C.O. Doc. MP/CONF/WP.35, amended by Protocol of 1978 Relating to the International Convention for the Prevention of Pollution from Ships, done at London, February 17, 1978, entered into force October 2, 1983, I.M.C.O. Doc. TSPP/CONF/11.

23. Antarctic Treaty, Article IX, paragraph 2 stipulates the essential condition for a Contracting Party becoming a Consultative Party is for that government to demonstrate "its interest in Antarctica by conducting substantial scientific activity there, such as the establishment of a scientific station or the despatch of a scientific expedition."

24. See Committee on Fundamental Science, National Science and Technology Council, "Antarctica: A Unique Laboratory for Science," in *United States Antarctic Program* (Washington, D.C.: Office of Science and Technology, April 1996), 13–28. See generally the selections in Hempel, ed., *Antarctic Science and Global Concerns*.

25. In 1997 U.S. Antarctic policy is guided by four fundamental national interests: (1) protecting the relatively unspoiled environment of Antarctica and its associated ecosystems; (2) preserving and pursuing unique opportunities for

scientific research to understand Antarctica and global physical and environmental systems; (3) maintaining Antarctica as an area of international cooperation reserved exclusively for peaceful purposes; and (4) assuring the conservation and sustainable management of the living resources in the oceans surrounding Antarctica. *The United States Antarctic Program*, 9. Of these interests, scientific research is clearly essential to numbers 1, 2, and 4, which contribute to number 3.

Australia asserts in its official study on Antarctic Science that its first priority as defined by the government is "to preserve our sovereignty over the Australian Antarctic Territory (AAT), including our sovereign rights over adjacent off-shore areas." Antarctic Science Advisory Committee, *Antarctic Science—The Way Forward*, 4.

26. Since 1963 at least thirty-one inspections of stations in the Antarctic have been conducted by governmental teams from fourteen different states. These include inspections by New Zealand (3), the United States (10), Australia (5), United Kingdom (2), Chile (3), Argentina (2), the Soviet Union (1), France/Germany (1), Norway (1), Brazil (1), China (1), the United Kingdom/Italy and Republic of Korea (1), and Sweden (1). "Report of Working Group II to the XVIIIth ATCM," Ant.Doc. XVIII ATCM/WP 36 (April 21, 1994), 21–25 (Annex A: Inspections by Year, Nationality, and Location Carried Out under Article VII of the Antarctic Treaty). See Pietro de Desari, "Inspections under the Antarctic Treaty," in Francesco Francioni and Scovazzi, eds., *International Law for Antarctica*, 459–74.

27. See Greenpeace Antarctica Tour: Press Release, "Penguin Population Declines Due to Climatic Changes," February 9, 1997 (on file at the Antarctica Project, Washington, D.C.).

28. Committee on Antarctic Policy and Science, Polar Research Board, *Science and Stewardship in the Antarctic* (Washington, D.C.: National Research Council, 1993), 6

29. Committee on Fundamental Science, *United States Antarctic Program*, 14.

30. See generally Drewry, "The Future of Antarctic Scientific Research," 37–44.

31. See generally SCAR, *The Role of Antarctica in Global Change. Part II: An International Plan for a Regional Research Programme* (Cambridge: International Council of Scientific Unions, 1992).

32. In an era of tightening budgets, the costs of Antarctic science have come under criticism. See "Pressure on Budget Triggers Review of Antarctic Program," *Science* 270 (December 1, 1995): 1433; Malcolm W. Browne, "Leaner Budgets Curtail Plans for South Pole," *New York Times*, April 15, 1997, p. C-1.

33. On remote sensing of ice-covered areas by satellites, see the special issue of *Polar Record* 31(177) (April 1995), especially Robert Massom, "Satellite Remote Sensing of Polar Ice and Snow: Present Status and Future Direction," 99–115.

34. Committee on Fundamental Science, *United States Antarctic Program*, 16.

35. Bill Dietrich, "Antarctica: Shelter Means Survival," *Seattle Times*, January 29–February 1, 1995, pp. 4–7 (Special Series).

36. Parsons, *Antarctica*, 48. These formations may date back 3.5 billion years.

37. Office of Polar Programs, National Science Foundation, *Facts about the United States Antarctic Program* (October 1994), 7. See also Tom Walters, "The Icy Secrets of Antarctica," *Earth* (November 1994): 37–45; and Committee on Fundamental Science, *United States Antarctic Program* (Sidebar on "West Antarctic Ice Sheet Stability and Global Sea Level"), 16–17.

38. National Science Foundation, *Facts about the United States Antarctic Program*, 8.

39. Kim A. McDonald, "Antarctic Dig Finds Fossils from Ancient Catastrophe," *Chronicle of Higher Education*, November 3, 1995, pp. A10, 21.

40. See "Antarctica and Remote Sensing: Understanding Earth's Atmospheric Chemistry and Climate Change," in Committee on Fundamental Science, *United States Antarctic Program*, sidebar between 20 and 21.

41. Ibid., 8.

42. National Science Foundation, *Facts about the United States Antarctic Program*, 8.

43. See generally Antarctic Science Advisory Committee, *Antarctic Research Priorities for the 1990s: A Review* (Canberra: Commonwealth of Australia, 1991.)

44. Committee on Fundamental Science, *United States Antarctic Program*, 15.

45. See Ruth Flanagan and Tom Yulsman, "On Thin Ice," *Earth Magazine* (April 1996): 44–50; and Jane Ellen Stevens, "Exploring Antarctic Ice," *National Geographic* 189 (May 1996): 36–53.

46. See Farman, Gardiner, and Shanklin, "Large Losses of Total Ozone in Antarctica Reveal Seasonal CIOx/NOx Interaction," 207–10; Bill Dietrich, "Antarctica Under the Ozone Hole," *Seattle Times*, April 6, 1997, p. A-1.

47. See Pyle, G. Carver, J. L. Grenfell, J. A. Kettleborough, and D. J. Larry, "Ozone Loss in Antarctica: The Implications for Global Change," *Philosophical Transactions of the Royal Society of London*, Series B (1992): 219–26.

48. See Malcolm W. Browne, "Laser at South Pole to Track Ozone Depletion," *New York Times*, January 1, 1995, p. C4; "Seasonal Hole In Ozone Grows at Record Rate," *Washington Post*, September 13, 1995, p. A7; "New Data Point to the Ultimate Recovery of the Ozone Layer," *New York Times*, May 31, 1996, p. A14; and "Effect of the Ozone Hole on Ocean Life," in Committee on Fundamental Science, *United States Antarctic Program*, sidebar between pp. 18 and 19.

49. See J. Priddle, V. Smetacek, and U. Bathmann, "Antarctic Marine Primary Production, Biogeochemical Carbon Cycles and Climatic Change," *Philosophical Transactions of the Royal Society of London*, Series B, 338 (1992): 289–97.

50. The oldest ice cores, extending back more than three hundred thousand years, have been taken by an international drilling project jointly sponsored by Russia, the United States, and France at the Vostok Station, far inland in East

Antarctica. Vincent Kiernan, "Breakdown Freezes Ice Core Project," *New Scientist*, January 13, 1996, p. 10.

51. See Corrina Wu, "Ice's Age? More than 8 Million Years," *Science News*, August 5, 1995, p. 87. Research into paleoclimatic studies involves drilling deep into ice mantle to depths up to four kilometers to obtain a record of changes in the ice sheet, global climate atmospheric gases, and volcanic fallout. Such research can provide extensive information on global climate change back several 400,000 years. *Antarctic Research Priorities for the 1990s*, 9. Indeed, some drilling programs for Antarctica have been designed to provide improved understanding of the Antarctic icecap using glaciological analogues such as ice sheets that covered the Northern Hemisphere during the last ice age and have revealed historical data about the Antarctic surface over the past 250,000–400,000 years.

52. "West Antarctic Ice Sheet and Global Sea Level," sidebar in Committee on Fundamental Science, *United States Antarctic Program*, 16–17.

53. See Michael D. Lemonick, "One Big, Bad Iceberg," *Time* (March 20, 1995): 65; and Sharon Begley, "Ice Cubes for Penguins," *Newsweek* (April 3, 1995): 56. But compare William K. Stevens, "Ice Shelves Melting as Forecast, But Disaster Script Is in Doubt," *New York Times*, January 30, 1996, p. C4.

54. See Harvey Merchant, "Antarctic Marine Life and Climate Change—A Critical Relationship?," *ANARE News* (Winter 1992): 21–22. Global warming is already having notable impacts upon Antarctic wildlife. See Roger Atwood, "Penguins Burned by Antarctic Sun: Some Species Recede with Ice in Warmer Weather," *Washington Times*, March 31, 1997, p. A14. The increased intensity of ultraviolet rays caused by aggravated ozone depletion is also seriously affecting Antarctic life. See Roger Atwood, "Ozone Hole Wreaks Havoc on Food Chain's Bottom Link, *Washington Times*, March 31, 1997, p. A14.

55. See Committee on Fundamental Science, *United States Antarctic Program*, 18.

56. See Jane E. Stevens, "Life on a Melting Continent," *Discover* (August 1995): 71–75.

57. Jane E. Stevens, "Martin's Sense of Ice," *Sciences* (July/August 1995): 14–17.

58. National Science Foundation, *Facts about the United States Antarctic Program*, 8.

59. Rudolf Merget, "Bits of Universe's Secrets Trapped in Antarctic Ice," *Washington Times*, February 1995, reprinted in National Science Foundation, *Antarctic News Clips 1995* (Arlington, Va.: NSF, 1995), 11 and Mike Sajna, "Meteor Man," *Sunday Tribune Review*, January 7, 1996, Focus 8–9, reprinted in National Science Foundation, *Antarctic News Clips 1995*, 122–23.

60. See Christopher C. Joyner, "Antarctic Resources and Remote Sensing by Satellite: The Interplay of Technology, Mission and Law," in Wolfrum, *Antarctic Challenge III*, 191–225.

61. National Science Foundation, *Facts about the United States Antarctic Pro-*

gram, 6–7; Donald Goldsmith, "Astronomy's Hot Spot," *Air & Space* (October/ November 1995): 40–46.

62. See Vincent Kiernan, "Sun Never Sets on Balloon Telescope," *New Scientist* (January 13, 1996): 10; and Lawrence Spohn, "Scoping Out the Sun," *Albuquerque Tribune*, August 8, 1995, p. C1.

63. See Bill Dietrich, "Antarctica; The Coldest Laboratory," *Seattle Times*, January 29–February 1, 1995 (Special Series), 9. Nearly nine thousand meteorites have been recovered from the Antarctic ice, some which may be four to five billion years old. Ibid. Also see Kim A. McDonald, "Scientists Battle Antarctica's Elements to Find Ideal Meteorites for Research," *Chronicle of Higher Eduction*, January 21, 1997, p. A10–12.

64. See Jane E. Stevens, "The Antarctic Pack-Ice Ecosystem," *BioScience* 45 (March 1995): 128–32.

65. Mary Aegerter, "Scientists Study Ozone Effect on Food Chain," *Weekend Daily News* (Washington State University),

January 13 and 14, 1996, reprinted in National Science Foundation, *Antarctic News Clips 1996* (Arlington, Va.: NSF, 1996), 44–45; Roger Atwood, "Ozone Hole Wreaks Havoc on Food Chain's Bottom Link," *Washington Times*, March 31, 1997, p. 14.

66. National Science Foundation, *Facts about the United States Antarctic Program*, 7.

67. *Antarctic Research Priorities for the 1990s*, 37–38.

68. Ibid.

69. In aiming to conserve the entire marine ecosystem, CCAMLR has assumed responsibility for conservation of whales and seals. CCAMLR accommodates this obvious duplication of effort by recognizing the rights and obligations of contracting parties under the Whaling and the Seals Conventions, and contains specific provisions requiring cooperation between CCAMLR, IWC, and ATCPs. See CCAMLR, Articles 6 and 22.

70. See generally Commission for the Conservation of Antarctic Marine Living Resources, *CCAMLR Ecosystem Monitoring System* (Hobart, Tasmania: CCAMLR, 1991).

71. Ibid.

72. See Manheim, "On Thin Ice."

73. Boleslaw Boczek has defined tourists as: "Private individuals travelling without remuneration individually or in a group for pleasure, recreation or personal curiosity rather than for scientific or other professional purposes. "The Legal Status of Visitors, Including Tourists, and Non-Governmental Expeditions in Antarctica," 455–90.

74. Enzenbacher, "Antarctic Tourism: An Overview of 1992/93," 107. The 100,000 figure is this author's estimate from the combined total of cruise-ship passengers and "flightseers" who have flown over the continent.

75. See generally Enzenbacher, "Tourists in Antarctica," 17–22.

76. R. J. Reich, "The Development of Antarctic Tourism," *Polar Record* 20(126) (1980): 210–11.

77. Enzenbacher, "Tourists in Antarctica," 19.

78. Wace, "Antarctica; A New Tourist Destination," *Applied Geography* 10 (1990): 331. See generally Swithinbank, "Airborne Tourism in the Antarctic," 103–10.

79. Enzenbacher, "Antarctic Tourism: An Overview of 1992/93," 107. Added to Enzenbacher's figures are the additional tourists totals for 1994–96.

80. Ibid.

81. Enzenbacher, "Tourists in Antarctica," 19. Scientific personnel in Antarctica number around 4,000; tourists visiting the continent in 1991 reached a reported number of 4,842. Ibid., 17–19.

82. "More People Travel to Antarctica in 1995–96 Than Ever Before," *IAATO News* (July 1996): 1.

83. Interview with Beth Marks Clark, director of The Antarctic Project, Washington, D.C., February 28, 1997.

84. Enzenbacher, "Tourists in Antarctica," 19. According to IAATO, the "Ten Most Visited Antarctic Sites, 1995–96" were Whalers Bay, Half Moon Island, Cuverville Island, Brown Station, Port Lockroy, Petermen Island, Hannah Point, Pendulum Cove, Paulet Island, and Waterboat Point. *IAATO News* (July 1996): 1.

85. Antarctic Treaty, Article VIII, paragraph 1.

86. Ibid.

87. ATCM Recommendation IV-27, Effects of Antarctic tourism (1966).

88. Ibid. See also ATCM Recommendation I-IV, Exchange of information on operations (1961), which recommended to ATCP governments that they should furnish "notice of any expeditions to Antarctica not organized by the party but organized in, or proceeding from the party's territory." Ibid., paragraph 10.

89. ATCM Recommendation VI-7, Effects of Tourists and Non-government Expeditions to the Antarctic Treaty Area (1970).

90. Ibid., Paragraph 1.

91. ATCM Recommendation VII-4, Effects of Tourists and Non-governmental Expeditions in the Antarctic Treaty Area (1972), paragraph 3.

92. Ibid., Paragraph 4.

93. ATCM Recommendation VIII-9, Effects of Tourists and Non-governmental Expeditions in the Antarctic Treaty Area (1975), reprinted in Heap, ed., *Handbook of the Antarctic Treaty System*, 2298–94.

94. For example, among these requests are included the following: do *not* walk on vegetation, touch birds or seals, collect eggs or fossils, use sporting guns, or paint names or graffiti on rocks or buildings. *Do* retain all litter, take care of historic monuments, and keep together with your party.

95. See generally Richard A. Herr, "The Regulation of Antarctic Tourism: A Study in Regime Effectiveness," in Stokke and Vidas, eds., *Governing the Antarctic*, 203–23.

96. The Protocol plainly asserts that tourist activities undertaken in the Antarctic Treaty area "shall . . . be modified, suspended or canceled if they result in or threaten to result in impacts upon the Antarctic environment or dependent or associated ecosystems inconsistent with those principles." Madrid Environmental Protocol, Article 3, paragraph 4(b).

97. Ibid., Articles 14, paragraph 1 and 15, paragraph 1(a).

98. Ibid., Article 12, paragraph 1 (e) and (g).

99. The annex separates human activities into three broad categories according to their possible impacts on the environment: activities that have (1) less than a minor or transitory impact; (2) a minor or transitory impact; or (3) more than a minor or transitory impact. Unfortunately, no precise standards or definitions of degree are furnished to differentiate between these categories of "minor," "transitory," or "more than minor or transitory" impacts. This determination is left up to national procedures, which of course may vary from state to state. Normal, uneventful tourist activities would probably fall under the first category.

100. Annex II to the Protocol on Environmental Protection Protocol to the Antarctic Treaty, Article 3. Special permits are required to authorize any taking of such specimens. Ibid.

101. Ibid., Article 3, paragraph 4. See also Appendix A attached to Annex II.

102. Of especial concern here are live poultry or other birds and nonsterile soils. Ibid., Article 4 and Appendix C to Annex II.

103. Annex III to the Protocol on Environmental Protection Protocol to the Antarctic Treaty, Article 1 (2) (4).

104. Annex IV to the Protocol on Environmental Protection Protocol to the Antarctic Treaty, Article 2.

105. Annex IV, Articles 3(1), 4, and 5.

106. Ibid., Article 10.

107. At the XVIIth ATCM in Venice in November 1992, the issue of tourism became especially polemical. Suggestions were made (and supported by the "Venice Group of Five"—Chile, France, Germany, Italy, and Spain— that a special annex to the Madrid Protocol was needed to deal with tourism. This was vigorously challenged by the United States, Australia, and the United Kingdom. The upshot was carrying the issue over to the Kyoto ATCM where it was resolved. See Vidas, "The Antarctic Treaty System and Antarctic Tourism," 22–31. For an incisive assessment of the tourism issue as a concern of the ATS, see Vidas, "Antarctic Tourism," 187–224.

108. See the discussion in "Report of Working Group I to the Plenary of the XVIIIth ATCM," Antarctic Treaty Doc. XVIII ATCM/WP 35 (April 21, 1994), 7–9 and attachments at 14–28.

109. ATCM Recommendation XVIII-1 (1994), reprinted in "Report of Working Group I," 12–13.

110. See the discussion in the text *infra* at notes 130–39.

111. "First Tourists Arrive," *Antarctic* 5(1) (March 1968): 52.

112. E. McDonald, "Antarctic Tourism in 1967," *Antarctic Journal of the United States* 3 (1967): 82–83.

113. "Grounded Ship Not Seriously Damaged," *Antarctic* 6(6) (1972): 219.

114. See "Argentina's Bahia Paraiso Sinks Off Anvers Island," *Antarctic Bulletin* 11(9–10) (August 1989): 391–93; "Bahia Paraiso: Sunken Argentinean Supply Vessel: A Continued Concern," *Antarctic Bulletin* 11(11) (1989): 441–42; "Long Term Monitoring of Bahia Paraiso," *Antarctic Bulletin* 11(12) (March 1990): 476–78; "Argentine Ship Sinks Near Palmer Station," *Antarctic Journal of the United States* 24(2) (1989): 3–12.

115. See Margaret E. Johnston, "Polar Tourism Regulation Strategies: Controlling Visitors Through Codes of Conduct and Legislation," *Polar Record* 33: 184 (1997): 13–20.

116. See ATCM Recommendation IV-27, Effects of Antarctic Tourism (1966), Paragraphs 2 and 3.

117. Ilse Louise Kiessling, "An Evaluation of Interdependence between Antarctic Science and Tourism," Honours Thesis submitted to Institute for Antarctic and Southern Ocean Studies, University of Tasmania, November 1993, p. 25.

118. Interview with Beth Marks Clark, director, The Antarctica Project, February 28, 1997, Washington, D.C.

119. International Union for the Conservation of Nature and Natural Resources (IUCN), *Report: A Strategy for Antarctic Conservation* (1991), 55–56.

120. S. V. Levich and N. S. Fal'kovich, "Recreation and Tourism in the Southern Ocean and Antarctica," *Polar Geography and Geology* 11 (April 1987): 94–102.

121. Reich, "The Development of Antarctic Tourism," 203–14.

122. P. D. Hart, "Bound for 60 South—Taxes, Tips and Transfers Included: The Growth of Antarctic Tourism," *Oceanus* 31(2) (1988): 97, 93–100. See also Francisco Orrego Vicuña, "Air Traffic in Antarctica—The Need for a Legal Regime," in Wolfrum, *Antarctic Challenge III*, 397–423.

123. See generally House of Representatives Standing Committee on the Environment, Recreation and the Arts, *Tourism in Antarctica: Report of the House of Representatives Standing Committee on Environment, Recreation and the Arts* (Canberra: Australian Government Publishing Service, 1989).

124. See National Science Foundation, "Agenda/Handouts" (Antarctic Tours Operators Meeting, Washington D.C., July 8, 1992); Auburn, *Antarctic Law and Politics*, 279.

125. C. Monteath, "Voyage to the South Sandwich Islands," *Antarctic* 12(10): 361, 359–63.

126. See SCAR, "Fifteenth Meeting of SCAR," *Polar Record* 19(120) (1983): 295–326. See also B. A. Culik, "The Effect of Disturbance on the Heart Rate and Behaviour of Adelie Penguins (Pygoscelis adeliae) during the Breeding Season," in Kerry and Hempel, *Antarctic Ecosystems*, 177–82.

127. C. M. Harris, "Environmental Effects of Human Activities," 193–204.

128. Kiessling, "Interdependence between Antarctic Science and Tourism," 62; and House of Representatives (Australian), *Tourism in Antarctica Report*, 9.

129. Wace, "Antarctica," 327–41.

130. Kiessling, "Interdependence between Antarctic Science and Tourism," 54.

131. IAATO, *Membership Directory 1996–97* (New York: Office of the IAATO Secretariat, 1996), cover. See also "IAATO Objectives," Ibid., inside front cover. The author wishes to thank Darrel Schoeling in IAATO's Office of the Secretariat for providing information on IAATO's membership and responsibilities in touring the Antarctic.

132. In 1998 full IAATO members included the following travel companies: Abercrombie & Kent/Explorer Shipping Corporation (USA); Adventure Network International (USA); Aurora Expeditions (Australia); Hanseatic Tours GmbH (Germany); Marine Expeditions (Canada); Mountain Travel Sobek (USA); Quark Expeditions (USA); Society Expeditions (USA); Southern Heritage Expeditions (New Zealand; Travel Dynamics (USA); WildWings (United Kingdom); and Zegrahm Expeditions (USA). The associate members were: Hapag Lloyd Tours GmbH (Germany); JES Japan Euro-Asia Service (Japan); Latour Chile (Chile); LifeLong Learning (USA); Natural Habitat Adventures (USA); Overseas Adventure Travel (USA); Park East Tours (USA); Plancius-Oceanwide (Netherlands); and Playguide Tours (Japan). IAATO, *Membership Directory, 1996–97*, 4–8.

133. See IAATO, "Guidance for those Organising and Conducting Tourism and Non-Governmental Activities in the Antarctic" (pamphlet, 1996).

134. See L. H. Stephenson, "Managing Visitors to Macquarie Island—A Model for Antarctica?," *ANARE News* 73 (1993): 8–9. See also IAATO, "Guidelines of Conduct for Antarctic Visitors and Tour Companies (1992–93)" (1993). These "Guidelines" are not legally binding, however.

135. IAATO, "Guidelines of Conduct for Antarctic Visitors," reprinted in Committee on Antarctic Policy and Science, *Science and Stewardship in the Antarctic*, 96–98 (Appendix A). See also IAATO, "Guidence for Visitors to the Antarctic" (brochure, 1996).

136. See IAATO, "Guidance for Those Organising and Conducting Tourism and Non-Governmental Activities in the Antarctic."

137. Ibid. See also an earlier version of IATTO guidelines in IAATO, "Guidelines of Conduct for Antarctic Tour Operators," reprinted in Committee on Antarctic Policy and Science, *Science and Stewardship in the Antarctic*, 101–3 (Appendix A); and compare Enzenbacher, "Antarctic Tourism: 1991/92 Season Activity," 240–42.

138. IAATO, "Guidelines of Conduct for Antarctic Tour Operators," 103 (Guideline 15).

139. See Australian Antarctic Division, *A Visitor's Introduction to the Antarctic and its Environment* (Canberra: Australian Government Publishing Service, 1986). Interestingly enough, this guidebook advocates common sense as the mindset for conservation in the Antarctic.

140. SCAR, SCAR GOSEAC V, *Report of the Fifth Meeting*, GOSEAC V Universita Goriza, Italy (April 21, 1993) (1993), 1.

141. Heap, *Handbook of the Antarctic Treaty System*, 261.

142. Ibid.

143. Ibid., 262.

144. See the discussion and exchanges on SCAR, COMNAP, and SCALOP in Robert Rutford, "Relations between Elements of the Antarctic Treaty System," in Jackson, ed., *On the Antarctic Horizon*, 57–68.

145. Davis, "Antarctica Visitor Behaviour," 327–34, at 333. In answering her title's query, Davis asserts that guidelines are "inadequate to prevent adverse impacts to flora and fauna" by tourists in the Antarctic. Ibid., 332. She recommends a comprehensive management plan that provides positive guidance about experiences that visitors will have in the polar South. Ibid., 333. But compare John Splettstoesser and M. C. Folks, "Environmental Guidelines for Tourism in Antarctica," *Annals of Tourism Research* 21(2) (1994): 231–44.

146. Enzenbacher, "Antarctic Tourism: An Overview of 1992/93," 107.

147. Georges Duquin, "New Areas for Cooperation—Logistics, Communications, Research and Tourism," in Jackson, *On the Antarctic Horizon*, 23–32. Also see G. Budowski, "Tourism and Environmental Conservation: Conflict, Coexistence, and Symbiosis?," *Environmental Conservation* 3(1) (1976): 27–31; and Kiessling, "Interdependence between Antarctic Science and Tourism," 76–78. For a useful analysis of various Antarctic Treaty parties' official attitudes toward tourism, see Kiessling, 79–86.

148. A. P. Crary, "The Long Look Ahead," in Lewis and Smith, *Frozen Future*, 307. See also Manheim, *On Thin Ice*, which carefully documented environmental degradation in and around U.S. scientific stations in the Antarctic.

149. See, e.g., "Cost, Future Savings, and Additional Options," in Committee on Fundamental Science, *United States Antarctic Program*, 29–41.

150. See D. J. Enzenbacher, "Tourism in Polar Areas," *Polar Record* 28(164) (1992): 17–22.

151. See Kiessling, "Interdependence between Antarctic Science and Tourism," 54.

152. See Sean Kearns, "An Antarctic Sojourn: With Krill, Chill, Gales, Whales, Penguins, and the *Polar Duke*," *Humboldt State* (Spring 1994): 9–12, reprinted in National Science Foundation, *Antarctic News Clips 1995*, 198–201.

153. See Tim Higham, "The Biggest Chill," *Forest & Bird* (August 1995): 36–42.

154. See generally Ron Naveen, "The Promise of Antarctic Tourism: On the Cutting Edge of Ecotourism, or a Blight on Earth's Last Pristine Wilderness?," *Antarctic Century* no. 7 (December 1991).

Chapter 8: Common Heritage

1. Article 38, Statute of the International Court of Justice.

2. Statement before the Legal Sub-Committee of COPUOS, Sixth Session, June 19, 1967, U.N. Doc. A/AC, 105/C.2/SR. 75 (1967), 7. (Statement of Ambassador Cocca).

3. Ambassador Pardo's definition of common heritage of mankind is contained in U.N. Doc. A/C.PV. 1515–1516, November 1, 1967.

4. Keyuan, "The Common Heritage of Mankind and the Antarctic Treaty System," 173–98.

5. See Larschan and Brennan, "The Common Heritage of Mankind Principle in International Law," 17–318.

6. See Dolman, *Resources, Regimes, and World Order*, 241–53.

7. Keyuan, "Common Heritage and Antarctic Treaty System," 176.

8. See the discussion in Dolman, *Resources, Regimes, and World Order*, 223–67.

9. Brown-Weiss, *In Fairness to Future Generations*.

10. See generally Joyner, "Nonmilitarization of the Antarctic," 83–104. But compare Peter J. Beck, "Antarctica as a Zone of Peace: A Strategic Irrelevance?," in Herr, Hall, and Haward, *Antarctica's Future*, 193–224.

11. See Herber, "The Common Heritage Principle," 391–406.

12. See the discussion in chapter 2 *supra*.

13. See Bernard P. Herber, "Economic Theory and the World Common Heritage Principle," Paper presented to Southwestern Economic Association Conference, Little Rock, Arkansas, March 29–April 1, 1989.

14. The tragedy of the commons suggests the following scenario for communal spaces: Imagine a pasture that was common land open to all herdsmen for grazing. For each individual herder exploiting the pasture commons, there appears every reason to add to his herd. While grass is limited, he will get a larger share if he has a larger herd. If his animals do not eat the grass, someone else's will. Such reasoning is of course followed by each user of the commons. Individuals struggle to increase their herds until at some point the carrying capacity of the commons is exceeded and destroyed by overgrazing. See Hardin, "The Tragedy of the Commons," 1243–48 and the discussion in chapter 2 *supra*.

15. For a discussion concerning the debate in the General Assembly over the status of Antarctica, see the text *infra* at notes 40–78.

16. J. Hatcher and E. Miller, *Medieval England: Rural Society and Economic Change, 1086–1348* (London: Longman, 1978), 38.

17. "New Solidarity" rights refers to those rights that are 18. Declaration of Principles Governing the Sea-Bed and Ocean Floor, and the Subsoil Thereof, Beyond the Limits of National Jurisdiction, December 17, 1970, U.N. GA Res. 2749 (XXV), 25 UN GAOR Supplement (No. 28) 24, U.N. Doc. A/8028 (1971), reprinted in *International Legal Materials* 10 (1971): 220.

19. Ibid., Paragraph 1.

20. See Christopher C. Joyner, "U.N. General Assembly Resolutions and International Law: Rethinking the Contemporary Dynamics of Norm-Creation," *California Western International Law Journal* 11 (Summer 1981): 445–78.

21. The vote on the Declaration of Seabed Principles was 108 in favor, none opposed, with 14 abstentions. The United States voted in favor.

22. Agreement Governing the Activities of States on the Moon and Other Celestial Bodies, opened for signature December 10, 1979, entered into force July 11, 1984, Article 11(1), U.N. Doc. A/34/664, reprinted in *International Legal Materials* 1979, 1434.

23. Ibid., Article XI, paragraph 1.

24. As of 1998, the only nine states to have ratified the Moon Treaty are Austria, Chile, Morocco, the Netherlands, the Philippines, Uruguay, Pakistan, Mexico, and Australia.

25. Convention on the Law of the Sea, opened for signature December 10, 1982, U.N. Doc. A/CONF.62/122, reprinted in United Nations, *Official Text of the United Nations Convention on the Law of the Sea with Annexes and Index,* U.N. Sales No. E.83.U.5 (1983) and in *International Legal Materials* 21 (1982), 2161.

26. See General Assembly Resolution 48/263 (July 28, 1994), Agreement relating to the Implementation of Part XI of the United Nations Convention on the Law of the Sea of December 10, 1982.

27. This declaration was made on the occasion of commissioning a new research vessel, the *Oceanographer.* Statement of July 13, 1966, quoted in Shigeru Oda, "International Law of the Resources of the Sea," *Recueil des Cours de l"Adademie de Droit International* 2 (1969): 464.

28. The Nixon statement was attached to a letter dated May 25, 1970, from the representative of the United States to the United Nations addressed to the Chairman of the Committee on the Peaceful Uses of the Seabed, U.N.Doc. A/AC.138/22, May 25, 1970, reprinted in *International Legal Materials* 9 (1970), 806. In relevant part, President Nixon said:

> I am today proposing that all nations adopt as soon as possible a treaty under which they would renounce all national claims over the natural resources of the sea-bed beyond the point where the high seas reach a depth of 200 meters . . . and would agree to regard those resources as the common heritage of mankind. The treaty should establish an international regime for the exploitation of the sea-bed resources beyond this limit. The regime should provide for the collection of substantial mineral royalties to be used for community purposes, particularly for economic assistance to developing countries.

Ibid., 806.

29. It is true nonetheless that the economic and ideological implications associated with deep seabed mining vis-à-vis a New International Economic

Order were strong influences on the Reagan administration to reject the 1982 Convention on the Law of the Sea. See generally Schmidt, *Common Heritage or Common Burden?* and Joyner, "The United States and the New Law of the Sea," 41–58.

30. See Schmidt, *Common Heritage or Common Burden?*, 277–88.

31. For an insightful treatment of this point, see Brown-Weiss, *In Fairness to Future Generations.*

32. Stephen Gorove, "The Concept of 'Common Heritage of Mankind': A Political, Moral or Legal Innovation?," *San Diego Law Review* 9 (1972): 390–403.

33. Kiss, "The Common Heritage of Mankind," 422–41.

34. U.N. Doc. A/30/PV 2380 (1975), 13–15.

35. United Nations General Assembly Official Records, 37th Session, U.N. Doc. A/37/PV.10 (1982), 17–20 (Statement of Mahathir Bin-Mohammad).

36. Ibid.

37. *Record of the Third Conference on the Law of the Sea*, A/CONF. 62/PV.189, pp. 81–82; A/CONF 62/ PV. 192, p. 12 (1982) (Statement of Ghazali Shafie).

38. For various statements by Malaysia before the First Committee of the United Nations General Assembly, see United Nations Official Records, 40th Session, U.N. Doc. A/C.1/40/PV.48 (1985), 2–17 (Statement by Mr. Abdul Kadir); Ibid., 40th Session, U.N. Doc. A/C.1/40/PV.55 (1985), 34–42 (Statement by Mr. Zain); Ibid., 41st Session, U.N. Doc. A/C.1/41/PV.49 (1986), 13–26 (Statement of Mr. Hitam); Ibid., U.N. Doc. A/C.1/41/PV.51 (1986), 22–31 (Statement of Mr. Yusof); Ibid., 42nd Session, U.N. Doc. A/C.1/42/PV.46 (1987), 16–26 (Statement of Mr. Hitam); Ibid., 42nd Session, U.N. Doc. A/C.1/42/PV.48 (1987), 49–53 (Statement by Mr. Hitam); Ibid., 43rd Session, U.N. Doc. A/C.1/43/PV.44 (1988), 13–23 (Statement of Mr. Ismail); Ibid., 44th Session, U.N. Doc. A/C.1/41/PV.44 (1989), 7–26 (Statement by Mr. Razali).

39. United Nations General Assembly Official Records, 43rd Session, U.N. Doc. A/43/C.1 PV.44 (1988), 23.

40. U.N. Doc. A/38/1325/15625, "Economic Declaration," paragraphs 122–23 (1983).

41. U.N. General Assembly Official Records, 38th Session, 46th Meeting of the First Committee, November 30, 1983, A/C.1/38/PV 46 (1983), 13.

42. U.N. Doc. A/38/PV.97 (1983), 30–31.

43. On the role of Malaysia, see Beck, "Antarctica: A Case for the UN?," 171.

44. U.N. General Assembly Official Records, 39th Session, *Study on the Question of Antarctica*, U.N. Doc. A/39/583 (1984).

45. U.N. Doc. A/39/583, p. 44.

46. Ibid., 49.

47. U.N. Doc. A/39/583 (Part II), 107–11.

48. Ibid., 110.

49. Ibid., 111.

50. See United Nations General Assembly Official Records, 40th Session, U.N. Doc. A/C.1/40/PV.48 (1985), 43–50 (Statement of Mr. Wijewardane); Ibid., 41st Session, U.N. Doc. A/C.1/41/PV.49 (1986), 36–39 (Statement of Mr. Wijewardane); Ibid., 42nd Session, U.N. Doc. A/C.1/42/PV.46 (1987), 26–31 (Statement of Mr. Wijewardane); Ibid., 43rd Session, U.N. Doc. A/C.1/43/PV.44 (1988), 28–35 (Statement of Mr. Jayasinghe); Ibid., 44th Session, U.N. Doc A/C.1/44/PV.46 (1989), 6–12 (Statement of Mr. Mr. Jayasinghe).

51. See *Question of Antarctica, Study Requested under General Assembly Resolution 38/77, Report of the Secretary-General* (PART TWO: Views of States), Vol. III (1984), U.N. Doc. A/39/583 (Part II) (1984), 32–36 (Pakistan); United Nations General Assembly Official Records, 40th Session, U.N. Doc. A/C.1/40/PV.55 (1985), 42–45 (Statement of Mr. Saeed); Ibid., 41st Session, U.N. Doc. A/C.1/41/PV.50 (1986), 20–25 (Statement of Mr. Mohiuddin); Ibid., 42nd Session, U.N. Doc. A/C.1/42/PV.46 (1987), 31–36 (Statement of Mr. Chohan); Ibid., 43rd Session, U.N. Doc. A/C.1/43/PV.45 (1988), 18–22 (Statement of Mr. Chohan); Ibid., 44th Session, U.N. Doc. A/C.1/44/PV.42 (1989), 22–27 (Statement of Ahmad Kamal).

52. See *Question of Antarctica, Report of the Secretary-General,* U.N. Doc. A/39/583 (Part II: Vol. I) (1984), 92 (Bangladesh); United Nations General Assembly Records, 40th Session, U.N. Doc. A/C.1/40/PV.50 (1985), 12–19 (Statement of Mr. Ali); Ibid., 42nd Session, U.N. Doc. A/C.1/42/PV.48 (1987), 2–12 (Statement of Mr. Siddiky); Ibid., 44th Session, U.N. Doc. A/C.1/44/PV.45 (1989), 8–12 (Statement of Mr. Mohiuddin).

53. See *Report of the Secretary-General,* U.N. Doc. A/39/583 (Part II: Vol. II), 93 (Indonesia); United Nations General Assembly Official Records, 40th Session, U.N. Doc. A/C.1/40/PV.52 (1985), 42–48 (Statement of Mr. Wisnoemoerti); Ibid., 41st Session, U.N. Doc. A/C.1/41/PV.49 (1986), 56–63 (Statement of Mr. Alatas); Ibid., 42nd Session, U.N. Doc. A/C.1/42/PV.48 (1987), 12–22 (Statement of Mr. Alatas); Ibid., 43rd Session, U.N. Doc. A/C.1/43/PV.45 (1988), 36–42 (Statement of Mr. Sutresna); Ibid., 44th Session, U.N. Doc. A/C.1/44/PV.44 (1989), 2–7 (Statement of Mr. Poernomo).

54. See United Nations General Assembly Official Records, 42nd Session, U.N. Doc. A/C.1/42/PV.48 (1987), 41–45 (Statement of Mrs. Namgyel); Ibid., 43rd Session, U.N. Doc. A/C.1/43/PV.45 (1988), 14–17 (Statement of Mr. Penjor); Ibid., 44th Session, U.N. Doc. A/C.1/44/PV.45 (1989), 12–15 (Statement of Mr. Tshering).

55. See United Nations General Assembly Official Records, 40th Session, U.N. Doc. A/C.1/40/PV.53 (1985), 26–28 (Statement of Mr. Josse); Ibid., 41st Session, U.N. Doc. A/C.1/41/PV.49 (1986), 63–67 (Statement of Mr. Josse); Ibid., 42nd Session, U.N. Doc. A/C.1/42/PV.47 (1987), 22–28 (Statement of Mr. Josse); Ibid., 43rd Session, U.N. Doc. A/C.1/43/PV.44 (1988), 24–27 (Statement of Mr. Rana); Ibid., 44th Session, U.N. Doc. A/C.1/44/PV.42 (1989), 6–11 (Statement of Mr. Josse).

56. See United Nations General Assembly Official Records, 43rd Session, U.N. Doc. A/C.1/43/PV.44 (1988), 43–48 (Statement of Mr. Tiogson); Ibid., 44th Session, U.N. Doc. A/C.1/44/PV.44 (1989), 26–27 (Statement of Mrs. Reyes).

57. See G.A. Resolution 38/77, United Nations General Assembly Official Records, 38th Session (Supplement No. 47), p. 69, U.N. Doc. A/38/47 (1984) and G.A. Resolution 39/152, United Nations General Assembly Official Records (Supplement No. 51), p. 94, U.N. Doc. A/39/51 (1984).

58. The sovereignty situation was complicated even more by the formal insistence of the United States and the Soviet Union that each retain a basis of claim to the continent that might be exercised at some later time. This insistence was actually attached to the 1959 Antarctic Treaty by both governments as a formal reservation to their signing of the treaty.

59. G.A. Resolution 40/156 A, United Nations General Assembly Official Records, 40th Session (Supplement No. 53), pp. 203–4 (1985), U.N. Doc. A/44/53. Resolution A was adopted by a vote of 96–0–11.

60. G.A. Resolution 41/88 A, United Nations General Assembly Official Records, 41st Session (Supplement No. 53), p. 190 (1986), U.N. Doc. A/41/53. The General Assembly approved Resolution "A" by a vote of 94–0–12.

61. G.A. Resolution 42/46 B, United Nations General Assembly Official Records, 42nd Session (Supplement No. 49), pp. 179–80 (1987), U.N. Doc. A/42/49. Resolution "B" was adopted by a vote of 100-0-10.

62. As put by Malaysia in its statement for the UN Study, the inequities within the Antarctic Treaty System make for a volatile international situation:

> The system with its two tiered membership is unacceptable because of its exclusivity, its unaccountability, and its secrecy. Membership as Consultative Parties requires the ability to meet stringent qualification . . . which can only be met by rich and scientifically developed countries . . . while the Consultative Parties assert that they have managed Antarctica in the interests of mankind, it is obvious that the interest of mankind can only be defined and managed by mankind itself. The coincidence of the interest of mankind and the intent of the Consultative Parties is not inevitable or pre-ordained.

UN Doc. A/39/583 (Part II), p. 110.

63. See Heap, ed., *Handbook of the Antarctic Treaty System*, 18–19 (contracting parties). The developing ATCP states in 1986 included Argentina, Chile, Brazil, Uruguay, China, and India.

64. As articulated in its statement for the *UN Study on Antarctica*, Malaysia asserted that:

> Antarctica as the common heritage of mankind requires a regime that is truly universal in character and committed to serving the interest of the entire international community. In this respect, the exploration of Antarctica and its resources must be carried out for the benefit of mankind.

Ibid., p. 111. The white-minority government in South Africa was hardly considered representative of that ambition.

65. G.A. Resolution 40/156 C, United Nations General Assembly Official Records, 40th Session (Supplement No. 53), pp. 205–6 (1985), U.N. Doc. A/44/53. While most Antarctic Treaty parties did not participate, the General Assembly voted 100–0–12 for this resolution.

66. G.A. Resolution 41/88 C, United Nations General Assembly Official Records, 41st Session (Supplement No. 53), p. 192 (1986), U.N. Doc. A/41/53.

67. G.A. Resolution 42/46 A, United Nations General Assembly Official Records, 42nd Session (Supplement No. 49), pp. 178–79 (1987), U.N. Doc. A/42/49.

68. G.A. Resolution 43/88 B, United Nations General Assembly Official Records, 43rd Session (Supplement No. 49), p. 205 (1988), U.N. Doc. A/43/49. The vote on Resolution "B" was 111–0–10.

69. On this issue, see Joyner, "The Antarctic Minerals Negotiating Process," 888–905.

70. G.A. Resolution 40/156 B, United Nations General Assembly Official Records, 40th Session (Supplement No. 53), pp. 204–5 (1985), U.N. Doc. A/44/53. The vote was 92 in favor, with none opposed and 14 abstentions.

71. 0. G.A. Resolution 41/88 B, United Nations General Assembly Official Records, 41st Session (Supplement No. 53), pp. 191–92 (1986), U.N. Doc. A/41/53.

72. G.A. Resolution 43/83 A, United Nations General Assembly Official Records, 43rd Session (Supplement No. 49), pp. 203–5 (1988), U.N. Doc. A/43/49. Emphasis in original. On Resolution "A," the vote was 100–0–6.

73. It must be noted that the merits of these criticisms have today been rendered moot. Significant changes have occurred in the Antarctic Treaty's structure and procedure over the past decade. The decision-making process has been made more public, and observers are permitted to attend Consultative Party meetings. Since 1981 the number of Consultative Parties has increased to include leading members of the developing world, among them Brazil, India, China and Uruguay. South Africa now has a black majority government. And there will be no minerals regime in the foreseeable future, since the Antarctic minerals agreement has been abandoned by the ATCPs in favor of the 1991 Protocol to the Antarctic Treaty on Environmental Protection.

74. G.A. Resolution 44/124 B, United Nations General Assembly Official Records, 44th Session (Supplement No. 49), pp. 181–82 (1989), U.N. Doc. A/44/49. The General Assembly vote on Resolution "B" was 101–0–8.

75. G.A. Resolution 44/124 A, United Nations General Assembly Official Records, 44th Session (Supplement No. 49), p. 180 (1989), U.N. Doc. A/44/49. Resolution "A" was adopted by a vote of 114–0–7.

76. G.A. Resolution 45/78 A, United Nations General Assembly Official Records, 45th Session (Supplement No. 49), pp. 143–45 (1990), U.N. Doc. A/45/49.

77. G.A. Resolution 45/78 B, Ibid., pp. 145–46.

78. See G.A. Resolution A/46/41 A, United Nations General Assembly Official Records, 46th Session (Supplement No. 49), U.N. Doc. A/46/49, adopted December 6, 1991, by a vote of 101–0–7, with 53 nonparticipating.

79. See G.A. Resolution A/46/41 B, in Ibid., U.N. Doc. A/46/49, adopted December 6, 1991, by a vote of 107–0–6, with 48 nonparticipating.

80. G.A. Resolution A/47/57, United Nations General Assembly Official Records, 47th Session (Supplement No. 49), U.N. Doc. A/47/49, adopted December 9, 1992, by a vote of 96–0–10, with 62 nonparticipating. Compare G.A. Resolution A48/80, United Nations General Assembly Official Records, 48th Session (Supplement No. 49), U.N. Doc. A/48/49, adopted December 16, 1993, by a vote of 96–0–7, with 66 nonparticipating. For insightful discussions of the debate and issues surrounding these measures, see Beck, "The 1991 UN Session," 307–14; Beck, "The United Nations and Antarctica, 1992," 313–20; and Beck, "The United Nations and Antarctica, 1993," 257–64.

81. G.A. Resolution 49/79 United Nations General Assembly Official Records, 49th Session (Supplement No. 49), U.N. Doc. A/49/49, adopted December 15, 1994. The report subsequently appeared as U.N. Doc. A/51/390 (1996).

82. See G.A. Resolution A/51/56, United Nations General Assembly Official Records, 51st Session (Supplement No. 49), U.N. Doc. A/51/56, adopted December 10, 1996.

83. Antarctic Treaty Consultative Parties: Final Act of the Eleventh Antarctic Treaty Special Consultative Meeting and the Protocol on Environmental Protection to the Antarctic Treaty, reprinted in *International Legal Materials* 30 (1991): 1455. See the discussion in chapter 6 *supra*.

84. Madrid Environmental Protocol, Article 2.

85. Ibid., Article 3.

86. Ibid., Article 25.

87. "Remarks by William R. Mansfield," *American Society of International Law Proceedings*, vol. 79 (1985): 61.

88. See the discussion on regime formation in chapter 4 *supra*.

89. See Herber, "The Common Heritage Principle," 391–406.

90. See Brown-Weiss, *In Fairness to Future Generations*, 289–91.

CHAPTER 9: CONCLUSION

1. See Agnew, "Distribution of Krill," 287–303.

2. Lentz, "Effective Legal Mechanisms for Protection of the Antarctic Environment," 3–4.

3. See "Report of Working Group I to the Plenary of the XVIIIth ATCM," ANT Doc. XVIII ATCM/WP 35 (April 21, 1994), 9–11 (mimeographed).

4. See "U.S. Opposes Antarctic Mining Ban Now," *New York Times,* June 23, 1991, p. 3.

5. See generally Joyner, "CRAMRA's Legacy of Legitimacy."

6. See Joyner, "CRAMRA: The Ugly Duckling of the Antarctic Treaty System?," 161–73.

BIBLIOGRAPHY

BOOKS

Alexander, Lewis M., and Lynne Carter Hanson, eds. *Antarctic Politics and Marine Resources: Critical Choices for the 1980s.* Kingston: University of Rhode Island, 1985.

Amundsen, Roald. *The South Pole: An Account of the Norwegian Antarctic Exploration in the "Fram" 1910–1912.* Vol. 2. London: John Murray, 1912.

Antarctic Science Advisory Committee. *Antarctic Research Priorities for the 1990s: A Review.* Canberra: Commonwealth of Australia, 1991.

———. *Antarctic Science—The Way Forward.* Canberra: Commonwealth of Australia, 1992.

Auburn, F. M. *Antarctic Law and Politics.* Bloomington: Indiana University Press, 1982.

———. *The Ross Dependency.* The Hague: Martinus Nijhoff, 1972.

Barnes, James N. *Let's Save Antarctica!* Richmond: Greenhouse Pub., 1982.

Beck, Peter J. *The International Politics of Antarctica.* New York: St. Martin's Press, 1986.

Benninghoff, William S., and W. N. Bonner. *Man's Impact on the Antarctic Environment: A Procedure for Evaluating Impacts from Scientific and Logistic Activities.* Cambridge: Scientific Committee on Antarctic Research, 1985.

Bertrand, Kenneth J. *Americans in Antarctica, 1775–1948.* New York: American Geographical Society, 1971.

Birnie, Patricia W. *International Regulation of Whaling.* Dobbs Ferry, N.Y.: Oceana Publications, 1985.

Black, Henry C. *Black's Law Dictionary.* 6th ed. St. Paul, Minn.: West, 1990.

Bond, Creina, and Ron Siegfried. *Antarctica, No Single Country, No Single Sea.* New York: Mayflower Books, 1979.

Bonner, W. N., and D. W. Walton. *Key Environments: Antarctica.* New York: Pergamon Press, 1985.

Brewster, Barney. *Antarctica: Wilderness at Risk.* Wellington: Friends of the Earth, 1982.

Brown-Weiss, Edith. *In Fairness to Future Generations*. Dobbs Ferry, N.Y.: Transnational Publishers, 1989.

Center for Oceans Law and Policy. *The Polar Regions: Proceedings from the Eleventh Annual Seminar*. Ocean Policy Studies Series. Charlottesville: University of Virginia School of Law, 1987.

Central Intelligence Agency. *Polar Regions Atlas*. Washington, D.C.: Central Intelligence Agency, 1978.

Charney, Jonathan I., ed. *The New Nationalism and the Use of Common Spaces*. Totowa, N.J.: Allanheld, Osmun, 1982.

Child, Jack. *Antarctica and South American Geopolitics: Frozen Lebensraum*. New York: Praeger, 1988.

Christy, Francis T., and Anthony Scott. *The Common Wealth in Ocean Fisheries*. Baltimore: Johns Hopkins Press, 1965.

Churchill, R. R., and A. V. Lowe. *The Law of the Sea*. Manchester: Manchester University Press, 1988.

Churchill, R. R., Samuel Lay, and Myron Nordquist, eds. *New Directions in the Law of the Sea*. Dobbs Ferry, N.Y.: Oceana, 1977.

Commission for the Conservation of Antarctic Marine Living Resources. *CCAMLR Ecosystem Monitoring System*. Hobart, Tasmania: CCAMLR, 1991.

De Wit, Maarten J. *Minerals and Mining in Antarctica: Science and Technology, Economics and Politics*. Oxford: Clarendon Press, 1985.

Elliott, Lorraine M. *International Environmental Politics: Protecting the Antarctic*. London: Macmillan, 1994.

———. *Protecting the Antarctic Environment: Australia and the Minerals Convention*. Canberra: Australian Foreign Policy Publications Program, Australian National University, 1993.

El-Sayed, S., ed. *Biological Investigations of Marine Antarctic Systems and Stocks. Vol. II: Selected Contributions to the Woods Hole Conference on Living Resources of the Southern Ocean*. Cambridge: Scott Polar Research Institute, 1981.

Francioni, Francesco, and Tullio Scovazzi, eds. *International Law for Antarctica*. Milan: Guiffre Editore, 1987.

———. *International Law for Antarctica*. 2nd ed. The Hague: Kluwer Law International, 1996.

Handmer, John, and Martijn Wilder, eds. *Towards a Conservation Strategy for the Australian Antarctic Territory*. Canberra: Centre for Resource and Environmental Studies, Australian National University, 1993.

Hardin, Garett, and John Baden, eds. *Managing the Commons*. San Francisco: W. H. Freeman, 1977.

Harris, Colin M., and Bernard Stonehouse, eds. *Antarctica and Global Climate Change*. London: Belhaven Press, 1991.

Harris, Stuart, ed. *Australia's Antarctic Policy Options*. Melbourne: Centre for Resource and Environmental Studies, Australian National University, 1984.

Hempel, G., ed. *Antarctic Science and Global Concerns*. Stuttgart: Springer-Verlag, 1994.

Herr, R. A., and B. W. Davis. *Asia in Antarctica*. Canberra: Australia National University, 1994.

Herr, R. A., H. R. Hall, and M. G. Haward, eds. *Antarctica's Future: Continuity or Change?* Hobart: Australian Institute of International Affairs, 1990.

Holdgate, M. W., and John Tinker. *Oil and Other Minerals in Antarctica: The Environmental Implications of Possible Mineral Exploration and Exploitation in Antarctica*. The Bellagio Report. Cambridge: Scientific Committee on Antarctic Research, 1979.

Holdgate, M. W., ed. *Antarctic Ecology*. London: Academic Press, 1970.

International Union for Conservation of Nature and Natural Resources, World Conservation Union. *A Strategy for Antarctic Conservation*. Cambridge: Burlington Press, 1991.

Jørgensen-Dahl, Arnfinn, and Willy Østreng, eds. *The Antarctic Treaty System in World Politics*. Oslo: Macmillan/Fridtjof Nansen Institute, 1991.

Joyner, Christopher C. *Antarctica and the Law of the Sea*. Dordrecht, The Netherlands: Martinus Nijhoff, 1992.

Joyner, Christopher C., and Sudhir K. Chopra, eds. *The Antarctic Legal Regime*. Dordrecht, The Netherlands: Martinus Nijhoff, 1988.

Joyner, Christopher C., and Ethel Theis. *Eagle Over the Ice: The U.S. in the Antarctic*. Hanover, N.H.: University Press of New England, 1997.

Keohane, Robert. *After Hegemony: Cooperation and Discord in the World Political Economy*. Princeton: Princeton University Press, 1985.

Kerry, K. R., and G. Hempel. *Antarctic Ecosystems: Ecological Change and Conservation*. Berlin: Springer-Verlag, 1990.

Kish, John. *The Law of International Spaces*. Leiden: A. W. Sitjhoff, 1973.

Laws, R. M., ed. *Antarctic Ecology*. London: Academic Press, 1984.

Lewis, Richard S., and Philip M. Smith, eds. *Frozen Future: A Prophetic Report from Antarctica*. New York: Quadrangle Books, 1973.

Lovering, J. F., and J. R. V. Prescott. *Last of Lands: Antarctica*. Carlton: Melbourne University Press, 1979.

Manheim, Bruce S. Jr. *On Thin Ice: The Failure of the National Science Foundation to Protect Antarctica*. Washington, D.C.: Environmental Defense Fund, 1988.

May, John. *The Greenpeace Book of Antarctica: A New View of the Seventh Continent*. Frenchs Forest, NSW: Child and Associates, 1988.

Mitchell, Barbara. *Frozen Stakes. The Future of Antarctic Minerals*. London: International Institute for Environment and Development, 1983.

———. *The Management of Antarctic Mineral Resources*. London: International Institute for Environment and Development, 1982.

Mitchell, Barbara, and Richard Sandbrook. *The Management of the Southern Ocean*. London: International Institute for Environment and Development, 1980.

Mosley, Geoff. *Antarctica: Our Last Great Wilderness*. Hawthorn, Melbourne: Australian Conservation Foundation, 1986.

Myhre, Jeffrey D. *The Antarctic Treaty System: Politics, Law, and Diplomacy*. Boulder, Colo.: Westview Press, 1986.

Ophuls, William. *Ecology and the Politics of Scarcity: A Prologue to a Political Theory of the Steady State*. San Francisco: W. H. Freeman, 1977.

Orrego Vicuña, Francisco. *Antarctic Mineral Exploitation: The Emerging Legal Framework*. Cambridge: Cambridge University Press, 1988.

———, ed. *Antarctic Resources Policy: Scientific, Legal, and Political Issues*. Cambridge: Cambridge University Press, 1983.

Ostrom, Elinor. *Governing the Commons: the Evolution of Institutions for Collective Action*. Cambridge: Cambridge University Press, 1990.

Parker, B. C., and M. C. Holliman, eds. *Environmental Impact in Antarctica*. Blacksburg: Virginia Polytechnic Institute and State University, 1978.

Parsons, Sir Anthony. *Antarctica: The Next Decade*. Cambridge: Cambridge University Press, 1987.

Peterson, M. J. *Managing the Frozen South: The Creation and Evolution of the Antarctic Treaty System*. Berkeley: University of California Press, 1988.

Pinochet de la Barra, Oscar. *Chilean Sovereignty in Antarctica*. Santiago: Edit. del Pacifico, 1955.

Quigg, Philip W. *A Pole Apart: The Emerging Issue of Antarctica*. New York: McGraw-Hill, 1983.

Rose, Lisle A. *Assault on Eternity: Richard E. Byrd and the Exploration of Antarctica, 1946–47*. Annapolis, Md.: Naval Institute Press, 1980.

Ross, Frank J. Jr. *Partners in Science: The Story of the International Geophysical Year*. New York: Lothrop, Lee and Shepard, 1960.

Rothwell, Donald R. *The Polar Regions and the Development of International Law*. Cambridge: Cambridge University Press, 1996.

Schatz, Gerald S., ed. *Science, Technology, and Sovereignty in the Polar Regions*. Lexington, Mass.: Lexington Books, 1974.

Schmidt, Markus G. *Common Heritage or Common Burden?* Oxford: Clarendon Press, 1989.

Shapley, Deborah. *The Seventh Continent: Antarctica in the Resource Age*. Washington, D.C.: Resources for the Future, 1985.

Siple, Paul A. *90° South*. New York: Putnam's, 1959.

Smedal, Gustav. *Acquisition of Sovereignty over Polar Areas*. Oslo: J. Dybwad, 1931.

Splettstoesser, J., and G. Dreschhoff, eds. *Mineral Resources Potential of Antarctica, Antarctic Research Series, Vol. 51*. Washington, D.C.: American Geophysical Union, 1990.

St. John, Bill, ed. *Antarctica as an Exploration Frontier— Hydrocarbon Potential, Geology, and Hazards*. Study No. 31. Tulsa: American Association of Petroleum Geologists, 1991.

Stokke, Olav Schram, and Davor Vidas, eds. *Governing the Antarctic: The Effectiveness and Legitimacy of the Antarctic Treaty System.* Cambridge: Cambridge University Press, 1996.

Stone, Christopher D. *The Gnat is Older than Man: Global Environment and Human Agenda.* Princeton, N.J.: Princeton University Press, 1993.

Sullivan, Walter. *Assault on the Unknown: The International Geophysical Year.* New York: McGraw-Hill, 1961.

———. *Quest for a Continent.* New York: McGraw-Hill, 1957.

Suter, Keith. *Antarctica: Private Property or Public Heritage?* London: Zed Books, 1991.

Triggs, Gillian, ed. *The Antarctic Treaty Regime: Law, Environment and Resources.* Cambridge: Cambridge University Press, 1987.

———. *International Law and Australian Sovereignty in Antarctica.* Sydney: Legal Books, 1986.

U.S. Polar Research Board. *Antarctic Treaty System, An Assessment.* Washington, D.C.: National Academy Press, 1986.

———. Committee on Antarctic Policy and Science. *Science and Stewardship in the Antarctic.* Washington, D.C.: National Research Council, 1993.

Von Glahn, Gerhard. *Law Among Nations.* 7th ed. New York: Macmillan, 1996.

Walton, D. W. H. *Antarctic Science.* Cambridge: Cambridge University Press, 1987.

Westermeyer, William E. *The Politics of Mineral Resource Development in Antarctica: Alternative Regimes for the Future.* Boulder, Colo.: Westview Press, 1984.

Wolfrum, Rüdiger, ed. *Antarctic Challenge.* Berlin: Duncker & Humblot, 1984.

———. *Antarctic Challenge II.* Berlin: Duncker & Humblot, 1986.

———. *Antarctic Challenge III.* Berlin: Duncker & Humblot, 1988.

———. *The Convention on the Regulation of Antarctic Mineral Resource Activities.* Berlin: Springer-Verlag, 1991.

World Commission on Environment and Development. *Our Common Future.* New York: Oxford University Press, 1987.

Young, Oran R. *International Cooperation: Building Regimes for Natural Resources and the Environment.* Ithaca: Cornell University Press, 1989.

———. *Resource Regimes: Natural Resources and Social Institutions.* Berkeley: University of California Press, 1982.

ARTICLES AND BOOK CHAPTERS

Agnew, David. "Distribution of Krill (*Euphausia Superba* Dana) Catches in the South Shetlands and South Orkneys." In *Selected Scientific Papers 1992*, SC-CAMLR SSP/9. Hobart: CCAMLR, 1993.

Alexander, Frank C. Jr. "A Recommended Approach to the Antarctic Resource Problem." *University of Miami Law Review* 33 (1978): 371–423.

Alexander, Lewis M. "The Ocean Enclosure Movement: Inventory and Prospect." *San Diego Law Review* 20:3 (1983): 561–91.

Anderson, Frederick R. "Of Herdsmen and Nation States: The Global Environmental Commons." *American University Journal of International Law and Policy* 5 (1990): 217–26.

Anderson, John B. "Geology and Hydrocarbon Potential of the Antarctic Continental Margin." In *Mineral Resources Potential of Antarctica, Antarctic Research Series, Vol. 51,* edited by J. Splettstoesser and G. Dreschhoff, 175–201. Washington, D.C.: American Geophysical Union, 1990.

"Antarctica." In *The New Encyclopaedia Britannica (Macropaedia), 15th ed.* Chicago: Encyclopaedia Britannica, Inc., 1991.

"Antarctica." In *The New Encyclopaedia Britannica (Macropaedia), 15th ed.* Chicago: Encyclopaedia Britannica, Inc., 1994.

Auburn, F. M. "Legal Implications of Petroleum Resources of the Antarctic Continental Shelf." *Ocean Yearbook* 1 (1978): 500–521.

———. "Offshore Oil and Gas in Antarctica." *German Yearbook of International Law* 20 (1977): 139–73.

Barnes, James N. "The Emerging Antarctica Living Resources Convention." *Proceedings of the American Society of International Law* (1979): 272–92.

———. "The Emerging Convention on the Conservation of Antarctic Marine Living Resources: An Attempt to Meet the New Realities of Resource Exploitation in the Southern Ocean." In *The New Nationalism and the Use of Common Spaces,* edited by Jonathan I. Charney, 239–86. Totowa, N.J.: Allanheld, Osmun, 1982.

———. "The Future of Antarctica—Environmental Issues and the Role of NGO's." In *Antarctic Challenge II,* edited by Rudiger Wolfrum, 413–45. Berlin: Duncker & Humblot, 1986.

———. "Legal Aspects of Environmental Protection in Antarctica." In *The Antarctic Legal Regime,* edited by Christopher C. Joyner and Sudhir Chopra, 241–68. Dordrecht, The Netherlands: Martinus Nijhoff, 1988.

Barratt-Brown, Elizabeth P., Scott A. Hajost, and John H. Stearne. "A Forum for Action on Global Warming: The U.N. Framework Convention on Climate Change." *Colorado Journal of International Environmental Law and Policy* 4 (1993): 103–18.

Beck, Peter J. "Another Sterile Annual Ritual? The U.N. and Antarctica 1987." *Polar Record* 24:148 (1988): 207–21.

———. "The Antarctic Minerals Regime Negotiations." *Polar Record* 24:148 (1988): 59–61.

———. "Antarctica: A Case for the UN?" *The World Today* (April 1984): 165–72.

———. "Antarctica at the U.N. 1988: Seeking a Bridge of Understanding." *Polar Record* 25:155 (1989): 329–34.

————. "Antarctica at the United Nations, 1985: The End of Consensus?" *Polar Record* 23:143 (1986): 159–66.

————. "Antarctica Enters the 1990s: An Overview." *Applied Geography* 10 (1990): 247–63.

————. "Antarctica, Viña del Mar and the 1990 UN Debate." *Polar Record* 27:162 (1991): 211–16.

————. "Britain's Antarctic Dimension." *International Affairs* (London) 59:3 (1983): 429–44.

————. "Convention on the Regulation of Antarctic Mineral Resource Activities: A Major Addition to the ATS." *Polar Record* 24:152 (1989): 19–32.

————. "The 1991 U.N. Session: The Environmental Protocol Fails to Satisfy the Antarctic Treaty's System's Critics." *Polar Record* 28:167 (1992): 307–14.

————. "Preparatory Meetings for the Antarctic Treaty 1958–59." *Polar Record* 22 (1985): 653–64.

————. "The United Nations and Antarctica." *Polar Record* 22:137 (1984): 137–44.

————. "The United Nations and Antarctica, 1992: Still Searching for That Elusive Convergence of View." *Polar Record* 29:171 (1993): 313–20.

————. "The United Nations and Antarctica, 1993: Continuing Controversy about the U.N.'s Role in Antarctica." *Polar Record* 30:175 (1994): 257–64.

————. "The United Nations' Study on Antarctica, 1984." *Polar Record* 22:140 (1985): 499–504.

Behrendt, John C. "Are There Petroleum Resources in Antarctica?" In *Antarctic Politics and Marine Resources: Critical Choices for the 1980's,* edited by Lewis M. Alexander and Lynne Carter Hanson, 191–201. Kingston: University of Rhode Island, 1985.

Bell, D. E. "The 1992 Convention on Biological Diversity: The Continuing Significance of U.S. Objections at the Earth Summit." *George Washington Journal of International Law & Economics* 26 (1993): 479–537.

Bergin, Anthony. "The Politics of Antarctic Minerals: The Greening of White Australia." *Australian Journal of Political Science* 26:2 (July 1991): 216–39.

————. "Recent Developments in Australia's Antarctic Policy." *Marine Policy* 9:3 (1985): 181–91.

Bernhardt, J. Peter A. "Sovereignty in Antarctica." *California Western International Law Journal* 5:2 (1975): 297–349.

Bilder, Richard B. "The Present Legal and Political Situation in Antarctica." In *The New Nationalism and the Use of Common Spaces,* edited by Jonathan I. Charney, 167–205. Totowa, N.J.: Allanheld, Osmun, 1982.

Blij, Harm J. de. "A Regional Geography of Antarctica and the Southern Ocean." *University of Miami Law Review* 33 (1978): 299–314.

Boczek, Boleslaw Adam. "The Legal Status of Visitors Including Tourists and Non-Governmental Expeditions in Antarctica." In *Antarctic Challenge III,* edited by Rüdiger Wolfrum, 455–90. Berlin: Duncker & Humblot, 1988.

———. "The Protection of the Antarctic Ecosystem: A Study in International Environmental Law." *Ocean Development and International Law* 13 (1983–84): 347–425.

———. "The Soviet Union and the Antarctic Regime." *American Journal of International Law* 78 (1984): 834–58.

———. "Specially Protected Areas as an Instrument for the Conservation of the Antarctic Nature." In *Antarctic Challenge II,* edited by Rudiger Wolfrum, 65–102. Berlin: Duncker & Humblot, 1986.

Burton, Steven J. "New Stresses on the Antarctic Treaty: Toward International Legal Institutions Governing Antarctic Resources." *Virginia Law Review* 65 (1979): 421–512.

Bush, W. M. "The Antarctic Treaty System: A Framework for Evolution, The Concept of a System." In *Antarctica's Future: Continuity or Change?*, edited by R. A. Herr, H. R. Hall, and M. G. Haward, 119–80. Hobart: Australian Institute of International Affairs, 1990.

Canmann, Mary Lynn. "Antarctic Oil Spills of 1989: A Review of the Application of the Antarctic Treaty and the New Law of the Sea to the Antarctic Environment." *Colorado Journal of International Environmental Law and Policy* 1 (1990): 211–21.

Carroll, James E. "Of Icebergs, Oil Wells, and Treaties: Hydrocarbon Exploitation Offshore Antarctica." *Stanford Journal of International Law* 19 (1983): 207–27.

Chandler, Melinda. "The Biodiversity Convention: Selected Issues of Interest to the International Lawyer." *Colorado Journal of International Environmental Law and Policy* 4 (1993): 141–75.

Charney, Jonathan I. "Future Strategies for an Antarctic Mineral Resource Regime—Can the Environment Be Protected?" In *The New Nationalism and the Use of Common Spaces,* edited by Jonathan I. Charney, 206–38. Totowa, N.J.: Allanheld, Osmun, 1982.

Christol, Carl. "The Common Heritage of Mankind Provisions in the 1979 Agreement Governing the Activities on the Moon and Other Celestial Bodies." *International Lawyer* 14 (1980): 429–83.

Colson, David A. "The Antarctic Treaty System: The Mineral Issue." *Law and Policy in International Business* 12 (1980): 841–901.

———. "The United States Position in Antarctica." *Cornell International Law Journal* 19:2 (1986): 291–300.

Constable, A. J. "CCAMLR Ecosystem Monitoring and a Feedback Management Procedure for Krill," WG-KRILL/CEMP-92-4. In Scientific Committee for the Conservation of Antarctic Marine Living Resources, *Selected Scientific Papers* 1992, SC-CAMLR-SSP/9 (1993).

Croxall, J. P. "Use of Indices of Predator States and Performance in CCAMLR Fishery Management." *Selected Scientific Papers* SC-CAMLR-VIII/9 (1989).

Bibliography

Daniel, J. "Conflict of Sovereignties in the Antarctic." *The Year Book of World Affairs* 3 (1949): 241–72.

Davis, Pamela. "Antarctica Visitor Behaviour: Are Guidelines Enough?" *Polar Record* 331:178 (July 1995): 327–34.

Drewry, D. J. "The Challenge of Antarctic Science." *Oceanus* 31:2 (Summer 1988): 5–10.

———. "The Future of Antarctic Scientific Research." *Polar Record* 29:168 (1993): 37–44.

Dugger, John A. "Exploiting Antarctic Mineral Resources—Technology, Economics, and the Environment." *University of Miami Law Review* 33 (1978): 315–39.

ECO, occasional newsletter of the Antarctic and Southern Ocean Coalition, 1983–97.

Edwards, David M., and John A. Heap. "Convention on the Conservation of Antarctic Marine Living Resources: A Commentary." *Polar Record* 20:127 (1981): 353–62.

El-Sayed, Sayed Z. "Living Resources: The BIOMASS Program." *Oceanus* 31:2 (Summer 1988): 75–79.

Enzenbacher, Debra J. "Antarctic Tourism: An Overview of 1992/93 Season Activity, Recent Developments, and Emerging Issues." *Polar Record* 30:173 (April 1994): 107–10.

———. "Antarctic Tourism: 1991/92 Season Activity." *Polar Record* 29: 170 (August 1993): 240–41.

———. "Tourists in Antarctica: Numbers and Trends." *Polar Record* 28:164 (1992): 17–22.

Farman, J. C., B. G. Gardiner, and J. D. Shanklin. "Large Losses of Total Ozone in Antarctica Reveal Seasonal ClOx/NOx Interaction." *Nature* 315 (1985): 207–10.

Francioni, Francesco. "Legal Aspects of Mineral Exploitation in Antarctica." *Cornell International Law Journal* 19:2 (1986): 163–88.

Frank, Ronald F. "The Convention on the Conservation of Antarctic Marine Living Resources." *Ocean Development and International Law* 13 (1983–84): 291–345.

Goldwin, Robert A. "Common Sense vs. 'The Common Heritage.'" In *The Law of the Sea: U.S. Policy Dilemma*, edited by Bernard H. Oxman, David O. Caron, and Charles L. O. Buderi. San Francisco: ICS Press, 1983.

Greig, D. W. "Territorial Sovereignty and the Status of Antarctica." *Australian Outlook* 32 (1978): 117–29.

Gulland, J. A. "The Development of the Resources of the Antarctic Sea." In *Antarctic Ecology*, edited by M. W. Holdgate, 217–23. London: Academic Press, 1970.

Guyer, Roberto E. "The Antarctic System." *Recueil des Cours de l'Academie de Droit International* 139 (1973): 149–226.

Haas, Peter M. "Do Regimes Matter?: Epistemic Communities and Mediterranean Pollution Control." *International Organization* 43:3 (Summer 1989): 377–403.

Hanessian, John. "The Antarctic Treaty 1959." *International and Comparative Law Quarterly* 9 (1960): 436–80.

Hardin, Garrett. "The Tragedy of the Commons." *Science* 162 (1968): 1243–48.

Haron, Mohamed. "Antarctica and the United Nations—The Next Step?" In *Antarctic Challenge II*, edited by Rüdiger Wolfrum, 321–32. Berlin: Duncker & Humblot, 1986.

Harris, C. M. "Environmental Effects of Human Activities on King George Island, South Shetland Islands, Antarctica." *Polar Record* 27:162 (1991).

Hayashi, Moritaka. "The Antarctica Question in the United Nations." *Cornell International Law Journal* 19:2 (1986): 275–90.

Hayton, Robert D. "The 'American' Antarctic." *American Journal of International Law* 50 (1956): 583–610.

———. "The Antarctic Settlement of 1959." *American Journal of International Law* 54 (1960): 349–71.

Hempel, G. "Antarctic Marine Food Webs." In *Antarctic Nutrient Cycles and Food Webs*, edited by W. R. Siegfried, P. R. Condy, and R. M. Laws. Berlin: Springer-Verlag, 1985.

Herber, Bernard P. "The Common Heritage Principle: Antarctica and Developing Nations." *American Journal of Economics and Sociology* 50:4 (October 1991): 391–406.

Hofman, Robert I. "The Convention on the Conservation of Antarctic Marine Living Resources." In *Antarctic Politics and Marine Resources: Critical Choices for the 1980's*, edited by Lewis M. Alexander and Lynne Carter Hanson, 113–22. Kingston: University of Rhode Island, 1985.

Holdgate, M. W. "Environmental Factors in the Development of Antarctica." In *Antarctic Resources Policy*, edited by Francisco Orrego Vicuña, 77–101. Cambridge: Cambridge University Press, 1983.

———. "The Use and Abuse of Polar Environmental Resources." *Polar Record* 22:136 (1984): 25–49.

Honnold, Edward E. "Thaw in International Law? Rights in Antarctica Under the Law of Common Spaces." *Yale Law Journal* 87 (1978): 804–59.

Howard, Matthew. "The Convention on the Conservation of Antarctic Marine Living Resources: A Five-Year Review." *International and Comparative Law Quarterly* 38 (1989): 104–49.

Jain, Subhash C. "Antarctica: Geopolitics and International Law." *The Indian Year Book of International Affairs* (1974): 249–78.

Joyner, Christopher C. "Anglo-Argentine Rivalry after the Falkland/Malvinas War: Laws, Geopolitics, and the Antarctic Connection." *Lawyer of the Americas* 15 (Winter 1984): 467–502.

———. "The Antarctic Minerals Negotiating Process." *American Journal of International Law* 81 (October 1987): 888–905.

———. "Antarctica and the Indian Ocean States: The Interplay of Law, Interests, and Geopolitics." *Ocean Development and International Law* 21:1 (1990): 41–70.

———. "Antarctica and the Law of the Sea: Rethinking the Current Legal Dilemma." *San Diego Law Review* 18 (1981): 415–42.

———. "CRAMRA: The Ugly Duckling of the Antarctic Treaty System?" In *The Antarctic Treaty System in World Politics,* edited by Arnfinn Jørgensen-Dahl and Willy Østreng, 161–85. New York: Macmillan, 1991.

———. "CRAMRA's Legacy of Legitimacy: Progenitor to the Madrid Environmental Protocol." *Antarctic and Southern Ocean Law and Policy Occasional Papers* No. 7. University of Tasmania, Institute of Antarctic & Southern Ocean Studies, 1995.

———. "The Effectiveness of CRAMRA." In *Governing the Antarctic: The Legitimacy and Effectiveness of the Antarctic Treaty System,* edited by Olav Schram Stokke and Davor Vidas, 152–73. Cambridge: Cambridge University Press, 1996.

———. "The Evolving Antarctic Legal Regime" (Review Article). *American Journal of International Law* 83 (1989): 603–22.

———. "The Evolving Antarctic Minerals Regime." *Ocean Development and International Law* 19 (1988): 73–95.

———. "The Exclusive Economic Zone and Antarctica." *Virginia Journal of International Law* 21 (1981): 691–725.

———. "Fragile Ecosystems: Preclusive Restoration in the Antarctic." *Natural Resources Journal* 34 (Fall 1994): 879–904.

———. "Introduction." In *The Antarctic Legal Regime,* edited by Christopher C. Joyner and Sudhir Chopra, 1–6. Dordrecht, The Netherlands: Martinus Nijhoff, 1988.

———. "Legal Implications of the Common Heritage of Mankind." *International and Comparative Law Quarterly* 35 (1986): 190–99.

———. "The Legitimacy of CRAMRA." In *Governing the Antarctic: The Legitimacy and Effectiveness of the Antarctic Treaty System,* edited by Olav Schram Stokke and Davor Vidas, 246–67. Cambridge: Cambridge University Press (1996).

———. "Maritime Zones in the Southern Ocean: Problems Concerning the Correspondence of Natural and Legal Maritime Zones." *Applied Geography* 10 (1990): 307–25.

———. "The 1988 Antarctic Minerals Convention." *Marine Policy Reports* 1:1 (1989): 81–98.

———. "The 1991 Madrid Environmental Protection Protocol: Contributions to Marine Pollution Law." *Marine Policy* 20 (1996): 183–97.

———. "Non-militarization of the Antarctic." *Naval War College Review* 42 (1989): 83–104.

———. "Oceanic Pollution and the Southern Ocean: Rethinking the International Legal Implications for Antarctica." *Natural Resources Journal* 24:1 (1984): 1–40.

———. "Protection of the Antarctic Environment: Rethinking the Problems and Prospects." *Cornell International Law Journal* 19:2 (1986): 259–74.

———. "Security Issues and the Law of the Sea: The Southern Ocean." *Ocean Development and International Law* 15:2 (1985): 171–95.

———. "The Southern Ocean and Marine Pollution: Problems and Prospects." *Case Western Reserve Journal of International Law* 17 (1985): 165–94.

———. "The United States and the New Law of the Sea." *Ocean Development and International Law* 27 (1996): 41–58.

———. "United States Domestic Politics and the Antarctic Treaty System." In *Governing the Antarctic: The Legitimacy and Effectiveness of the Antarctic Treaty System,* edited by Olav Schram Stokke and Davor Vidas, 409–31. Cambridge: Cambridge University Press, 1996.

Joyner, Christopher C., and Blair G. Ewing Jr. "Antarctica and the Latin American States: The Interplay of Law, Geopolitics and Environmental Priorities." *Georgetown International Environmental Law Review* 4 (Spring/Summer 1991): 1–46.

Joyner, Christopher C., and Peter J. Lipperman. "Conflicting Jurisdictions in the Southern Ocean: The Case of an Antarctic Minerals Regime." *Virginia Journal of International Law* 27 (1986): 1–38.

Joyner, Christopher C., and Ethel Theis. "The United States and Antarctica: The Interplay of Law and National Interests." *Cornell Journal of International Law* 20:1 (1987): 65–102.

Keyuan, Zou. "The Common Heritage of Mankind and the Antarctic Treaty System." *Netherlands International Law Review* 38 (1991), 173–98.

Kimball, Lee A. *Antarctic Minerals Convention.* Washington, D.C.: International Institute for Environment and Development—North America, July 1988.

———. "Environmental Issues in the Antarctic Minerals Negotiations." In *Antarctic Politics and Marine Resources: Critical Choices for the 1980's,* edited by Lewis M. Alexander and Lynne Carter Hanson, 204–14. Kingston: University of Rhode Island, 1985.

———. "The Future of the Antarctic Treaty System. Environmental Community Suggestions." In *Antarctic Politics and Marine Resources: Critical Choices for the 1980's,* edited by Lewis M. Alexander and Lynne Carter Hanson, 237–47. Kingston: University of Rhode Island, 1985.

———. "Report on Antarctica." Washington, D.C.: International Institute for Environment and Development, June 19, 1987.

———. "Report on Antarctica." Washington, D.C.: International Institute for Environment and Development, December 1987.

———. "Report on Antarctica." New York: World Resources Institute, November 1989.

————. "Report on Antarctica." Washington, D.C.: World Resources Institute, 1991.

————. "Report on Antarctica, 1985." Washington, D.C.: International Institute for Environment and Development.

————. "Report on Antarctica: United Nations Focus 1984 and Recent Developments in the Antarctic Treaty System." Washington, D.C.: International Institute for Environment and Development, November 1, 1984.

————. "Special Report on the Antarctic Minerals Convention." Washington, D.C.: International Institute for Environment, 1988.

Kiss, Andre. "The Common Heritage of Mankind: Utopia or Reality?" *International Journal* 10 (Summer 1985): 422–41.

Knox, George A. "The Living Resources of the Southern Ocean: A Scientific Overview." In *Antarctic Resources Policy*, edited by Francisco Orrego Vicuña, 21–60. Cambridge: Cambridge University Press, 1983.

Kock, Karl-Hermann. "Fishing and Conservation in Southern Waters." *Polar Record* 30:172 (1994): 3–22.

Krasner, Stephen. "Structural Causes and Regime Consequences: Regimes as Intervening Variables." In *International Regimes*, edited by Stephen Krasner, 1–21. Ithaca: Cornell University Press, 1983.

Kriwoken, Lorne, and Peter Keage. "Antarctic Environmental Politics: Protected Areas." In *Antarctica Policies and Policy Development*, CRES Resource and Environmental Studies No. 1, edited by John Handmer. Canberra: Centre for Resource and Environmental Studies, Australian National University, 1989.

Lagoni, Rainer. "Antarctica's Mineral Resources in International Law." *Zeitschrift fur Auslandisches Offentliches Recht und Volkerrecht* 39 (1979): 1–37.

Larschan, Bradley, and Bonnie C. Brennan. "The Common Heritage of Mankind Principle in International Law." *Columbia Journal of Transnational Law* 21 (1983): 305–37.

Laws, Richard M. "Antarctic Politics and Science are Coming into Conflict." *Antarctic Science* 3:3 (September 1991): 231.

————. "The Ecology of the Southern Ocean." *American Scientist* 73 (January–February 1985): 26–40.

————. "Science, the Treaty and the Future." In *Antarctic Science*, edited by D. W. H. Walton. Cambridge: Cambridge University Press, 1990.

Lentz, Sally A. "Effective Legal Mechanisms for Protection of the Antarctic Environment." In Greenpeace International, *A Realistic Dream for Antarctica—Background for an Eighth U.N. Debate*, October 30, 1990.

Levin, Harvey J. "Regulating the Global Commons." *Research in Law and Economics* 12 (1989).

Llano, George A. "Ecology of the Southern Ocean Region." *University of Miami Law Review* 33 (1978): 357–69.

Luard, Evan. "Who Owns the Antarctic?" *Foreign Affairs* 62:5 (1984): 1174–93.

Lundquist, Thomas R. "The Iceberg Cometh?: International Law Relating to Antarctic Iceberg Exploitation." *Natural Resources Journal* 17:1 (1977): 1–41.

Lyons, David. "Environmental Impact Assessment in Antarctica under the Protocol on Environmental Protection." *Polar Record* 29:169 (1993): 111–20.

Marcoux, J. Michael. "Natural Resource Jurisdiction on the Antarctic Continental Margin." *Virginia Journal of International Law* 11 (1971): 374–404.

McLaughlin, Richard J. "UNCLOS and the Demise of the United States' Use of Trade Sanctions to Protect Dolphins, Sea Turtles, Whales, and Other International Marine Living Resources." *Ecology Law Quarterly* 21:1 (1994): 1–78.

Miller, D. G. M. "Commercial Krill Fisheries in the Antarctic, 1973 to 1988." In *Antarctic Krill*, SC-CAMLR-VIII/BG/11. Hobart: CCAMLR, 1989.

Mitchell, Barbara. "Resources in Antarctica. Potential for Conflict." *Marine Policy* 1 (1977): 91–101.

———. "The Southern Ocean in the 1980's." In *Ocean Yearbook 3*. Chicago: Chicago University Press, 1982, 349–85.

Mitchell, Barbara, and Lee Kimball. "Conflict over the Cold Continent." *Foreign Policy* 35 (1979): 124–41.

Moneta, Carlos J. "Antarctica, Latin America, and the International System in the 1980's. Toward a New Antarctic Order?" *Journal of Interamerican Studies and World Affairs* 23:1 (1981): 29–68.

Mouton, M. W. "The International Regime of the Polar Regions." *Recueil des Cours de l'Academie de Droit International* 107 (1962): 169–284.

Nicol, S. "Management of the Krill Fishery: Was CCAMLR Slow to Act?" *Polar Record* 28:165 (1992): 155–57.

Olson, Mancur. "Environmental Indivisibilities and Information Costs: Fanaticism, Agnosticism, and Intellectual Progress." *American Economic Review* 72 (May 1982): 262–66.

Orrego Vicuña, Francisco. "The Effectiveness of the Decision-making Machinery of CCAMLR: An Assessment." In *The Antarctic Treaty System in World Politics*, edited by Arnfinn Jørgensen-Dahl and Willy Østreng, 25–42. Oslo: Macmillan/Fridtjof Nansen Institute, 1991.

Orrego Vicuña, Francisco, and Maria Teresa Infante. "Le Droit de la Mer dans l'Antarctique." *Revue Generale de Droit International Public* 84 (1982): 340–50.

Oxman, Bernard. "The Antarctic Regime: An Introduction." *University of Miami Law Review* 33:2 (December 1978): 285–97.

Pallone, Frank. "Resource Exploitation: The Threat to the Legal Regime of Antarctica." *Connecticut Law Review* 10 (1978): 401–17.

Peterson, M. J. "Antarctic Implications of the Law of the Sea." *Ocean Development and International Law* 16:2 (1986): 137–81.

———. "Antarctica: The Last Grand Land Rush on Earth." *International Organization* 34:3 (Summer 1980): 377–403.

Pinto, M. C. W. "The International Community and Antarctica." *University of Miami Law Review* 33 (1978): 475–87.

Pontecorvo, Giulio. "The Economics of the Resources of Antarctica." In *The New Nationalism and the Use of Common Spaces*, edited by Jonathan I. Charney, 155–66. Totowa, N.J.: Allanheld, Osmun, 1982.

Prescott, J. R. V. "Boundaries in Antarctica." In *Australia's Antarctic Policy Options*, edited by Stuart Harris, 83–111. Melbourne: Australian National University, 1984.

Reeves, J. S. "Antarctic Sectors." *American Journal of International Law* 33 (1939): 519–21.

Reid, David E., and John B. Anderson. "Hazards to Antarctic Exploration and Production." In *Antarctica as an Exploration Frontier—Hydrocarbon Potential, Geology, and Hazard*. Study No. 31, edited by Bill St. John, 31–38. Tulsa: American Association of Petroleum Geologists, 1991.

Rigg, Kelly. "'Environmentalists' Perspective on the Protection of Antarctica." In *The Future of Antarctica: Exploitation Versus Preservation*, edited by Grahame Cook. Manchester: Manchester University Press, 1990.

Rose, Julia. "Antarctica Condominium: Building a New Legal Order for Commercial Interests." *Marine Technology Society Journal* 10:1 (1976): 19–27.

Rothwell, Donald R. *A World Park for Antarctica? Foundations Developments and the Future*. Antarctic and Southern Ocean Policy Center Occasional Paper No. 3. Hobart, Australia: Institute of Antarctic and Southern Ocean Studies, University of Tasmania, 1990.

Scott, David Clark. "Australia Advocates No Mining in Antarctica." *Christian Science Monitor* (World Edition Weekly), June 1–7, 1989.

Scully, R. Tucker. "The Antarctic Mineral Resource Negotiations." *Oceanus* 31 (Summer 1988): 20–21.

———. "The Antarctic Treaty System: Overview and Analysis." In *Antarctic Politics and Marine Resources: Critical Choices for the 1980's*, edited by Lewis M. Alexander and Lynne Carter Hanson, 3–11. Kingston: University of Rhode Island, 1985.

———. "The Evolution of the Antarctic Treaty System—The Institutional Perspective." In *Antarctic Treaty System, An Assessment*, U.S. Polar Research Board, 391–411. Washington, D.C.: National Academy Press, 1986.

———. "The Marine Living Resources of the Southern Ocean." *University of Miami Law Review* 33 (1978): 341–56.

Scully, R. Tucker, and Lee A. Kimball. "Antarctica: Is There Life After Minerals?" *Marine Policy* 13:2 (1989): 87–98.

Shusterich, Kurt M. "The Antarctic Treaty System: History, Substance, and Speculation." *International Journal* 39 (1984): 800–827.

Simma, Bruno. "The Antarctic Treaty as a Treaty Providing for an 'Objective Regime.'" *Cornell International Law Journal* 19:2 (1986): 189–209.

Smith, R. I. Lewis. "Terrestrial Plant Biology of the Sub-Antarctic and Antarctic." In *Antarctic Ecology*, edited by R. M. Laws, 61–162. London: Academic Press, 1984.

Snidal, Duncan. "Limits of Hegemonic Stability Theory." *International Organization* 39 (Autumn 1985): 579–614.

Soroos, Marvin J. "The Commons in the Sky: The Radio Spectrum and Geosynchronous Orbit as Issues in Global Policy." *International Organization* 36 (Summer 1982): 665–77.

Stokke, Olav Schram, and Davor Vidas. "Effectiveness and Legitimacy of International Regimes." In *Governing the Antarctic: The Effectiveness and Legitimacy of the Antarctic Treaty System*, edited by Olav Schram Stokke and Davor Vidas, 1–2. Cambridge: Cambridge University Press, 1996.

Stonehouse, B. "Monitoring Shipbourne Visitors in Antarctica: A Preliminary Field Study." *Polar Record* 28:156 (1990).

Sullivan, Walter. "Antarctica in a Two-Power World." *Foreign Affairs* 36 (1957–58): 154–66.

Swithinbank, Charles. "Airborne Tourism in the Antarctic." *Polar Record* 29:169 (1993).

Taubenfeld, Howard J. "A Treaty for Antarctica." *International Conciliation*. No. 531 (1961): 249–55.

"The Commons: Where the Community Has Authority." *The Ecologist* 22:4 (July/August 1992): 123–30.

Thornton, Brenda Sue. "A New Model for Antarctic Conservation." *Polar Record* 26 (October 1990): 329–30.

Tinker, Jon. "Antarctica: Towards a New Internationalism." *New Scientist* 83 (September 13, 1979): 799–801.

Toma, Peter A. "Soviet Attitude toward the Acquisition of Territorial Sovereignty in Antarctica." *American Journal of International Law* 50 (1956): 611–26.

Triggs, Gillian. "The Antarctic Treaty Regime: A Workable Compromise or a 'Purgatory of Ambiguity'?" *Case Western Reserve Journal of International Law* 17:2 (1985): 195–228.

———. "Australian Sovereignty in Antarctica: Traditional Principles of Territorial Acquisition versus a 'Common Heritage.'" In *Australia's Antarctic Policy Options*, edited by Stuart Harris, 29–66. Melbourne: Australian National University, 1984.

Van der Heydte, F. A. F. "Discovery, Symbolic Annexation and Virtual Effectiveness in International Law." *American Journal of International Law* 29 (1935): 448–71.

Vidas, Davor. "Antarctic Tourism: A Challenge to the Legitimacy of the Antarctic Treaty System?" *German Yearbook of International Law* 36 (1993): 187–224.

———. "The Antarctic Treaty System and Antarctic Tourism: Towards a Legal Regime?" *International Challenges* 14:2 (1994): 22–31.

————. "The Legal Status of Antarctica with Special Reference to the Antarctic Sea-bed and its Subsoil." In *Essays on the New Law of the Sea*, edited by Budislav Vukas, 504–36. Zagreb: Sveu cili snanaklada Liber, 1985.

Wace, N. "Antarctica; A New Tourist Destination." *Applied Geography* 10 (1990): 327–42.

Waldock, C. H. M. "Disputed Sovereignty in the Falkland Islands Dependencies." *The British Year Book of International Law* 25 (1948): 311–53.

Waller, Deborah Cook. "Death of a Treaty: The Decline and Fall of the Antarctic Minerals Convention." *Vanderbilt Journal of Transnational Law* 22:3 (1989): 631–68.

Watts, Arthur D. "Liability for Activities in Antarctica—Who Pays the Bill to Whom?" In *Antarctic Challenge II*, edited by Rüdiger Wolfrum, 147–61. Berlin: Duncker & Humblot, 1986.

Westermeyer, William. "Resource Allocation in Antarctica. A Review." *Marine Policy* 6 (1982): 303–25.

"Whose Common Future: A Special Issue." *The Ecologist* 22 (July/August 1992): 125.

Wijkman, Per Magnus. "Managing the Global Commons." *International Organization* 36 (Summer 1982): 511–36.

Wilkes, O., and R. Mann. "The Story of Nukey Poo." *Science and Public Affairs* (or *Bulletin of Atomic Scientists*) (October 1978): 32–36.

Wilson, Gregory P. "Antarctica, The Southern Ocean, and the Law of the Sea." *JAG Journal* 30 (1978): 47–85.

Wolfrum, Rüdiger. "The Principle of the Common Heritage of Mankind." *Zeitschrift fur auslandisches offentliches Recht und Volkerrecht* 43:2 (1983): 312–37.

Young, Oran R. "International Regimes: Problems of Concept Formation." *World Politics* 23 (April 1980): 331–56.

————. "International Regimes: Toward a New Theory of Institutions." *World Politics* 39 (October 1986): 104–14.

————. "The Politics of International Regime Formation: Managing Natural Resources and the Environment." *International Organization* 43 (Summer 1989): 349–75.

Zegers, Fernando. "The Antarctic System and the Utilization of Resources." *University of Miami Law Review* 33 (1978): 426–73.

Zorn, Stephen A. "Antarctic Minerals: A Common Heritage Approach." *Resources Policy* 10 (March 1984): 2–18.

Zumberge, James H. "The Antarctic Treaty as a Scientific Mechanism—SCAR and the Antarctic Treaty System." In U.S. Polar Research Board, *Antarctic Treaty System, An Assessment*, 153–68. Washington, D.C.: National Academy Press, 1986.

————. "Mineral Resources and Geopolitics in Antarctica." *American Scientist* 67 (January/February 1979): 68.

————. "Potential Mineral Resources Availability and Possible Environment

Problems in Antarctica." In *The New Nationalism and the Use of Common Spaces*, edited by Jonathan I. Charney, 115–54. Totowa, N.J.: Allanheld, Osmun, 1982.

DOCUMENTS

Antarctic and Southern Ocean Coalition. *Annex on Liability and Compensation for Antarctic Activities*, ASOC Information Paper 1991–92, April 22, XVI ATCM/INFO 55, October 9. Wellington, New Zealand: Antarctic and Southern Ocean Coalition, 1991.

———. *Antarctic Minerals Negotiations: The Second Draft* (October 22). Wellington, New Zealand: Antarctic and Southern Ocean Coalition, 1984.

———. *A Critique of the Protocol to the Antarctic Treaty on Environmental Protection*, ASOC Information Paper No. 1, October 8, XVI ATCM/INFO 21. Wellington, New Zealand: Antarctic and Southern Ocean Coalition, 1991.

———. *Environmental Assessment*. ASOC Paper No. 1, ANT/SCM 8, Minerals Negotiations, Hobart, Australia, April 16. Wellington, New Zealand: Antarctic and Southern Ocean Coalition, 1986.

———. *The Place of Science on an Environmentally Regulated Continent*, ASOC Information Paper No. 4, October 8, XVI ATCM/INFO 79, October 11. Wellington, New Zealand: Antarctic and Southern Ocean Coalition, 1991.

———. *The Regulation of Tourism in Antarctica*, ASOC Information Paper No. 6, XVI ATCM/INFO 77, October 11. Wellington, New Zealand, 1991.

———. *The World Park Option for Antarctica*, ASOC Information Paper No. 4, ANT SCM/8, April 21. Wellington, New Zealand: Antarctic and Southern Ocean Coalition, 1986.

Antarctica Project, "Status of Antarctic Minerals Negotiations," *Antarctic Briefing*, No. 5, October 4. Washington, D.C.: Antarctica Project and Greenpeace International, 1984.

———. "Status of Antarctic Minerals Negotiations," *Antarctic Briefing*, No. 13, June 30. Washington, D.C.: Antarctica Project and Greenpeace International, 1987.

Australian Antarctic Division. *A Visitor's Introduction to the Antarctic and Its Environment*. Canberra: Australian Government Publishing Service, 1986.

Australian House of Representatives Standing Committee on the Environment, Recreation, and the Arts. Australian Parliament. *Tourism in Antarctica: Report of the House of Representatives Standing Committee on Environment, Recreation and the Arts*. Canberra: Australian Government Publishing Service, 1989.

Beddington, John, and W. N. Bonner. *Conservation in the Antarctic*. Report of the Joint IUCN/SCAR Working Group on Long-Term Conservation in the Antarctic. Cambridge: SCAR/IUCN, 1986.

Behrendt, John C., ed. *Petroleum and Mineral Resources of Antarctica*. Geological Society Circular 909. Washington, D.C.: U.S. Government Printing Office, 1983.

Bibliography

Bush, W. M., ed. *Antarctica and International Law: A Collection of Interstate and National Documents.* Vols. 1–3. London: Oceana Publications, 1982.

Convention for the Conservation of Antarctic Marine Living Resources. Commission. *Reports of Meetings.* Hobart, Australia: CCAMLR, 1982–97.

Everson, Inigo. *The Living Resources of the Southern Ocean.* UNDP/FAO Southern Ocean Fisheries Survey Programme. GLO/SO/77/8 (1977).

Foreign Relations of the United States. A collection of State Department historical documents published regularly by the U.S. Government Printing Office, Washington, D.C.

French, F. *After the Earth Summit: The Future of Environmental Governance.* Worldwatch Institute, Worldwatch Paper 107 (March 1992).

Greenpeace. *The French Airstrip: What the ATCPs Should Do.* ATCM 13/NGO/5, Greenpeace International.

———. *Greenpeace Antarctica: The World Park Option for Antarctica.*

———. *The World Park Option for Antarctica.* Greenpeace Briefing Paper. London: Greenpeace UK, 1986.

———. *The World Park Option for Antarctica: Background for a Fourth U.N. Debate,* November 17. Lewes: Greenpeace International, Stichting Greenpeace Council, 1986.

Heap, John. ed., *Handbook of the Antarctic Treaty System.* 8th ed. Washington, D.C.: U.S. Department of State, April 1994.

Nansen Foundation. *Antarctic Resources, Report from the Informal Meeting of Experts, 30 May–9 June 1973.* Polhogda, Norway: Fridtjof Nansen Foundation, 1973.

National Science and Technology Council, Committee on Fundamental Science. *United States Antarctic Program.* Washington, D.C.: NSTC, April 1996.

National Science Foundation. *Antarctic Conservation Act of 1978.* Arlington, Va.: NSF, October 1995.

———. *Antarctic News Clips, 1995.* Arlington, Va.: National Science Foundation, July 1995.

———. *Antarctic News Clips, 1996.* Arlington, Va.: National Science Foundation, July 1996.

———. *Facts About the United States Antarctic Program.* Washington, D.C.: Office of Polar Programs, October 1994.

———. *The Role of The National Science Foundation in Polar Regions.* NSB-87–128. Washington, D.C.: National Science Foundation, 1987.

———. *Safety in Antarctica: Report of the U.S. Antarctic Program Safety Review Panel.* NSF Publication 88–78, June 30, 1988.

Polar Research Board. *Antarctic Treaty System: An Assessment.* Proceedings of a Workshop Held at Beardmore South Field Camp, Antarctica, January 7–13, 1985. Washington, D.C.: National Academy Press, 1986.

Sands, Peter. *Marine Environment Law in the United Nations Environmental Programme,* Natural Resources and the Environment Series, Vol. 24. London: Tycooly, 1988.

United Nations. General Assembly. *Agreement Governing the Activities on the Moon and Other Celestial Bodies*, text annexed to U.N.G.A. Res. 34/68, 34 U.N. GAOR Supp. (No. 46), at 77, U.N. Doc. A/Res/34/68 (1979).

―――. General Assembly. *Declaration of the United Nations Conference on the Human Environment* (Stockholm Declaration). U.N. Doc. A/Conf. 48/14/Rev. 1 (1973).

―――. General Assembly. *Question of Antarctica: Study Requested under General Assembly Resolution 38/77. Report of the Secretary-General.* U.N. Doc. A/39/583 (October 31, 1984).

―――. General Assembly. *Question of Antarctica, Study Requested under General Assembly Resolution 38/77, Report of the Secretary-General* (PART TWO: Views of States), Vol. III. U.N. Doc. A/39/583 (PART II) (1984).

―――. *Global Outlook 2000: An Economic, Social, and Environmental Perspective.* U.N. Doc. ST/ESA/215/Rev. 1 (1990).

United States. Congress. House. Committee on Interior and Insular Affairs. *Antarctica Legislation, 1960: Hearings before the Subcommittee on Territorial and Insular Affairs,* 86th Cong., 2d sess., June 13 and 14, 1960.

―――. Committee on Interior and Insular Affairs. *Antarctica Report—1965: Hearings before the Subcommittee on Territorial and Insular Affairs,* 89th Cong., 1st sess., April 12 and 13; May 6 and 7; and June 15, 1965.

―――. Committee on Interior and Insular Affairs. *Establish an Antarctica World Park: Hearing before the Subcommittee on Insular and International Affairs,* 101st Cong., 2d sess., September 18, 1990.

―――. Committee on Science and Technology. *NSF Antarctic Environment Act of 1991: Hearing before the Subcommittee on Science,* 102nd Cong., 1st sess., May 14, 1991.

―――. Congress. Office of Technology Assessment. *Polar Prospects: A Minerals Treaty for Antarctica.* OTA-0–428. Washington, D.C.: U.S. Government Printing Office, September 1989.

―――. Senate. Committee on Commerce, Science, and Transportation. *Antarctica: Hearing before the Subcommittee on Science, Technology, and Space,* 98th Cong., 2d. sess., September 24, 1984.

―――. Committee on Commerce, Science, and Transportation. *Protecting Antarctica's Environment: Hearing before the Subcommittee on Science, Technology and Space,* 101st Cong., 1st sess., September 8, 1989.

―――. Committee on Foreign Affairs. *U.S. Policy with Respect to Mineral Exploration and Exploitation in the Antarctic: Hearing Before the Subcommittee on Oceans and International Environment,* 94th Cong., 1st sess., May 15, 1975.

―――. Department of State. *Conference on Antarctica.* Washington, D.C.: U.S. Government Printing Office, 1960.

―――. Department of State. *Environmental Impact Statement on the Convention for the Conservation of Antarctic Seals.* Washington, D.C.: U.S. Government Printing Office, 1974.

Bibliography

————. *Final Environmental Impact Statement for a Possible Regime for Conservation of Antarctic Marine Living Resources.* Washington, D.C.: Bureau of Ocean Affairs, 1978.

————. *Final Environmental Impact Statement on the Negotiation of an International Regime for Antarctic Mineral Resources.* August 1982.

————. *Treaties in Force: A List of Treaties and Other International Agreements of the United States in Force on January 1, 1997.* Washington D.C.: U.S. Government Printing Office, 1997.

U.S. Naval War College. *International Law Documents, 1948–49* 46 Washington, D.C.: U.S. Government Printing Office, 1950.

Wright, N. A., and P. L. Williams, eds. *Mineral Resources of Antarctica.* Geological Survey Circular 705, 1974.

INDEX

Index